The Teacher's Toolkit

Raise Classroom Achievement with Strategies for Every Learner

Paul Ginnis

Illustrations by Les Evans

Crown House Publishing
www.crownhouse.co.uk

First published by

Crown House Publishing Ltd
Crown Buildings, Bancyfelin, Carmarthen, Wales, SA33 5ND, UK
www.crownhouse.co.uk

and

Crown House Publishing Ltd
P.O. Box 2223, Williston, VT 05495-2223, USA
www.CHPUS.com

© Paul Ginnis 2002

First published 2002.
Reprinted 2002 (twice), 2003.

British Library Cataloguing-in-Publication Data
A catalogue entry for this book is available
from the British Library.

International Standard Book Number
1899836764

Library of Congress Control Number
2002109646

Printed and bound in the UK by
Bell & Bain Limited
Glasgow

"We should be as concerned with how
we teach as we traditionally have been
concerned with what we teach."

John Bruer, *Schools for Thought*

Dedicated to those closest to me

Sharon, Helen, Steven, Clare

Table of Contents

Acknowledgments   v
Foreword   vii
Introduction   ix

Section 1
Design Tools   1

  Why?   3
  There Are Similarities Between Learners   12
  There Are Also Differences Between Learners   33
  There Are Other Agendas Too   50
  The Recipe   58

Section 2
Tools for Teaching and Learning   61

  Introduction   63
  Ambassadors   65
  Assembly   67
  Back to Back   69
  Beat the Teacher   71
  Bingo   73
  Bodily Functions   75
  Broken Pieces   78
  Calling Cards   81
  Centre of the Universe   83
  Circus Time   85
  Conversion   87
  Corporate Identity   89
  Delegation   91
  Dicey Business   93
  Discussion Carousel   95
  Distillation   97
  Dominoes   99
  Double Take   101
  Dreadlines   103
  Forum Theatre   105
  Go Large   107
  Guess Who   109
  Hide 'n' Seek   111
  Hierarchies   113
  Hot-Seating   116
  Information Hunt   118
  Mantle of the Expert   120
  Marketplace   122

Masterminds   126
Memory Board   128
Multisensory Memories   130
On Tour   133
One-to-One   135
Pairs to Fours   137
Pass the Buck   139
Question Generator   141
Question Time   143
Quick on the Draw   145
Ranking   148
Scrambled Groups   150
Silent Sentences   152
Spotlight   154
Stepping Stones   156
Still Image   158
Thumbometer   161
Value Continuum   163
Verbal Football   166
Verbal Tennis   168
Wheel of Fortune   170
Where There's a Will ...   172

Section 3
Tools for Managing Group Work, Behaviour and Personal Responsibility   175

Introduction   177
Murder Hunt   179
Framed   182
Observer Servers   185
Learning Listening   187
Sabotage   190
Games   192
Maintenance   195
Assertiveness   199
Groups Galore   207
Step On It   209
Help! How Do We Hold A Group Discussion?   212
Help! How Do We Make Decisions?   214
Proportional Representation   216
Triple Check   218
Think About It   220
Settled Starts   222
Tricks of the Trade   223

Section 4
Operating Tools   **225**

    Introduction   227
    Overtime   228
    Extended Horizons   231
    Upwardly Mobile   234
    Menu   246
    Sole Search   253
    Blank Cheque   261

Section 5
Audit Tools   **271**

    Introduction   273
    Check Your Lesson Plans   274
    Check Your Students' Learning Styles   279
    Check Your Impact On Students' Self-Esteem   289
    Check Your Delivery Of Independent Learning Skills   297
    Check Your Language   307
    Check Your Professional Development   314
    Check Your Management Of Change   321

Appendix A: Starting Points for Research   331
Appendix B: Learning Styles Analyses   333
References   337
Select Bibliography   345
Index   353

Acknowledgments

My deepest appreciation goes to my family and friends without whose love and support this book would not have been written. They waited patiently while *The Teacher's Toolkit* took time and energy that should have been given to them:

My wife Sharon, beautiful and intelligent, my companion and co-worker who has given so much to see this project through.

My three multi-talented children, Helen, Steven and Clare to whom I wish all the happiness in the world.

My mother Jean, stepfather Cliff, sisters Trish and Debs, brothers-in-law Andy, John and John, nieces Nicola and Amy, nephew Dan, mother-in-law Monica and sister-in-law Mary.

My inspiration, Donna Brandes.

My dear friends, Peter Batty and Steve Munby.

I am thankful to all those who have shared their wisdom, skills and friendship with me over the years. From you I have learned many lessons, most of which are now between the covers of this book:

Lindsey and Ted Hammond and the boys
Roland and Janet Meighan, Philip and Annabel Toogood and all in the Education Now network
Clive Carroll, John Peatfield and all the academic and administrative staff at the Education Development Unit of St Martin's College
Jane Ryan Caine and John Caine
Peter Duncan, Dai Power and everyone in the Dynamix team
Ian and Jane Pickles and family
Ted Harvey
Mike and Pam Cousins
Roy Kent and Janet Briggs
Tony Salmon
John McAleavey

Of the 450 schools with which I've worked, some have particularly helped me to develop and trial new practice. Thanks for providing the challenge and the opportunity:

The Harwich School, Essex
Villiers High School, Southall
The Ferrers School, Northamptonshire
Thistley Hough High School, Stoke-on-Trent
Radcliffe School, Oldham
Stamford High School, Ashton-under-Lyne
All Saints Catholic High School, Huddersfield

Likewise, my long-term relationship with several Education Authorities has given me the chance to try out and refine key ideas. Thanks for taking me on:

Birmingham, Pembrokeshire, Sandwell, Solihull, Stoke-on-Trent, Salford, Swansea, Jersey and Middlesbrough

Thanks to all the colleagues involved and a particular thanks to the Pembrokeshire Project Leaders Group for putting such energy into the work, for sustaining genuine change and for giving me valuable feedback and encouragement.

Thanks to one or two teachers who have given permission for me to publish examples of their work:

Alan Cadman
Jim Bradshaw
Roger Hamer
Paul Stewart

A big thanks to Jane Ryan Caine for carefully scrutinising Section 2 and providing many helpful suggestions.

Foreword

Over the past ten years there has been a cautious but profound revolution taking place in schools and in broader debates about education. At the centre of this change are the fundamental questions about the nature of learning and, linked to this, the role of the teacher and the organisation of classrooms and schools. Paul Ginnis has been at the heart of this debate and this book represents an important synthesis of his contribution to our shared understanding of the impact of learning on children's education.

The change is perhaps best represented by the change in the language we use about what happens in classrooms. The emphasis has switched from 'teaching', through 'teaching and learning' to the situation where *learning* is seen as the key activity. The impact of this change should not be underestimated; it alters the fundamental premises about the status of children, the nature of pedagogy and the whole architecture of learning. The curriculum becomes a vehicle to support learning rather than an end in itself.

What Paul has done in this book is to provide a powerful conceptual framework to justify the strategies he describes. Perhaps one of the most significant changes has been the emergence of the 'science of learning': the discovery of a neurological foundation for the work of learners and teachers. This is as profound a change as any in medical or electronic science in the past 50 years. When linked with new insights into cognitive psychology and the social aspects of learning, it becomes clear that the status quo in the classroom is not an option.

Some of the activities that Paul describes will be recognised by many teachers; others will be seized on as innovative and exciting – others may be rejected as too radical. However, every single activity described is firmly rooted in a coherent and systematic strategy based on a real understanding of the difficult balance between the science of learning and the art of teaching for learning.

The Teacher's Toolkit is an important and welcome resource because of the emphasis that it places on *how* we learn and teach rather than *what* we learn and teach. The book also focuses on raising achievement but balances the concern for performance with the development of understanding of learning *how to learn* and this, perhaps, is the greatest legacy of formal schooling. This book provides numerous opportunities for individual teachers to develop their own classroom practice; it will serve as a powerful stimulus for professional learning; but, and most importantly, it has the potential to make learning exciting and fun for teachers and students alike.

John West-Burnham
Professor of Educational Leadership
University of Hull

Introduction

I have packed into *The Teacher's Toolkit* almost everything I know about teaching and learning.

For years, as a profession, we have been trying to raise levels of student achievement. Given that the challenge is still on to pursue excellence day by day, often in testing circumstances, this seems like a good time to gather my favourite practices together and share them.

Teachers want practical ideas. There are loads of them in this book, but that's not all. My experience has been that the quality of teaching and learning improves most readily when practice and theory inform each other. It is helpful for us to know why things work, or don't; it is helpful to have principles to guide the design of lessons; it is helpful to know how students learn so we don't always operate unthinkingly from expediency or unquestioningly from political directive.

On the wall of Pontin's Conference Centre in Blackpool, of all places, there's a plaque:

> Insanity – doing the same thing the same way and expecting a different result!

Making the same point, Frank Zappa, the great American rock musician, once said:

> Without deviation, progress is not possible.

We have to do things differently if we want achievement to improve further. But what? Fortunately, we no longer have to depend on guesswork, trial and error, ideology or flights of philosophical fancy. We can now rely on some fairly secure truths about the learning process. It seems that there are natural laws of learning, some givens, some universal principles that provide a firm foundation for effective practice. These provide us with compass directions to follow, indicating the best, though not necessarily the easiest, ways forward.

Where have they come from? In recent years a huge amount of scientific information about the brain has become available thanks to new neuroscanning technologies. This has been popularised in accelerated learning and through the wealth of print and Internet material on brain-based approaches (see Appendix A and Bibliography for details). What is impressive, and reassuring, is the extent to which this "new" stuff affirms and refines earlier practices based on the principles of humanistic psychology, holism, cooperation and democracy. Many older educationalists who held only quasi-scientific notions about teaching and learning – Dewey, Holt and Rogers, for example, whom we shall meet later – have been proved largely right. This current convergence of thinking from a variety of old and new sources – neuroscientific, psychological, sociological and moral – suggests that the main thrust of national policy needs to be rethought. It seems to be barking up the wrong tree.

Be that as it may, the principles that underpin *The Teacher's Toolkit* are sufficiently down-to-earth for individual teachers such as yourself to adjust your practice no matter what the big wide world outside your classroom is up to. The practical techniques inspired by current thinking are sufficiently self-contained to be conducted within the confines of your own four walls. In some cases the strategies of yesteryear belonging to the older, recently reaffirmed thinking, can be dusted down and reused with confidence.

Classroom techniques created in the days of active learning, student-centred learning, drama across the curriculum, flexible learning and supported self-study, and belonging to initiatives such as the Technical and Vocational Education Initiative, Active Tutorial Work, even Raising of the School-Leaving Age (well before my time!), are found to be compatible with the latest findings of the neuroscientists. These ideas always were effective, and now we know why. They just got buried under the pile of prescription that is the national curriculum. So, where is this particular collection from?

Over the 22 years that I have worked in schools – as a teacher, head of department, advisory teacher, staff development tutor and freelance trainer – I have learned my craft from many remarkable people. Without doubt the deepest and most pervasive influence has been Dr Donna Brandes, the internationally renowned student-centred educator. Donna brought into my young professional life, at a time when I am ashamed to say that students called me "Hitler", a coherent person-centred philosophy and skill set. The ideas stretched me to the limit but resonated strongly with the deep values of my theological training and so created the kind of congruence in my teaching that I had been seeking. Over the years that we worked and wrote together she taught me how to trust students, how to be myself in the classroom, how to pursue the goals of self-esteem and personal responsibility above all and let everything else fall into place. A master practitioner herself, she showed me the power of optimism, unconditional regard and self-belief. Donna's insights continue to influence my work, fundamentally, day by day.

The second greatest influence on my thinking has been my good friend Professor Roland Meighan. Roland taught me to see the big picture, to understand what is happening socio-economically and politically within and beyond schools. He showed me the true nature of democracy and cooperation, the value of nonconventional and free-spirited thinking and the place of pioneering action. He continues to model the winning combination of hard-hitting analysis, humane values, sharp wit and genuine warmth.

Then there is my wife Sharon. She taught me how to use drama, how to trust intuition, how to think laterally and how to be daring in the classroom. She showed me what it's like to have a learning style and intelligence profile that doesn't fit the system, what it's like to be on the outside and what happens to self-esteem and life chances when teachers do not have the will or the skill to meet individual learning needs. Her creativity and spontaneity I aspire to.

The fourth, but by no means least, significant influence is my close friend and colleague Peter Batty, the ultimate reflective practitioner and man of integrity. Peter has taught me to slow down, to make room for learning, not just teaching. He has shown me how to trust the process, how to value reflection and review, how to let principles be the guide to practice, and how to live a little.

So, you will no doubt get to know these characters as you read between the lines of the pages that follow. Beyond them are countless teachers, headteachers, advisers and trainers who have taught me, often unknowingly, crucial lessons. Therefore, many of the ideas in *The Teacher's Toolkit* are not mine. Credit is hard to apportion, though, as many strategies have their origins somewhere in the mists of time, so forgive me if you read something that you thought you'd invented! The ones that *are* mine have been fashioned from experiences in thousands of classrooms in hundreds of secondary schools of all types around the country. In fact, every practical suggestion has been thoroughly road-tested, often with difficult classes and always in a variety of subjects and with different age groups. In the hands of skilful teachers, they have almost always had positive effects on motivation, discipline and the quality of learning. Ideas that didn't work have been ditched.

By the way, don't use the ideas slavishly; the intention is to stimulate your own creativity. Don't underestimate the power of enthusiasm; it lifts lessons to a higher plane, and your enthusiasm will always be greatest for ideas that you invent yourself. I hope you enjoy using *The Teacher's Toolkit* as much as I have enjoyed writing it. Now, at last, I can get back to listening to my jukebox and going to some home games at the Britannia Stadium.

Paul Ginnis
Birmingham

Section 1

Design Tools

Why?

In his bestselling book The *Seven Habits of Highly Effective People*[1] Stephen Covey suggests that a habit is formed whenever a person knows *what* to do, knows *how* to do it and has a good reason for doing it – in other words knows *why*. Understanding why helps to create motivation. Covey says "A habit is the overlapping of *what* to do, or knowledge, *how* to do or skill, and *why* to do – want to or attitude. Where they overlap you'll see a habit."[2]

Knowing *what* to do = awareness

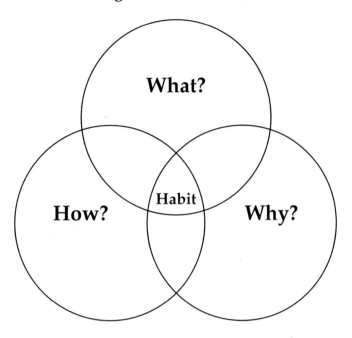

Knowing *how* to do it = skill　　　　**Knowing *why* to do it = motivation**

Those who work in the field of professional development, or whose job it is to manage change, know the truth of this. Simply exhorting people to alter their ways doesn't work. Telling them what they should do differently, without giving them the necessary skills, leads to feelings of frustration and failure. Nor does it work in the long term to give people new techniques without a convincing rationale. Innovation is then short-lived. On the whole, new practice is not sustained unless people have:

- a **motivation** to keep doing it, which comes from conviction
- an **understanding** of the principles that underpin the practice so that the new methodology can be continually refreshed and reinvented.

Much of this book is about *how*. This, I hope, makes it attractive to teachers and trainers who are understandably eager for new practical ideas. The risk, though, is that it provides no more than a "box of chocolates". Once the chocolates have been enjoyed, the box is likely to be thrown away and a fresh one demanded. The more taxing but ultimately more productive intention of *The Teacher's Toolkit* is for readers to internalise the recipe so they can make their own confectionery when this particular selection runs out.

So this first section is about *why* – the rationale. Why push the boat out and do things differently? Why not just carry on as normal? My basic premise is that learning in schools is likely to be at its best when teachers follow the natural laws of the learning process. This idea is presented strongly by the Scottish Consultative Council on the Curriculum in the introduction to their excellent *Teaching For Effective Learning*:

> Some would argue that teaching is a different job depending on where you teach and whom you teach. Obviously there are differences but [we] believe that the basic principles of learning apply no matter where you teach and no matter what the needs or the age of the learners you teach.[3]

The title of Mike Hughes's book, *Closing the Learning Gap*,[4] says it all. In the past, teaching tended to be hit-and-miss because as a profession we were less certain about learning. Even now the way many teachers teach is out of step with the way most learners learn. The task of the modern, aware teacher and school manager is to bring teaching methods increasingly in line with the learning process. Herein lies the real solution to the apparent problems of under-attainment (measured narrowly) and underachievement (more broadly).

The difference between attainment and achievement is more than semantic. In *Effective Learning in Schools* Christopher Bowring-Carr and John West-Burnham stress

> that learning must have a consequence for the learner. By "consequence" we mean that by learning x, the learner will see the world in a slightly different way, will alter his or her behaviour or attitude in some way. If the "learning" that has taken place is merely capable of being reproduced at some later date in answer to the demands of some form of assessment which replicates the original problem, and the context for that problem, then what is being learnt is "shallow learning" only.[5]

Deep learning involves the development of an increasingly sophisticated personal reality with matching competencies and disciplines. *The Teacher's Toolkit* attempts to provide some of the means of arriving at "deep learning" (achievement), even within a culture concerned largely with "shallow learning" (attainment).

There are many excellent books currently available providing surveys of modern learning theory. Alistair Smith's *Accelerated Learning in the Classroom*,[6] *Accelerated Learning in Practice*[7] and his myth-busting *The Brain's Behind It*,[8] along with Colin Rose's and Malcolm J. Nicholl's *Accelerated Learning for the 21st Century*[9] and Robin Fogarty's *Brain Compatible Classrooms*,[10] are ideal starting points. *The Learning Revolution*[11] by Gordon Dryden and Jeanette Vos is a recognised classic, and the many books by Eric Jensen, especially *The Learning Brain*,[12] *Teaching with the Brain in Mind*,[13] and *Brain-Based Learning*,[14] provide crisp, readable and, above all, applied insights into recent research.

Fuelled by the latest ideas, their journey began. Instinctively they knew...the future wasn't what it used to be.

Behind all this is biology. For the last couple of decades neuroscientists have been telling us with increasing confidence about the workings of the brain. This is a direct consequence of advances in scanning technology, particularly fMRI (Functional Magnetic Resonance Imaging) and PET (Positron Emission Tomography), which allow us to see the brain in action to a very precise degree. For those who are not very familiar with all the bits of the central nervous system, visit Eric Chudler's fresh and frequently updated website *Neuroscience for Kids* at http://faculty.washington.edu/chudler/neurok.html

For more advanced technical stuff about the structure of the brain, go to www.vh.org/Providers/Textbooks/BrainAnatomy/BrainAnatomy.html

Alternatively, familiarise yourself with Susan Greenfield's work. Professor of Pharmacology at Oxford and a popular TV presenter, she describes the inner secrets of the grey matter in very readable texts such as *The Private Life of the Brain*,[15] *Brain Story*[16] and *The Human Brain, a Guided Tour*.[17] If you're ready for a detailed and fairly technical account of shifts in brain research from the 1940s to the present day, read John McCrone's *Going Inside: A Tour Round a Single Moment of Consciousness*. Towards the end of the text he sums up: "This book has tried to track what would be a fundamental change in the science of the mind: a shift from reductionism to dynamism."[18]

Nowadays the brain is thought of as dynamic, not as some sort of computer crunching its way through billions of inputs per second. It is considered to be a flexible, self-adjusting, unique, ever-changing organism that continually grows and reconfigures in response to each stimulus. Early in the 1990s researchers such as the neurobiologist Karl Friston of London and the psychologist Stephen Kosslyn of Harvard were instrumental in formulating this new paradigm. They realised that the brain operates rather like the surface of a pond. New inputs provoke a widespread disturbance in some existing state. The brain's circuits are drawn tight in a state of tension and when a pebble is thrown in (a sensory input) there are immediate ripples of activity. New pebbles create patterns that interact with the lingering patterns of previous inputs. Then everything echoes off the sides. Nothing is being calculated. The response of the pond to the input is organic, or more accurately *dynamic*.

Elissa Newport, psycholinguist at the University of Rochester in New York, uses another image: the brain can now be seen as working more like a beehive, its swarm of interconnected neurons sending signals back and forth at lightning speed. Sir Charles Sherrington, who has been described as "the grandfather of neurophysiology", says of the brain, "It is as if the Milky Way entered upon some cosmic dance". However you choose to describe it, the brain is characterised by activity, plasticity, responsiveness, interplay, speed, adaptability, continual reshaping and inexhaustible resources – a far cry from the computer-like comparisons of the not-too-distant past.

Aware of the vitality and fluidity of the brain, all made nakedly apparent by imaging, McCrone suggests that a complete understanding of consciousness can be achieved only if insights from a number of disciplines are combined:

> Scanning technology has already had the beneficial effect of forcing the beginnings of a marriage between psychology and neurology … But if the human mind is a social as well as a biological phenomenon, then yet further marriages are required with the "soft" sciences of sociology and anthropology, and their many sub-disciplines.[19]

Therefore, in our rush to embrace the main messages from brain science, it is vital that we do not bypass more established cultural and socioeconomic insights as if they were now old hat. Roland Meighan's *A Sociology of Educating*,[20] for instance, is as important as it ever was. The classic perspectives of Ivan Illich and Paulo Friere, along with the popular works of John Holt, most crucially *How Children Fail*,[21] and Postman and Weingartner in *Teaching As a Subversive Activity*,[22] may be middle-aged and unfashionable, yet they combine to present a powerful agenda for personal, social and ultimately political empowerment that is entirely relevant to our modern needs. In assessing Illich in *The Trailblazers*, for example, Professor Edith King of Denver concludes:

As the educational issues that Ivan Illich espoused now seem familiar at the close of the 20th century, teachers and parents can find strength … from his writings in their advocacy of the democratic school and alternative educational futures.[23]

What next?

Revolutionary insights into the brain are only part of a more general overhaul of thinking that has gathered momentum in the last fifteen years. An increasing number of commentators are now weaving global social, economic, commercial and technological "megatrends" together with modern insights into the brain to present us with new visions of the future. Dryden and Vos's "16 major trends that will shape tomorrow's world"[24] provides as good an overview as any, while Charles Handy, the internationally renowned business and social commentator, established some time ago that change is now discontinuous. He said, "the success stories of yesterday have little relevance to the problems of tomorrow … The world at every level has to be reinvented to some extent. Certainty is out, experiment is in."[25] Guy Claxton's reflective *Wise Up: The Challenge of Lifelong Learning*[26] makes the persuasive case for major shifts in our thinking about learning, schooling, training and parenting. He argues that the ultimate life skill for the 21st century is the ability to face difficult and unprecedented challenges calmly and resourcefully.

Worldwide, information and communications technology is being increasingly understood and utilised by ordinary people. This brings two major, positive benefits to learning. First, teachers are gradually being released from having to be the main transmitters of information, ideas and skills, enabling them instead to concentrate on the facilitation of learning, on being learning coaches. Second, students are being empowered to learn independently. They can access most of the information they need, and often whole courses, on CDs or online. Learning, even of regular examination subjects, can take place in the school's learning centre, at home or in the local cyber café, meaning that students can control when and where they learn, and often how. The visual and interactive nature of most hi-tech resources makes them appealing to learners who struggle with academic routines. Information and communications technology (ICT) is free of time, space and tradition. All students need to do is learn how to learn.

In fact, Doug Brown, chairman of the British Computer Society's School of the Future Project, commenting on his final report back in 1998, said:

> The current school model, with its rigid classroom, has been useful only because there was no alternative. The millennium school will be vastly different … the concept of a nine-to-four school day will become obsolete … In order to use ICT successfully, schools must change their culture – how students learn and how teachers teach.[27]

In the United States, Don Glines, director of the California-based Educational Futures Project, has argued for years that "there is only one overriding issue facing educators today: the transformation to communication age learning systems."[28] In Britain, John Abbott and Terry Ryan's superb *The Unfinished Revolution: Learning, Human Behaviour, Community and Political Paradox* presents a complete raft of compelling reasons for declaring that "the current structures of formal education are fundamentally flawed" and that "societies now stand at an evolutionary crossroads where the way ahead must be to capitalise on fresh understandings and remedy … upside down and inside out education."[29] The 21st Century Learning Initiative (www.21learn.org) sums up the situation in its published vision:

> New understandings about the brain; about how people learn; about the potential of information and communications technologies; about radical changes in patterns of work as well as deep fears about social divisions in society, necessitate a profound rethinking of the structures of education.

This UK network and others like it, such as Education Now (www.gn.apc.org/ educationnow) give penetrating insights into the shortcomings of the current education system and offer constructive, radical alternatives.

Such thoughts raise big questions – two in particular. In this day and age, **what** should be the purpose of education? And **how** should it be organised? Over recent decades a view has crept to dominance in Britain that education exists primarily to serve the economy. This premise currently drives almost all current policy. Early in the reign of New Labour, Tony Blair declared in *The Learning Age: A Renaissance For a New Britain*[30] that "Education is the best economic policy we have." At the start of his second term of office the Prime Minister sounded the same note: "The world's fourth largest economy cannot advance without a world-class education system."[31] The economy has become the politician's first and foremost, and unquestioned, reason for pursuing quality in education, but where does such functionalism lead?

Even educationalists in the "learning-to-learn" camp often argue their case on economic grounds – they say that people are often required to learn on the job and will inevitably have to retrain at least once in their working lives, so they need the skills to do it. It's true, companies increasingly expect employees to learn, and employees increasingly expect companies to provide for their learning. Many multinationals now have their own in-house universities and even a relatively small outfit such as Bulmer's Cider in Hereford has a learning centre open 24 hours a day. The British government's University for Industry, Learning Direct advice service and Lifelong Learning Partnerships, along with the Learning and Skills Councils, are designed to facilitate continuous work-based or work-related education.

Clearly, education and the economy are in a mutually dependent relationship: each needs the other, and this will remain so. Individual livelihoods and the continuance of national life depend on it. But there are two issues to debate. First, the *prominence* of the economy in the nation's thinking about education: currently it dominates and dictates. National education and training targets are set explicitly to improve competitiveness; the national numeracy and literacy strategies and the current attention given to thinking and learning skills are intended to serve the same purpose. The second debate concerns the nation's understanding of *what* the economy now needs from education. According to Abbott and Ryan,

> Today's social and economic needs argue for a new model of learning that entails:
>
> 1. mastery of basic skills;
> 2. the ability to work with others;
> 3. being able to deal with constant distractions;
> 4. working at different levels across different disciplines;
> 5. using mainly verbal skills, and;
> 6. problem-solving and decision-making.[32]

By contrast, most political thinking about education is driven by an out-of-date understanding of business needs. Current education policy is way behind the times, serving the old factory age, not the new information age. Attendance, punctuality, compliance, acceptance of the "manager's" decisions, an understanding of one's place in the pecking order, a sufficient general knowledge and the ability to use a few basic skills make up the current curriculum (as they did a hundred years ago), whereas businesses are currently crying out for flexibility, responsiveness, creative problem-solving, teamwork, self-management and sophisticated communication skills. The reason for the yawning gap is clear. The modern business agenda chimes with the modern learning agenda, and there's a deep-seated stubbornness about accepting modern educational ideas, even those grounded in the most credible neuroscientific research. Why? Because they resemble the progressive child-centred practices that have been so successfully rubbished in the popular mind. In a private conversation with Professor

Howard Gardner, a recent British Secretary of State for Education irrationally said, "I simply don't believe in your multiple intelligence theory." End of story.

Compounding the problem is the simplistic idea that educational outcomes can be fundamentally altered by changing the curriculum and its content. This of course is nonsense. Since the UK's Education Reform Act of 1988 there has been nothing but curriculum change, and yet the outcomes that matter – attitudes and skills – remain more or less the same. The kind of changes required for modern economic success, for a healing of social ills and for personal fulfilment are rooted in the *way* learning is conducted, not in *what* is learned. In other words changes to teaching and learning methodology and to education structures are required. No wonder John Bruer, a cognitive scientist, said that "we should be as concerned with how we teach as we traditionally have been concerned with what we teach".[33]

Take creativity, for example. *All Our Futures: Creativity, Culture and Education,*[34] the report of the National Advisory Committee for Creative and Cultural Education, headed by Professor Ken Robinson of Warwick, points out that employers are "saying that a degree is not enough, and that many graduates do not have the qualities they are looking for: the ability to communicate, work in teams, adapt to change, to innovate and be creative". Robinson concluded that:

> this is not surprising … the traditional academic curriculum is not designed to promote creativity. Complaining that the system does not produce creative people is like complaining that a car doesn't fly … It was never intended to. The stark message, internationally as well as nationally, is that the answer to the future is not simply to increase the amount of education, but to educate people differently.[35]

Once free of the Earth's gravitational pull, many things became possible.

He provides a clear way forward: "Creative learning is made possible by creative teaching. This is not an easy process and calls for sophisticated skills in teachers."[36] Robinson argues that substantial changes to the curriculum, to assessment and to teacher training will be needed to support this.

Presently teachers tell us that creativity is crushed in Key Stage 2 as they focus on preparation for SATs, and we see the natural learning processes of childhood – free play and random exploration, for example – abandoned by zealous teachers and parents in their desperate attempts to give children an "advantageous" start. Secondary schools are using increasingly bizarre bribes (such as offering McDonald's meals and mountain bikes as prizes) to get students to attend. The national teacher shortage suggests that adolescents are not the only ones who don't want to go to school any more. How long will this position be tenable in a country that still harbours deep divisions (the North of England race riots of summer 2001) and signs of serious disaffection (the turnout in the 2001 General Election was a shocking 59%) and in which we now know enough about learning to address these issues successfully? The snag is that politicians get stuck. Once they've declared their course they can't backtrack. They fall prey to a great British habit: if something doesn't work, do it harder and more often (homework clubs, holiday schools, evening revision classes). Politicians are simply not allowed by the media and the public to learn from mistakes and adapt to fresh evidence – what a role model for a "learning society"!

Perhaps I'm being too harsh. Estelle Morris, on becoming the UK Education Secretary in 2001, declared, "We want to give schools more freedom. We want to put the fun and creativity back and we want them to be innovators for our next round of reforms."[37] We'll keep our fingers crossed and see what happens. I wonder if she has in mind what Tom Bentley, Director of the independent think tank Demos, said: "A sustained transformation of the education system needs a guiding purpose. I have suggested that this goal should be creativity, at the individual, organisational and societal level."[38]

Those who break with the economy-driven view of education and propose fundamentally different purposes are few and far between, but include Bowring-Carr and West-Burnham: "We see the development of the mind as the overriding purpose of education."[39] Professor Clive Harber of the University of Birmingham on the other hand speaks strongly of education for democracy that is "as much about the *way* in which people think and behave, *how* they hold their political opinions, as it is about *what* they actually think". He quotes Carl Rogers, the inventor of client-centred counselling and student-centred learning: "People who can't think are ripe for dictatorship."[40] This begs us to ask whether the British government's simultaneous interest in thinking skills and citizenship is joined-up policy, or a fluke!

If we are to break from the shackles of "shallow learning", navigate these uncertain times and fashion a morally sound and fruitful future for all, then purposes such as "the development of the mind" and the "preservation of democracy", or others such as "the creation of an inclusive and egalitarian society" or "the fulfilment of the whole person" will have to become driving rather than half-hearted concerns. As I hope you will come to recognise, these intentions underlie the practical strategies presented in Sections 2, 3, 4 and 5.

Then there is the question of **how** education should be organised. It all depends on the dominant purpose, of course. If education were supposed to *secure acceptance of the social order and working habits of old*, then we'd probably want the kind of schools we have now. Writing a few years ago, Anita Higham OBE, formerly principal of Banbury School, puts this point strongly: "My thesis is that we are in the death-throes of secondary schools as we know them because we are attempting to educate adolescents of the late 20th Century within the style and structure of the late 19th Century school and its teachers' contractual conditions."[41] In Britain we have never quite shaken off the idea that schools are primary agents of socialisation; we've stuck with them because they do this job rather well. Sadly, as Bill Lucas and Toby Greany put it: "Schools as we know them are fast becoming an anachronism … their very traditions and structures mean that they are educating young people for a world which no longer exists."[42]

If instead, the prime purpose of education were to *meet learners' individual needs*, we would follow the lead of Valerie Bayliss, director of the RSA project Redefining the Curriculum: "Implicit in these [modern] ideas is a greater emphasis on the individual. A competence-led curriculum, together with the liberating capacity of technology, has the potential to open up much more individualised learning."[43]

If the prime purpose were to *help people learn how to learn*, we'd be asking serious questions along with Sir Christopher Ball, patron of the Campaign for Learning:

In a foolish attempt to cling to what they had left behind, they religiously prepared the young for a world they would no longer inherit.

> Is it going to be possible to adjust traditional school education to satisfy pupils – or should we think about replacing it with something altogether different? The true learning society we all seek will require a new breed of teachers – more like guides than instructors, more part-time than full-time, more philosophers than pedagogues.[44]

If the purpose were to *promote democracy*, we'd have democratic schools, as in Denmark, for example.[45]

It is significant that calls for fundamental change are no longer being made by radicals alone, but increasingly by mainstream, and in many cases Establishment, figures.

Part of the reason for sticking with what we've got is that there are no large-scale models to copy. In America there are many individual examples of reconstructed "schools". Ted Sizer's Coalition for Essential Schools with its 1,000 institutional members (www.essentialschools.org), for example; schools redesigned along the lines of multiple intelligence; the chain of schools modelled on Daniel Greenberg's Sudbury Valley School in Massachusetts (www.sudval.org); the One Room Schoolhouse in Alameda, San Francisco – these are just some of the welcomed "experiments". The alternative education movement in the States is buoyant, as is clear from *Creating Learning Communities*,[46] a stimulating collection of examples of grassroots innovation, summaries of underpinning ideas and insights into key thinkers in which American contributions outnumber the rest by nine to one. Visit the website: www.creatinglearningcommunities.org

In the UK, by contrast, alternative schools have been systematically crushed over the years, or have committed suicide by poor management and chronic public relations. The attempt in 2000 to close Summerhill School in Suffolk (with its many faults) was staved off only at the eleventh hour. A few marginalised innovations survive outside the system: Sands School in Devon; a number of small schools affiliated to the Human Scale Education movement (www.hse.org.uk); one or two virtual cyberschools that have sprung up recently and struggled; English Experience in Kent, a school set up to pioneer brain-friendly teaching; and that's about it. For a full account of the rise and fall of progressive schools in Britain see John Shotton's *No Master High Or Low: Libertarian Education and Schooling 1890–1990*.[47] No wonder that an increasing number of parents are turning to home education and organising educational cooperatives such as the Brambles Centre in Sheffield, the Otherwise Club in London, the Learning Studio in Bishop's Castle and Planet Learning Zone, Warrington.

There are those in Britain who talk about reconstruction – the Tomorrow Project recently submitted its recommendations for education in the year 2020 to the Department for Education and Skills (DfES) (www.tomorrowproject.net); there are those who fantasise about it – see John Adcock's *In Place of Schools*[48] and his more recent and more detailed *Teaching Tomorrow: Personal Tuition as an Alternative to School*;[49] and there are many who argue cogently for it – see particularly Phil Street's, Bob Fryer's, Tony Hinkley's and Guy Claxton's contributions to the impressive collection of essays, *Schools in the Learning Age*,[50] and Professor Roland Meighan's *The Next Learning System*.[51] But there's no one with the clarity of vision who is also in a position to generate sufficient political will to make anything happen. Yet. The real problem is that our preoccupation with the economy has constrained our thinking. The language ("delivery", "hard outcomes", "driving up standards", for example), the procedures (measuring, target setting, inspecting, comparing, bidding, performance-related pay) and the values (materialism, competition, capitalism) have created a "national normality". Few people inside the system now seem able, or willing, to think outside the box.

Therefore, there is huge resistance to contrary ideas. Radical proposals from the brain scientists, the sociologists and the philosophers – people who know about learning – are generally batted off. At the same time, the government's own initiatives haven't amounted to much.

Potentially exciting possibilities have been suffocated by the blanket domination of targets and league tables. On the whole, Education Action Zones in Britain haven't risen to the original challenge to explore real alternatives – they have at best tinkered with existing provision. Learning centres within the Excellence in Cities initiative stand a better chance of breaking new ground. Transforming Teaching and Learning in the Foundation Subjects, part of the Key Stage 3 Strategy, will only nibble at the edges unless it is led with vision and courage. The Specialist School Programme just gives more money, which certainly buys welcome facilities, but at the price of imposing a specialism on students who happen to live in a given area.

The ultimate answer is of course to base policy *on what we know about learning*. Professor Robert Sylwester of Oregon sums up the position with a voice that rings true over the years and across the miles:

> The brain is a biological system, not a machine. Currently we are putting children with biologically shaped brains into machine-oriented schools. The two just don't mix. We bog the school down with a curriculum that is not biologically feasible.[52]

Return to the Forbidden Planet?

So this is the political and professional arena into which the theoretical and practical ideas in *The Teacher's Toolkit* are pitched. But the majority of ideas presented in this book are not that new after all. For example, some of the currently fashionable "neuroscientific" applications to education actually have their origin in Neuro-Linguistic Programming. NLP promotes a set of principles, attitudes and techniques that enable people to change or eliminate behaviour patterns by focusing on the dynamic relationship between mind and language. Apart from the obvious visual, auditory and kinaesthetic modalities model and its detection through predicates and eye patterns, other examples of the transference of NLP into education include the notion of

The further they travelled, the stronger the sense that their distant destination was strangely familiar.

"states", "anchoring" and the idea of "chunking" (short-term memory can cope with between only five and nine bits of information at a time). For those who want to check out NLP, which is among the primary sources of accelerated learning, one of the most complete introductions is *The User's Manual For The Brain* by Bodenhamer and Hall.[53]

NLP itself has a direct historical connection with humanistic psychology and the human-potential movement. Richard Bandler and John Grinder, developers of NLP, actually began by deconstructing and modelling the language used by two therapists: Fritz Perls of Gestalt fame and Virginia Satir, the leading family therapist. So it's no surprise that many of the "brain-friendly" ideas, simply confirm older notions. Much of humanistic psychology, with its optimistic view of human capacity, its mission to overcome barriers to personal growth and its holistic agenda, has been affirmed by neuroscientists and neurolinguists. As a young teacher in 1985, I had the privilege of writing *A Guide to Student-Centred Learning*[54] and in 1990 *The Student-Centred School*[55] with Dr Donna Brandes, the internationally acclaimed and exceedingly gifted educator and therapist. Inspired by Carl Rogers's client-centred work, many of the books' central themes, such as the need for emotional safety, the fundamental significance of self-esteem and the power of personal responsibility, are now commonplace within the emergent new orthodoxy. The importance of mental and physical activity, clarified by our modern understanding of the neocortex and the role of kinaesthetics in learning, is in direct line with "active learning" of old. Developmental group work, flexible learning and supported self-study all find reflections in the mirror of modern-day teaching and learning.

John Abbott, the determined and erudite commentator on educational futures, writing with Terry Ryan at the dawn of the new millennium, makes a similar point that would have John Dewey, the father of experiential learning, rejoicing in his grave:

> The mass of evidence that is now emerging about learning and brain development is spawning a movement towards educational practice which confirms the earlier intuitive understanding about learning through direct involvement with the activity.[56]

In other words, the only way to learn *how* to do something is by doing it!

So the basis of good practice may have shifted from psychology and philosophy to biology, and many new insights have been added, but in some key respects ideas that disappeared underground with the rise of the reductionist thinking that has dominated political visions of education since the mid-1980s have now been given fresh impetus and value. This is encouraging for many established teachers who might otherwise feel resistant to "yet another set of new-fangled ideas".

Head in the clouds, feet on the ground

So far, I have attempted to paint a picture of the background to the practical ideas in this book. It is at once an exciting and depressing sight. And it's easy to get carried away with the discussion, but let's keep things in perspective. *The Teacher's Toolkit* has its feet firmly on the ground, it is rooted in the here and now and suggests only strategies that can be tried today, tomorrow or next week in regular classrooms in ordinary schools. However, it is not just a novel collection of expediences. It is more than a random and aimless set of "tips for teachers". Its core purposes are in line with the best of modern thinking and these now need to be clarified. They say that a journey of a thousand miles starts with a single step – but that step has to be in the right direction! Fortunately, modern researchers and commentators have given us compass bearings and a map.

So let's now look at a modern agenda for learning in more detail. This will give us the specifications for the design of effective learning strategies, even within the limitations of the present system. From the wealth of insight available I have selected certain key ideas on the basis that they translate directly into the construction of concrete classroom activities. The first two groups of points, dealing initially with *similarities* and then with *differences* between learners, draw largely on the brain sciences. But beware: this is nowhere near the full game of "brain-compatible learning", just a few edited highlights. Find out more via the Bibliography and Appendix A.

There Are Similarities Between Learners

Emerging from the latest neuroscientific research are several truths about the way that all brains seem to function. Four of the *similarities* are presented in this section, the ones that have particularly informed the preparation of *The Teacher's Toolkit*'s practical ideas. In the next section we look at key *differences* between learners. Before any of it will make sense, though, we need to familiarise ourselves with the brain's processing method: the biology of learning.

The biology of learning

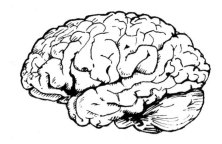

Susan Greenfield, Professor of Pharmacology at Oxford and one of the UK's best-known neuroscientists, likens the brain to the Amazonian Basin.[57] She says that the number of neurons in the human brain is about equivalent to the number of trees and plants in the 2.7-million-square-mile rainforest. The number of dendrites (the fibrous extensions from the neuron cell body that act as "receptors") is more or less equivalent to the number of leaves on those plants and trees. In the jungle that is the brain, all these are busily and continuously connecting with each other. Other images come to mind. The number of neurons in the brain is about the same as the number of stars in the Milky Way or three times the number of people on Planet Earth. One cubic millimetre of brain tissue has more than a million neurons, which means that all the world's telecommunications systems could fit into an area of the human brain about the size of a pea.

The good news is that you have the same number of brain cells as Albert Einstein! Everyone does, unless their brain is diseased or damaged. The even better news is that every student in your school has the same number of brain cells as you! There is, therefore, a biological basis for optimism. One hundred billion neurons per person, up to twenty thousand dendrites per neuron, all multiplied together means that the number of potential connections between brain cells in any brain is 10 to the 100 trillionth power, actually far greater than the number of particles in the known universe, according to Paul Churchland, Professor of Philosophy at the University of California.[58] In fact, if you were to count the actual connections in an adult neocortex alone, that is in the thin outer covering of the brain, at a rate of one per second, it would take you 32,000,000 years!

Neurons are responsible for processing information. Each neuron has one axon, a thin fibre that can be up to a couple of metres in length (and operate your big toe, for example), but is more often a centimetre or so long. The axon is the transmitter, passing information on in the form of electrochemical stimulation. Its job is to connect with the dendrites of other neurons, thousands of them, which means it has to subdivide itself to create lots of terminals. Each neuron is in effect a tiny battery powered by the difference in concentration between sodium and potassium ions across the cell membrane. An electrical charge, the action potential, is generated in the cell body of the neuron, which travels down the axon at a rate of between 1 and 100 metres per second.

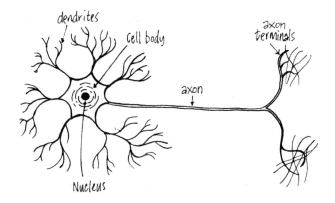

Dendrites, meanwhile, are the branch-like extensions from the neuron cell body that act as receptors. The information flow between neurons is only ever one way: from the cell body, down the axon and then via synaptic connections to the dendrites of other neurons, which carry the signal to their own cell bodies. The axon terminal never touches the dendrite. There is always a tiny gap, the synaptic cleft. The electrical pulse travelling down the axon reaches the terminal and activates neurotransmitters (chemical cocktails stored in vesicles in the tip of the axon) that carry the message across the synapse and stimulate (or inhibit) the electrical charge in the receiving dendrite.

A single neuron can simultaneously receive signals from thousands of other neurons. The sum total of all the signals arriving from all the dendrites to the cell body determine whether or not the neuron will itself fire a charge. Because its axon can branch repeatedly, a firing neuron can send the signal on to thousands of other neurons.

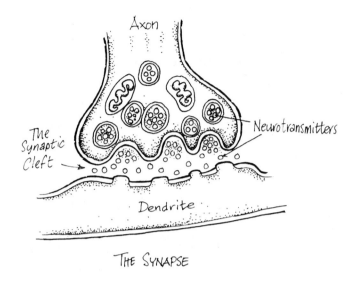

THE SYNAPSE

So, this is learning: new mental or motor experiences provide stimuli that are converted to nervous impulses that travel to sorting stations such as the thalamus (in the midbrain area). From here signals are sent to specific areas of the brain. Repeated stimulation of a group of neurons causes them to develop more dendrites and therefore more connections, and so a whole forest-like network of neurons is established that creates a grasp, an understanding, a mastery. In time these neurons "learn" to depress "wrong" connections and to respond positively to weaker signals – in other words to do the same mental or motor process with less "effort". In other words, cells change their receptivity to messages based on previous stimulation.

The teacher's job is to support students in translating their brains' remarkable biological potential into actual performance. It is of course a "mission impossible", since only a fraction of the brain's total power can ever be used within a lifetime. It is estimated that we use less than 1 per cent of 1 per cent of our brain's projected processing capacity which is around 10^{27} bits of data per second according to psychiatrist and sleep expert Allan Hobson of Harvard.[59] When scientists cut into Einstein's brain after his death they discovered that he had no more brain cells than anyone else, just more connections between them, and, even so, there was loads of capacity left.

In pursuit of excellence in learning, then, it seems that the skilled educator faces three tasks:

- First, to *encourage new* neural connections through challenges that create high levels of stimulation.
- Second, to *consolidate existing* connections. The more a neural pathway is used, the more efficient it becomes. Axons become insulated with a white fatty substance called myelin, which speeds up the electrical-chemical-electrical signalling process, and neurons respond with less effort to the original prompt. On the other hand, unused connections are eventually lost, they are pruned away.
- The educator's third task is to ask learners to *reconfigure* existing webs of neural connections by taking on board data that will straighten out a misunderstanding, refine a concept, complete an understanding or hone a skill.

This last one sometimes feels like quite an effort. Eric Jensen sums up the job: "The key to getting smarter is growing more synaptic connections between brain cells and not losing existing connections. It's the connections that allow us to solve problems and figure things out."[60]

In order to achieve best results, it's obviously important to work with the brain's natural processes, to teach in a way that is compatible with the student's natural learning methods. Some of these points, a selection of the similarities and differences between learners, will be discussed shortly. But, generally, learning should get off to a great start because it appears that everyone is born with several predispositions, including

- a desire to work cooperatively with others
- the inclination and ability to learn language
- the will and skill to make patterns
- a natural propensity to learn mathematics, according to Brian Butterworth, Professor of Cognitive Neuropsychology at University College, London.

Butterworth argues that "… our genes contain a set of instructions for building a mathematical brain, and this is why, without benefit of teaching, human beings are born to count".[61]

However, it's not all plain sailing. Some of the factors that affect the translation of potential into performance are outside of the teacher's control, so let's get the depressing bits out of the way first.

One obvious example is lifestyle during pregnancy. A developing foetus is very sensitive to stress and nutrition. The mother's emotional state, diet and intake of substances have an effect on the development of the brain, which is creating neurons at a rate of up to 15 million per hour between the fourth and seventh month of gestation.

A second example is nutrition. Mothers' breast milk appears to contain certain nutrients that stimulate the production of neurotransmitters, which are essential to the efficient firing of synapses. Also, fast foods and most cheaply-produced packaged foods simply don't contain enough of the items that the brain needs for optimum performance: proteins, unsaturated fats, complex carbohydrates, sugars and trace elements such as boron, selenium, vanadium and potassium. Conversely, the negative effects of many soft drinks and most food additives is well known.

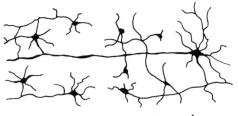

Few connections through lack of stimulation

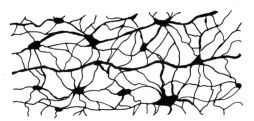

A young, stimulated brain rich in neural connections.

A third area is early-years stimulation. In middle-class homes, for example, twice as many words per day on average are spoken by parents to toddlers, compared with working-class homes. Such enrichment in early years is crucial to the construction of the brain's basic architecture. So is the amount of early-years laughter, touch, freedom, visual stimulation, tactile manipulation, music, motor stimulation, environmental variety and cooperative play. The infant brain is utterly plastic and begins to customise itself from the moment a child is born. It configures itself to its environment and experiences. Over 50 trillion neural connections are already in place at birth, and millions more are added moment by moment, but unused connections begin to be cut away by the billion. Take emotional and social development. The evidence suggests that emotional intelligence develops early, perhaps even in the first year, and that the school years are only the last resort for nurturing emotional literacy.

Professor Philip Gammage, de Lissa Chair of Early Childhood, South Australia, is clear:

> At birth there are far more potential connections than the child can use, and by the age of three or so pruning has already started and systems of connection that are seldom or never used are being slowly eliminated. We are born, for instance, capable of learning phonemic combinations not common in our native language, but will lose that capability relatively soon … By about five (or earlier) many predictive and causal social, as well as physical/locational attributions, have become quite settled. In a real way, the brain is then almost "cooked".[62]

It's a real case of "use it or lose it". Even the first two years of life can decide between dramatically different possible futures. This is why Ernest Boyer, the late President of the Carnegie Foundation for the Advancement of Teaching, offered a sobering thought: "To blame schools for the rising tide of mediocrity is to confuse symptom with disease. Schools can rise no higher than the expectations of the communities that surround them."[63]

A fourth example is sleep. Lots of children simply don't go to bed early enough or, during puberty, they wake up too early! Modern thinking suggests that during deep sleep the brain sorts and files the day's inputs. Consequently, learning is consolidated and memories are laid down.

Finally, we come to genetics. Currently, the extent to which intelligence is inherited is hotly debated. There are researchers who fiercely argue that it is, among them Professor Sandra Scarr, famous for her identical-twin studies, and also Professor Robert Plomin, who claims to have virtually isolated the elusive gene for "general intelligence". One area is fairly clear: Tonegawa and Kandel have identified a specific gene that activates the critical memory function of neurons and this may explain why some people have a better memory than others. Overall, it's now thought that 30–60 per cent of the brain's wiring is due to heredity and 40–70 per cent is the result of the environment, depending on what type of behaviour is being considered.

Now let's flip the coin over and see what's on the optimistic side. The good news is more powerful than the bad. Within the teacher's control are *expectations*. We have known since Rosenthal's and Jacobsen's *Pygmalion in the Classroom*,[64] published in 1968, that teachers' internalised views of students' capabilities have a direct impact on students' actual performance. In the studies students were grouped randomly, but the teachers were told they differed in ability. Guess what. The results of the group that were mistakenly believed to be high flyers rose and the results of the "low achievers" went down. Rosenthal identified six ways in which the teachers communicated high expectations:

1. the teacher expressed confidence in her ability to help the student
2. the teacher expressed confidence in the students' ability
3. her nonverbal signals were consistent with what she said: tone of voice; eye contact; level of energy
4. feedback from the teacher was specific and ample and mentioned both good and bad
5. the teacher gave detailed input to individual students
6. the teacher encouraged individual improvement through challenge.

Teachers communicate expectations through the energy they bring into the classroom, through the words they say and the way they say them, through the effort they put into developing a good relationship with a class, and perhaps most powerfully, through the design of learning tasks. Together, these impact on students' self-image and self-esteem (page 292 for a detailed checklist). The resultant self-belief either drives or depresses motivation and perseverance. Expectations are received by students from other sources, too –

family, peers, the culture of a local community, the media, and in many cases teachers have to work doubly hard to reverse negative messages. It is critical that we maintain high expectations even in the face of contrary evidence. Reading scores, base-line tests and value-added procedures can so easily limit our expectations of pupils.

Also within the teacher's control is the *culture of the classroom* – the psychological and emotional environment for learning (the whole of Section 3 is devoted to this). Likewise, we control the *physical environment of learning*. The brain needs a continual supply of oxygen (it uses one-fifth of the body's supply), cool temperature (open the windows), and preferably negatively ionised air (buy an ioniser unit for the classroom, or have a waterfall installed!). It absorbs a surprising amount of information from peripheral material (have lots of displays). Colours, aromas, light and furnishings (lay carpets, redecorate) have a profound effect on mood, and music can make a big difference. The brain turns music into electrical energy; it literally feeds the brain. Different types of music appear to have different effects (the Mozart debate). The type of food offered in the canteen at lunchtime is within the school's control, as is the provision of pure chilled water (have plenty of dispensers around the building). A hundred and ninety-eight gallons of blood passes through the brain every 24 hours. If it is insufficiently hydrated, the electrolytic balance of the brain is affected and mental performance suffers. Eight to ten glasses of water a day are required for optimum functioning. All in all, learners' "states", to use the technical term, can be altered. Learners can be made more "ready" for learning.

Alistair Smith gives us a further reason to be cheerful: children can become cleverer through the teacher's *skilled intervention*. He explains how Sternberg, Vygotsky, Feuerstein and Rand "pioneered work on cognitive modifiability through cognitive mediation and created a structure for developments such as 'thinking skills'. They showed that 'intelligence' could be modified and thus expended and developed."[65] Michael Howe, Professor of Psychology at Exeter, who is on the "environmentalist" side of the debate about intelligence, also encourages us to believe that the conditions we create make a profound difference: "It is not true that a young person's intelligence cannot be changed. There is abundant evidence that the intelligence levels of children increase substantially when circumstances are favourable."[66]

So, overall, the prospects for raising achievement look good. Of course, there are major challenges, especially in difficult socioeconomic and sociocultural circumstances. However, teachers can make a difference, and will do so if they follow some simple guidelines. At last we can begin to spell them out. Here are the promised four *similarities* between learners:

1. Everyone needs to work things out for themselves
2. Experiences that are multi-sensory, dramatic, unusual or emotionally strong are remembered for longer and in more detail than ordinary, routine experiences
3. Everyone needs to feel emotionally secure and psychologically safe
4. Learners are more motivated, engaged and open when they have some control over their learning.

1. Everyone needs to work things out for themselves

Learning occurs through the brain in making its own meaning, making its own sense of things. Many researchers distinguish between two types of meaning: "pointer" meaning and "sense" meaning (Kosslyn), or "surface" meaning and "deeply felt" meaning (Caine and Caine). Take, for example, knowing about Pythagoras's Theorem. *Pointer* or *surface* meaning refers to the ability to name and reference an idea, so you would know that the square on the hypotenuse is equal to the sum of the squares on the other two sides. You might even be able to use this formula to conduct simple, standard calculations. You would certainly be able to quote the definition in a game of Trivial Pursuit.

Sense or *deeply felt* meaning is different. It involves understanding *why* the square on the hypotenuse is what it is. It's a conceptual grasp, probably the result of hearing the idea explained several times by different people, seeing it presented visually, happening to catch a TV programme about its importance in architecture, "doing" it with bits of cut-up card, reading about what prompted Pythagoras to make his discovery in the first place. These separate fragments weave together in your mind and suddenly it all makes sense: the penny drops. You can now explain the Theorem to someone else and use it in a range of contexts. This deeper meaning, or internalised understanding, is the kind of learning that concerns us here.

As long ago as 1983 Leslie Hart[67] found that such pattern-making is one of the innate characteristics of the neocortex. The neocortex, or cerebral cortex, is the convoluted outer covering of the brain (*cortex* is Latin for bark or rind). Only three millimetres thick, comprising six layers of neurons, with the total surface area of a closed broadsheet newspaper, this

> is what makes human beings what they are. Within the vast human cortex lies a critical part of the secret of human consciousness, our superb sensory capacities and sensitivities to the external world, our motor skills, our aptitudes for reasoning and imagining, and above all our unique language abilities.[68]

The cerebral cortex is home to rationality, logic and conceptualisation.

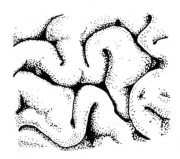

The convoluted surface of the neocortex

It is clear from the research that students create personal concepts by recognising "gestalts", not by adding up bits of information in a digital manner. According to the dictionary a "gestalt" is a "perceived organised whole that is more than the sum of its parts". Biologically, these are in fact physical interconnections of neurons, webs, neural fields, axon–synapse–dendrite networks created by existing neural groups suddenly connecting up. It's like a whole series of light bulbs coming on together – in fact we often use the light bulb image when someone finally gets an idea that we've been wanting them to grasp for some time.

Hart says, "It can be stated flatly … the human brain is not organised or designed for linear one-path thought". Earlier we said that the modern scientists see the brain as dynamic and responsive, not computer-like. Gestalts form unpredictably when a number of realisations occur together, triggered by who knows what? So, it's no use explaining first about squares, then about square numbers, then about triangles, then about the relationship between the three sides and expecting every student to be with you every step of the way. Rather, students form gestalts by deciphering clues, indexing bits of information and recognising relationships across a range of sources. They don't necessarily grasp things just because you've explained them.

In fact, Hart goes as far as to say that "learning is the extraction of meaningful patterns from confusion". And "there is no concept, no fact in education, more directly important than this: the brain is, by nature's design, an amazingly subtle and sensitive pattern-detecting apparatus". Concept formation depends on what students do, in their heads, not what the teacher does. So, it's obvious: make learning mentally active and set up investigative, problem-solving types of activities that invite the brain to operate according to its natural inclination – to play detective. Section 2 is full of strategies designed to get students to think and come to conclusions for themselves.

Obviously, "pattern recognition depends heavily on what experience one brings to a situation", says Hart. This is why students grasp ideas at different times and learn at different rates. Back to our earlier discussion about the Theorem of Pythagoras: a student who was taught about square numbers in primary school or who plays a lot of games where triangles matter, such as pool, or whose father is a maths teacher and has pointed out lots of applications of geometry since the student was a toddler, will "get it" faster than a student who has never had these experiences. How often do you, as a teacher, have to go back and back with a student, scraping away conceptually until you find a firm foundation of understanding to build on? This makes the fundamental case for the differentiation and personalisation of learning. (See Section 4 for some practical possibilities such as "Extended Horizons" (page 231) and "Upwardly Mobile" (page 234).)

Since Hart's pioneering work, many researchers have restated and refined the point. Jane Healey, the famed educational psychologist, for example: "I am increasingly convinced that patterns are the key to intelligence. Patterning information means really organising and associating new information with previously developed mental hooks."[69]

In *Descartes' Error: Emotion, Reason and the Human Brain*[70] Antonio Damasio, Professor of Neurology at the University of Iowa School of Medicine, explains further. As we are presented with new information, he says, the brain recalls past experience and references the new stuff to base data from different locations simultaneously. The new material is integrated into existing neural networks, which are consequently changed, giving us an enriched template of experience. "Some circuits are remodelled over and over throughout the lifespan, according to the changes an organism undergoes", he writes. "Other circuits remain mostly stable and form the backbone of the notions we have constructed about the world outside."

So, as the brain becomes more experienced, as it takes in more and more data, misconceptions get sorted out, half-understood ideas are completed and erroneous notions are ditched. Again, this gives us clues about how to teach effectively: work from students' prior knowledge; accept their misunderstandings and half-baked ideas; start from where the students are, not from where you think they should be because of their age. Create both the climate and the opportunity for them to be honest about their confusions, frustrations and struggles. Create time for reflection. Expect conceptual leaps to occur at different times for different students for different reasons.

This pattern-based explanation of the learning process is known as constructivism. Abbott and Ryan:

> Constructivism holds that learning is essentially active. A person learning something new brings to that experience all of their previous knowledge and present mental patterns. Each new fact or experience is assimilated into a living web of understanding that already exists in that person's mind. Constructivist learning is an intensely subjective, personal process and structure that each person constantly and actively modifies in light of new experiences … With a constructivist form of learning, each child structures his or her own knowledge of the world into a unique pattern, connecting each new fact, experience, or understanding in a subjective way that binds the child into rational and meaningful relationships to the wider world.[71]

To support students' individual mental patterning, which is the key to concept formation and internalised understanding, I offer six guidelines.

One principle kept them sane;
When in doubt check a List.

19

(a) Encourage students to find things out, and work things out, for themselves

Make the implicit, natural function of the neocortex explicit. Capitalise on its innate curiosity and desire to make connections. At the simplest level, reverse the usual process and have students ask you the questions. Use "Question Generator" (page 141), "Question Time" (page 143) or "Hot-Seating" (page 116), for example. Make them work for information, don't hand it to them on a plate; research strategies include "Information Hunt" (page 118), "Circus Time" (page 85), "Double Take" (page 101) and "Sole Search" (page 253). And structure opportunities for them to work things out, to come to conclusions by pulling together several threads of information, by deducing, rationalising and intuiting. The best examples in Section 2 are "Broken Pieces" (page 78), "Assembly" (page 67), "Silent Sentences" (page 152), "Ranking" (page 148) and "Guess Who" (page 109).

(b) Encourage students to articulate "draft ideas"

Checking something out, talking something through, getting it off our chest, speaking off the top of our heads – these all play natural and key roles in the process of concept formation. We are social creatures, our brains develop in a social environment and we often make meaning through social intercourse. So, discussion, peer teaching, draft writing, presentations to others and think-talk-respond are classic ways of getting students to articulate their thinking, and thereby speed up the process of sorting and connecting in their heads. In the process, language itself is being clarified. Students are not using language just to "do the activity": they are "using" the activity to develop language. "Back-to-Back" (page 69) is a crystal clear example of this.

What's more, William Glasser suggests that people retain 95% of what they teach to someone else.[72] In many classrooms this means fundamentally shifting the ratio of teacher talk to student talk. Alistair Smith suggests that we "adopt a policy of no more than 16 minutes an hour of direct instruction".[73] Section 2 of *The Teacher's Toolkit* contains many ideas for structuring peer teaching and "articulation". "Scrambled Groups" (page 150), "Pairs to Fours" (page 137), "One-to-One" (page 135), "Corporate Identity" (page 89), "Discussion Carousel" (page 95) and Centre of the Universe" (page 83) are just some of the classics on offer.

Articulating draft ideas needn't be verbal, though. It's possible to take "draft action", that is "have a go", even though you're not sure whether you can do it or how it will turn out. Encourage students to use trial and error as a deliberate learning strategy and encourage them to demonstrate what they've got so far, even though it may not be the finished article. The most structured versions of this in *The Teacher's Toolkit* are "Forum Theatre" (page 105) and "Value Continuum" (page 163).

(c) There's little point in giving students "ready-made meaning"

By this I mean such things as printed notes, dictation, copying, predrawn mind maps, fill-in-the-gaps-type exercises (which are usually corruptions of the original "Cloze Procedure"). Such material might be filed neatly in students' folders and give everyone the comforting impression that work has been done, but little deep learning will have occurred. Instead, teach students different ways of arriving at and recording their own patterns of meaning. Use what are sometimes known as "graphic organisers": key-word plans, mind-maps from scratch (see Tony Buzan's extensive and much-copied work), flowcharts, sketches, diagrams, spidergrams, bullet-pointed lists, graphs, storyboards and so on. Eric Jensen makes the point strongly: "Humans never really cognitively understand or learn something until they can create a personal metaphor or model."[74] *Ready for Revision*[75] offers some practical suggestions. See "Conversion" (page 87), "Distillation" (page 97) and "Hierarchies" (page 113) for more details. The strategy that combines the first three guidelines, which is therefore both complex and powerful, is the demanding "Marketplace" (page 122). Try it if you dare.

(d) Come at the same key concepts from different angles in different ways

Building a logical and linear series of steps towards a concept, and then moving on to the next, will not work for most students. They usually need to have lots of examples and applications along with several explanations in different media if they are to "get it" (deep), rather than just rote-learn it (shallow). Continually moving from the Big Idea to the details, and back again, drawing it, miming it, speaking it, charting it, saying it, singing it, demonstrating it, modelling it, listing it, hot-seating it (ever had a conversation with the water cycle?), dancing it, writing it – unusual combinations of these techniques presented in rapid succession help the left and right hemispheres of the neocortex to work together and encourage that penny to drop. The most efficient way for some students to "get" a concept is to see pictures and "do" the idea rather than listen to it or read about it. For suggested ways of creating multisensory routes to conceptualisation see "Bodily Functions" (page 75), "Go Large" (page 107) and "Multisensory Memories" (page 130).

(e) Provide interactive feedback that's specific and immediate

Think of what happens in computer games: students learn to progress through levels quickly because they get instant and precise feedback on the decisions they make. The brain is exquisitely geared for feedback – it decides what to do next based on what has happened before. It is self-referencing and self-rectifying; it readily builds feedback that's "hot", in other words relevant and immediate, into its developing concepts and skills. Of course, it's not easy for the teacher to get round to everyone quickly enough (see "Dreadlines" on page 103), but there are ways of checking students' understanding collectively so that you can make appropriate interventions. Methods include "Calling Cards" (page 81), "Thumbometer" (page 161), "Beat the Teacher" (page 71) and "Spotlight" (page 154).

Apart from the teacher's feedback, the reactions of peers, verbal and nonverbal, are vital sources of information for the learner. These can be spontaneous, a by-product of the cut and thrust of regular classroom activity, or can be planned, as in the case of peer redrafting peer-assessment activities such as "Pass the Buck" (page 139), "Stepping Stones" (page 1 and "Wheel of Fortune" (page 170).

Feedback has maximum effect when it is controlled by the learner – they choose when receive it and how much to receive. This builds another case for democratic and student-ce tred practice of the kind described in "Blank Cheque" (page 260).

(f) Punctuate the learning

According to Jensen, there are three reasons for this:

> First, much of what we learn cannot be processed consciously; it happens too fast. We need time to process it. Second, in order to create new meaning, we need internal time. Meaning is always generated from within, not externally. Third, after each new learning experience, we need time for the learning to "imprint".[76]

The brain continues to process information long after we are aware that we're doing it. The snag is that further external inputs can get in the way. According to Allan Hobson, Professor of Psychiatry at Harvard University,[77] association and consolidation processes can occur only during "downtime" when other external stimuli are shut out. In practical terms, this means having a few mini-breaks within a double lesson. Two to five minutes every ten to fifteen minutes is recommended for heavy, new material and a couple of minutes every twenty for more familiar stuff. Teachers who relentlessly get through the syllabus often find that they have to reteach a lot of the content before the exam – now we know why.

On top of all this, didactic-transmission teaching is simply inefficient. When students are asked to be passive they are using only a fraction of their brains' power. That's why there's a lot of doodling, daydreaming and surreptitious chitchat in "boring" lessons – students are using spare capacity. By contrast, when a brain is asked to solve a problem, decipher a code, fathom a mystery, unravel a puzzle, respond to a curiosity, answer a creative request, it immediately bursts into life. Nancy Denney, the late Professor of Psychology at Wisconsin University, has shown that "problem-solving is to the brain what aerobic exercise is to the body".[78] The brain needs novel, complex and challenging tasks for its health. Scans show that, as soon as the brain is asked to work actively on problems, there's a virtual explosion of neural activity, causing synapses to form, neurotransmitters to activate and blood flow to increase.

The neocortex of the human brain is designed to operate in this active, investigative way. It is irrepressible in its automatic search for the best answer to a question in which it is interested, and it continually scans to resolve unfinished business. It's like a nonstop search engine. This is why we sometimes wake up in the middle of the night with an unexpected solution to a worrying issue. Working with the "grain of the brain" – teaching via intriguing questions, challenges, conundrums and creative activities – does everyone a favour. Students become more engaged and achieve deeper levels of understanding. Teachers therefore have to press less. Clearly these insights support the current interest in thinking skills.

The snag is that many teachers feel that they can't afford the time to teach like this because they've got "a syllabus to get through". Yet many of the same teachers complain that the students don't remember what they've covered! The answer may lie with the headteacher of a Swansea secondary school who recently told his moaning science department to cut the GCSE syllabus by 20 per cent. His argument was: if you cut 20 per cent of the content and give yourselves time to teach properly, then the 40 per cent that the students currently learn by covering 100 per cent of the syllabus will become 60 per cent even though they'll do only 80 per cent of the total. Confused? More is less! How does that work?

2. Experiences that are multisensory, dramatic, unusual or emotionally strong are remembered far longer and in more detail than ordinary, routine experiences

There are three points to make about this. **First,** the brain has an attentional bias for novelty. It is far more interested in what's new than what's normal. Sylwester and Cho[79] discovered that the brain has a built-in bias for certain types of stimuli. Since it can't give attention to *all* types of incoming data, it sifts out those bits that are less critical to our survival. Any stimulus introduced into our immediate environment that is either new (novel) or sufficiently different in emotional intensity (high contrast) immediately gets our attention. For example, when a recent Year 8 geography class in Southall in the UK saw house bricks and pieces of chalk, rubber, wood and stone waiting for them on the desks, they started beaming and chattering with anticipation. During the lesson, on rates of erosion, everyone was focused and stayed on task pretty well the whole time. According to the end-of-term test, this was a far more memorable experience than the regular lessons of teacher talk, textbooks and worksheets.

Clearly, the immediate minimum requirement is to ensure that there is plenty of variety within a lesson and over a series of lessons. Mix it. See "Overtime" (page 228), "Upwardly Mobile" (page 234) and "Menu" (page 246) for details. A number of studies in the 1980s by Prigogine & Stengers,[80] Gleik[81] and Doll[82] found that students actually achieve a richer understanding of "content" in a climate of suspense, surprise, disequilibrium, uncertainty and disorder! Prigogine goes as far as to say that the brain is designed for chaos: "instability creates purposeful activity and direction." Because the brain loves to sort things out for itself, and loves variety, super-ordered behaviouristic approaches are actually the least likely to produce desired results. Most effective learning is either real-life learning or designed like real life, which leads the Scottish Consultative Council on the Curriculum to conclude that "learning is messy".[83]

The **second** point that needs to be made concerns retention. There is no single part of the brain used to store memories. It used to be said that we have two types of memory, short-term and long-term, but nowadays it's generally thought that we have at least five! *Working memory*, situated in the prefrontal and parietal cortices is extremely short, only a few seconds long. *Implicit memory*, sometimes divided into "reflexive" and "procedural", is stored in the cerebellum. This enables us still to juggle or ride a bike after years of inactivity, or drive a car on "autopilot". The remaining three are collectively known as *explicit* or *declarative* memory: *remote memory*, spread around the neocortex, is the lifetime collection of data about a whole range of topics – ideal for Trivial Pursuit; *episodic memory*, the record of specific personal experiences (i.e. locations, events, personnel involved, circumstances), is stored in the hippocampus; *semantic memory*, created in the hippocampus and stored in the angular gyrus, retains the meaning of words and symbols from textbooks, people, videos, films, diagrams, computer programs, written stories and so on, and gives us our general knowledge about the workings of the world and is the stuff of exams.

These different types of memory explain why some people are good at remembering what they did on holiday ten years ago (episodic), but can't remember the name of someone they met two days ago (semantic). In addition, peptide molecules, circulating throughout the body, also store and transfer information. Memory is hard to pin down.

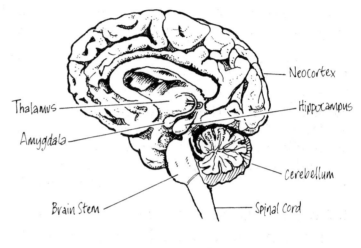

Inside the brain

So, how are memories made? Memories appear to be the result of a rapid alteration in the strength of the synaptic connections, a process known as long-term potentiation, which is activated by specific genes and a protein molecule known as CREB (cyclic AMP-response element binding protein).[84] The physical evidence of memory is stored as changes in neurons along specific pathways. Some researchers such as William Calvin,[85] a University of Washington neurobiologist, and Michael Gazzaniga,[86] Director of the Center for Cognitive Neuroscience at the Dartmouth College, USA, have fathomed the retrieval process: when enough of the right type of neurons are firing in the right way, dormant neurons are activated and successful retrieval occurs. The process is triggered by association. The word "birthday" for example will activate not just one memory of one birthday, but hundreds of neural fields connected with many experiences of your own and other people's birthdays and patterns abstracted from those experiences. Some studies have shown that we can retrieve almost everything we paid attention to in the first place, but only when we are in the right state and in the right context. We all know how a song we haven't heard for years will bring memories flooding back, usually with associated smells and feelings. Tony Buzan reckons that "There is now increasing evidence that our memories may not only be far better than we ever thought, but may in fact be perfect."[87]

The strength of a memory, and therefore the ease with which it is retrieved, seems to depend on the strength and processing of the initial input. Now the importance of multisensory learning becomes clear. When several senses are simultaneously involved, the message is being received through a number of different channels and stands a better chance of remaining prominent. There are also more ways to trigger the memory: location (where were we?); feelings (what was it like?); movements (what did we do?); the names and faces of other people (who else was there?); as opposed to just words (what did the teacher/textbook say?).

Proving the point, Ekwall and Shanker[88] discovered that people can generally recall about

- 10% of what they read
- 20% of what they hear
- 30% of what they see
- 50% of what they both see and hear
- 70% of what they say
- 90% of what they simultaneously say and do

Therefore, to maximise learning, make it active, make it episodic. Design, where possible, activities that involve students in *physical doing* as well as speaking, listening, reading and looking. Create learning experiences that really are *experiences*. Episodic learning is effortless, it happens all the time quite naturally. By contrast, semantic recall requires huge amounts of internal motivation, is triggered by language alone, and is the weakest of our retrieval systems because in the long haul of evolution it is the most recently developed.

Beyond this, make learning experiences dramatic, give them an emotional edge. According to journalist Jill Neimark "a memory associated with emotionally charged information gets seared into the brain".[89] Highly charged events, whether positive or negative, are remembered well because the chemicals released, such as adrenaline, noradrenaline, enkephalin, vasopressin, ACTH (adrenocorticotrophic hormone), act as memory fixatives. They tell the brain to retain events that might be vital points of reference in the future. Use learning strategies such as "Still Image" (page 158) and "Bodily Functions" (page 75). Ask the students to take risks, to take part and try things they haven't done before. Tell strong stories, use analogies that excite the imagination, create tension and suspense.

The more the amygdala (the almond shaped, "emotional" organ in the midbrain area) is aroused, the stronger the imprint will be. The pioneering studies of the University of California psychobiologist Dr James McGaugh have led him to conclude that emotions and hormones "can and do enhance retention".[90] His research clearly shows that even relatively ordinary emotions improve memory, so we don't always have to put students through shocks, horrors and life-threatening situations to get them to learn!

In fact, at Stanford University Medical School, Professor William Fry's research[91] even suggests that the body reacts biochemically to laughing. He says "Having a laugh while you're studying is a good idea because it increases the brain's alertness."[92] The chemical balance of the blood is altered, and this may boost the body's production of neurotransmitters. So it's OK to have fun. Some *Toolkit* ideas are designed to do just that. Check out "Games" (page 192), "Bingo" (page 73), "Verbal Football" (page 166), "Dicey Business" (page 93), "Quick on the Draw" (page 145) and "Verbal Tennis" (page 168).

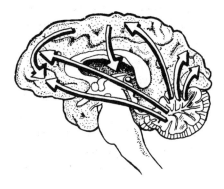

The relationship between movement and cognition

The **third** point is the importance of movement. The old idea that mind and body are separate has recently gone out of the window, for strong biological reasons. For example, various studies of the cerebellum, classically considered to be concerned only with motor function, have revealed that it is closely associated with spatial perception, language, attention, emotion, decision making and memory. It's only 10 per cent of the brain by volume, but it possesses over half of the brain's neurons. It is now understood that it sends signals to many parts of the cerebral cortex, not just to the motor cortex as earlier thought. Professor Susan Greenfield of Oxford declares that there is no single movement centre in our brain. Movement and learning are in a continual and complex interplay.

The implication is clear: make sure that there is sufficient physical movement, even within an "academic" learning situation, which is the reverse of what most teachers have been brought up to believe. But will movement raise achievement? Yes! In a Canadian study of over 500 students reported by Dr Carla Hannaford, author of *Smart Moves: Why Learning is Not All in Your Head*, those who spent an extra hour each day in a gym class far outperformed in exams those who didn't exercise.[93]

Apart from anything else, physical activity increases blood flow to the brain. Sometimes it's helpful to ask students to do a quick bit of physical exercise in the middle of a lesson – jog on the spot for a minute for instance, stretch or do one or two cross-laterals[94] – just to liven things up. According to Dr Max Vercruyssen, Associate Professor at the University of Hawaii School of Medicine, simply having students stand up while you talk to them means they take more in! Sometimes at the start of a lesson, play a physical game such as "Caterpillar" (page 194) or "Giants, Dwarfs and Wizards" (page 193). For a full account of the role of the body in the learning process, and how to make the most of it, consult Hannaford's *Smart Moves*. By way of introduction she says:

> We have attempted to explain the mind from the glimpses and pieces we are able to put together as we focus our attention and research on the brain. But we have missed a most fundamental and mysterious aspect of the mind: learning, thought, creativity and intelligence are not processes of the brain alone, but of the whole body.[95]

Similarly, Roy Anderson in his *First Steps To A Physical Basis Of Concentration*[96] suggests that many behavioural and apparent learning difficulties can be resolved by attending to the physical origins of inattention and deploying a range of specific physical exercises, stimuli and postures. For further practical insights into educational kinesiology see *BrainGym* by the Dennisons (www.braingym.com), *Every Body Can Learn* by Marilyn Nikimaa Patterson[97] and *Learning with the Body in Mind* by Eric Jensen.[98]

3. Everyone needs to feel emotionally secure and psychologically safe

We can thank Daniel Goleman and his concept of emotional intelligence for bringing this point to international prominence. The author of many books, Goleman for years covered the behavioural and brain sciences for *The New York Times* and was senior editor at *Psychology Today*. However, he wasn't the first to describe the significance of the emotions. Joseph LeDoux, Candace Pert, Jerome Kagan and Antonio and Hannah Damasio paved the way. Goleman, summarising some of their key findings, explains that in the Western world:

> We have gone too far in emphasizing the value and import of the purely rational – of what IQ measures – in human life. Intelligence can come to nothing when the emotions hold sway ... To better grasp the potent hold of the emotions on the thinking mind, consider how the brain evolved ... From the most primitive root, the brainstem, emerged the emotional centres. Millions of years later in evolution, from these emotional areas evolved the thinking brain or "neo-cortex" ... Because so many of the brain's higher centres sprouted from or extended the scope of the limbic area, the emotional brain plays a crucial role in neural architecture. At the root from which the newer brain grew, the emotional areas are entwined via myriad connecting circuits to all parts of the neurocortex. This gives the emotional centres immense power to influence the functioning of the rest of the brain – including its centres for thought.[99]

Our clever neocortex might enable us to *think* about our feelings, and might allow us to choose from a range of subtle responses, but, when the emotional chips are down, the thinking brain defers to the limbic area and midbrain. Emotion is stronger than thinking. We all know how hard it is to concentrate on a difficult letter we're trying to write when we've just received some tragic news or had a row. Emotions are different from feelings. They include joy, fear, surprise, disgust, anger and sadness – these are universal phenomena, entirely biological and travel the brain's superhighways. Feelings are culturally and environmentally developed responses to circumstances and take a slower, more circuitous route around the body.

In extreme cases, when we feel seriously at risk, for example, pure instinct takes over. The most ancient part of the brain, the "reptilian brain" as Paul MacLean (former Director of the US Institute of Mental Health) called it years ago, activates both predetermined and learned survival behaviours. The desire to survive dominates. For example, if someone shouted "Fire!" right now, you wouldn't carry on reading this fascinating section: you'd throw the book down and bolt for the nearest exit. The brain is designed primarily for survival, not for learning.

Three biological truths explain this. First, there are more neural connections going from the emotional limbic area to the intellectual neocortex than vice versa. This means that the limbic organs can pull rank. Second, the thalamus deep inside the brain acts as a switchboard, or relay station, sending incoming sensory information to the neocortex for rational processing. However, the faster route is not "up" to the thinking cap, but "down" to the amygdala (the "seat of emotions") and the reptilian "survival" area. If the brain even *suspects* that an input signals danger – the footsteps behind us *may* mean that we are being followed, the sound of breaking glass in the middle of the night *could* mean that a burglar has broken into the house – it immediately sends the information "downwards". The amygdala, which is at the centre of all fear and threat responses, is called into action. It activates the entire sympathetic system, releasing adrenaline, vasopressin and the peptide cortisol, which collectively change the way we think, feel and act. Our blood pressure rises, our large muscles tense and our immune system becomes depressed. This instinctive reaction results in running to get away or hiding under the bedclothes!

This is our *first* response, just in case. Later, if further sensory inputs do not confirm our fears (the footsteps become more distant, the house remains silent), we might rationalise and investigate. The thalamus will start to send signals to the cortex for more thoughtful, considered responses. Then we discover that the predator was actually an innocent pedestrian who turned off down a side street. And the glass? Well, it was only the cat, who'd knocked over an empty milk bottle on the doorstep.

The third fact is to do with the distribution of blood. Under "normal" conditions, blood flows evenly to all parts of the brain, including the neocortex. In the instant that the brain perceives threat, blood concentrates in the reptilian area. Heart rate and blood pressure increase, exaggerating the supply to the base of the brain, and blood is drained from the neocortex, debilitating higher-order thought processes. Consequently, survival behaviours take over: walking away from the problem; burying your head in the sand; being defensive; counterattacking; ganging up; playing dead; lashing out. In other words, fight, flight, flock or freeze. The tendency is to do what's worked before in similar situations; all attention becomes focused on the source of the threat; peripheral vision and rationality go out of the window. Lateral thinking? No chance. At this point the brain is closed to hearing or trying anything new. Learning is impossible. Leslie Hart called this process "downshifting".

The kinds of threats that trigger this sort of behaviour may be physical, such as the possibility of being bullied, or of not being able to get from room to room because there are no ramps. They may be psychological and emotional – the fear of being ignored, of being the last one to be picked, of being shown up in class, of being name-called, exposed, belittled, ridiculed, caught out, told off, excluded. Here at home, for example, my son Steven declared that he wasn't intending to get more than C grades in his GCSE mock exams because he'd be in for so much stick from his mates if he did really well. Whenever she's asked what kind of a day she's had at school, my younger daughter Helen doesn't talk about lessons, but how she's getting on with her friends, whether she's "in" or "out" with this person, that group, or the other teacher. For both of them acceptance is the big issue.

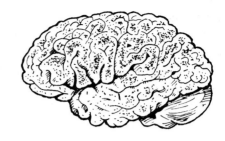

Blood distribution under normal Conditions

Threat can also come from the prospect of failure. A task that is perceived to be too difficult, or for which the resources are inadequate or inaccessible, is likely to be refused. The threat of punishment can actually exaggerate the behaviour it's designed to eradicate: inattentiveness, for example. Even rewards can be anxiety-creating and threatening: will I have done enough to deserve it? With every reward there is the implied lack of reward, which is essentially a covert punishment. Whatever the source of threat, the reaction is always the same: play safe. Recent research

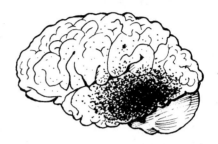

Under threat : blood Concentrated in the ancient parts of the brain

suggests that, in stressful environments, levels of seratonin (the ultimate modulator of our emotions) are reduced. This often results in increased violence. Continued stress leads to a depressed immune system and the increased risk of physical illness. In *Accelerated Learning in Practice*, Alistair Smith quotes an interesting finding: "A recent Medical Research Council study reported that only 10 per cent of low serotonin amongst depressives is caused by genes … it is the social environment which is crucial."[100]

Professor Roland Meighan, in many ways the British John Holt, has clear and sharply worded insights into the fear that pervades schools. In particular read "How Many Peers Make Five?"[101] and "In Place of Fear".[102] These and other of his columns for the UK journal *Natural Parent* are available on the Roland Meighan pages of www.gn.apc.org/edheretics, and in book form: *Natural Learning and the National Curriculum*.[103]

This said, human emotions don't just have a negative relationship with the learning process. Take motivation. People want more of what they experienced as pleasurable, and less of what was boring or painful. The brain has its own internal reward system, producing opiates that attach a sense of pleasure to a satisfying behaviour. Students who succeed feel good. Often, at the end of a particularly enjoyable lesson, students will say, "Can we do that again?" and will frequently turn up next time full of anticipation, asking excitedly, "What are we doing today?" Beyond this, the joint and separate studies of O'Keefe and Nadel have shown that we make better conceptual maps when we feel positive.[104] The happier we are, the faster and more accurately we sort and connect incoming data. Who said learning shouldn't be fun?

Compared with the Central Nervous System, in which axon–synapse–dendrite connections travel along only fixed pathways, chemicals are much more pervasive. We now know that the chemicals that create emotions are produced and distributed throughout the body. Peptide messenger molecules (ligands) are released into the blood stream and access all areas: every cell has countless receptor sites for ligands, creating "feelings" or "moods" throughout the whole body. We might get a "gut feeling" because the peptides that are released in the brain are simultaneously released into the intestines. It has even been suggested recently by Miles Herkenham of the US National Institute of Mental Health[105] that 98 per cent of all communication within the body may be through peptide messengers. This has led some to regard the bloodstream as the body's second nervous system. The effect is that emotions create distinct mind–body states that strongly influence behaviour. Richard Bergland, a neurosurgeon, goes as far as to say that "thought is not caged in the brain, but is scattered all over the body".[106] The brain operates more like a gland than a computer. It produces hormones, is bathed in them and is run by them: in other words emotions rule, OK.

What we know about the dominance of emotions leads us to examine three aspects of practice.

(a) Classroom rules

Learning occurs most efficiently when the learner is *not at all* fearful of being bullied, mocked, ridiculed, ignored, left out, name-called, belittled or shown up. Firm classroom ground rules, made *with* students, can secure positive behavioural norms based on listening and the elimination of put-downs. The idea of creating this kind of harmonious, civilised community connects strongly with the current concern for citizenship and the national drive for inclusion. It is so fundamental that the whole of Section 3 of *The Teacher's Toolkit* is devoted to it. Beyond your own classroom, start to work on whole school behaviour and ethos.

The ship would often make its extensive range of feelings known.

(b) Our own demeanour and manner

This means the way we come across to students. The researcher R. C. Mills discovered that learners pick up on the particular emotional state of the teacher, which impacts on their cognition. Teachers who use humour, give warm smiles, have a joyful demeanour and take genuine pleasure in their work will have learners who outperform those students whose teachers do not demonstrate these qualities.[107] Encouragement, positive feedback and acknowledgment all seem to release serotonin – an essential neurotransmitter that aids neural interconnection.

NLP tells us that most communication is nonverbal, so the way we look, how we speak and what we do, combined with what we actually say, make the total impact. The effect of "the way the teacher is" on students is twofold: first, directly on their own feelings of wellbeing, and, second, on their perception of what's acceptable; we model norms to them, they take their lead from us. So, if we are sarcastic, for example, students are likely to feel nervous *and* are likely to use sarcasm themselves. It's easy to see how the teacher can affect the "state" of the learner as NLP and accelerated learning would describe it. Of course, this calls for teachers to be self-aware and skilled, in other words to be emotionally intelligent themselves.

Here's an example. Soon after *A Guide to Student-Centred Learning* was published in 1985, Dr Donna Brandes and I received a remarkable essay from Alan White, a science teacher in Sunderland. He wrote about his commitment to developing a student-centred approach and recognised the need to attend to his own attitudes and skills first:

> I can identify strongly with the essential beliefs and attitudes which underscore student-centred learning. At the same time I am aware of my own limitations in terms of being able to translate and communicate through behaviour, my attitudes and beliefs. My immediate goal is to develop my own interpersonal skills in such a way that I am able to provide the facilitative conditions for personal growth in a student-centred classroom.[108]

Again we see that the pursuit of excellence to which *The Teacher's Toolkit* is committed takes us beyond the superficial level of classroom techniques and into the more personal territory of teachers' language and skills, and further into the domain of their attitudes and beliefs values – and ultimately their own self-esteem. See "Check your Professional Development" on page 314, and the "Onion Rings" model in particular, on page 317, for further details.

In the meantime, here's an example of a school currently taking these matters very seriously. When candidates are interviewed for the post of learning assistant, they are observed at work with students and assessed on a five-point scale.

	1	2	3	4	5	
Offers success						denies success
Is enthusiastic						is reserved
Asks questions						lectures
Praises						is critical
Is patient						is impatient
Is optimistic						is pessimistic
Is supportive						is alienating
Sets at ease						discomforts
Is acceptive						is hostile
Has sense of humour						is over serious

Harwich School

(c) The teaching of emotional intelligence

Apart from students and teachers behaving well towards one another, which has been the essence of our discussion so far, there's more. There's the prospect of students being able to identify, name and describe feelings. Then there's their ability to manage their own, and respond to other people's, emotions appropriately. And, further, there is the development of desirable qualities such as impulse control, perseverance and social deftness, plus desirable values such as honesty and a commitment to justice. Underpinning these is the acceptance of personal responsibility: the willingness to see life is a series of moment-by-moment choices; and the willingness to change behaviours, feelings and beliefs based on an awareness of personal potential and self-imposed limitations. Remarkably, all this can be taught.

Using a slightly different term, but defining the same territory, Stephen Bowkett says, "Self-intelligence is about equipping children with an emotional toolkit, and giving them the skills to pick the right tool for the job. Emotional resourcefulness … is the capacity to know and understand yourself and make best use of that understanding."[109] Many resources in this growing field, such as *Teaching Emotional Intelligence* by Adina Bloom Lewkowicz,[110] take their structure from Goleman's five emotional competencies:

- self-awareness
- managing emotions
- self-control/self-motivation
- empathy
- handling relationships/social arts

Mike Brearley's book *Emotional Intelligence in the Classroom*[111] defines emotional intelligence as "the ability to control and use our emotions to enhance our success in all aspects of our lives", and offers a suite of structured classroom activities to develop what he calls the "five emotions of success": self-awareness; ambition; optimism; empathy; integrity.

All this material resonates strongly with the Personal, Social and Health Education programmes, and active learning initiatives of the 1980s. A lesson learned then was that teaching such issues only through separate dedicated lessons, no matter how well designed and delivered, always fails. To stand a chance, these concepts, beliefs and skills have to be part of the fabric of school life at every level.

Developing emotional intelligence is an intention of *The Teacher's Toolkit* and surfaces most strongly in activities such as "Discussion Carousel" (page 95), "Silent Sentences" (page 152) and "Value Continuum" (page 163). The subject gets explicit attention in Section 3, where self-discipline and relating skills are tackled through "Murder Hunt" (page 179), "Framed" (page 182), "Observer Servers" (page 185), "Learning Listening" (page 187) and "Assertiveness" (page 199). Personal responsibility is tackled in "Sabotage" (page 190) and throughout the increasingly independent operating systems of Section 4.

To conclude, some years ago Nathaniel Branden, a practising clinical psychiatrist, related what we now call emotional intelligence to self-esteem. He suggested that self-esteem can be defined as "the disposition to experience oneself as competent to cope with the basic challenges of life and as worthy of happiness", and is fed by six characteristics of living:

- living consciously
- self-acceptance
- self-responsibility
- self-assertiveness
- living purposefully
- personal integrity

These behaviours are in a relationship of "reciprocal causation" with self-esteem, he argues. In other words they are both the *products of* healthy self-esteem and they *create* healthy self-esteem.[112] After well over thirty years of work in this field, Branden concludes: "It is cruel and misleading to tell people that all they need do to have self-esteem is decide to love themselves. Self-esteem is built by practices, not by emotions."[113]

To find out more about self-esteem, and to check your impact on students, see page 289.

4. Learners are more motivated, engaged and open when they have some control over their learning

Imagine you want to buy a new car. You visit several showrooms and, after a lot of umming and ahhing, you eventually set your heart on a shiny red Mazda 323. For the next few days you're driving your old car while you await delivery, and suddenly the roads are full of Mazda 323s – they are everywhere! Where have they all come from? They've always been there, of course, but only now do you "see" them.

Another example: you are going on holiday with your family. It's a long drive and after a while your children start to get hungry and thirsty. The more desperate they become, the more they spot Little Chefs, chip shops, McDonald's restaurants, pizza places – even a garage that sells sandwiches and sausage rolls will do. Just stop!

What directs our attention to Mazda 323s and eating opportunities? The answer: the reticular activating system, or RAS. Since the classic research of Scheibel, and of Scheibel, Kilmer,

McCulloch & Blum in the 1960s, and 1980s, the RAS has been regarded as the central command system of the brain, operating as a "gating mechanism" for sensory inputs and causing a person to focus their attention.

At its base, the RAS is connected to the spinal cord, where it receives information projected directly from the ascending sensory tracts. In fact, it serves as a point of convergence for signals from your exterior and interior worlds. This is where the world outside of you, and your thoughts and feelings "inside" you, meet. In the other direction, the reticular activating system sends axons (transmitters) to the cerebral cortex and other forebrain structures, giving it the power to "switch on" your brain and control its levels of arousal.

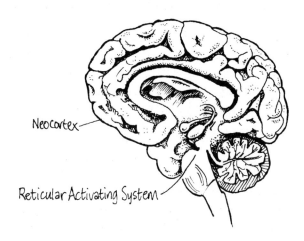

The Reticular Activating System

As more and more is discovered about this ancient bit of the brain, it is clear that the situation is not quite as simple as the early research suggested. Whatever the detail, the effects are the same. The area in and around the old RAS exercises a dynamic influence on the activity of the cortex, including the frontal lobes and motor activity centres. Consequently, it plays a significant role in determining whether a person is impulsive or self-controlled, active or inactive, highly motivated or bored. This is the centre of balance for the other systems involved in learning. When functioning normally, it provides the neural connections needed for the processing and learning of information, and the ability to stay on task.

Naturally enough, in cases where the reticular activating system doesn't excite the neurons of the cortex as much as it ought, the results are inattention, slow learning, poor memory and little self-control. In fact, if the RAS is sufficiently damaged, or disconnected altogether, the consequence is irreversible coma. On the other hand, overstimulation can lead to hyperactivity, hypervigilance and anxiety. The reticular activating system must be activated to normal levels for the rest of the brain to function as it should.

Clearly, the RAS acts as a filter. From all the incoming data, both external and internal, it decides what is important enough to send through to the cerebral cortex. In other words it decides what gets our attention. It decides what is filtered in and out of "consciousness". A new or surprising input is generally given priority – the door of the classroom opens in the middle of a lesson and everyone looks up, for example. A house alarm goes off accidentally and we immediately look through the curtains to make sure everything is all right. After a while, though, we don't "hear" it any more, although it's still ringing. Our RAS eventually decides that it's not relevant to our needs or purposes.

Conversely, on a school training day, as long as you are fascinated by the presenter's input you don't notice the noise of traffic outside, the clanking in the school kitchen, the fluttering curtains or the changing weather conditions through the window. However, if the trainer talks for too long you start to lose interest and pay attention instead to these peripheral stimuli. Your mind then turns to more pressing matters such as what you're going to cook for tea and all the jobs you've got to do that evening. So, attention depends fundamentally on what *we* perceive to be meeting *our needs* or to be relevant to *our purposes* at any particular moment.

This is why the children going on holiday spotted food outlets so readily – they had a *reason* for noticing them. Their brains were alert to food outlets because they were receiving increasingly strong hunger signals. Likewise the Mazda 323s. Now you've made a decision to get one, you have a "reason" for spotting them. Mazda 323 information is suddenly "relevant". Before, it was of no consequence. To sum up: the RAS will readily let information through that is new or unusual, that helps to meet "felt" physical or psychological needs, or that connects with a choice we have made.

There are at least five implications of this for teaching and learning.

First, provide novelty and variety to sustain attention, both within and between lessons. This has already become a recurring theme of the *Toolkit*.

Second, understand that the brain will give first priority to basic needs – if a student is hungry, thirsty, cold or dying to go to the loo, they are not going to pay attention to Pythagoras's Theorem, no matter how important we tell them it is.

Third, the "big picture". If students understand the purpose of the lesson or scheme, what it contains, how it fits in with what's gone before, what it will lead to later, and why it's necessary for some future assessment, then their RAS will begin to "open". If they *accept* that this purpose is *personally important* – in other words they want it, they take "ownership" of it – then their RAS becomes wide open. See the fifth point for how this might happen.

One by One they mastered the natural laws of their New World.

Fourth, personal goals. In most schools, target-setting with students is done badly. There's not enough time given to the diagnostic discussion; there's no real relationship between the teacher and student in the first place; the targets end up being general (such as "I will improve my writing") or trivial (such as "I will bring a pen to lessons"); there's no flexibility in the system to allow students to concentrate on more meaningful learning targets anyway (they still have to go through the lock-step lesson regime with all lesson content and process sewn up by the teacher) and it all feels like a bit of a ritual.

Deeply internalised personal goals, however, are a different matter. These are the result of people identifying an ambition and catching a sense of what it will be like to get there. The process takes time: it involves recognising wants and needs, weighing up pros and cons, sifting options and making genuine priorities. The result is an internalised goal, a clarified personal purpose. From then on the reticular activating system automatically spots opportunities, marshals energies, scouts for resources and eliminates distractions. It navigates you towards your goal, operating as a kind of autopilot. This degree of personal desire results in self-motivation, self-sufficiency and perseverance. In schools, for this to work fully, there would need to be a substantial overhaul. The teacher would need to be more like counsellor and coach, relationships between teachers and students would need to be authentic, the prescribed curriculum would have to go and learning resources, including time and space, would need to be used much more flexibly to enable personal pathways to be followed. For further insight into the role of the RAS and the power of personal goals, study the *Investors in Excellence* programme run by the Pacific Institute. Visit them at www.pac-inst.com

As things stand, most teachers do all the planning *for* learners, then they wonder why students are not attentive or motivated! Which brings us to …

Fifth, plan *with* learners. This is the route to ownership and self-motivation and is possible even within the prescriptions of the national curriculum and exam syllabi. There are four levels at which this can take place

1. At the scary deep end lies open negotiation with learners: "Blank Cheque" (page 261). As the nickname suggests, some details of the deal are already written in – what has to be learned is non-negotiable – but *how* it is learned is determined by the students collectively and democratically. This, for me, is the pinnacle of practice. This method delivers a multiplicity of outcomes simultaneously – learning to learn, emotional intelligence and citizenship – and is the most inclusive practice in the whole *Toolkit*.

2. Then there's "Sole Search" (page 253). The idea here is to combine prescribed learning with the student's own interests and to work out a personal learning plan to suit each student's inclinations and style.

3. Waist-deep is "Menu" (page 246), which involves organising a series of options (based perhaps on different learning styles) and asking students to make individual choices. The destination (the learning outcome) is the same for everyone, there are just different ways of getting there.

4. The shallowest, toes-in approach is "Upwardly Mobile" (page 234). This involves mapping out a differentiated learning route for all learners and giving individual students some control over the pace and depth, but not the direction, of their progress.

The reticular activating system is no doubt why Eric Jensen maintains that "the easiest way to reach all of your learners is simple – provide both variety and choice".[114] Many studies confirm the importance of students having some control over their learning. Deci and Ryan,[115] Deci, Vallerand, Pelletier and Ryan[116] conclude that motivation and standards decrease in situations where learners have no choice. Likewise, Mager and McCann[117] show that motivation is in direct proportion to feelings of control.

What's more, deciding personal goals and accepting responsibility for negotiating, or at least choosing, learning strategies is the essence of *life-long learning*. So, the earlier people get used to it, the better. Finally, the connections with *citizenship* are clear. Choice, negotiation, collective decision making and personal responsibility are at the heart of democracy. These attitudes and skills can be acquired only experientially.

There Are Also Differences Between Learners

Key issues

People are different. People react differently to the same circumstances, they have different likes and dislikes, they have different default behaviours, they perceive and process experience differently. Biologically, each person's brain is as individual as their fingerprint, the result of a fantastic process of neural interconnection running at a rate of between 300,000,000 and 500,000,000 new synapses per second in the earliest phase of life. During this period the basic architecture of the brain is established and, not surprisingly, preferred learning styles are determined. According to Michael Grinder, a person's preferred style is the one they learned to use for survival as an infant, so their brain gives it first priority for the rest of their lives. Dr Anthony Gregorc, on the other hand, believes that the mind is separate from the brain and that differences in style are the outward manifestations of differences of mind, not physical differences in the brain's structure and neural pathways.

Whenever a problem arose, there were always six different ways of tackling it.

Either way, faced with such diversity, a teacher can easily feel overwhelmed, and this is where learning-style *models* come in. They simplify the complexity and enable us to manage the territory. According to Rita Dunn, "Learning style is the way in which each learner begins to concentrate on, process and retain new and difficult information". It can be seen as "a biologically and developmentally imposed set of personal characteristics that make the same teaching method effective for some students and ineffective for others. Every person has a learning style; it's as individual as a signature".[118] Similarly, Robert Sternberg defines learning style as: "A preferred way of using one's abilities. It is not in itself an ability but rather a preference."[119]

And J. W. Keefe describes it as "an individual's characteristic and consistent approach to organizing and processing information".[120]

Since the early 1970s numerous attempts have been made to categorise these natural and learned differences. I have detected at least seven broad approaches, each with its own frame of reference, key researchers and variations:

1. Approaches based on **information processing** – defining different ways of perceiving and processing new material. For example, Kagan, Kolb, Honey & Mumford, Gregorc, Butler, McCarthy.
2. Approaches based on **personality** – defining different character types. For example, Myers-Briggs, Lawrence, Keirsey & Bates, Simon & Byram, Singer-Loomis, Grey-Wheelright, Holland, Geering.
3. Approaches based on **sensory modalities** – defining different degrees of dependence on particular senses. For example, Messick, Bandler & Grinder.
4. Approaches based on **environment** – defining different responses to physical, psychological, social and instructional conditions. For example, Witkin, Eison, Canfield.
5. Approaches based on **social interaction** – defining different ways of relating to others. For example, Grasha-Reichman, Perry, Mann, Furmann-Jacobs, Merrill.
6. Approaches based on **intelligence** – defining different socially recognised talents. For example, Gardner, Handy.
7. Approaches based on **cerebral geography** – defining the relative dominance of different parts of the brain, the two hemispheres, for instance. For example, Sperry, Bogen, Edwards, Herrmann.

For a succinct survey of some of the more prominent of these approaches, and links to more specific websites, visit: http://www.universaleducator.com/LearnStyle/index.html, the "Learning Styles" section of the *Universal Educator* website. For many more research possibilities see Appendix B.

There is such overlap between some of these approaches that a different commentator would probably label the field and place the researchers differently to the way I have done it. In fact, Rita and Ken Dunn of St John's University, New York, have created a learning styles framework that brings several of these approaches together. They propose five "strands" or "stimuli" and twenty-one "elements". A person's learning style is a combination of features from all five categories:

- **Environmental**: sound, light, temperature, design
- **Emotional**: motivation, persistence, responsibility, structure
- **Sociological**: self, pair, peers, team, adult, varied
- **Physical**: perceptual, intake, time, mobility
- **Psychological**: global/analytic, hemisphericity, impulsive/reflective

Other attempts to combine approaches include Eric Jensen's catalogue of 28 possible learning styles[121] and the Israeli scholar Aaron Aviram's list of 32![122] Some suggest that there is a *hierarchy* of factors determining a person's learning style. The most fundamental influence, they say, is personality type – these characteristics are least likely to change. The next strongest influence is sensory preference (the way you take information in), then information processing style (the way your mind works on that incoming data), then social interaction style (ways of involving others, or not, in your learning process) then instructional preference (preferences for certain types of content, or the drive for information acquisition compared with the drive for grades and marks) and learning environment (your response to physical and emotional conditions).

Even though people develop their dominant style early in their lives, or may indeed be born with it as part of their pre-written "life-script", some researchers (Torrance and Ball, for example) suggest that these natural styles can be changed as a result of intense experience. For some people it is desirable that they do make changes – their future success may depend on it. Patricia Kirby's evidence suggests that learning style *flexibility* leads to higher levels of achievement.[123]

Similarly, Dr Anthony Gregorc found that most successful professionals learn, somewhere along the way, to operate in a variety of styles. However, he argues that the changes are superficial. People never change their dominant Mind Style™, as he calls it, or the shape of their Mind Field (see below), only their behaviour. Such superficial changes might be the result of "a phase they are going through" (most evident in childhood), or the result of external demands (the requirements of a job, for instance) or internal ambitions, or simply the consequence of trying to survive in a noncompatible environment.

Given the way that schools and the big wide world operate, student success and life chances are clearly at stake. Students, and for that matter most employees, cannot afford always to plough their own furrow – it usually leads to trouble of one sort or another. Learning and working institutions are not sufficiently person-centred, nor are they likely to become so in the current political and economic climates, to accommodate diverse individuality. Getting the balance right between supporting and challenging students' modes of learning is therefore crucial. If students are allowed always to work within their preferred style, they will remain narrow and ill-equipped. On the other hand, if they are forced too early or too often to work in nonpreferred and uncomfortable ways, they are bound to underachieve and may well become alienated.

The solution to this is twofold.

First, ensure that each learner experiences sufficient success to create a platform of personal confidence. This requires us to be sensitive to their personal style. Study after study in the heyday of learning styles research found that, whenever learners are taught in their own style, their motivation, initiative and results improve: Carbo,[124] De Bello,[125] Della Valle,[126] Hodges,[127] Shea,[128] Shipman & Shipman,[129] Virostko,[130] White.[131] For many more up-to-date studies on the relationship between learning styles and attainment, visit: www.learningstyles.net/bib.html

This compelling point is found at the heart of the statutory Statement of Inclusion, a central plank of the British National Curriculum 2000 (page 57). The issue of learning styles is, at root, an equal-opportunities issue.

Second, students who have been sufficiently successful, and therefore believe themselves to be capable learners, are likely to rise to and master the challenge of working in nonpreferred ways. Encourage them to do so. Provide opportunities for students to work in "new" ways. Provide training – show them how to do it. Provide information – explain why it's a good idea. Do it with sensitivity, self-awareness and a firm intention to inflict no harm. The "operating systems" in Section 4 provide various ways of structuring this.

Before looking at three learning-styles models in more detail, let's register the practical implications so far.

1. Recognise that your own preferred style can get in the way of effective learning

Over the years researchers have consistently found that teachers' own dominant learning styles tend to determine the plans they make for children: the way they structure a topic; the selection of teaching methods and resources; the design of tasks; the allocation of time; the type of evidence of learning to be produced by students; the assessment method. More than this, teachers' underlying mindsets determine the way they organise the learning environment, the value they place on homework, tests, grades and pecking orders, their reaction to misbehaviour, their creation of unwritten classroom norms, their subtle nonverbal communications, as well as their explicit "delivery" of information and instructions.

Therefore, the first base for the concerned teacher to get to, clearly, is increased self-knowledge. Bruno Bettelheim, the psychologist, said, "There are ... utterly destructive consequences of acting without knowing what one is doing." Beyond this, aim for base two: the will to accommodate students' individuality.

To recognise your own style, I recommend Gregorc's excellent book *An Adult's Guide to Style*[132] and his "Gregorc Style Delineator" instrument. Both are available from Gregorc Associates at www.gregorc.com. These tap into your mindset, not just your preferred learning or teaching strategies, so they provide information about deep rather than surface style issues. However, it's important to get feedback from lots of sources, so surf the Internet and find ways of working out your intelligence profile, your sensory dominance and whether your left or right brain is boss. Try Peter Honey's quick and easy questionnaire at www.campaign-for-learning.org.uk/aboutcfl/whatkind. Or try the full version of

To learn how to encourage individuality, they regularly practised on visitors from Planet Uno.

Honey and Mumford available at www.psi-press.co.uk/lss2.htm. See Appendix B for lots more options. All of these tools build personal awareness and will help you to recognise the relationship between your own learning style and your natural teaching instincts. They may well reveal the difference between your natural teaching style – the one you would use if left to your own devices – and your role-based teaching style, in other words the ones you use because of some constraint or forceful expectation. Where there is strong dissonance between the two, frustration and distress build up, as many readers know.

Above all, discovering your own Mind Style or learning style gives you the wherewithal to resist the temptation to operate automatically from habit, instead to stop, to think empathetically and to begin to break out of your own mould.

By the way, it's important to recognise that different models have different roots, different underlying assumptions and principles. They cannot be integrated successfully. So try a few and feel for the one that provides the most self-awareness and the most valid personal challenge. Beware also that some of the models and instruments on offer are scientifically untested, that is they have been knocked together only to give a rough and ready indication of how you stand against a framework such as VAK (see below) or multiple intelligence or left-brain/right-brain. Many of their prompts are context-specific, which limits the self-knowledge they return. The most established and thoroughly researched instruments usually have to be bought, and most are readily available via the Internet. Money well spent in my view.

2. Understand learners' preferred styles, but don't pigeonhole

For this I suggest Cynthia Ulrich Tobias's *The Way They Learn*.[133] This slim volume, written for parents, neatly presents the visual-auditory-kinaesthetic (VAK) model, plus Gregorc's Mind Styles as well as Gardner's Multiple Intelligence Theory. Better still, consult the "Gregorc Mind Styles Learner Extenda-Charts", which provide detailed information about different dominant learning types (again, available from the website). Alternatively, try Priscilla L. Vail's *Learning Styles*,[134] which describes her own eclectic and insightful idea of six learning styles dimensions with down-to-earth examples. Or see Bernice McCarthy's *The 4MAT System*,[135] which is presented in an extremely readable and highly visual form.

It is important not to get hung up on just one model: none of them is an adequate description of reality, each is only a simplified projection of its creator's view of reality. Familiarise yourself with several. Be aware that not every model will suit every teacher. Gregorc makes the point:

> My experience says that anyone can gain topical information about any model. But, each fully practiced model will make further specific mental demands on the implementor. As a result, some people, because of the natural strengths and limitations of their Mind Styles, will not be able to fully utilize certain models with ease and integrity.[136]

Therefore, choose a model that passes three tests of "rightness" for you:

> First, is it a coherent system which addresses your needs? Second, does the theory and practice of the model work in the crucible of the everyday world and help to improve it? And third, do your mind and Self accept the model so that the theory and practice become silent guides to harmless behaviors?[137]

Finally, remember that everyone uses more than one style. "Since people are multi-faceted, each person has more than one way of learning. But most of us have predominant clusters, preferred channels, and secondary, subordinate approaches," says Priscilla Vail.[138] Therefore, aim to sensitise yourself to differences rather than to categorise students. For four practical ways of spotting students' styles, go to "Check Your Students' Learning Styles" on page 279.

3. Accommodate different styles, but don't try to be too precise

Beyond increased self-knowledge, a will to accommodate individuality and an understanding of students' style types lies the delivery of diversity. The key to this is to have lots of practical teaching techniques at your fingertips. Not all teachers feel that they have. The answer is to read books such as this one, or *The Active Learning Handbook*.[139] Or plan with colleagues whom you don't normally work with. At a Pembrokeshire school recently, as part of the county-wide *Learning Learning Project*, the experienced head of physics planned a series of lessons on renewable energy with a young art teacher. Afterwards he said, "This has been the most productive meeting I have been to in my whole career" – it resulted in exciting and workable classroom ideas that he confessed he would never have thought of himself. Too often we meet with the same old colleagues, usually in the department group. Mix it. Arrange to brainstorm and plan with colleagues who teach quite different subjects and who probably have different learning styles from your own.

Planning became a wild and dangerously productive business

Use a learning-styles construct to audit and then stimulate your practice. Many people these days like the simplicity of VAK, though Gregorc is more penetrating. It's probably best to keep two or three on the go so your thinking does not get too narrow and pernickety. Run your chosen model(s) past your existing schemes of work; this will expose any style gaps in methodology. Check out your assumptions. I recently worked with a science department who told me, "We do lots of variety". On closer inspection their Year 7 scheme was full of nothing but Abstract Sequential and Concrete Sequential lessons (the meaning of these terms will become apparent later). Of course, the science teachers were all strongly AS and CS themselves and they could not see it. They were shocked and quickly set about identifying lessons that could be rewritten in more random modes. When they taught these lessons, they reported higher levels of achievement among "mischievous pupils". Learning style constructs help to pull thinking and planning in unfamiliar directions.

Armed with loads of practical and diverse ways of achieving the learning objectives, you then decide how to present these strategies to students. Sequencing learning activities so that different styles are accommodated *over time* is the simplest, and for many teachers the most comfortable, way of going about things. I regard this as the minimum professional response to the challenge of learning-styles research, to guarantee all learners a regular dose of their preferred modus operandi. Beyond it are more sophisticated ways of delivering personal styles: by building them into differentiated route ways ("Upwardly Mobile"), through structured choices ("Menu"), through personal learning plans ("Sole Search") and through open negotiation ("Blank Cheque"). See Section 4 for details and take your pick.

4. Begin to address the bigger issues

Schools are still, on the whole, geared for certain types of learners. Bernice McCarthy's research led her to ask, "If 70% of our students learn most comfortably in ways not generally attended to in our schools, how should we proceed?"[140] In training sessions, teachers often say to me, "The exams require students to demonstrate abstract and sequential learning, therefore we must teach in this way." Of course the logic is flawed, but the continued dominance of narrow forms of assessment does create enormous injustice, and signals to teachers and students alike the value placed by the nation on certain learning styles compared to others. Then there is the issue of resources. Textbooks, worksheets and exercise books still dominate the "deskscape" of most classrooms. In fact, the rooms themselves are a problem. Often there's just enough space for students to sit cramped behind desks for a whole lesson, lesson after lesson. The boxlike nature of the building resonates with the gridlike nature of the timetable. Times are fixed, subjects are fixed, teachers are fixed, even movement is fixed, life is compartmentalised; everything feels tight and contained. No wonder that 80% of excluded pupils in the UK have kinaesthetic learning needs and pupil referral units up and down the country are full of Concrete Random students.

Three popular models

Having surveyed the key issues, it's now time to look at three well-used learning styles models in a bit more detail.

1. Sensory preferences: visual, auditory, kinaesthetic

This construct has come to prominence through accelerated learning, but was originally developed by Richard Bandler (a computer programmer) and John Grinder (a linguist), the inventors of Neuro-Linguistic Programming (NLP) in late 1970s America. The basic idea is that everyone has a dominant sense. Everyone prefers to use this sense to let in and deal with new information – some will prefer to look at, others will prefer to listen to, others will prefer to engage actively with new data. The dominant sense creates the preferred channel for receiving and processing material and consequently the most efficient and default way of learning.

Naturally, for everyone all three senses continually work in concert, with information from one being supplemented and complemented by information from another. Also, different combinations of senses are required in different situations. Therefore, no one can be said to be entirely visual or auditory or kinaesthetic (physical). However, the research suggests that everyone *does* have a dominant and preferred sense, to one degree or another, and that the opportunity to use this preference for learning has a significant effect on their level of achievement and feelings of competence.

Research conducted by Specific Diagnostic Studies of Rockville, Maryland, with 5,300 students[141] revealed that in any class in any subject in any school there are on average

- 29% of students with a visual dominance
- 34% with an auditory dominance
- 37% with a kinaesthetic dominance

Some of those with a visual preference respond to the visual impact of *words*, while others are attentive to graphics shown on the overhead projector, to a slide sequence or a PowerPoint presentation, to a video, a poster, or field trip, or to a diagram, photograph or drawing in a textbook. They engage most readily with visual material and learn most efficiently through this channel.

Those with an auditory preference engage with, and learn most easily from, sound – the sound of the teacher's voice, or fellow students in discussion, peer presentations, the commentary of a video, an audio cassette, or a guest speaker.

The largest group, those with a kinaesthetic inclination, need to "do" the learning. Some are happy with tactile activity – making models, sorting cards, folding, cutting, sticking, arranging, handling artefacts. Others need to be up and doing. They are "with it" only when they are physically active, demonstrating a process, rehearsing a role-play, preparing a still image, standing on a value continuum line, miming, moving between resources, going on a visit. These students tend to give us most grief if their needs are not met; they easily become restless. These are the ones most at risk of underachievement and exclusion, largely because most UK secondary school teachers have not been trained to teach them effectively. Mike Hughes says:

> Kinaesthetic learners are the students who are most disadvantaged in secondary schools, simply because so many learning activities are based upon reading, writing and listening. This is partly because most teachers, who themselves have been successful in the reading, writing, listening world of formal schooling, are visual or

auditory learners and predominantly teach in their preferred style … Kinaesthetic learners generally find that opportunities to work in their preferred style significantly decrease as they get older.[142]

Rita and Ken Dunn's research in regard to retention suggests that in a well-taught ordinary lesson you can expect at best about 30% of students to remember up to 75% of what they hear. About 40% will remember around 75% of what they read and see. Of the remaining 30%, they suggest that half are tactile learners and will remember best what they touch, feel and move. The final 15% will remember only what they physically do. This gives us strong clues about ways to raise levels of achievement for all.

The Dunns suggest that everyone has a dominant sense and a secondary sense. If the teacher is not catering for the use of their dominant sense, most students compensate by using their fallback position. Although there are many students whose sensory modalities are sufficiently balanced for them to adapt and take in information however it's presented, there are some (Michael Grinder suggests about 20%) who have such a strong single dominance that they will absorb information only if it is presented in their favoured style. Unless their learning-style needs are sufficiently met, these students quickly become frustrated, bored, alienated and mischievous. They then generally end up in lower sets. There is still a great deal of confusion in Britain between ability, behaviour and learning style.

Skilled as they were at juggling priorities, sensory preferences proved a bit more of a handful

The implications for teachers are clear. The obvious minimum requirement is to check that all lessons have sufficient elements of all three modalities. Naturally, some topics appear to lend themselves to one or two senses and not the third. For example, it's not easy to imagine how you present quadratic equations kinaesthetically. The key is to think laterally and imaginatively, to consider rather than dismiss wacky ideas, to look at the lesson through the eyes of a student whose learning style is the opposite to your own, to start with the assumption that there are multisensory ways of doing everything and that you have to be convinced otherwise. Each topic in every subject is innocent until proven guilty, as it were. Check out ideas such as "Assembly" (page 67), "Bodily Functions" (page 75), "Go Large" (page 107), "Hide 'n' Seek" (page 111), "Quick on the Draw" (page 145), "Value Continuum" (page 163) and "Multisensory Memories" (page 130) to stimulate your thinking about tactile and kinaesthetic possibilities.

Beyond this balancing act, consider offering structured choices to students. Ask them individually to choose between a visual, an auditory and a kinaesthetic way of reaching the learning outcome (see the "Menu" approach, page 246). If you feel confident enough, go even further and negotiate learning with students. Take into account what they say about their preferred style and see if it can be built into the programme by using the "Sole Search" (page 253) or "Blank Cheque" (page 261) operating systems.

There are various ways of detecting students' sensory preferences. Consult "Check your Students' Learning Styles" on page 279.

2. Cognitive predilections: Gregorc's analysis

For Dr Anthony Gregorc, previously of the University of Connecticut, learning involves the dual processes of *perceiving* and *ordering* information. He distances himself from the brain-based learning crowd, believing mind and brain to be separate. "The **mind** is the instrument by which and through which we interact with the world. It is the primary medium for the learning/teaching process," he says.[143] The mind arises from the individual's psyche, like a tree growing from a seed. All minds are *similar* in that they are made of the same "stuff", various qualities such as abstractness, concreteness, sequentialness and randomness.

> On the other hand, each mind is also **inherently different** because of a natural variance in the amount of "stuff" that is at our disposal. Some of us have more of the Concrete Sequential qualities. Others have more Abstract Sequential, etc. These quantitative differences account for our specialized abilities and our inability, beyond the basics, to understand and relate to all others equally well.[144]

He explains that "**Style** is the outward product of the mind and psyche,"[145] and goes on:

> the human mind has channels through which it receives and expresses information most efficiently and effectively. The power, capacity, and dexterity to utilize these channels are collectively termed "mediation abilities". The outward appearance of an individual's mediation abilities is what is popularly termed "style".[146]

The **brain**, meanwhile,

> is a physical organ which serves as a vessel for concentrating much of the mind substances. Along with the spinal cord, nerves and individual cells, it comprises the "machinery of the mind" for receiving and transmitting data to various parts of the body. It is part of the essential hardware that permits the software of our spiritual forces to work through it and become operative in the world.[147]

Gregorc suggests an analogy. Imagine a telephone system. The brain is the hardware, in other words the switchboard, cables, telegraph poles, and handsets. These are the tools that make communication possible. The mind is the caller's voice and message.

After almost three decades of phenomenological research, Gregorc confidently proposes that there are differences in the way people both *perceive* (let in, grasp) and *order* (organise, store and reference) data. These differences in mental operation are the result of possessing common mental qualities to different degrees. Take perception first, the differences can be plotted on a continuum from *concrete* to *abstract*.

Concrete └──┘ **Abstract**

PERCEPTION

Extremely *concrete* people are focused on physical reality. They are sensate. They concentrate on what they can see, feel, hear, smell and touch. They have little patience with arty-farty ideas and waffle. They are down-to-earth and live in the here and now. They have a strong tendency to be objective. When it comes to learning, the experience has to be physical. If the learning can't be seen, touched and "done", nothing goes in. Extremely *abstract* students, on the other hand, quickly and naturally turn experience into abstract thought. They live in their heads: they think; they feel; they look for patterns; make connections; seek generalities; want ideas; love theories and big principles. They "see" the invisible. They tend to be subjective. Remember, this is a continuum with most people occupying positions somewhere between the two ends.

Ordering refers to the way in which people organise and store data in their heads. Again there are big natural differences, from *sequential* to *random*.

Sequential |_____| **Random**

ORDERING

Strongly *sequential* people store ideas and facts systematically. They seem to have filing cabinets in their heads, they are logical and precise. To get from A to E mentally, they first go from A to B, then B to C, then C to D and finally arrive at E – and can describe all the steps clearly. They are linear, structured, step-by-step thinkers who will pursue only one idea or line of thought at a time. They are telescopic rather than kaleidoscopic. By contrast, strongly *random* people seem mentally chaotic. They appear to store things all over the place, without rhyme or reason, yet can make intuitive connections and creative leaps that sequential people never do. They can go from A to E in one go, but have no idea how they got there! They store information in categories that makes sense to them but to no one else! They tend to deal in big chunks, make connections this time that aren't the same as last time, see the whole rather than the parts and weave many strands together simultaneously. They are kaleidoscopic rather than telescopic. Again, these are extreme positions and most people are somewhere in between.

Gregorc combines these mental qualities to form four distinctive styles and designates them: Concrete Sequential (CS); Abstract Sequential (AS); Concrete Random (CR) and Abstract Random (AR).

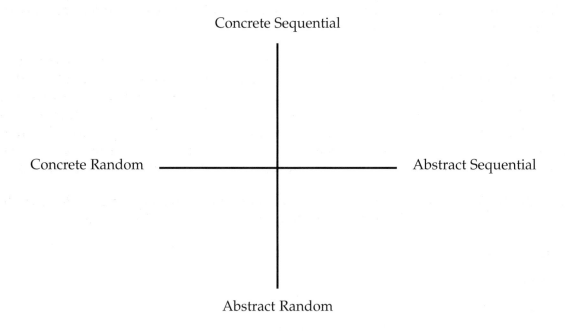

He is keen to stress that everyone has all four of these styles, but usually in different proportions. Some people might be fairly well rounded and have more or less equal facility in all four modes, but most have a natural inclination to one or two. Some people favour one style very strongly. If you imagine plotting your personal position on each of the four "points of the compass" and then joining the dots with straight lines to form a kite or diamond shape, the area enclosed by the lines is your Mind Field. This territory is deeply rooted in your psyche, it is to be honoured and nurtured, it is not changeable, it is *you*. It could be said to be your comfort zone.

Although Gregorc does not have precise percentages for each category, his extensive research across the two genders, across all age ranges, abilities, socioeconomic backgrounds and ethnicities suggest that *any* class you teach will comprise students of all kinds. Some will have a strong preference, others a mild preference and a few (Gregorc's initial studies indicated about 5%) will have no significant preference at all.

This model and the consistency of findings over the years provide us with an excellent way of planning for diversity.

Students with a dominant Concrete Sequential Mind Style learn best through structured practical activities. They relish hands-on learning with step-by-step instructions such as following a computer program, playing a game with clear rules, making a model from a set of instructions, completing a list of short tasks, following a prescribed route, painting by numbers, observing and imitating an expert, working through a manual.

Students with a dominant Abstract Sequential Mind Style learn best through structured academic research. They like to be guided to see the connection between ideas, the reasons for such-and-such being the case, the theory behind a concept. Preferring to work alone, they welcome structured worksheets, books and exercises in logic and detail such as "find the missing link", "extract the core concepts", "present the key words", "compare x with y". They take pride in carrying out instructions thoroughly. They like to think things through.

Students with a dominant Abstract Random Mind Style learn best through unstructured group work. They love to talk, to brainstorm, to reflect, to imagine, to explore ideas, to go off at tangents and make personal connections. The freedom to use images, sounds and movement, to be dramatic, to use a range of resources are important to Abstract Random learners. Tasks that value feelings, impressions and whole ideas are particularly suitable, for example, "Together, find a way of presenting the main idea of joint stock companies and how they affect all our lives."

Students with a dominant Concrete Random Mind Style thrive on open-ended practical work. They tend to resist prescription, deadlines and guidelines. Typically, they want to work out their own method and timescale. They usually want to explore alternatives, experiment and use trial and error to find things out: "See if you can work out a way of ..."; "Come up with the best design for ..."; "Can you find the answer to such and such? Off you go ..."; "Prepare some teaching resources to get this across to eight-year-olds ..." are the best kinds of task. Concrete Random learners like to have finished, tangible outcomes to show for their efforts.

Insightfully, Diane Gregorc, Anthony's wife, captures the essential qualities of the four Mind Styles by suggesting correlations with the four elements of the ancient world:[148]

CS = earth

AS = air

AR = water

CR = fire

There are two levels at which we do well to respond to these differences. The *first* is to incorporate these Mind Styles into our lesson plans. The simplest way of doing this is to check that over a series of, say, four lessons all four styles have been accommodated. Alternatively, different learning strategies can be prepared and offered to students as a menu of options. Or learning strategies can be negotiated with students so that their natural preferences are built directly into democratically created learning plans. See Section 4 for details.

To help you consider the teaching and learning characteristics of each style, here's my attempt at a summary:

Abstract Sequential		Concrete Sequential	
reading	analysis	hands on	maps
ideas	evaluation	concrete examples	diagrams
reasoning	sit down and work	doing things	short explanations
theories	lectures	clear-cut objectives	lists
debate	libraries	structured	follow rules and
note taking	academic work	step-by-step	conventions
content	research	data and figures	tried and tested
logical	intellectual	checklists	methods
knowledge	essays	clear instructions	specific answers
thinking	quiet	attention to detail	tangible outcomes
individual study	comprehension	computers	methodical
tests	philosophy	charts	honesty
structured	documentation	outlines	field trips
mental exercises	objectivity	deadlines	consistency
hypothesising	comparisons	manuals	plans
vicarious		real experiences	
experiences			

Concrete Random		Abstract Random	
problem solving	creating models	group work	intuition
investigation	own timetable	humour	self-expression
ingenuity	up and doing	games	own timetable
finished products	practical	movies	imagination
choice	broad guidelines	non-linear	peer teaching
independence	tangible outcomes	relationships	open-ended tasks
experiential	connected to real	own ideas	art
risks	world	belonging	discussion
exploration	experiments	music	drama
open-ended	creativity	human angle	media
questions and tasks	trial and error	emotions	creativity
big picture, not	options	colour	fantasy
details	challenge	spontaneity	personalised work
curiosity	mini-inputs	flexibility	poetry
originality	games	stories	time for reflection
exploration	flexibility	cooperation	subjectivity
invention	lots of resources	visualisation	
few restrictions		movement	

The *second* level of response is to take account of Mind Style differences in our interventions with individual students. Consider for example a student who is off task. If the student is dominantly Abstract Sequential, she will probably respond to knowing why the work needs to be finished, what it's leading to, how it connects conceptually with what's been done already and what will be done later. A strongly Concrete Sequential student is likely to benefit from having the task broken into small steps, each with a clear deadline, while a dominantly Abstract Random learner might be best teaming up with one or two other like-minded students for a few minutes and letting off some steam about how boring it all is and then be asked to tackle it together. Try asking the strongly Concrete Random learner to find their own way of getting the learning finished by the start of next lesson; they can change the task as long as the learning outcomes are achieved in time.

However, it's not necessarily as easy as it sounds, as Dr Gregorc pointed out to me in private correspondence:

> Please note that the individual Mind Styles of teachers can prevent them from understanding and reaching all children equally well. As a matter of fact, some teachers can't fully connect with some students no matter how hard they try. This is a point where I differ from most other style model developers.

If you genuinely want the best for all students, and are excited about the insights provided by learning styles research, it is tempting to believe that you can be trained to reach all students. The risk, though, is that you end up feeling anxious and guilty because you *should* be able to meet the needs of all learners but find that the limitations of your own Mind Style genuinely prevent it. This is no excuse for not trying!

Dr Gregorc's work more than anyone else's, I believe, sheds light on some uncomfortable management and policy issues. Most school managers remain unaware of Mind Style differences and make demands on their colleagues that reflect their own way of doing things. For example, a headteacher with a dominant Concrete Sequential style might insist on a uniform way of writing schemes of work and lesson plans, or instigate a uniform approach to discipline; they might value punctuality at meetings above ideas and cut short a creative discussion because it's time to move on to the next item; they might make a big fuss about the tidiness of classrooms, the neatness of displays and the orderliness of movement around the building. Conversely, a strongly Concrete Random headteacher might have a million ideas a minute and expect everyone to live in a state of continual experimentation, when what they really want is some stability and continuity for a while. I know of many battles that have been fought between managers and teachers, and of colleagues who have left the profession, over issues that were really matters of style and neither side could let the other just "be".

Nationally, we have been in the grip of Concrete Sequential thinking for many years. The imposition of a rigid "one-size-fits-all" curriculum with a standard, linear notion of progression is one product. The idea of a standard "good" lesson that always begins by explaining learning objectives in advance, the insistence on neat and tidy documentation and neat and tidy classrooms, all peddled by Ofsted, are further manifestations. The sidelining of the arts in education, the introduction of rigid lesson structures for numeracy and literacy,

Some crew members struggled to fit the new regime:- many began to wonder if the machine itself was faulty.

the deconstruction of teaching into a series of tick-list competencies, the increase in prescriptions for this and guidelines for that – all are hallmarks of the Concrete Sequential mindset. And we wonder why we cannot currently persuade people to enter or, more significantly, remain in the profession!

3. Intelligence profiles: Howard Gardner of Harvard

We have come long way in our thinking about intelligence since the days of Galton, Binet, Stern, Terman and Yerkes, who were collectively responsible for the creation of intelligence tests purporting to measure the "intelligence quotient". For a start, intelligence is no longer regarded as fixed at birth: it can be enhanced by every person. In fact, the process of improving intelligence can be taught – read for example Harvard Professor of Education David Perkins's *Outsmarting IQ*.[149] What's more, intelligence now comes in different shapes and sizes. For example, Jerome Bruner, former Professor of Psychology at Harvard and Oxford Universities, proposes two types of intelligence, cognitive and narrative; Charles Handy suggests logical, spatial, musical, practical, physical, intrapersonal, interpersonal; David Perkins defines neural, experiential and reflective types; Denis Postle, the psychotherapist and counsellor, offers emotional, intuitive, physical and intellectual. Robert Sternberg, Professor of Psychology and Education at Yale, has a Triarchic Theory with "componential" intelligence (the kind of linguistic, logical and mathematical abilities most typically valued in schools), "contextual" (the source of creative insight) and "experiential" (street-smart intelligence).

Peter Salovey of Yale and John Mayer of New Hampshire were the first to formulate the idea of emotional intelligence, a concept recently expanded and popularised by Daniel Goleman. On a different tack, Arthur Costa, Professor Emeritus at California State University and co-director of the Institute for Intelligent Behavior, proposes the notion of "intelligent behaviour", in other words intelligent thought transposed into action. He argues that some apparently bright students don't have a sufficient repertoire of skills with which to apply their intelligence, but that these skills can, and must, be taught in order for a person to be actively intelligent. While we're at it, let's not forget Cole's moral intelligence and Zohar and Marshall's spiritual intelligence.[150]

Currently, the best-known thinker about multiple intelligence (often referred to as MI) is Professor Howard Gardner of Harvard. As early as 1983 in *Frames of Mind*,[151] he proposed what was then a radical break with tradition:

> There is persuasive evidence for the existence of several relatively autonomous human intellectual competencies or "frames of mind". The exact nature of each intellectual frame has not so far been satisfactorily established, nor has the precise number been fixed. But the conviction is that there exist at least some intelligences, and that these are relatively independent of one another.

He went on to define seven distinct types of intelligence (or "frames of mind"), each, he claimed, traceable to a separate area of the human brain. Previously, many of these had been called gifts, talents, skills, capacities, abilities or human faculties, but never *intelligences*. In making this well-researched and deliberate linguistic switch, Gardner seriously expanded the world's thinking and broke the shackles imposed by the psychometricians. Many years, ten books and numerous articles later, he now claims that all humans have *eight* types of intelligence:

- **linguistic**
- **logical-mathematical**
- **spatial**
- **musical**
- **bodily-kinaesthetic**

- **interpersonal**
- **intrapersonal**
- **naturalistic**

Gardner has strict criteria for defining intelligence. In 1983 he called it "the ability to solve problems or to create products that are valued within one or more cultural settings". In *Intelligence Reframed*, he offers a more refined definition. "I now conceptualise an intelligence as a biopsychological potential to process information that can be activated in a cultural setting to solve problems or create products that are of value in a culture". He goes on:

> … intelligences are not things that can be seen or counted. Instead they are potentials – presumably, neural ones – that will or will not be activated, depending upon the values of a particular culture, the opportunities available in that culture and the personal decisions made by individuals and/or their families, school teachers and others.[152]

The debate is far from settled though. For example, in the widely read *The Bell Curve*,[153] Herrnstein and Murray re-presented the idea that intelligence is a singular, measurable commodity distributed among the population along a bell-shaped curve and passed on genetically from one generation to the next. With a dubious analysis of data, they drew the sinister conclusion that many social ills are due to the behaviours of people with relatively low intelligence. Professors Sandra Scarr and Robert Plomin argue that intelligence is genetically inherited, and Professor Alan Smithers of Liverpool argues for a core intelligence that underlies success across all fields, claiming that Gardner has misused the word "intelligence". Meanwhile, Professor John White of the London Institute of Education has voiced serious misgivings about Gardner's definition and underpinning rationale, describing his theory as "decidedly flaky".[154]

The questions of inherited intelligence, the definition of intelligence(s), the measurability of intelligence and the relationship between intelligence and social class will continue to be the subjects of fierce debate. In the meantime, in classrooms around the country students' achievements and self-esteem are being raised by the optimistic and positive message that everyone is intelligent, but in different ways. White himself concedes that

> MI theory has recently become a liberating force in school improvement projects across the country … It is not difficult to see why such a notion should appeal to policy-makers working in deprived areas and faced with underachievement. Many children in these areas are held back by a low self-concept. They see themselves as dim or thick. But this is within the framework of the traditional version of intelligence – they are poor at the kind of abstract logical thinking that IQ tests target. Broaden the picture and their perceptions are transformed.[155]

A friend and colleague of mine, Tony Salmon, when he was a Secondary Curriculum Project Worker in Sandwell, put to Howard Gardner during a seminar: "The strength we get from your work is that you do use the word 'intelligence', because the kids have been told so often – not explicitly, but they have picked up the message – that they are not intelligent."[156] Tony was expressing just one of the benefits of Gardner's work, the flattening of the ancient hierarchy of educational values. The upgrading of ordinary household abilities to the status of "intelligence" suddenly gives everyone a place in the world. Nobodies become somebodies overnight. Self-images and self-expectations are transformed. What's more, the fact that this idea has a credible, internationally renowned, academic, weighty source makes it easier to persuade teachers to bring their habits into line with the new order, on three counts: their *thinking* (they can't write anyone off any more); their *language* (drop the limiting language of ability); and their *classroom techniques* (broaden learning and assessment strategies). These three thrusts characterise the high-aspiration strategies adopted by raising achievement initiatives all over the country. Mums and dads are also benefiting from briefings on the theory and its practical parenting implications.

Even *Mensa Magazine* is attracted to the idea of multiple intelligence. The cover of the March 2000 edition[157] carries a photograph of the British soccer star David Beckham with the teasing question, "Is Beckham brighter than Einstein?" The lead article goes on to explain how the "controversial theory" dares us to put the two men not on the same pedestal but on neighbouring pedestals.

Finally, it all made sense; imagination is greater than knowledge

Apart from MI theory's power to persuade grown-ups, it can be used directly with students. Its upbeat message is appealing and easy to communicate, and the differing characteristics of the various intelligences can be used to help students with self-study. Once they've got the idea that they have their own individual intelligence profiles, that each of them is capable in their own way, students can start to select appropriate learning methods. This is particularly applicable to home study and revision, where the teacher's imposed methodology doesn't apply. Many modern revision courses and study guides offer notemaking, organising and memorising techniques across the full range of intelligences. Students are encouraged to sample various methods and then settle on the ones that work best for their personal disposition. One example, arising from innovative Key Stage 4 work at the Ferrers School in Northamptonshire, is the folder of study-skills lesson plans: *Ready for Revision*.[158] Like the Ferrers, many schools claim improvements to exam results as a consequence of encouraging students to base their preparation on MI theory.

This chart could be used to give students, parents and even teachers a rough-and-ready guide to the eight intelligences. Remember, everyone has all eight, but to varying degrees.

Type of intelligence	With this intelligence you ...
Linguistic intelligence	• think in words • like to read and write • like stories • like to play word games • have a good memory for names, places, dates, poetry, lyrics and trivia • find spelling easy • have a well developed vocabulary
Logical and mathematical intelligence	• see patterns easily • like abstract ideas • like strategy games and logical puzzles • work out sums easily in your head • ask big questions e.g. "where does the universe end" • use computers • devise experiments to test out things you don't understand • think in categories and see relationships between ideas
Spatial intelligence	• think in images and pictures • easily remember where things have been put • like drawing, designing, building, daydreaming • read maps and diagrams easily • do jigsaw puzzles easily • are fascinated by machines • reproduce images accurately
Musical intelligence	• often sing, hum or whistle to yourself • remember melodies • have a good sense of rhythm • play an instrument • are sensitive to sounds in the environment • need music on when studying
Bodily/kinaesthetic intelligence	• remember through bodily sensations • find it difficult to sit still for long • have "gut feelings" about exam answers • are good at sports or dance or acting or mime • have excellent coordination • communicate well through gestures • learn best through physical activity, simulation and role play • mimic people easily
Interpersonal intelligence	• understand people well • learn best by interacting and cooperating with others • are good at leading and organising • pick up on other people's feelings • mediate between people • enjoy playing social games • listen well to other people
Intrapersonal intelligence	• like to work alone • motivate yourself • are intuitive • have a sense of independence • are strong-willed and have strong personal opinions • set your own goals • are self-confident • are reflective • are aware of your personal strengths and weaknesses
Naturalistic intelligence	• recognise flora and fauna – make distinctions and notice patterns in the natural world • use common and distinguishing features to categorise and group phenomena • use criteria consistently • use this ability productively, e.g. farming, pet keeping, conservation

The final benefit of multiple intelligence theory is its usefulness as a lesson-planning tool. A huge amount of secondary literature has grown up around the idea. There are numerous books offering practical strategies to suit different intelligences; see the Bibliography for material by David Lazear, Sally Berman, James Bellanca, Bonita DeAmicis, Carolyn Chapman, Ellen Arnold and others. The cataloguing and categorising of techniques wears a bit thin after a while, but the principle is sound: use MI as another way of thinking about differences between students, use it to increase your empathetic understanding of students and, if the notion feels comfortable, use it to help you plan your varied provision alongside, or instead of, the models described above. Ensure that over a series of lessons you have required students to use the full range of intelligences. As with learning styles it's important to encourage students to operate within their comfortable range initially, but then to challenge them over time to push the boat out and begin to strengthen intelligences that are currently weak. To support you, the activities in Section 2 cover different intelligences in different combinations.

There Are Other Agendas Too

The final group of items that inform current thinking about learning arises from two sources: the current desire to address a number of pressing social and economic concerns; and firm belief in certain values. This creates a combination of pragmatism and ideology. Take citizenship, for example. This is where belief in democracy meets a concern about the state of the nation's youth. Inclusion is the marriage of social justice with a drive to stop wasting the nation's economically valuable talent. Learning to learn combines the ideal that everyone should make the best of their lives with the need for commercial competitiveness.

The introduction to the UK's National Curriculum 2000 suggests this mixture:

> By providing rich and varied contexts for pupils to acquire, develop and apply a broad range of knowledge, understanding and skills, the curriculum should enable pupils to think creatively and critically, to solve problems and to make a difference for the better. It should give them the opportunity to become creative, innovative, enterprising and capable of leadership to equip them for their future lives as workers and citizens.

1. Learning to learn

In Britain, we are being swept towards a national acceptance of the need to learn how to learn. Together, the accelerating pace of technological change, the increasingly fragmented nature of work and career patterns, and the expansion of leisure time (and therefore pursuits) create a need for people to possess skills that will enable them to retrain professionally and make the most of their lives personally. These learning skills, along with underpinning attitudes such as the will to defer gratification and perseverance, can be acquired only over time, with lots and lots of practice. As things stand in schools at the moment, this doesn't seem to happen – at least not consistently. Have a look at "Check Your Delivery of Independent Learning Skills" (page 297) and see whether you think I'm right.

Mike Roberts, vice-principal of Cadbury Sixth Form College in Birmingham, published an interesting study a few years ago. He noticed that most of his post-16 students were not coping well with "autonomous" or "self-managed" learning. After two years of detailed investigation he concluded that two skill sets are required:

Information processing skills
1. planning
2. gathering
3. processing
4. presenting

Underlying core skills
1. time management
2. social skills
3. reflective skills
4. self-appraisal skill
5. the skill of seeking help

In fact, he found that "autonomous learning was a novel experience for most learners which demanded skills they did not possess". Why? Because "the scale, breadth, depth and complexity of skills demanded for autonomous project management were neither understood nor appreciated by teachers".[159] Most sixth-form tutors and college lecturers that I meet around the country tell me that they face a similar situation. But it needn't be this way. Frequently using strategies such as "Marketplace" (page 122), "Circus Time" (page 85), "Sole Search" (page 253) and "Blank Cheque" (page 261) at Key Stages 3 and 4 would fix the problem, or even the "milder" stepping stones to independence such as "Dreadlines" (page 103), "Step On It" (page 209), "One-to-One" (page 135), "Double Take" (page 101) and "Information Hunt" (page 118).

Under continued pressure to get good exam results above all, most schools don't have the courage or the energy to take independent learning seriously. However, two current trends support the cause. First, *liberating technology*. Students can access most of the information and many of the skills they need for exam success through online or media-based resources. They can study at least as well at home or in the cyber café as they can in school. They can follow personalised learning pathways and take diagnostic assessments when they are ready. Teachers are increasingly putting lesson and homework materials onto school websites or intranets for students to follow. E-tutoring is catching on. Learning, even formal learning, is no longer teacher-dependent. Given sufficient hardware resources, teachers can now become managers and facilitators, counsellors and coaches. At the hi-tech One Room Schoolhouse in Alameda on the outskirts of San Francisco, teachers don't even have to do the organising: they are simply "on hand".

The second supportive trend is the *national interest in thinking skills*. To be fully independent, students need to be able to think in a whole variety of ways. CASE (Cognitive Acceleration through Science Education) and CAME (Cognitive Acceleration in Maths Education) have developed thinking through science and maths over the years. Somerset Thinking Skills, Robert Fisher's work at Brunel University,[160] David Leat's work at the University of Newcastle, Matthew Lipman's Philosophy for Children,[161] and Professor Carol McGuinness's report from Queen's University, Belfast,[162] have gradually focused the nation's attention on thinking. So, what are these skills? Christopher Bowring-Carr and John West-Burnham offer a helpful definition. They say[163] that "cognitive skills, and thus the basis for the thinking curriculum" can be summarised as follows:

- problem-solving
- critical thinking
- reasoning
- creative thinking

They go on to say that more specific strategies might include

- recognition and clarification of a problem
- mapping and ordering relevant information
- generating alternative solutions
- applying logical criteria
- implementing a solution

- monitoring
- communicating
- evaluating outcomes
- generating conclusions
- transfer to other situations

Check out how many of these ten specific skills are rehearsed by students doing "Broken Pieces" (page 78). I reckon eight or nine, which isn't that bad for a twenty-minute exercise. With a little imagination it's possible to design learning activities that cover the curriculum efficiently and do thinking skills *at the same time*. Other examples in *The Teacher's Toolkit*, just to get your own creative thinking going, include "Assembly" (page 67), "Calling Cards" (page 81), "Guess Who" (page 109), and "Ranking" (page 148).

For a more detailed analysis of cognitive skills and their integration into school life check out Bowring-Carr's and West-Burnham's book *A Curriculum for Learning*.[164]

Another useful tool for the design of "thinking" tasks is Benjamin Bloom's old Taxonomy of Educational Objectives.[165] As you move from bottom to top, you demand increasingly sophisticated skills of your students.

Evaluation	assess, judge, weigh, rate, determine, rank, assay, decide, arbitrate, grade, appraise, classify
Synthesis	combine, build, originate, regroup, conceive, blend, develop, mix, compound, structure, make, generate, join
Analysis	break down, examine, dissect, scrutinise, inspect, sort, analyse, separate, investigate, compartmentalise, classify, take apart
Application	apply, adapt, transfer, adopt, transcribe, solve, use, transform, employ, manipulate, utilise, transplant, relate, convert
Comprehension	reword, convert, outline, explain, define, interpret, reconstruct, paraphrase, transpose, understand, conceive, calculate
Knowledge	what, who, when, where, recall, locate, repeat, name, recite, list, find, identify, label

If you fancy a change from Bloom, another taxonomy worth considering is that proposed by Edys Quellmalz, Senior Educational Researcher at the Center for Technology in Learning.[166]

As always, the temptation is for us to focus mainly on logical thinking involving the processes of analysis and deduction. Creative thinking, lateral thinking, intuitive thinking (if there can be such a thing), random thinking and spiritual "thinking" all have a vital place in the complete life and the complete society. In our rational, empirical world, we don't value them half enough. Just look at the status of drama, dance, religious education, even music and art in the school curriculum. "Still Image" (page 158), for example, involves more layers and types of thinking than any of the ideas mentioned above.

Of course, there's more than just thinking: there's *meta-cognition*, which is the sophisticated business of thinking about thinking, involving ongoing debrief and reflection. According to Robin Fogarty in *How To Teach for Metacognitive Reflection*,[167] "metacognition is awareness and control over your own thinking behaviour". This involves making implicit skills explicit, learning new ones and making choices. Arthur Costa defines metacognition as being

> conscious of our own thinking and problem solving during the act of thinking and problem solving ... It is a uniquely human ability occurring in the cerebral cortex of the brain. Interestingly, it has been found that good problem solvers do it; they plan a course of action before they begin the task. They monitor themselves during the execution of the plan, they consciously back up or adjust the plan, and they evaluate themselves upon completion.[168]

But why bother with metacognition? Because it supports the independent learning process. Back to patterning and constructivism, which were discussed above.

> Constructivists view learning as the process individuals experience as they take in new information and make sense of that new information. By making meaning, they are acquiring knowledge. However, individuals who construct knowledge and are aware of the gaps in their understanding of that knowledge are actively using both their cognitive and their metacognitive strategies. In their awareness of what they know and what they don't know, they take the first step in remedying the deficit areas.[169]

Or, as Jean Piaget, the Swiss psychologist known for his pioneering work on intelligence, said, "Intelligent behaviour is knowing what to do when you don't know what to do"!

This connects with the view of Professor David Perkins of Harvard[170] that there are three types of intelligence: neural (genetically inherited, there's nothing we can do about it); experiential (the result of our experiences as we attempt to navigate our world); and reflective. This last can be developed – it is within our control. It amounts to the ability to make better use of our minds. We can *learn* better strategies for dealing with problems and better ways of remembering details for example. Metacognition is the process by which we become more intelligent in the reflective sense.

So, the advance of information and communications technology, the pursuit of thinking skills, along with socioeconomic expediencies, are edging us towards an inevitable future. But are things moving fast enough and far enough? As I write, the national Key Stage 3 Strategy, the Excellence in Cities programme, along with energetic initiatives such as Learning to Learn (part of the Campaign for Learning) provide the opportunities and resources to develop learning skills more systematically and at more depth in schools.

2. Cooperation, democracy and citizenship

Citizenship is now a statutory part of the secondary school curriculum. Why? The Crick Report[171] listed a whole raft of reasons, including social ills such as juvenile crime and political apathy among young voters. These concerns and the current British government's policy of pushing responsibility back to the people (care in the community and stakeholder pensions, for example) are the driving forces. And at a deep level what John Dewey (writing in 1916!) said is true:

> We have taken democracy for granted; we have thought and acted as if our forefathers had founded it once for all. We have forgotten that it has to be enacted anew in every generation, in every year and day in the living relations of person to person in all social forms and institutions.[172]

Consequently, Crick's ambition is to be applauded: "We aim at no less than a change in the political culture of this country both nationally and locally."[173]

I am a great supporter of citizenship education, but I find it difficult to see how this high aim can be realised, for several reasons. For starters there are strong contradictory messages in the system. F. Clarke:

> I think in terms of experiential learning and wonder how pupils are expected to grasp the ideas of democracy and citizenship when they have been trapped in a totalitarian educational system which does not recognise their right to choose what they learn or how they learn it. Isn't the whole of their schooling a lesson in living under a dictatorship?[174]

In this regard we in Britain are far behind countries such as Denmark, Germany, Holland and Sweden.[175] Professor Clive Harber of the University of Birmingham sums up the problems:

> At the moment citizenship education looks like the seed that did not fall on fertile ground. The main problem is that it is being introduced into an education system that is currently undemocratic and does not have anything like the congruent structures, procedures, values, assessment and staffing required to make it a significant contribution to changing British political culture.[176]

What we need for starters are "citizenship schools" as Titus Alexander calls them.[177]

However, it's important that we do what we can and seize the opportunity presented by citizenship education to develop the habits of democracy. The good news is that the Key Stage 3 Orders require, among other things, that "Pupils should be taught to:

- think about topical political, spiritual, moral, social and cultural issues, problems and events by analysing information and its sources
- justify orally and in writing a personal opinion about such issues, problems or events
- contribute to group and exploratory class discussions, and take part in debates
- negotiate, decide and take part responsibly …
- reflect on the process of participating"

Many of the *Toolkit* techniques in Sections 2 and 4 contribute to these outcomes in various combinations. Take "Broken Pieces" (page 78), "Value Continuum" (page 163), "Corporate Identity" (page 89), "Ambassadors" (page 65) and "Delegation" (page 91), for example. The whole of Section 3 is devoted to the creation of a civilised, participatory, self-regulating mini-society. In addition, the tone of the whole book supports the more general points about the type of teaching methods required for effective "active citizenship" education:

CITIZENSHIP? EDUCATION?

> The learning outcomes will be best achieved through a broad range of teaching approaches and learning opportunities.
>
> It is vital that pupils are provided with structured opportunities to explore actively aspects, issues and events …
>
> It is difficult to conceive of pupils as active citizens if their experience of learning in citizenship education has been predominantly passive.[178]

Clearly, citizenship learning has to be experiential. Underpinning a flourishing democracy are interdependent, mutual behaviours. Of course, procedures and constitutions are required to keep everything in place in large democratic groups, but they can become cold, combative and abused. A democratic *will*, which shows itself through cooperative attitudes and skills, brings life to the dead hand of procedure. Neuroscientists say that people are born with such a will, a cooperative instinct, and if it's not exercised and nourished in the first few years of life, then, like other neural facilities, it deteriorates.

In secondary schools we can do our best to regenerate the will to be cooperative and to provide training in democratic skills. Even when the institution itself is undemocratic and the attitude of government towards education is dictatorial, we can still use lots of collaborative group work and interdependent learning activities in our own classrooms. Over the years the research of Robert Slavin at Johns Hopkins University, the Johnson brothers at the University of Minnesota[179] and the classic work of Spencer Kagan[180] have defined the practice and the benefits of cooperation. As long ago as 1984 Johnson and Johnson's extensive studies led them to conclude:

> The results indicate that cooperative group learning experiences tend to promote higher achievement than do competitive and individualistic learning experiences. The results hold good for all ages levels, for all subjects areas, and for tasks involving concept attainment, verbal problem solving, categorisation, spatial problem solving, retention and memory, motor performance, guessing, judging and predicting.[181]

We can go further, if we have the courage, and create relative democracy in our classrooms. Lesley Browne did at Park Hall School in Solihull. Her Year 12 A-level sociology group were asked to choose one of four different ways of studying the course:

- teacher-directed
- consultative model
- democratic learning cooperative
- individual study programmes

They chose the democratic learning cooperative (DLC), immediately spent time thrashing out a set of thirteen principles and procedures, and then set about organising and monitoring their own learning. They called on the teacher as a resource for subject knowledge, exam requirements and advice about the learning process. In the end they did well in the A-level exams, but looking back one of the students, James Baldaro, says:

> The relative success of the group in external examinations, despite seeming to mean "everything" at the time, is actually secondary. The real success of the democratic learning cooperative lies in how it instilled key notions of cooperation, mutual support and tolerance in a group of 16–18 year olds. These are skills which reach far beyond the short term goals of A-Level examinations and university graduation. Coupled with the confidence developed through the DLC's reliance on continued public speech and teaching and discussion with others, I believe our experiences equipped us with essential transferable skills.[182]

Browne herself implies that there are two further, automatic benefits to teaching democratically – students *learn how to learn* and *develop cognitive and metacognitive* skills:

> Possibly one of the most important practices in democratic learning environments is that of dialogue between students and teachers, questioning and discussing together how they might improve their practice. If democracy in the classroom is about anything, it is the free exchange of ideas. Without this open continuous debate, power-sharing is pointless.[183]

We can begin to see how it all fits together. There are some types of classroom practice that do actually deliver most of the current agendas simultaneously and quite naturally. "Blank Cheque" (page 261) is the prime example. It is a demanding "operating system" for both teacher and student, but offers rich rewards.

Key aspects of citizenship can be delivered through academic lessons by choosing the right methods. Traditional teacher-dictated teaching simply cannot do the business. It can only ever tinker with thinking skills, learning how to learn, citizenship and inclusion because the method is fundamentally incongruent with the purposes.

By the way, you can find a full account of Lesley Browne's experience in *Developing Democratic Education*,[184] and, of the many other books now available on citizenship education, I recommend the practical *Activate! – Teacher Starter File* by Adam Newman-Turner and Lee Jerome.[185]

3. Inclusion

The concern for inclusion has a moral basis. It is a matter of social justice and equal opportunity. Too many students are still excluded from real success for a range of complex reasons. Apart from the most obvious, some form of disability or learning impairment that has traditionally kept them separate, there is the mismatch between students' language, behaviour or cultural norms and those of the institution; there is low self-esteem and anger about failures of the past; there is poor basic skills … and so on. In *Understanding Barriers to Learning*,[186] Peter Maxted helpfully categorises the problems into cultural, structural and personal issues. Although summarising ten years of research into why people don't continue their learning beyond school, the analysis and main messages are entirely pertinent to pre-16 provision.

While inclusion is first a principle, it quickly becomes a resource issue. Laying on the right courses, providing the necessary facilities and personnel, supplying appropriate materials and equipment all require money. Even so, they only get us to Base One. Resources create the *possibility* that learning will occur. For example, hearing loops make it possible to hear, large print makes text easier to see, ramps make it possible to get into a classroom, specialist teachers and learning assistants make it possible for personal needs to be met. Beyond Base One is the challenge of translating possibility into solid achievement.

As a minimum, this requires the teacher to create an acceptant learning community within which each and every student, no matter what, is guaranteed freedom from ridicule and belittlement. As we have already discussed, students' full participation in learning is dependent upon such conditions. Section 3 spells out the steps that need to be taken. In addition to this minimum, the teacher will need to follow the "natural laws of learning" proposed above. Otherwise, students who are physically present in the classroom will still be effectively excluded from the achievements of which they are capable.

One of these principles is of course the accommodation of different learning styles. Thomas Armstrong, in his provocative book *In Their Own Way*, positions learning styles as the solution to most "special needs":

> Six years ago I quit my job as a learning disabilities specialist. I had to. I no longer believed in learning disabilities … It was then that I turned to the concept of learning differences as an alternative to learning disabilities. I realised that the millions of children being referred to learning disabled classes weren't handicapped, but instead had unique learning styles that the schools didn't clearly understand. Furthermore, it seemed to me that the reason so many millions of additional children were underachieving, experiencing school phobias, or just plain bored in the classroom was because no one had recognised and used what they really had to offer in the learning place – their special talents and abilities.[187]

This self-same issue is now placed centre stage in the Statutory Statement on Inclusion found in all National Curriculum 2000 subject orders. It says:

Teachers secure pupils' motivation and concentration by

- using teaching approaches appropriate to different learning styles
- using a range of organisational approaches
- varying subject content and presentation

Teachers use appropriate assessment approaches that

INCLUSION?

- allow for different learning styles and ensure that pupils are given the chance and encouragement to demonstrate their competence and attainment through appropriate means.

Though not in itself the answer to inclusion, the accommodation of diverse learning styles is an example of the lengths that teachers need to go to. Offering students choices of strategy, consulting them about their needs, negotiating deadlines and assessments, actively raising self-esteem through the careful use of language all contribute to the possibility of success for all.

4. Literacy, numeracy and key skills

There's not much to say about literacy, numeracy and key skills that's not already been said; they've been major talking points over the last few years. Whatever you think of the national strategies, these skill sets are among the essential tools of the learning trade. They are important to personal growth as well as to the national economy. Aspects of literacy, as defined by the Key Stage 3 National Literacy Strategy Framework for Teaching English, are clearly supported by many *Toolkit* strategies, especially in regard to the reading, writing, speaking and listening domains. So are parts of Key Skills "Communication and Improving Own Learning and Performance". But let's not overstate the case. Literacy and numeracy are only tools. They are not the goal in themselves, just among the instruments that we use to help us get there.

The Recipe

The size of the issues discussed in this opening section invites us to rethink our practice and structures on a huge scale. However, *The Teacher's Toolkit* does not set out to redesign the education system, desirable though that might be. It does not even attempt to revolutionise classroom practice. Rather, it simply puts into the hands of teachers the means by which they might begin, or continue, to move in the "right" direction. When all the brain research, the socioeconomic, political and philosophical considerations have been put through the mill of critical thought there emerges, remarkably, a set of consistent conclusions about the way to go.

We can have confidence in the practical ideas in this book because they serve *a number* of *converging* purposes. In sum, they are designed to do the best for all students, irrespective of learning style, background and previous attainment in an age when qualifications appear to matter most. They are designed to support students in becoming socially skilled, independent thinkers and self-sufficient learners with a strong sense of personal and collective responsibility. Consequently they are designed to equip individuals and society with the means of creating a fruitful and morally sound future.

The learning principles behind these high ambitions – the theoretical ideas discussed above – shake down into a handful of *planning purposes*. These have guided the design of the learning activities. By planning purposes I mean the reasons for approaching learning in a particular way, the intentions behind the activity, the aims that the activity is seeking to achieve. There are seven:

1. **thinking**: students actively processing data creatively, logically, laterally, imaginatively, deductively and so on
2. **emotional intelligence**: learning to manage emotions and relate to others skilfully; developing positive personal qualities such as self-control and values such as justice
3. **independence**: students acquiring the attitudes and skills that enable them to initiate and sustain learning without a teacher
4. **interdependence**: students engaging in mutuality, which is the essence of cooperation and the basis of democracy
5. **multi-sensation**: students experiencing through a number of senses simultaneously, in effect seeing, hearing *and doing*
6. **fun**: sheer enjoyment
7. **articulation**: students speaking or writing thoughts, often in "draft" form, as an essential part of the process of creating personal understanding

Just a quick word about number six. Not all learning can be fun, nor should we try to make it so. Nor does learning always have to be heavy. Teachers who undertake pupil pursuits often report that students' days in secondary schools are filled with huge doses of sitting, listening, reading and writing. For concentration and interest to be sustained over a day, never mind a week, the human mind requires variety and contrast. It requires learning experiences to be variously serious and light, active and passive, individual and collective, controlled and loose, noisy and silent. Kept in perspective, fun is a serious business.

These seven planning purposes are effectively the *ingredients of the recipe* of *The Teacher's Toolkit*. In Section 2 they are presented alongside each activity as a "ready reckoner" of its intended benefits. By being made explicit, they enable you to go on to create your own strategies – simply mix the same underpinning ideas and mentally bake.

However, the theory also suggests that there are four additional factors to take into account. These create the environment for optimum learning. The techniques described in Sections 2 and 3 and the operating systems in Section 4 will be truly successful only if these *contextual characteristics* are in place and refreshed day by day:

1. **The communication of optimism and high expectations**: achieved by exuding energy, using positive language and designing challenging tasks.
2. **The creation of a conducive physical environment**: achieved by paying attention to the basics of oxygen, ionisation, temperature, hydration and access, plus aesthetics, aroma, sounds, furnishings and peripheral learning materials.
3. **The accommodation of diverse learning styles**: achieved by providing variety (the minimum requirement), by offering choices and by negotiating learning strategies with students.
4. **The preservation and enhancement of students' self-esteem**: achieved by establishing ground rules, by using affirming language, by turning mistakes into positive learning and by following all the other guidelines in "Check Your Impact on Students' Self-Esteem" in Section 5.

The seven **planning purposes** and four **contextual characteristics** combine to create a simple model for the design and delivery of effective learning experiences:

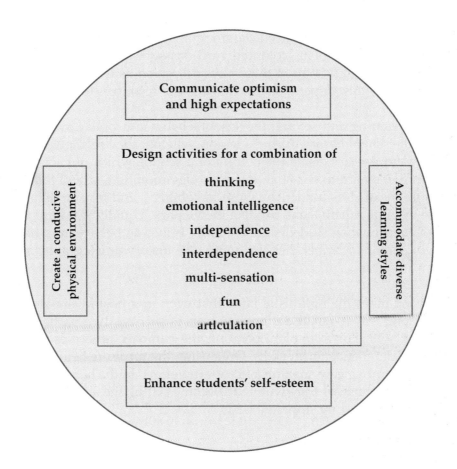

Why not?

This section began with the question Why? We have surveyed a number of answers and are left with the question Why not? Simply, if we don't begin to make fundamental changes to our educational practices we're in trouble. Nationally, our education policies are not going in the right direction – research from neuroscience, sociology, anthropology, philosophy and psychology tells us so. But what can you do? Begin by checking your own methodology against the evidence. Be willing to make whatever adjustments are needed to bring your teaching more and more in line with natural features of the learning process and students' and society's future needs, as far as the school and the system allow.

Let the last word on the matter go to John Abbott and Terry Ryan:

> The reforms of the 1980s and 1990s simply shifted the balance of power within the system away from those who work directly with children without effectively questioning the underlying structure and purposes of the system itself. The politics of reform have resulted in an old model of education being coerced to work more efficiently, and – in the best of circumstances – towards higher academic standards. On the surface this may seem like a great success, but the sense of accomplishment quickly fades when it is measured through the lens of our current knowledge about learning and human development. It fades even more quickly when one contrasts what current systems of education are achieving with what are emerging as the challenges and opportunities of the 21st century.[188]

Yes, but ...

Sometimes a teacher will take a *Toolkit* technique and come back with, "I tried that and it didn't work." Why not? Clearly there are lots of requirements for the successful implementation of the ideas in this book. A decently sized classroom that allows furniture to be reconfigured, enough large paper and felt pens, coloured card, scissors and a generous photocopying budget are needed for starters. Some of these physical prerequisites cannot be conjured up by the individual teacher – they depend on the allocation of resources to, and within, schools.

Decisions about streaming and setting, the school's behaviour policy, whether students are allowed to go to the school library during a lesson, whether they're allowed in at break – all these procedures and policies create the culture of a school, which impacts on student attitudes. For instance, it's hard to create an inclusive classroom in a school that locks students out, segregates by social class (under the guise of "ability") and favours those with 100 per cent attendance by giving them a day trip to a theme park. Equally, it is hard to establish the habits of independence when students are blatantly bribed to behave, and have all the real decisions (except perhaps whether they are going take history or geography at GCSE) made for them.

However, this book takes the optimistic view that even in a hostile climate the individual teacher can go a long way to create a dignified oasis of success. Two particular qualities are required: skill and will. For example, operating the complex processes of "Marketplace" requires fine classroom management skills. Organising the furniture beforehand and putting it back afterwards simply means making a bit of extra effort. In the hands of skilful and willing teachers, or at least those who are willing to become skilful, the techniques can be remarkably successful, even against the apparent odds.

So, if you're up for it, read on.

Section 2

Tools for
Teaching and Learning

Introduction

The fifty learning activities presented here cover a wide variety of styles and purposes. Variety is important in itself. It's the spice of life, everyone needs it to keep their concentration and motivation alive – students and teachers alike!

Beyond this, the activities are deliberately designed to accommodate a mixture of learning styles. The natural instinct of professional teachers is to do the best for each and every student, but in view of the fact that every human brain is as unique as a fingerprint the task can feel overwhelming. Learning-styles constructs help us to make sense of this diversity and give us the means of plotting and planning our provision.

There are lots of models available these days. Take your pick. The three that have informed the preparation of this section are:

- **Visual, auditory, kinaesthetic**: the sensory-preferences model that goes back to the invention of Neuro-Linguistic Programming by Bandler and Grinder.
- **Anthony Gregorc's Mind Styles**: an information-processing model similar to David Kolb's, Honey and Mumford's and Bernice McCarthy's, and the basis of Kathleen Butler's RAPID system.
- **Multiple Intelligence Theory**: the acclaimed creation of Professor Howard Gardner.

Consequently, in this Section you will find group work and individual work, academic and practical, up-and-doing and sitting still, open-ended investigation and structured research, drama, analysis of text, competition, cooperation, fun, careful concentration, debate, peer teaching, construction, deconstruction and more.

Some of the items are no more than useful novelties, such as "Bingo", "Memory Board" and "Verbal Tennis", while others are substantial and demanding learning experiences such as "Marketplace", "Scrambled Groups" and "Still Image". All have their place in the modern classroom, where the design of lessons is informed by the latest understanding of how the brain works.

But there's more. Other agendas need to be addressed. For a range of sound social and moral reasons we want to create genuine inclusion, promote citizenship and develop thinking skills. In fact, the grand aims of the broad-based approach to education suggested by the *Toolkit* are

- to help people become skilled, self-aware and independent learners
- to help people become skilled, socially aware, inclusive and democratic citizens

Of course such learning can occur only experientially. These aims are achieved only if they determine the character of learning experiences on a regular basis. The good news is that it's possible to address several of these learning agendas simultaneously. Through cleverly designed activities you can cover the content of your curriculum efficiently and do thinking skills and citizenship at the same time! Look at the various types of learning in "Marketplace", for example.

Four further points:

First, not all of these activities will work with all classes. Different exercises require different levels of social and study skill. Use your judgment. If you regard a technique as too ambitious, identify the enhancements needed and work on these with your class for a while. For example, notemaking and presentation skills are needed for "Scrambled Groups" to work properly. These can be developed through "Distillation" and "Hierarchies". It should be possible to mix and match the activities in this section to build a programme that's tailor-made for your group.

Second, many readers will recognise a number of these activities. Some have been in circulation for years, having been invented in the mists of time when experiential learning, discovery learning, active learning and student-centred learning were in their prime. It's been fascinating in recent years to see how the new thinking about the brain has validated such older strategies. I've drawn on this heritage, trialled techniques in hundreds of classrooms around the country, rejected ideas that didn't work, adapted others and invented new ones. This is a collection of my current favourites.

Third, many teachers complain that interactive teaching techniques need lots of resources that take lots of time to prepare. Sometimes this is true, but not always. For many of the activities, students don't need anything at all, or just pen and paper.

Fourth, these fifty activities are only for starters. They attempt to show how modern learning theory can be turned into classroom practice. They make certain principles concrete. But they are only examples. The sophisticated teacher will get under the surface of the techniques, identify the principles upon which they are based and create their own practice. This is the ultimate intention of the *Toolkit*, not to provide "teaching by numbers", but to indicate directions, offer examples and reasons, and then set you on your own way.

Just a final word about the panels in the margin of each activity. These summarise:

- the **purpose** of the activity (related to theory in Section 1 – see "The Recipe" on page 58)
- the **particular** character of the activity (how much noise and movement there will be)
- the **room layout** (if a specific one is required)

To find out more about the dramatic techniques described – from "Forum", "Theatre", "Hot Seating" and "Still Image" – and to discover other ways in which drama can be a powerful learning medium, consult the work of Jonothan Neelands.[1]

Ambassadors

Ambassadors go to foreign lands on behalf of their countries. They represent and report. All this can be re-created in the kingdom of the classroom.

Purposes (what the activity is designed to achieve)	
Thinking	* * * *
Emotional Intelligence	* *
Independence	* * *
Interdependence	* * * *
Multi-sensation	* *
Fun	*
Articulation	* * * *

Particulars (what the activity contains)	
Individual work	* *
Group work	* * * *
Moving about	*
Speaking	* * * *
Listening	* * * *
Reading	*
Writing	* *
Looking	* * * *
Choice	*

How?

1. Students work in groups of four. In each group, one student is nominated to be the *ambassador*.
2. The ambassadors leave the classroom together to watch a demonstration elsewhere. This could be conducted by a willing colleague in the hall. Or the group could be overseen by the librarian in the learning resource centre watching a PowerPoint presentation or a video of *you* demonstrating the technique!
3. Meanwhile, the rest of the class get on with the theory connected with the demonstration, taught by the teacher in the classroom.
4. While watching the demonstration, the ambassadors are expected to make notes so they can repeat and explain the demo to their groups. They may need to see the demo more than once and may need some time to prepare teaching aids.
5. Ambassadors return to the classroom, by which time, ideally, the theory work has been completed. They now teach the demonstration to their respective groups explaining, and if necessary repeating, the steps.
6. The recipients return the compliment by teaching the theory that they have just learned to their ambassador.
7. Everyone's learning is then checked by the teacher. This can be done through a formal test, or by using "Spotlight" (page 154), or by the teacher spontaneously dropping on individuals to explain or show the technique.

Specific room layout (Yes) No	

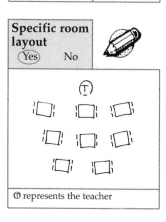

ⓣ represents the teacher

Applications

- Ideal for **art, PE** and **technology**, where precise techniques and processes have to be learned.
- In **science**, to introduce the procedure for an experiment that everyone then has to carry out in the lab.

- How to structure an essay in **English**.
- Fieldwork techniques in **geography**, research techniques in **sociology**.
- Conventions and procedures in **maths**, business planning techniques in **business studies**.
- As a means of introducing new language structures and vocabulary in **modern languages**; ideal use of a language assistant.

Why do it?

- The activity reinforces interdependent and mutual behaviours, which are among the foundation stones of citizenship.
- The exercise requires students to internalise, memorise and articulate. These are the basics of the learning process and are deliberately taught in this exercise. If the process is debriefed adequately, it helps students become just a bit more self-aware and independent.
- By requiring students to take degrees of responsibility, it addresses the problem faced by many teachers: that students tend not to sustain interest for long when passively watching a demonstration.
- It frees the teacher to become the quality controller, rather than the performer.

Variations

1. Instead of practical demonstrations, any piece of teaching can be used. On video the teacher can be giving information or explaining a concept or showing something "in the field" filmed on location. It doesn't have to be practical.
2. Use a commercial video – the easiest option.
3. Instead of watching teachers or videos, ambassadors can carry out research using the Internet, then go back and disseminate the results.
4. Instead of using video or a colleague to do the demonstration, use a "star" student who has been briefed by the teacher, or it can be led by an older student who has enough knowledge and experience in the area, a sixth-former for example.
5. Have groups of three instead of four to make sure everyone is involved.

Assembly

Everyone loves assembly. No, not the early-morning get-together in the school hall, rather the human instinct to put things together, to make a finished product from bits and pieces.

Purposes (what the activity is designed to achieve)	
Thinking	* * * * *
Emotional Intelligence	*
Independence	* * *
Interdependence	* * * (variable)
Multi-sensation	* *
Fun	* *
Articulation	* * *

Particulars (what the activity contains)	
Individual work	* * * *
Group work	* * * (variable)
Moving about	*
Speaking	* * * (variable)
Listening	* * * * (variable)
Reading	* * * * (variable)
Writing	
Looking	* * * *
Choice	

Specific room layout	
Yes (No)	

How?

1. Students work on their own or in pairs to assemble logically coherent material that has been cut up into separate parts. Choose the material and the divisions carefully.
2. The simplest form of assembly is **sequencing**. There need to be enough clues in each separate piece for it to be possible to connect them in a logical sequence. The sequence could be provided by chronology (a timeline, for example), or by the correct order of steps in an experiment or technological process, or the order of events in the narrative of a story, or the logic of a mathematical calculation, or the rationality of a cumulative argument.
3. The material to be assembled might be text or pictures or symbols or a combination.
4. **Other forms** of assembly include:
   - put together a **picture**, e.g. select and position cut-out drawings of scientific apparatus for an experiment before it's carried out; position cut-out items based on comprehension of a text or spoken description in English or a foreign language, for example position furniture on a room plan, people in a scene, buildings on a street plan, settlements on a map.
   - **geometry**, e.g. construct five equally-sized squares from an apparent jumble of shapes.
   - insert **labels** correctly that have been cut out from diagrams.
   - show the connections between **causes and effects** by physically placing cards with key words on them in relation to each other, e.g. wars, crises and revolutions in history or fictional characters and their actions in an English novel or play. The distance between the cards symbolises the strength of the relationship between them – the further apart, the weaker the relationship.
   - physically map out an **action plan** with main tasks, small steps, dates and resources on separate cards – in technology or GNVQ (General National Vocational Qualification).

Applications

- **The big picture**: "Assembly" is an excellent way to help students get their heads round a *scheme of work* or an exam *syllabus*. Rewrite the syllabus in students' language, retaining as much of the official terminology as possible. Cut it up into logical sections, being careful to separate elements that go together, for example, category headings and their subdivisions, quotations and their references. Students, working in pairs, match and sequence the bits of paper to resemble the original document as closely as possible. Once the original and the students' attempt have been compared and adjustments made, ask each pair to mount the pieces of syllabus on sugar paper in a way that makes sense to them, using coloured lines or wool to make connections. This visual representation can then be displayed on the classroom wall or stored for easy reference.
- **Modern foreign languages (MFL)**: sequence the jumbled text of a story or sequence text-picture-text-picture – these activities force reading and comprehension.
- **PE**: using stick-figure drawings, set out the precise movements of a warm-up or skill or strategy in the correct order before doing it for real.
- **Technology, science**: predict, or record, the steps of a process or experiment, the knock-on events in a chain reaction, the sequence of atomic changes in a chemical reaction.

Why do it?

- The exercise rehearses key thinking skills such as sequencing, categorising, selecting, matching.
- It feeds off natural human curiosity and the brain's desire to make connections, to see how things fit together.
- Many students benefit from the tactile nature of the exercise, they remain motivated and focused through pushing pieces of paper round the desk compared with staring at a blank page, pen in hand.

Variations

1. Inject an element of competition – race against each other or the clock.
2. Students could work in threes for some jobs. For complex tasks where there could be differences of opinion, use "Pairs to Fours" (page 137) to compare results and discuss a final solution.
3. Students are given a ready-assembled piece in which there are mistakes and they have to find them. At a high level, there could be just one tiny mistake, forcing close attention to detail.

Back-to-Back

This is an easily applied and fun activity that promotes verbal skill, listening, observation, comprehension and cooperation. What more could you want?

Purposes (what the activity is designed to achieve)	
Thinking	* * * * *
Emotional Intelligence	* *
Independence	* *
Interdependence	* * * * *
Multi-sensation	* *
Fun	* * *
Articulation	* * * * *

Particulars (what the activity contains)	
Individual work	* *
Group work	* * * *
Moving about	
Speaking	* * * * *
Listening	* * * * *
Reading	
Writing	
Looking	* * * * *
Choice	

Specific room layout	
Yes (No)	

How?

1. Students sit in pairs "back-to-back" – the chair backs should touch so the students are close enough to hear each other above the noise that will follow. They decide who is A and who is B.
2. A is given visual material, which he holds close to his chest (so that prying eyes around the room can't see it). B is given a piece of plain paper and pencil.
3. A describes the visual to B, while B draws it, aiming to make a perfect replica which is exact in size shape and detail, complete with labelling. No peeking! Describers are not allowed to draw in the air with their fingers!
4. This is a cooperative exercise. B can ask as many questions as she likes and A's job is to be as helpful as possible.
5. When the time is up, partners compare the original with the attempted copy.
6. Partners swap roles and try it again, using different material, with B describing and A drawing.

Applications

- Almost any visual material, such as photographs of landscapes, settlements, historical monuments, works of art, maps, fashion garments, religious buildings …
- **Geography** – diagrams of different types of volcanoes, sketchmaps.
- **Geometry and trigonometry**, giving precise details of angles, lengths of lines, diameters.
- Scientific apparatus, circuit diagrams, sketches of equipment.
- Also in **science**, one person describes to their partner what they can see under the microscope.
- Flow diagrams, maps and plans.
- The exercise could be conducted in a **modern foreign language**. For example, the cross-section of a house showing the position of different rooms, or routes on a town plan, or the items on different shelves of a refrigerator, or furniture in a room, or descriptions of people.
- Designs in **technology** – to draw attention to features of different designs, various clock faces for example, prior to a design task.

Why do it?

- Lasting learning occurs through the focused attention to detail and the struggle to use appropriate language.
- Listening and questioning skills are deliberately developed – these are two of the essential ingredients of effective independent learning.
- Visual and interpersonal intelligences are required. By removing the need to read and write, this exercise gives nonacademic students a chance of success and satisfaction. It is inclusive.
- Those with a strongly visual learning style are satisfied.
- It's an exercise in cooperation – each student depends on the other for success. This is an ideal opportunity to get students working in "unusual" combinations across typical friendship and gender boundaries.

Variations

1. Try it with squared paper, thereby inviting students to use coordinates in the desire for accuracy.
2. Try it face-to-face rather than back-to-back with papers hidden behind boards or books. In this case students benefit from eye contact, but are not allowed to use gestures or trace shapes in the air. The describer should not be able to see the drawer's work during the process.
3. After a while stop the process and discuss with the class the technical terminology demanded by the exercise, for example, *apex, equilateral, isosceles*. Make a list on the board of terms and their meanings – this creates a word bank, which supports language learning and application. The students then get back to the activity and are expected to make greater use of the technical language. Wander round and make sure they do!
4. Use it for three-dimensional modelling – e.g. circuit boards, plasticine models, wire sculpture …
5. Use an overhead projector to present the image. One partner faces the screen, the other has their back to it.

Beat the Teacher

Go on, fulfil your fantasy!

How?

1. Explain that you are going to describe a procedure, read a text, write a passage on the board, demonstrate a practical activity, explain a concept, work through a calculation, draw a diagram on the overhead projector … and that you are likely to make some mistakes.
2. The students' job, working individually, is to spot and make a note of the mistakes.
3. At the end of the teacher's presentation students pair up, compare results and come up with their joint list.
4. The teacher goes round the class asking each pair to offer a mistake. Discussion follows to clarify the points.
5. To conclude, the teacher's "corrections" are written up by everyone.

Applications

- **Modern foreign languages**: teacher reads a passage in target language, or gives dictation, or provides a listening test. Mistakes can include mispronunciation, incorrect syntax, mixed tenses …
- **Technical vocabulary**: students have to spot where the teacher could have used a technical word but didn't, in science, technology, art, maths, geography, ICT (Information and Communication Technology), PE.
- **Science**: conduct an experiment without sufficient attention to health-and-safety details.
- Any demonstrable process, complicated drawing or calculation, substantial explanation or description.
- **English, history, religious education, art**: the teacher works in role, speaks in character and makes deliberate mistakes. Could use "Hot-Seating"(page 116) – in other words, the teacher responds to students' questions.

Purposes (what the activity is designed to achieve)	
Thinking	* * * * *
Emotional Intelligence	*
Independence	* *
Interdependence	* * * (variable)
Multi-sensation	*
Fun	* * * *
Articulation	* *

Particulars (what the activity contains)	
Individual work	* * *
Group work	* * *
Moving about	
Speaking	*
Listening	* * * *
Reading	
Writing	*
Looking	* * * * (variable)
Choice	

Specific room layout	
Yes (No)	

71

Why do it?

- Requires all students to be alert and thinking.
- Confirms understanding in the student's mind as the brain automatically compares what it thinks it knows with what is being seen and heard.
- The novelty value of students pitting their wits against the teacher is usually motivating.
- It can create a softer relationship between the class and the teacher.

Variations

1. Initially, students work in pairs. Then, after the teacher's presentation, pairs join up to make fours. They discuss, argue and decide on a definitive list.
2. Students can use "Calling Cards" (page 81) or "Thumbometer" (page 161) to signal the teacher's mistakes "live".
3. Beat the teacher in a different sense. Students have to do something faster than the teacher, e.g. conduct an experiment, do a calculation, come up with a design, write a model answer, translate a passage, make a set of notes on a passage. Students might be asked to work in pairs to give them an advantage.
4. Reverse the process. Students in pairs devise a presentation that contains deliberate mistakes. If the teacher doesn't spot them all, the teacher is beaten. Ideal for revision.
5. After an initial period of individual research, students pair up and devise questions to take their knowledge further. They put these to the teacher, who scores a point for each question she can answer off the top of her head. The class gets a point for every answer she has to look up.

Bingo

Eyes down for a novel and light-hearted way to reinforce key concepts and vocabulary.

Purposes (what the activity is designed to achieve)	
Thinking	* * * * *
Emotional Intelligence	
Independence	* *
Interdependence	* * * **(variable)**
Multi-sensation	
Fun	* * * *
Articulation	* **(variable)**

Particulars (what the activity contains)	
Individual work	* * * *
Group work	* * **(variable)**
Moving about	
Speaking	*
Listening	* * * *
Reading	* *
Writing	* *
Looking	* * *
Choice	*

Specific room layout
Yes   No

How?

1. Get everyone to draw, quickly and freehand, a blank nine-square "bingo" grid.
2. On the board write twelve key terms from the current topic.
3. Ask everyone to fill in their nine squares, putting their choice of nine of the twelve key terms in any order. If they're wise, they'll choose the ones they are most likely to get right!
4. Call "eyes down". Read out the definitions of the twelve terms, one at a time, in random order. One way to do this is to have the definitions written out on small cards beforehand. The pack is shuffled, or shaken in a bag, so everyone can see that the order is random as in real bingo.
5. Pupils cross off the terms on their card if and when they match the definitions. When someone calls a line (horizontal, vertical or diagonal), they read back the keys terms and their meanings. Then proceed to a full house. Again, the winner reads back the terms and meanings. The rest of the class are asked to agree or disagree with the student's answers.

Applications

- To revise a topic just covered.
- To assess prior knowledge of a topic before it is tackled.
- As a novel way to give a "test".
- An ideal end to a lesson that has introduced a number of technical terms.

Why do it?

- It's engaging, it's novel, it's painless!
- It tells you and the students a great deal about levels of understanding and retention. The diagnosis can then inform your choice of reinforcement and extension activities.
- It encourages students to realise that learning can be fun, as well as giving them a revision technique to use at home.

Variations

1. Use a sixteen-square grid with twenty-five terms.
2. Students can work in mixed-ability pairs instead of individually.
3. Instead of just reading out definitions, devise rather more demanding questions that reflect the standard of the official assessment.
4. Learning how to spell technical terms. Students are asked to learn twelve words, they then choose the nine that they are most confident about and write them in the boxes – from memory. The teacher then spells out the twelve words one at a time in random order. The students can cross them off only if they have spelled them correctly.

Bodily Functions

We all have them, naturally. But don't just go through the motions - make them a natural part of learning

How?

Use members of the class to represent component parts of a process, and get them to act it out. For example: **human reproduction**.

1. Clear the furniture from the middle of the room. Use tables, chairs or laboratory benches to make a passageway (a vagina!) from the classroom door into the middle of the room.
2. Ask half the class to wait outside in the corridor – they will be the sperm!
3. Most of the others stand in two lines to make up the Fallopian tube at the end of the passageway. Five students with backs to each other and arms tightly linked in a circle form the female egg cell membrane. The egg nestles in the Fallopian tube.
4. Chose the smallest student in the class to be the nucleus – he stands in the middle of the cell, quivering with anticipation.
5. Now ask the sperm in the corridor to pair up, head and tail. The tails wiggle and push. Explain that the passageway is tight, that it's a race and, to make it less chaotic, the sperm can only walk heel to toe or move in slow motion.
6. The sperm press against the closed door, which then bursts open and a great ejaculation of pairs of students jostle up the passageway to the waiting egg. If heads and tails become separated, they die.
7. The first sperm head to arrive is let in, the egg cell membrane immediately closes up, arms tightly linked again. The nucleus is fertilised and the rest of the sperm mill around and give up.

The placenta. String a badminton net across the room as the placenta wall. Divide the students into two large groups – the mother's and the foetus's blood supplies. The groups, on opposite

Purposes (what the activity is designed to achieve)	
Thinking	* * *
Emotional Intelligence	* *
Independence	* *
Interdependence	* * *
Multi-sensation	* * * * *
Fun	* * * *
Articulation	*

Particulars (what the activity contains)	
Individual work	*
Group work	* * * *
Moving about	* * * * *
Speaking	*
Listening	* *
Reading	
Writing	
Looking	* * * *
Choice	

Specific room layout (Yes) No

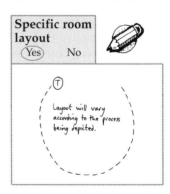

Layout will vary according to the process being depicted.

sides of the net, move in large circles. As they circulate, students pick up cards. The mother's students pick up large red-blood-cell cards and smaller white oxygen cards and green nutrition cards, one each. The foetus students pick up large red-blood-cell cards and smaller grey carbon dioxide cards and brown and yellow waste cards. As the circulating students approach the net, they attempt to pass cards through to students on the other side. The oxygen and nutrition cards pass to the foetus, and the brown and yellow waste cards pass to the mother. The red cards are too big and won't go through the net either way, showing that the blood supplies never mingle. Keep the process going, until the key teaching points have become clear.

Magnetism. Clear the furniture and make a circle of chairs. Place a table or bench in the middle of the circle as a bar magnet, labelled positive and negative. Invite a student to get up and walk the path of the magnetic field. Establish the route using discussion and guidance from the teacher. Gradually invite more and more students to take part until the full pattern of the magnetic field is in motion.

Applications

- **Geography**: mapwork – students stand in concentric circles, indicating the shape of a hill, and hold long circles of string at various heights to form contour lines. The string lines are then laid on the floor to show how height is represented on a flat surface. Develop into more complex landforms.
- **Maths**: coordinates. Especially easy on a tiled floor. Teams of students send delegates to stand in response to given coordinates. Can be done as a competition. Play noughts and crosses or draughts (with students sitting on chairs and the team leader giving instructions in the form of coordinates for each move). Or geometry: students in groups make given shapes and figures. Individual students then volunteer to "walk the line", for example, walk the route of a tangent, or a chord, or a diameter.
- **English**: individual students take characters from a novel or play and work out how to position themselves in relation to each other to represent relationships, tensions, conflicts, alliances – these then shift as different chapters or scenes are depicted.
- **Information and communications technology**: flowcharts. Students represent different functions in a process, linked by pointing students who represent arrows.
- **Business studies**: organisation charts with students representing positions and functions within a company, separated by hierarchical tiers and holding lengths of string to indicate lines of management.
- **Science**: voltage. Lay out an "electrical circuit" using rope or string. A few students are light bulbs and stand on the string, while another represents electrical power. Initially just one student is a "volt" and pushes the "power student" around the circuit. When the "power" passes the bulbs, their arms shoot up. Then two "volts" push the "power", who now moves faster so the lights come on more quickly. A third "volt" is added and so on until the point has been firmly made.
- **History**: timeline. Some students have large cards with dates written on, others with events. The "dates" organise themselves first and then the "events" stand behind them. The rest of the class instruct people to move if they feel they're incorrectly placed.

Why do it?

- Multisensory learning sticks in the mind more than monosensory learning. The experience goes in through more sensory channels.
- Experiences that have an emotional edge to them, that feel risky, exciting or fun, for example, involve the release of chemicals in the brain, which act as memory fixatives.
- "Bodily Functions" is an inclusive strategy – it provides for students who do not read and write well, whose learning styles are concrete, activist and random, or whose intelligences are predominantly kinaesthetic and spatial.

- It can break the ice and change the dynamic of classroom relationships. The teacher is often seen in a different light afterwards and students might be more prepared to work with each other in various combinations.

Variations

1. Go outside – use the playground or field for big demonstrations.
2. Have an advance party of students who research the topic and work out how the class can represent it physically. They then lead the lesson and organise everyone, instead of your having to do it! You simply make adjustments and comments.
3. Ask students to work in groups. Give them the challenge to work out, and physically demonstrate, the process for themselves in their groups. Groups then view each other's interpretations.

Broken Pieces

You'll have a smashing time with this. You break material up into bits - and get other people to put it back together. Very satisfying!

How?

Each student is given a key piece of information or responsibility that the group needs in order to complete a corporate task.

1. Best done in circles, but not impossible with conventional seating arrangements.
2. Explain the task to be completed by the group – a problem to be solved, a code to be cracked, a sequence to be decided, a conclusion to be drawn, a decision to be made, a solution to be found, a product to be created.
3. Explain the rules. For a typical talk-based "Broken Pieces" like "Codebuster" or "Mad Inventors' Society" (below); or "Murder Hunt" (on page 179):

   - You cannot show or physically give your information to anyone else. Nor can you take anyone's.
   - You exchange your contributions by word of mouth only.
   - Only one person can write.
   - You cannot move or leave your seat, except for one person who may be asked by the group to write notes on the board/flipchart.
   - From time to time the teacher will let you know how long is left, and will remind you of the rules if they are being broken. Apart from this, you have to organise yourselves.

   Adjust the rules for the nature of the activity. It is important that each student hold onto her information or resource or particular responsibility throughout the exercise.

4. Announce the deadline, which should create a sense of urgency, and let them start.
5. Teacher's role. The activity is designed to exercise the group's problem-solving skills. It is therefore important to allow the group to take charge of the process. If you sit back,

Purposes (what the activity is designed to achieve)	
Thinking	* * * * *
Emotional Intelligence	* *
Independence	* * *
Interdependence	* * * * *
Multi-sensation	
Fun	* * *
Articulation	* * * *

Particulars (what the activity contains)	
Individual work	*
Group work	* * * * *
Moving about	
Speaking	* * * * *
Listening	* * * * *
Reading	* * *
Writing	*
Looking	*
Choice	

Specific room layout (Yes)   No

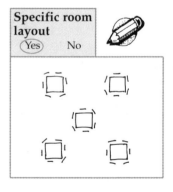

observing but not intervening, the true dynamics of the class will probably become evident: domination, withdrawal, poor listening, put-downs or whatever. It may be difficult to hold back, but this is experiential learning and will bear fruit only if the real state of affairs is witnessed by all. Intervene only if physical harm or emotional abuse is about to occur. Talking about what has happened afterwards with the group is as important as the exercise itself.

Applications

1. Maths: Codebuster

For example, as an introduction to algebra write this coded message on the board:

$$7\ 9\ 13\ 4\ 5\ 6\ 9$$
$$1\ 5\ 7\ 8\ 2\ 6\ 7\ 10\ 11\ 10\ 12\ 10\ 9\ 3$$

Students work in groups of five or six. Each group is given an envelope containing thirteen clue cards. These are distributed as evenly as possible.

o x e = i	n < 10
3 x d = 12	o + e = s
y – o = r	yd = u – r
3d = l	2 x p = n + i
o + y = e	3y + 2 = b
$y^2 = t$	2y = n
3 x o = n	

Explain: "On the board is a message, which you can solve as a group by using all the clues. Everyone stays in their seat (except for one person who can be nominated as 'writer' and can use the board). Everyone keeps hold of their own cards. People share their clues and ideas by talking. O is the letter, not the number." The exercise should take about fifteen minutes.

2. Science: Mad Inventors' Society

Students work in groups of four or five. Each group has to devise an experiment to separate alcohol and water. Clues include:

- alcohol is colourless
- the boiling point of water is 100°C
- the boiling point of alcohol is 78°C
- evaporation means …
- condensation is …
- a Liebig Condenser is … etc.

3. Business Studies: Settling Matters

Decide the best location for a new branch of a supermarket chain. The "pieces" are various factors to take into account in the decision-making process.

4. Pieces can be visual

For example:
History: give sections of the Bayeaux Tapestry to be organised into the correct sequence.
Modern languages: snippets of a story from a storyboard of cartoon-like scenes.

5. Pieces can be physical

For example:
● Build a bridge to certain specifications – one person has the straws, one the scissors, one the Sellotape, one the ruler etc.
● Each person has a particular dance step or position – these have to be put together into a performance piece.

6. Pieces can be in a foreign language

As detectives, work out the appearance, recent movements and psychological profile of a wanted man from various snippets of information and documents, all in target language.

7. Pieces can be sophisticated

Each piece can be a position or an argument or a personality in a debate. For example, "What is the path to peace in Northern Ireland?" or "What is the likelihood of intelligent life being discovered on other planets?" The aim is to come to a reasonable conclusion given all the positions around the table.

Or each piece can be a lengthy text that requires interpretation and deduction, in which case students should have some individual working time before coming together for the group exercise. This develops higher-order reading skills, especially if the deadline for the individual phase puts students under pressure to operate at speed.

8. Pieces can be a mixture

For example, in **geography**, students have to find where the treasure is located on an island, some with pictures of the landscape, some with coordinates, some with fragments of a map and others with written descriptions.

Why do it?

● The exercise works with the brain's natural desire to work out puzzles, unravel mysteries, resolve conundrums and generally make its own meaning.
● It strengthens linguistic, logical and interpersonal abilities.
● Distributing the pieces gives everyone a potential contribution, so no one is left out – this is helpful when you want students to learn the arts of participation and inclusion. It trains students in genuine group work.
● It draws everyone's attention to the need for listening skills and basic rules. This, in turn, creates the context and motivation for improving behaviour. It can lead to the creation or reinforcement of classroom ground rules (see p. 179 for further details).
● It reveals the starting point from which you can discuss with the class ways of taking increased responsibility for learning.
● The exercise requires a range of thinking skills, including hypothesising, ordering information, cross-referencing, lateral thinking, suspending judgment, monitoring …
● By overhearing the discussions, the teacher can carry out informal diagnostic assessments.

Variations

1. Video the exercise with the group's agreement. Watch the footage with the students, then discuss improvements to behaviour and problem-solving technique. A couple of weeks later run a similar exercise, video it again, watch it and discuss the extent to which improvements have been made. See "Framed" (page 182).
2. Vary the size of groups. Even try it with the whole class sitting round in a circle.

Calling Cards

Calling out is rude. In the polite social circles of your classroom, calling cards are much more civilised.

Purposes (what the activity is designed to achieve)	
Thinking	* * * * *
Emotional Intelligence	*
Independence	* * * *
Interdependence	
Multi-sensation	*
Fun	* *
Articulation	* *

Particulars (what the activity contains)	
Individual work	* * * * *
Group work	
Moving about	
Speaking	
Listening	* * * *
Reading	
Writing	
Looking	* *
Choice	

Specific room layout
Yes　(No)

How?

1. This simple idea allows students to signal a response by holding up, or placing out on the desk, a card.
2. Make cards, A5 or A6 size, and distribute to each student. For most purposes it's useful for students to have three cards each: red, green, amber; or different symbols: tick, cross, question mark.
3. The only rule is to be honest.

Applications

- They can be used to indicate **responses to questions**: "I know I know the answer" (tick or green), "I know I don't know" (cross or red), "I'm not sure whether I know or not" (question mark or amber). As everyone is required to show a card, this is more challenging and participatory than "hands up".
- They can be used to signal **confusion**: hold up the amber card when you're beginning to lose the thread of what I'm saying; hold up the red card when you've completely lost it! A good example is in **modern foreign languages**, when the teacher is giving instructions or explaining a concept in target language, or is reading a comprehension piece. It is an excellent diagnostic tool, enabling the teacher to fix students' problems very precisely.
- They can be used to signal that a student **wants to ask** a question, wants clarification or wants to make a statement – more grown up than putting their hand up. This is good for discussions and debates and is a more interactive way of listening to guest speakers.
- They can be used to make a **spot check on understanding** – at any point the teacher can stop and ask for a show of cards: completely understand everything so far; half understand; haven't got a clue.
- Ideal for school council meetings or form meetings (even staff meetings) as a quick way of gathering opinion and making decisions.

Why do it?

- The technique encourages participation. The cards create the expectation that everyone will take an active part in proceedings. They beg to be used.
- The fact that *everyone* has been issued with cards levels out the playing field. The strategy has an inclusive feel to it, especially as it removes the barriers of speaking, reading and writing.
- The cards suggest that it's OK not to understand everything, that we are here to learn, not just go through the motions of learning. They signal that learning involves confusion, mis-understanding and mental struggle, that this is natural and we learn most efficiently if we are honest and upfront about our state of mind!
- Above all, the cards demand that students think: they have to listen, absorb, synthesise, connect, check. The device supports the natural process of pattern-making, which is the route to internalised understanding.
- Consequently, the cards strengthen the idea of personal responsibility in learning.
- This is a fundamentally democratic procedure and therefore contributes to the Citizenship agenda.

Variations

1. If you don't have enough card, get students to use three different hand signals.
2. Or three different facial expressions!

Centre of the Universe

Few people know that the centre of the universe is actually Stoke-on-Trent, home of the world's greatest football team. Now, you can create the centre of the universe in the comfort of your own classroom.

Purposes (what the activity is designed to achieve)	
Thinking	* * * *
Emotional Intelligence	* *
Independence	* * * *
Interdependence	*
Multi-sensation	* * *
Fun	* * *
Articulation	* *

Particulars (what the activity contains)	
Individual work	* *
Group work	* * * *
Moving about	* * *
Speaking	*
Listening	* * * *
Reading	
Writing	
Looking	* * *
Choice	* * *

Specific room layout (Yes) No

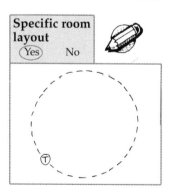

How?

1. Clear the desks and create a circle of chairs.
2. Have a round cardboard "bull's-eye", or a rope circle, about half a metre in diameter, on which students can stand. This should be placed in the centre of the circle and represents the "centre of the universe".
3. The first volunteer student stands at the "centre on the universe" and makes a statement about the topic in hand. All the other students respond. The more they agree with the statement, the closer to the middle they stand. If they totally disagree, they remain seated. Those who agree completely with the statement stand shoulder to shoulder at the "centre of the universe". Then they all sit down.
4. Another student takes over, stands in the middle and makes a fresh statement. The process continues with volunteer students taking turns to have their say.

Applications

- **Revise any topic**. Students at the centre state facts or better still explain concepts or give judgments, for example, "On balance we have to say that Churchill was Britain's greatest prime minister since Gladstone because …"
- **Explore prior knowledge** at the beginning of a new topic: "What do we already know, or think we know, about …?"
- **Initiate a whole-class discussion**, for example, "Sole trading is the most efficient type of business"; "We will never know the truth about the historical Jesus"; "Britain's climate is changing due to global warming."
- **Evaluate learning**, for example: "How could we improve the experiment we just carried out?"; "Next time we do group work, what should we do differently?"
- **Gather whole-class opinions quickly** on sensitive issues such as bullying, or to make decisions about where to go for the class outing; this is an ideal way for school council representatives to consult the class.

Why do it?

- It maximises participation – everyone is part of the process all the time.
- There's no hiding place, there are no passengers. Everyone is being asked to think and respond. There's always the prospect that the teacher will spot and challenge those who are just following the crowd.
- The physical aspect of the exercise is appealing to many students – and can come as a welcome relief to everyone.

Variations

1. As students stand in response to a statement, they can be challenged by the teacher or other students to justify their position. This cuts out students just "going through the motions".
2. The exercise can be used to start a formal debate.
3. Quick sketches can be made or digital photographs taken to create a record of each statement.
4. The teacher can join in too, as a respondent, or sometimes to make a statement of her own, especially if she feels that some crucial point has been overlooked.

Circus Time

Teachers are often juggling priorities, walking tightropes and jumping through hoops, so running a classroom circus shouldn't be a problem.

Purposes (what the activity is designed to achieve)	
Thinking	* * *
Emotional Intelligence	* *
Independence	* * * * *
Interdependence	* *
Multi-sensation	* * * (variable)
Fun	* *
Articulation	* *

Particulars (what the activity contains)	
Individual work	* * * *
Group work	*
Moving about	* * * *
Speaking	* *
Listening	* *
Reading	* *
Writing	* *
Looking	* *
Choice	* * * *

Specific room layout (Yes) No

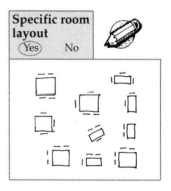

How?

The basic plan is for students to work through a series of set tasks in any order within a given timescale.

1. Design a number of tasks pertinent to the topic in hand. Preferably, these should cover a range of learning styles and differ in conceptual sophistication.

2. Set out the tasks in different locations around the room. If facilities allow, they might include watching a video for selected information (with the TV facing into a corner of the room), listening to an audio cassette (with a 'listening centre' and multiple headphones), CD-ROM or Internet exercise (on the classroom PCs or in the school resource centre), and various reading, writing, graphic and tactile activities laid out on desktops. If facilities or energy or time doesn't allow for such a range, then a smaller number of tasks doubled up could be provided. The key is to have enough stations to ensure that no one location becomes overcrowded.

3. Explain the learning objectives, and the assessment to be conducted at the end of the series of lessons. It's important that students be able to remain focused on the purpose and end point during the circus.

4. Show the large wall chart you made earlier on which all the tasks appear as columns in random order (it is important that they be random and not in some increasing order of difficulty) and all the students' names appear as rows. Students are also given an individual record sheet with all the tasks on. Progress will be recorded on both the public and private sheets. Each time a student completes a task to the teacher's satisfaction, both record sheets are signed and dated.

5. Then set the challenge: for example, "Let's see if everyone can achieve success in at least five out of the eight tasks within the next three lessons". It's important to give latitude in the number of tasks to be completed to allow for differentiation. Hence a minimum of five,

a maximum of eight (or whatever numbers are right for your students). You might offer some kind of celebration if everyone gets there: for example, in modern languages a French breakfast complete with croissants and hot chocolate (it's money well spent from the departmental budget), or in geography an orienteering treasure hunt. It's amazing how such a simple incentive can stimulate peer group pressure and support as students encourage each other to complete the minimum number of tasks.

6. Students set off, tackling tasks in an order that suits them. The teacher moves around monitoring, challenging and supporting. In some cases, students may be directed to certain tasks: for example, the more able students should be challenged to do the more difficult ones, and vice versa. This way, the teacher ensures that learning is personally appropriate for each student. When a student completes a task, the teacher has to validate the work and check the student's understanding before they are allowed to move on.

7. Some students might plan their route, others will go with the flow. However, they are not allowed to overcrowd workstations, so some negotiation will be needed.

8. At the end of the allocated time, learning is consolidated by the teacher, drawing on the knowledge and understanding achieved by students, and a concluding assessment is undertaken against the original learning objectives.

Applications

- Any subject that can be learned, or consolidated, through a number of independent tasks.
- Set out past exam questions as the tasks – excellent for revision and training students in exam technique. The questions could even have "bad" answers attached, using real anonymous examples from mock exams. The aim is to rework the answers until they are perfect.

Why do it?

- It is an example of structured independent learning and as such trains students in certain disciplines: managing time; using a range of resources; operating in a range of styles; moving unprompted from one task to the next; remaining on task (even when the teacher isn't looking); making choices.
- Students exercise a degree of control over their learning – they determine the order and pace of their work. Research suggests that motivation, initiative and results improve when students have relative control.
- At best, students will experience a range of learning styles. This will give them, and the teacher, insight into their natural preferences.
- The method is highly differentiated. Everyone is offered success at a level that is stretching, but within their reach.

Variations

1. A more structured version: put the students into groups and move them round at set intervals from one task to another. The exercise can still be differentiated if the groups are constructed according to "ability". Not all groups will do the same series of tasks, though there will be a common core.

2. Make it an exercise in cooperation. Expect the students to work collaboratively in pairs rather individually at the tasks.

Conversion

To maximise learning, convert your students to the idea that all material can be converted.

Purposes	
(what the activity is designed to achieve)	
Thinking	* * * * *
Emotional Intelligence	*
Independence	* * * *
Interdependence	
Multi-sensation	*
Fun	*
Articulation	* * * *

Particulars	
(what the activity contains)	
Individual work	* * * * *
Group work	
Moving about	
Speaking	
Listening	*
Reading	* * * *
Writing	* * *
Looking	* *
Choice	*

Specific room layout	
Yes (No)	

How?

1. Ask students to take material that is presented in one format and convert it into a different format.
2. Typical examples include:

   - turn text into a mind map
   - turn text into a flow diagram
   - turn text into a storyboard
   - turn text into a chart
   - turn text into a key-word plan
   - turn text into overlapping circles
   - turn text into a graph
   - turn text into ranked bullet points
   - turn mind maps, flow diagrams, storyboards, charts, graphs and bullet points into text
   - turn the teacher's explanation, or a video, into any of the above

3. Other formats to convert material into include "Still Image" (otherwise known as freeze-frame or tableau: page 158), drawing, model, arrangement of objects on the desk to represent component parts of an idea or process, "Bodily Functions" (page 75). Mix and match the combinations to suit the topic.

Applications

- Endless. For example, in **MFL** turn a story in target language into a storyboard or vice versa.
- In **PE** turn a complex movement or skill into a series of still images.
- In **maths**, turn a process or convention into a written description.
- In **history** turn a description of cause and effect into a flow diagram.
- In **English**, turn the theme of evil in *Macbeth* into a line graph, tracing the highs and lows of evil through each scene; turn relationships between characters into overlapping circles; turn the plot into a flow diagram and character studies into mind maps.

- In **geography**, turn climate graphs into a written description of the weather experienced by a resident throughout the year.
- In **business studies**, turn a job description into a storyboard.
- In **English**, **religious education** and **history** turn a narrative into a flow diagram and descriptions into a chart.
- In **science**, turn processes and reactions into "working models" using everyday items on the desktop.
- In **technology**, turn the teacher's verbal instructions into a flow diagram.

Why do it?

- Material can be converted only if it is understood. This technique ensures that deep learning takes place.
- If students are struggling with the conversion it reveals where their misconceptions and difficulties lie. In this sense, the exercise provides diagnostic assessment, and personal tuition from the teacher will be required.
- It equips students with a core independent learning and revision skill. This will stand them in good stead as they approach exams.
- The types of conversion suit different learning styles and intelligence profiles. The strategy encourages students to see that they can be successful with academic material whatever their style or profile, if only they adopt the right approach.

Variations

1. Students can be encouraged to take any material presented in lessons and convert it at home, even when the teacher doesn't require it. This will deepen learning and make revision much easier.
2. Give students a choice of formats. Over time demonstrate them all, teach them all, get the class to practise them all. Students will then be in a position to choose the ones that suit their learning style or type of intelligence independently.
3. Students can do conversions in pairs rather than on their own.

Corporate Identity

In this hi-tech age of competition, here's a lo-tech way of achieving cooperation.

Purposes (what the activity is designed to achieve)	
Thinking	* * *
Emotional Intelligence	* *
Independence	* * *
Interdependence	* * * * *
Multi-sensation	
Fun	*
Articulation	* * *

Particulars (what the activity contains)	
Individual work	* * * *
Group work	* * * *
Moving about	
Speaking	* *
Listening	* *
Reading	* *
Writing	* *
Looking	*
Choice	*

Specific room layout

(Yes)　　No

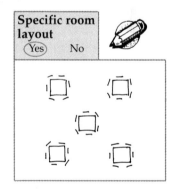

How?

1. Organise the class into mixed-ability groups of, say, six. These should be carefully selected so they comprise students with currently *different* levels of performance in your subject.
2. Within each group, members need to sit so they can all see and hear each other easily.
3. Work continues as normal, but members of the group are expected to support each other so that everyone understands all the material they are attempting. The responsibility is shared. Those who are having difficulty with a particular instruction or concept are expected to ask those who aren't. Those who do understand are expected to check that others also understand, and if not to offer help. If everyone's stuck, they ask the teacher.
4. The teacher can drop on any member of the group at any time to question their knowledge and understanding of material that has been covered. If answers are inaccurate or even half accurate, then *the group* has not fulfilled its duty.
5. This does not mean that everyone has to work at the same pace or even on the same material within the group. Faster workers can get ahead. The idea is to have groups large enough so that it's not always the same person being called on for help.

Applications

Any subject. "Corporate Identity" works best when students are following a sustained piece of individual work – a series of structured worksheets or a booklet, for example.

Why do it?

- Students often learn more efficiently from each other than from the teacher because they understand each other's confusions, and use more relevant language and examples.
- It builds both personal responsibility and interdependence, and demonstrates a model of both citizenship and inclusion.
- It frees the teacher to give substantial attention to those who need it most.

Variations

1. The method is most successful when sustained for several lessons. This gives students chance to get into the routine.
2. Although it detracts from the cooperative nature of the exercise, points can be awarded to groups for members successfully passing the teacher's spontaneous "tests".

Delegation

Get other people to do the learning for you. Now that sounds like a sensible idea.

How?

1. Set up resource stations around the room. These might include a combination of posters to examine, experiments to carry out, a short video to watch, pages of a text book to read, an audio cassette to listen to (using a listening centre with multiple headphones), a PowerPoint presentation to watch on a PC, an Internet site to visit …

2. Students form home groups of, say, five. Each group has the same objective: to understand and learn all aspects of the topic exhibited around the room.

3. Therefore, each group decides which student to send to which resource station, perhaps taking account of their preferred learning style. These envoys then go the their stations and work to a common deadline to understand the material and make notes to take back to base. Delegates from different groups help each other to master the resources, so everyone goes back to their home group feeling clear and confident.

4. On returning to their home group they take turns to teach each other. The teacher moves round monitoring the quality of teaching and responding to questions for clarification.

Purposes (what the activity is designed to achieve)	
Thinking	* * *
Emotional Intelligence	* *
Independence	* * *
Interdependence	* * * * *
Multi-sensation	* * (variable)
Fun	*
Articulation	* * *

Particulars (what the activity contains)	
Individual work	* *
Group work	* * * *
Moving about	* * *
Speaking	* * *
Listening	* * *
Reading	* *
Writing	* * *
Looking	* * (variable)
Choice	* *

Specific room layout (Yes) No

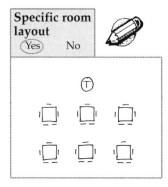

Applications

- **Science**: learning the tests for different food substances (starch, carbohydrate, sugar, fat); methods of separation and their commercial uses.
- **Technology**: the properties of different materials; the procedures and characteristics of different ways of joining materials; different types of finish for materials.
- **History**: the various causes of World War Two; different bits of evidence of Catherine the Great's "enlightenment".
- **English**: different stanzas of a poem to interpret; different characters to study; different scenes to analyse; different critical reviews to summarise; different positions to articulate.
- **Art**: examples of an artist's, or a genre's, work.
- **Business studies**: different leadership styles.

Why do it?

- A number of independent learning skills are being rehearsed, including managing a variety of resources, note making, collaboration, communication, presentation.
- The sense of challenge created by the ethos of this activity is usually motivating.
- Peer teaching is proven to be an efficient learning strategy.
- Group work and citizenship are being learned through the interdependence of the exercise. Every individual's learning is dependent on several other people, so everyone carries a lot of responsibility.

Variations

1. Build in a "double check". After the first round of delegation, everyone is sent out again to a different resource, to check the work of their colleague. This way, when the peer teaching takes place there is an expert and a seconder for each topic. This usually results in more confidence, clarity and coverage.
2. The resources need not be made by the teacher. They could be the work of students, either produced by small expert groups as the first phase of the exercise, or by last year's class as the end products of their learning, or by a parallel class (a top set producing materials for a middle set, for example).
3. Conclude the exercise with some form of individual assessment.
4. Differentiate. Make sure the resources differ in difficulty and predetermine mixed-ability groups. Decide in advance which students will go to which resource.

Dicey Business

Learning needn't be a lottery. Nor should it be dull and predictable. Just add a little spice with the dice.

How?

1. Prepare a set of connected prompts or questions to which the students should respond. These should be put in logical order, lettered A, B, C, D … on the back, and made up into packs of cards enough for one pack per group.
2. Students work in groups of six. Each group sits at a table with its pack of cards in the middle, face down, with card A on top. The group also has a die. Each person has a number, 1 to 6.
3. The group decides who goes first. The first player rolls the die and the person with the number shown picks up the first card and responds to the prompt or question.
4. The second player throws the die. The person with the number shown picks up card B and responds … and so on round the circle as often as it takes to get through the cards. As the prompts or questions are connected, and as no one knows whose number will be next, everyone has to pay full attention all the time.

Applications

- **Modern foreign languages**: ideal for prompting a spoken story, sentence by sentence. Each card has a word or phrase that must be included in the next sentence. Could be pictures instead of words. At a higher level the prompts could indicate which tenses, parts of speech or structures have to be used.
- **English**: ideal for prompting a piece of creative writing. Each card has an image or part of speech or new character that must be woven in. The group's collective verbal version models the idea for students' individual written efforts later.
- **Technology**: establishing the design-and-make sequence – what has to be done at each stage of this new project?
- **Science**: explaining the elements, substances, reactions and equations in a chemical process.
- **Maths**: several examples of the same mathematical technique, calculating angles for instance.

Purposes (what the activity is designed to achieve)	
Thinking	* * * *
Emotional Intelligence	* *
Independence	* *
Interdependence	*
Multi-sensation	*
Fun	* * * *
Articulation	* * *

Particulars (what the activity contains)	
Individual work	* *
Group work	* * * *
Moving about	
Speaking	* * *
Listening	* * * *
Reading	*
Writing	
Looking	*
Choice	

Specific room layout (Yes) No

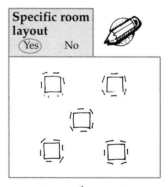

- **Citizenship, religious education, personal, social and health education (PSHE)**: discuss an issue or argue a point from various angles. Each card has a different character or outlook – for example, a Labour politician, a human rights activist, a clergyman, a headteacher, an atheist etc.
- A series of **consolidation or revision** questions on any topic in any subject.

Why do it?

- As a piece of structured group work it trains students in the disciplines of turn-taking, listening and collective responsibility.
- The randomising effect of the die is fun and usually motivating.

Variations

1. If numbers don't allow groups of six, have smaller groups with void numbers on the die (i.e. in a group of four, if number five or six comes up, everyone breathes a sigh of relief and the player rolls again).
2. Can be done as a whole class activity with everyone sitting round in a circle and a pack of large cards in the middle. A die on a tray is passed round, when a student throws a six, they're next. For best results, the person in the middle should have to keep talking to the prompt or question until the next six is thrown.

Discussion Carousel

A device for getting everyone to take part in productive, if not circular (!) discussion.

Purposes (what the activity is designed to achieve)	
Thinking	* * * *
Emotional Intelligence	* *
Independence	* *
Interdependence	* * *
Multi-sensation	* *
Fun	* * *
Articulation	* * * *

Particulars (what the activity contains)	
Individual work	*
Group work	* * * *
Moving about	* *
Speaking	* * * *
Listening	* * * * *
Reading	
Writing	
Looking	
Choice	

Specific room layout
(Yes)   No

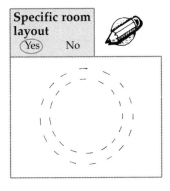

How?

1. Clear the desks.
2. Have the group sitting on chairs in two concentric circles, an "outer" and an "inner", of equal numbers. The inner circle faces outwards and the outer circle faces inwards. In other words, everyone is facing a partner.
3. The facing pairs are given a prompt and have a conversation for, say, three minutes. They are asked to make sure that each has a chance to speak. The teacher lets them know when it's half-time.
4. When the time is up, the outer circle stands and spins round (more accurately shuffles round) to the left until the teacher says stop. Students now sit down, facing a new random partner.
5. Before the new pair launch into *their* conversation, developing the subject further, each has to summarise to the other their **previous partner's** contribution. Listening skills to the fore!
6. Once again, when time is up, the outer circle "spins" and new pairs are formed. Students have to summarise both their first and second partners' contributions before conducting their third conversation.
7. This may be repeated as many times as is useful.

Applications

- Useful for any type of discussion. The discussion could be very academic: an A-level question; formulating a precise definition of a technical term or phenomenon; constructing a model paragraph answer to a GCSE question; planning a method to test a hypothesis.
- Use it to revise a topic or to find out what people already know before a new topic is begun.
- Use it to evaluate products (in **technology,** for example), or to evaluate the learning process itself.

- It is a way of "broadening the mind" whenever matters of opinion are to be discussed (in **English, religion, health, history**). It prepares for argumentative writing.
- Use it to help students formulate their own opinions with a degree of privacy. It helps them gain confidence before taking part in an open whole-class discussion or formal debate.
- It can be used to air class opinion about a matter of common concern, for example what to do about bullying, as part of **PSHE** or school council business.
- "Discussion Carousel" can be conducted in a **modern foreign language**.

Why do it?

- Creates maximum participation – half the class is talking at any one moment.
- Enables each student to hear a range of opinion quickly.
- Practises listening skills.
- Encourages empathy.
- Gets students used to working with others at random, which is likely to make group work easier in the future.
- Deepens individual students' thinking by making them test it out on others.

Variations

1. If the students are nervous and have poorly developed listening skills, they can be allowed to take notes on what their partners say as an aide-mémoire. This is a stage to grow out of quite quickly, though.
2. To give everyone a chance to move, at changeover times, have both circles "spinning", but in opposite directions.
3. If it's not possible or desirable to move the furniture, have shuffling lines or slinking snakes around the classroom. The principle intention is to randomise pairings.

Distillation

Now this is how you create a good "spirit" in the classroom. At least you get the pure meaning across.

Purposes (what the activity is designed to achieve)	
Thinking	* * * *
Emotional Intelligence	
Independence	* * * *
Interdependence	* *
Multi-sensation	
Fun	*
Articulation	* * *

Particulars (what the activity contains)	
Individual work	* *
Group work	* * *
Moving about	*
Speaking	* * *
Listening	* * *
Reading	* * * *
Writing	* * *
Looking	* *
Choice	*

Specific room layout	
Yes (No)	

How?

1. To completely mix scientific metaphors, distil the essential meaning of a text by using a process of filtration! Draw a large filter funnel and beaker on the board.
2. Students work on a given text in pairs. They are challenged to find the five (or ten, or whatever number is appropriate, given the length and density of the text) most important words. Some discussion of what is meant by "most important" might be needed.
3. As soon as a pair is ready, one of the two comes to the board and writes their proposed five words in the filter funnel.
4. Other pairs follow and from their selection can add only words that are not already in the funnel.
5. As soon as every pair has contributed, lead a debate with the class about which five (or ten, or whatever) words to let through the filter funnel into the beaker. These should be *the* essential words that capture or trigger the meaning of the whole passage.
6. The agreed, filtered words become the basis for notes, which everyone then makes individually.

Applications

- In any technical text – in **science, technology, business studies, geography** – the filtered words are likely to be technical terms.
- In **English** where the criteria for "most important" words might change. For example: the five adjectives that are key to the author's description of the scene or character; the words most typical of this author's style; the most persuasive, evocative, loaded, unexpected … words in the passage.
- In **English** and **history**, reduce narrative to its key moments in chronological order.
- In **drama**, reduce dialogue to key words to help actors to memorise their lines.

- Any factual resource in **religious education, sociology** ..., where the selected words capture key bits of information.
- In **modern foreign languages** – a text has to be thoroughly understood for the key words to be identified.

Why do it?

- Distillation is the basis of all good note making. This exercise helps students to gain the confidence to separate important from peripheral material.
- It demonstrates that time invested in selecting key words is repaid in reducing the volume of written material and in aiding memorisation.
- By showing how key pieces of information can be recorded quickly and lightly, this process encourages students to use a number of resources when researching rather than get bogged down in one.
- In all these ways it supports the skills of independent research, which are crucial to course work and individual assignments.

Variations

1. Instead of writing words on the board, students write them on cards and Blu-Tack them on the board. Then the teacher, or students, can physically move words around during the debate and final filtration.
2. Reverse the image. Instead of a filter funnel, draw a cauldron. All the words are "thrown in", then as the heat is turned up words are evaporated, eventually leaving a residue of essential items.
3. Instead of distilling or boiling images, allow students a number of centimetres. They can underline words and phrases in the text, up to the maximum length in total.
4. Instead of the most important words from the text, students have to choose words that summarise the meaning of the text from their own extensive vocabularies!
5. The notes that students consequently make could be in various formats. Ask students to experiment with bullet points, key-word plans, mind maps, spidergrams, flowcharts ...
6. As exams approach, encourage students to make notes of their notes. Use "Distillation" to reduce existing notes in exercise books and files so that final revision is done with minimum materials. Show them how to use key words as memory prompts.
7. Use exactly the same process with videos, audio cassettes or the teacher's exposition instead of text. It doesn't half sharpen students' listening skills!

Dominoes

No matter what your learning or teaching style, there's always room for some serious fun.

Purposes (what the activity is designed to achieve)	
Thinking	* * * *
Emotional Intelligence	*
Independence	*
Interdependence	* *
Multi-sensation	*
Fun	* * *
Articulation	*

Particulars (what the activity contains)	
Individual work	* *
Group work	* * *
Moving about	
Speaking	* * *
Listening	* * * *
Reading	* *
Writing	
Looking	*
Choice	

Specific room layout
Yes   (No)

How?

1. Prepare a set of cards, A6 or A7 size, each divided in half by a line like a domino tile. On one half of each card is a question, on the other half an answer. The question and answer on any card do not match.
2. The cards are shuffled and given out, one per person.
3. Anyone can begin by reading out their question. Someone in the room has the answer – they read it out and everyone else has to indicate whether they think it is right or wrong by sticking their thumbs up or down. If no one offers, the teacher asks for those who *think* they *might* have the right answer – consequently, several people offer answers and the class debate which one is correct.
4. Whoever had the right answer asks the question on their card ... and so on. When students have "played" their domino cards, they remain involved by judging whether other people's answers are right or wrong.

Applications

- Ideal for revision of a topic just covered.
- It can be used at the start of a topic to find out what people already know.
- It can be used part way through a topic to consolidate basic ideas and diagnostically assess the learning so far.

Why do it?

- It's novel and fun, therefore the material is more likely to be remembered.
- It requires students to think: to recall, predict, calculate, guess ...
- The exercise requires everyone to be involved. It helps shy students to contribute publicly.
- At a more advanced level questions can have particular angles and answers can have subtle differences, reinforcing the need to read the question properly and answer the question precisely. This is essential exam technique.

Variations

1. Instead of the teacher making the cards, students work in groups to produce a set of "dominoes". Different sets are used with the class at different times to revise the same topic. This reinforces the idea that material has to be revisited time and time again if it is to stick.

2. Allow students to look for the answers in their notes or in textbooks – use it to stimulate research and, again, to underline the idea of having to go back over work if it is to stick.

3. "Dominoes" can be played in small groups rather than the whole class. If groups have produced their own cards, they swap sets with each other.

4. Picture questions and answers can be used, for example naming bits of apparatus, labelling diagrams, identifying the correct equipment to use for a particular purpose, choosing between right and wrong movements or procedures, connecting adverbs or adjectives with drawings (in **MFL,** for instance).

5. At an advanced level, make the questions and answers less obvious. Use subtle nuances, angles and details to test the students' ability to distinguish between the finer points of the material.

Double Take

Good news for the busy teacher: you can be in two places at once! Double your presence, double your impact, double your time – without increasing your stress.

Purposes (what the activity is designed to achieve)	
Thinking	* * *
Emotional Intelligence	*
Independence	* * * * *
Interdependence	*
Multi-sensation	* * (variable)
Fun	
Articulation	

Particulars (what the activity contains)	
Individual work	* * * * *
Group work	
Moving about	*
Speaking	
Listening	* * * *
Reading	* * *
Writing	
Looking	* * (variable)
Choice	* * *

Specific room layout	
Yes (No)	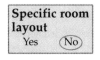

How?

1. Record key teaching points on audio cassettes, on video cassettes, as PowerPoint presentations, or as MP3, midi or wav files. If you have the facility, post them on the school's intranet or website.
2. During normal classroom activity, students who need an exposition or explanation again don't have to bother the busy teacher – they can access the independent resource. It's like having two teachers in the room.
3. Students may need training to use the hardware and may take some time to develop the habits of independent learning.
4. If video or PowerPoint is being used, it's best to have the TV or monitor facing into a corner of the room so that other students are not distracted. Audio cassettes can be played on personal stereos or through "listening centres" with multiple headphones. MP3 or wav files can be heard through personal headphones attached to a PC or via portable MP3 players.

Applications

- **Art**: PowerPoint presentation on Roy Lichtenstein as an introduction to a GCSE assignment. Three five-minute video programmes for Year 8 giving demonstrations and commentary by the teacher on: mixing watercolour paint; applying paint to paper; creating three-dimensional effects.
- **Maths**: explaining concepts and demonstrating procedures.
- **Business studies**: definitions of different types of business, various business concepts, procedures and roles each on a short length audio cassette, all numbered and catalogued on a shelf in the stockroom.

- **Modern foreign languages**: the teacher introducing and modelling new language structures and vocabulary on video – more or less the same as the "performance" done live with the class at the beginning of the topic.
- **Technology**: the safe use of equipment; standard measuring, cutting, forming, joining and finishing techniques.
- **Science**: demonstrations; instructions for conducting an experiment.
- Key concepts and facts in any subject.

Why do it?

- Students often have to wait some time for the teacher's attention. This is frustrating for students and teacher alike. "Double Take" means more students get more help more often.
- It facilitates differentiation – those who need more support can get it. No one is held back by slower learners.
- It promotes the attitudes and skills of independent learning – vital for students' future success.

Variations

1. Students can make the resources themselves as a legitimate part of their learning process. These can be reproduced, stored and used with future generations.
2. Resources can be placed in the school library or learning centre with added benefits: less distraction in the classroom; building the habit of using the central resources.
3. If hi-tech resources are not possible, make lo-tech versions: Help Sheets. These are large A2 or A3 sheets of paper with information, techniques, explanations, instructions, procedures presented in written and visual forms. Stored in a large folder, Help Sheets can be consulted by students whenever they get the urge. See page 259 for further information.

Dreadlines

Deadlines are dreaded by more or less everyone. They create pressure, instil panic and usually have terrible consequences attached. But, they're good for you.

Purposes (what the activity is designed to achieve)	
Thinking	* *
Emotional Intelligence	* * *
Independence	* * * * *
Interdependence	
Multi-sensation	
Fun	
Articulation	

Particulars (what the activity contains)	
Individual work	* * * * *
Group work	
Moving about	
Speaking	*
Listening	*
Reading	
Writing	
Looking	
Choice	* * (variable)

Specific room layout
Yes (No)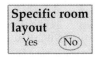

How?

1. This is the simplest way to increase the pace of learning: set challenging, just-achievable deadlines.
2. Equip yourself with a list of students' names on a clipboard. Move round the class looking at students' work and talking with them about progress. As you move from student to student agree with each of them a deadline by which the next stage of the task will be completed. Explain that you will return at that time. You make a note of the deadline on your list and the student makes a note in the margin of their exercise book or file.
3. Sometimes it will be important to allow the student to decide the deadline, perhaps because you want them to learn about the management of time and tasks, or because they are self-motivated and can be trusted. Sometimes you might need to impose a deadline to increase a student's sense of urgency, while at other times a negotiated deadline will be best. Remain flexible in your approach.
4. Make sure there's a clock in the room!
5. Return to each student at the stated time. If you're not there when you said you would be, they'll think you don't mean business. Look at what they've done and offer congratulations, challenge, support, rebuke ... as appropriate. Then set a new deadline for the next stage of learning.
6. Timescales for deadlines will vary. Some students will need short steps and frequent visits, perhaps because they are not self-motivated, or because they are struggling with this particular material, or because they have a strongly Concrete Sequential learning style. Others will need to see you less often.
7. To begin with, go to those students who are likely to need most help or most chivvying. Deal with them first. Once they are under way with the task, visit the students who are more self-sufficient.

Applications

- Any subject where students are working individually: worksheet, workbook, extended research task, extended writing.
- **Maths**: working through examples.
- **English**: silent reading – speed up the time it takes to get through text.
- **Technology, science** and **art**: practical work.
- **ICT**: individual work at the computers.
- **PE**: practising individual skills.

Why do it?

- It keeps up the pace of potentially tedious work.
- It provides external motivation for those who don't have much internal.
- It generally demonstrates to students that they are more capable than they thought. They can often work faster and learn faster than they normally do. It communicates high expectations, which strengthen self-belief, which in turn translates into improved performance.
- It allows for different learning styles. Those with Concrete Sequential or "pragmatist" tendencies can have short step-by-step instructions; those who are more "abstract" or "activist" can work for longer stretches without interference.

Variations

1. The same procedures apply to paired or small group work as to individual work.
2. Set deadlines not for a certain amounts of work to be done, but for certain learning points to be mastered. For example, "At 2.35 p.m. I'd like you to explain to me …/show me how you …/describe …/be able to …"
3. Instead of setting deadlines for individual students, set them for the whole class. Write or draw the lesson sequence on the board with clear steps to be completed by certain times … or else!
4. Use "Dreadlines" to speed up reading time. Challenge individuals to read the information sheet, or section of the text book, or chapter in two-thirds of the time it would usually take. Test them on it afterwards to prove that they can do it. Challenge the whole class to halve their normal reading time. Teach them speed-reading techniques. Encourage them to skim and scan rather than decode every word. This usually boosts confidence and shows that reading need not be time-consuming and laborious.

Forum Theatre

A truly dramatic technique for exploring all kinds of interactions and events - fictional or factual - past, present or future.

How?

1. Ideally sit the group in a circle or horseshoe around a working space.
2. Introduce the situation to be portrayed. It should involve a small number of players (e.g. how a family handles the sacking of the son: mum, dad, son and older sister). The situation will need some kind of **tension** (e.g. the sacking is for lateness and the father is very proud of his own punctuality).
3. Decide **where** the action is taking place (around the family tea table), **when** (the present) and **what** the opening line is to be (e.g. dad to son: "What are you looking so miserable about?").
4. Invite students to volunteer to take on the roles. The volunteers organise the furniture (in this case a desk as the tea table and a few chairs) and play the scene spontaneously for three or four minutes.
5. Once the scene is well under way, members of the audience are free to **stop the action** by raising a hand. They do this in order to suggest modifications. For example, someone might ask the dad to be tougher, or the son to cry or the mother to use this as an opportunity to say how she has always hated being hurried along by her husband. Specific lines can be suggested. In addition, audience members can ask to take over one of the roles, or to join the original player to form a "composite character". Likewise, players can stop the action and ask for advice from the audience, or can ask for someone to take over if they've had enough.
6. Like a piece of videotape, the action can be rewound and bits replayed in different ways – with more assertiveness on the son's part, for example. By the same token, the action can be wound on to new and interesting moments in the future. This enables consequences

Purposes (what the activity is designed to achieve)	
Thinking	* * * * *
Emotional Intelligence	* * * *
Independence	* *
Interdependence	* * *
Multi-sensation	* * *
Fun	* * *
Articulation	* * * *

Particulars (what the activity contains)	
Individual work	*
Group work	* * * * *
Moving about	* * *
Speaking	* *
Listening	* * * * *
Reading	
Writing	
Looking	* * *
Choice	* * * *

Specific room layout   (Yes)   No

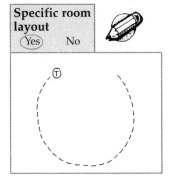

and effects to be examined. The drama can always be taken back again and a new course of action explored.

7. All this enables the drama to be moulded. It allows the group to understand the effect of different attitudes, languages and behaviours, and the consequence of different actions.

8. Key learning points can be brought out in debrief. The teacher needn't wait until the end. She can stop the action at any time and lead a discussion or make an input.

Applications

*   **History**: to examine the human issues in various moments of history: e.g. a cropper comes home having just lost his job because of new machines. To examine cause and effect by playing with alternative versions of events: "Let's imagine that ..."; "What would have happened if ...?"

*   **Science**: Louis Pasteur persuading sceptical colleagues about his latest discovery or a doctor being pressed to buy a new drug about which he has reservations.

*   **English**: to develop scenes suggested by poems, novels, newspapers, or to develop alternative scenes in established plays: "What if ...?"

*   **Business studies**: a manager has to handle a health-and-safety issue in the workplace – explore different management styles.

*   "Forum Theatre" could be conducted in a **modern foreign language** at A level. At GCSE two students play the scene – a waiter and a customer in a café at lunchtime – and the audience have to tell them what to say.

*   **Personal, social and health education (PSHE)**: as a way of handling the human issues around abortion, drugs, marriage, friendship, environment, health, employment ... Through "Forum Theatre" it is easy to raise awareness of choice and responsibility because cause and effect can be explored in the safety of a fiction.

*   **Religious education**: encounters between people of different beliefs, a fictional conversation between Jesus and a follower who is torn between loyalty to his family and loyalty to his new master; a Sikh family dispute over a teenage daughter who is taking a nontraditional stance on marriage.

Why do it?

*   Dramatic action brings ideas and information to life. It works at the level of feelings as well as thoughts and usually creates a lasting, detailed impression.

*   This particular technique allows students to experiment with their own ideas, so it is, in a sense, automatically student-centred. This degree of ownership usually generates a fair degree of commitment and motivation.

*   For some students whose preferred learning styles are experiential and creative and whose dominant intelligences are visual, kinaesthetic and interpersonal (the kind of kids who are often hard to handle!), drama can give easier access to many aspects of the curriculum.

Variations

1. Each character in the "play" can have a group of students to whom she is attached. They are her advisers. At intervals during the drama, the action is stopped and each player goes to her own group to take advice on what the character should say and do next.

2. Use "Forum Theatre" for skill acquisition – this was its original purpose among the oppressed classes of South America. Use it to explore, identify and practise the skills of assertiveness, conflict resolution, managing groups, persuasion, debate ... For the origins of "Forum Theatre", see *Theatre of the Oppressed* by Augusto Boal.[2]

Go Large

"The bigger the better" - for many students, size really does matter.

Purposes (what the activity is designed to achieve)	
Thinking	* * * *
Emotional Intelligence	*
Independence	
Interdependence	*
Multi-sensation	* * * *
Fun	* * *
Articulation	*

Particulars (what the activity contains)	
Individual work	* *
Group work	* * *
Moving about	* * *
Speaking	* *
Listening	* * * *
Reading	
Writing	
Looking	* * * * *
Choice	

Specific room layout (Yes) No

How?

1. Clear the desks and create a circle of chairs.
2. Use the central arena to demonstrate the teaching point on a large scale with a range of materials.
3. For example, the ignition system of a car. Place a large box on the floor to represent the battery, use rope and string as cables and wires, connect them with Blu-Tack (solder) to the ignition switch (an old padlock) and in turn to the overhead projector acting as the starter motor. This is finally connected to the engine – a desk. As you build up the model, use the students' suggestions and your own commentary to explain what goes where and why.
4. The intention is to make the learning visible and big. Abstract ideas can be represented by objects or by key words written on cards. Categories or sequences can easily be created by moving the cards. Connections between ideas can be created with string, masking tape, chalk or cardboard arrows. Thoughts can be presented as large speech-bubbles using flipchart paper. Large question marks and exclamation marks made of coloured card can be used to signal key questions and important points.

Applications

- **History**: use string to form a rough outline of Britain and the Normandy coast. Use various objects to show the movements of Harold, Hardrada, Tostig and William up to the Battle of Hastings.
- **PE**: depict strategies and tactics in almost any sport on a model court or playing field.
- **Maths**: large-scale geometry on the floor using chalk, string and sticks; arrange and rearrange large number cards, function cards and letter cards on the floor to demonstrate the conventions of algebra.

- **Science, technology** and **ICT**: most processes and procedures can be simulated in this way. Imagine that small, microscopic, even electronic, processes are being put under a magic microscope and being made available for all to see.
- **English**: lay out paragraph headings and subpoints on cards on the floor. Move them around to create essay plans with the class. Sequence the key events in a narrative or plot. Create the structure of a play on the floor, using masking-tape squares or sheets of sugar paper for scenes sequenced into acts. Then use objects or coloured cards for different characters and themes. Summarise the play by asking students to tell you which items to include and which to exclude as you move from scene to scene: "Who's in this scene?"; "How do the characters relate to each other?"; "So where shall I place them?"; "What is the dominant 'theme of the scene'?"
- **Geography**: make urban zones of development on the floor with masking tape or string
- **Business studies**: depict and compare different organisational structures.
- Use cards and string to demonstrate settlement sites and patterns in **geography**, timelines in **history** and **religious education**, sentence construction and syntax in **English** and **MFL**.
- If you pay close attention to the students' suggestions and their answers to your questions, the technique can provide a diagnostic assessment of a topic just covered, or of their prior knowledge of a topic just being introduced: "So what goes here?"; "Why have I put that there?"; "Who can tell me what to do next?"; "What is this meant to represent?"

Why do it?

- Many students, especially those with a "concrete" cognitive tendency, find abstract ideas hard to grasp. They benefit from seeing, rather than just being asked to listen and think. It aids their concentration and their understanding.
- The size of the demonstration does make a big impact. This, along with the dramatic and unusual nature of the technique, makes the material memorable.
- Such presentations are vital to those with a visual sensory dominance. Also, the technique allows for those with a kinaesthetic dominance to get up and be involved.

Variations

1. Instead of doing it yourself, ask students to conduct the demonstration either spontaneously, based on existing knowledge, or after research and preparation time.
2. Do the demonstration once, then ask one or two students to repeat it with everyone looking on. The audience gives feedback at the end; then, if there's enough time and interest, another couple of students have a go.

Guess Who

Even the most basic detective work requires interrogation skills, lateral thinking, wit, perseverance and speed of thought. No wonder this simple strategy has universal appeal.

Purposes (what the activity is designed to achieve)	
Thinking	* * * * *
Emotional Intelligence	*
Independence	* *
Interdependence	* * * *
Multi-sensation	* (variable)
Fun	* * *
Articulation	* * * *

Particulars (what the activity contains)	
Individual work	*
Group work	* * * *
Moving about	* * * * * (variable)
Speaking	* * *
Listening	* * * *
Reading	*
Writing	
Looking	* (variable)
Choice	*

How?

1. Students work in groups of four, sitting so that group members can easily see and hear each other.
2. Give each group a pack of cards, which is shuffled and placed face down in the middle of the table. The cards depict items that should have been learned, for example people or events (in history), equipment (science apparatus), places (in geography or leisure and tourism), processes (in technology), definitions (any subject).
3. Group members agree to take turns, or to have numbers and use a die to determine who goes next. The player whose turn it is picks the top card and looks at it, taking care not to let anyone else see.
4. The rest of the group ask questions. The player holding the card can answer only yes or no. If preferred, the number of questions, or the time, can be limited.
5. Once the item has been successfully identified by the group, the turn passes to the next player.

Specific room layout
(Yes) No

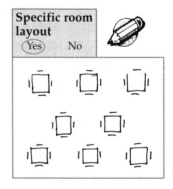

Applications

- Perfect for consolidation and revision in any subject. For example: characters in novels and events in plays in **English**; technical terms in **business studies**, **PE theory**, **geography**, **technology**; elements, compounds and mixtures in **science**, techniques in **PE**, random numbers in **maths**.
- The whole exercise can be conducted in a **modern foreign language**.

Why do it?

- This is a classic lateral and deductive thinking exercise.
- It provides training in group work: turn-taking, listening, thinking before you speak.

- It practises the art of asking the right question, a vital ingredient in independent learning.
- Students will remember items because they have worked them out in their heads.

Variations

Two major variations:

1. **Do it as a whole-class exercise.** For example, studying famous designers in art:

   - pictures of items designed by, and items that inspired, various designers are Blu-Tacked to the board
   - a volunteer sits at the front of the class and is given a prompt card, which supplies the designer's name, dates of birth and death, nationality, what they are famous for designing and what inspired their design
   - the class have to find out this information by using the visual clues and asking questions, to which the volunteer can answer only yes or no
   - there is a limit either to the number of questions, or to the amount of time
   - once the first designer has been identified, a new volunteer is sought and the process continues

2. **Do it as a party game.**

   - each member of the class wears a sticker on their back or forehead giving the name of the person or object to be identified; the wearer doesn't know what it says
   - class members mill around asking questions of each other, each student trying to find out what their own sticker says
   - answers can be only "yes", "no" or "don't know"
   - only one question can be asked of each student
   - the aim is to work out your sticker before you run out of people to ask
   - once you've guessed who, or what, you are, you stay in the game, continuing to answer other people's questions

Hide 'n' Seek

"Seek and ye shall find" – this is one sure way not to lose your memory.

Purposes 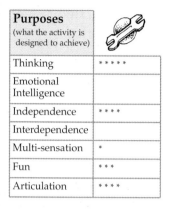(what the activity is designed to achieve)	
Thinking	* * * * *
Emotional Intelligence	
Independence	* * * *
Interdependence	
Multi-sensation	*
Fun	* * *
Articulation	* * * *

Particulars (what the activity contains)	
Individual work	* * * *
Group work	
Moving about	
Speaking	
Listening	
Reading	* * *
Writing	*
Looking	* * *
Choice	

Specific room layout
Yes (No)

How?

This is a basic memory technique, the foundation of many variations. When they first use it, students are often delighted that learning occurs as if by magic.

1. Supply to each student, or students each make for themselves, a pack of small cards, about the size of business cards.
2. On one side of the cards students write the items to be learned, one per card, and on the reverse their meanings or definitions.
3. Each student lays their cards out on the desk face up. The meanings/definitions are face down.
4. Ask students how long they think it will take them to turn all the cards over. The procedure is: look at a card, give its meaning or definition in your head, then turn it over to see if you are right. If you are, you turn the card over. If not, you leave it face down and can't return to it until you have been round all the other cards. You can turn a card over only when you have given the correct meaning or definition.
5. Of course, learning occurs effortlessly at the point where the offered answer in the student's head is compared to the answer on the back of the card.
6. Once all the cards are turned, ask students to reverse the process. How long will it take you to turn them back again?

Applications

*   **Modern foreign languages**: vocabulary.
*   **History**: dates, significance of key events and policies.
*   **Science**: formulae, diagrams of apparatus, technical terminology.
*   **Maths**: symbols, rules, conventions.
*   **PE**: names of muscles and bones.
*   **Art**: key features of artists' styles.
*   **Music**: musical genres and examples of works, instruments from around the world.
*   **Geography**: weather graphs and climate names.

Why do it?

- It's a very efficient and natural way of memorising hard information.
- It teaches the students an invaluable technique that can apply to many subjects.
- It thereby adds to their repertoire of independent learning skills.
- It helps students to realise that success can be achieved with a little effort and a little fun – it creates motivation for future learning.

Variations

1. Use pictures, diagrams or symbols on one side, words on the other.
2. To aid memorisation use different colours of card for different aspects of the topic: e.g. different parts of speech in **English** and **modern foreign languages**; positive and negative consequences of the Norman invasion in **history**.
3. Students can put the pack in an envelope, and they then have a ready-made revision aid to use at home.
4. Encourage students to make further packs for other topics; set pack-making homeworks.
5. Strengthen the level of challenge by getting students to set time targets for themselves. Then encourage them to beat their best time for turning a whole pack over.
6. Ask students to work in pairs. They put two identical packs together, one face up, the other face down. The cards are shuffled randomly around the desktop, and then they take turns to match pairs. When a pair is successfully matched, the player keeps it and goes again, and again until a mismatch is made. The player with the most pairs at the end "wins".

Hierarchies

More or less all nonfiction text is made up of hierarchies. Spot them, use them and you'll soon rise to the top.

Purposes (what the activity is designed to achieve)	
Thinking	* * * * *
Emotional Intelligence	
Independence	* * * *
Interdependence	
Multi-sensation	
Fun	*
Articulation	* * * *

Particulars (what elements the activity contains)	
Individual work	* * * * *
Group work	
Moving about	
Speaking	
Listening	*
Reading	* * * *
Writing	* * *
Looking	*
Choice	

Specific room layout	
Yes (No)	

How?

1. Each student draws a page-sized pyramid.

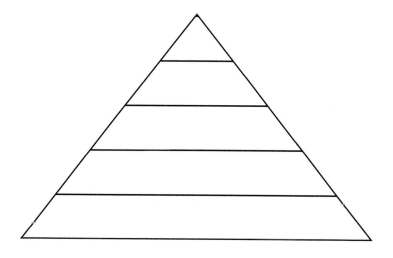

2. Explain that most nonfiction text is made up of hierarchies of information and that finding the hierarchies provides the structure for good notes. Show how newspapers make hierarchies explicit through the use of headlines, bold paragraphs, subheadings and smaller print. Well-written textbooks present information in a similar way. But not all texts are so helpful and it's up to students to detect the status of information in order to separate major from minor points.
3. Give out a nonfiction text appropriate to the topic in hand and to the reading ages of the students. While the "Hierarchies" technique is being learned, it's important that the vocabulary and syntax are not too difficult.
4. Ask students to find the big idea in the text: the headline. They write this in the apex of the pyramid.
5. Students then work out the next level of information – the main points – and note them in the next "layer" down.

6. Finally, the details are written into the base of the pyramid. The shape encourages students to recognise that there is usually one big idea, two or three main points and lots of detail.

7. Ask students to memorise the material by covering up different layers, attempting to recall what they contain, then looking to check. In time, they should be able to work just from the higher layers which prompt the recall of detail.

Applications

- Use with almost any **nonfiction** material.
- With **fiction**, use "Hierarchies" for character studies, interpretations, critiques and summaries.

Why do it?

- Passive reading is inefficient – the brain takes little in. For text to be understood, the material needs to be attacked with an active and purposeful mind. Deep learning occurs through understanding, not rote. Exercises such as this force understanding.
- The brain's neocortex is designed to work things out for itself, so this exercise goes with "the grain of the brain". Although taxing, the exercise should feel natural, especially if presented as a mystery to be fathomed or a challenge to be met.
- So much independent learning rests on the student's ability to deconstruct text and make useful, efficient notes. This exercise, if done often enough in different guises, helps to break the habit of copying or condensing text, and to establish the habit of discerning note making.
- Exam success depends on effective revision. Material has to be visited and revisited several times. This is much less daunting if notes are already in handy, revision-friendly formats.

Variations

1. Experiment with different shapes. For example, Target Notes:

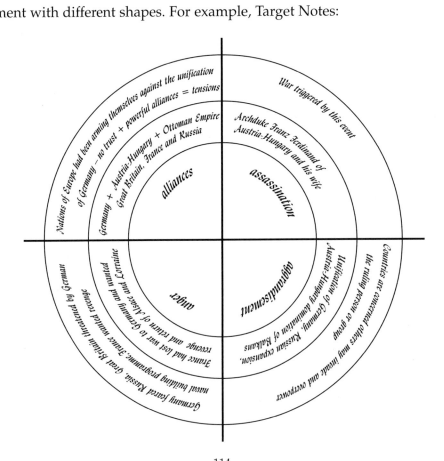

Take the causes of World War One. There are generally reckoned to be four causes: alliances, assassination, aggrandisement and anger. Each of these four headline words goes in a quarter of the bull's-eye. In the next layer out go key points. Take alliances, they were between Germany and Austria-Hungary, later joined by the Ottoman Empire; on the other side Great Britain, France and Russia. In the outer layer go the details of how these alliances contributed to the heightening of tension. For other topics, adjust the number of sectors as appropriate.

2. Instead of (or even as well as) shapes, use different colours for different "levels" of information.

3. Instead of text, ask students to work out the hierarchies of information within an **audio** cassette, a **video**, an **exposition** by the teacher, a **presentation by their peers**, or even a **diagram** in a book. Ideal as a listening exercise in **modern languages**. "Hierarchies" provides a way of focusing attention and sharpening the challenge in what might otherwise be quite "flat" tasks.

Hot-Seating

A nondidactic way for the teacher to give information to the class, without giving up the spotlight!

Purposes (what the activity is designed to achieve)	
Thinking	* * * *
Emotional Intelligence	* *
Independence	* * * *
Interdependence	* *
Multi-sensation	* *
Fun	* *
Articulation	* * *

Particulars (what elements the activity contains)	
Individual work	* * *
Group work	* * * (variable)
Moving about	
Speaking	* * *
Listening	* * * * *
Reading	
Writing	* * * (variable)
Looking	* * *
Choice	* *

Specific room layout
Yes   (No)

How?

Best done with the desks cleared and the class sitting in a horseshoe around the "Hot Seat", but also possible with a conventional classroom layout.

1. The teacher announces that she will play a character and will want to answer the class's questions. A small piece of costume such as a scarf, hat or bag helps everyone to tell when the teacher is in and out of role.

2. The reason for portraying the character is first explained: "I'll be the author of St Mark's gospel so we can understand more about the book and its background." Give the students time to get to grips with the precise learning objectives – write them up for all to see: "For the exam you need to know who wrote Mark's gospel, when it was written, why it was written, the social and political conditions in which it was written and the language used." If you feel it's necessary, give the students time to frame a few quick questions so the process gets off to a good start. Then spontaneity should take over.

3. Ground rules are established: no comments of any kind on either the students' questions or the teacher's answers, except by asking another question.

4. The teacher sits (or wanders around theatrically!) and takes questions in role, providing answers that, at best, invite further questions. If the role is hammed up too much, though, silliness can creep in and the power of the experience is lost.

5. It is crucial that the teacher hold the role, behaving and answering consistently in character. If belief in the character is broken, the strategy will quickly fall apart. Therefore, if the teacher wishes to speak to the class *as teacher* (to deal with discipline for instance) then she should get off the "Hot Seat" and remove the symbolic costuming to signal the change. She can always go back into role once the issue has been sorted.

Applications

- **Maths**: a ship's captain (coordinates); Pythagoras; a bookmaker!
- **Science**: Madame Curie; Louis Pasteur; a physiotherapist; a nuclear physicist; Einstein; Edison; a product designer.
- **Art:** Van Gogh; Picasso; Oldenberg; Mondrian; an art critic; a dealer; an art teacher.
- **Business studies:** Sir John Harvey-Jones; different roles within an organisation.
- **English:** characters in plays, novels and poems; authors; actors, directors; critics.
- **Geography:** a migrant worker; a founder member of Greenpeace; a politician facing a potential natural disaster; a relief worker; chair of the local planning committee.
- **Modern languages:** questions can be prepared beforehand; answers can be tape-recorded and translated later.
- **History:** any historical character; also fictional observer or messenger characters who are reporting and interpreting events.
- **Technology:** a famous fashion designer, chef, engineer; an expert in a particular process – a consultant or technician.

Why do it?

- Once under way, the process can be quite gripping, even moving.
- It gives everyone access to information, irrespective of reading ability.
- The exercise particularly suits learners with an Abstract Random or "reflective" learning style, but because of its "soap opera" feel it actually appeals to most students.
- As the students determine what information they receive they are practising the management of their own learning in general, and the framing of good questions in particular.
- The information is usually well-remembered because of the dramatic and relatively unusual (seeing the teacher "acting") nature of the experience.

Variations

1. Students can undertake research and prepare more sophisticated questions beforehand.
2. Students can write up the answers afterwards as a set of notes or a report. In order to record adequate information as they go along, students can operate in pairs: one asking the questions, the other making the notes. Periodically they swap over. Alternatively, you can ban all notemaking and force the students to rely on their memory – this tends to sharpen those listening skills!
3. Students can be set research tasks as a result of the *first* "Hot Seat" interview and be asked to bring the results to a *second* interview, when more detailed and complex questions are expected.
4. Individual students can take the "Hot Seat", especially after a period of research (done as a homework perhaps).
5. Group Hot Seat: students work in small groups to prepare the character. The group puts forward one student as the "front person" or "mouthpiece", with the others sitting behind as "alter egos" or "brain cells" ready to be consulted on what to say.
6. Objects rather than human characters can be hot-seated – especially good for science (an atom in a chemical reaction), technology (the properties and usefulness of a particular material), geography (a water droplet in the water cycle). How about a UCAS application form in sixth-form tutorials?
7. Instead of genuine hot-seating in which the questions are one-way, try "In Conversation With ...". The subject (played by the teacher or a knowledgeable student) could be Wenlock Edge, A Bunsen Burner or The Bible, for example. The conversation is two-way. The subject can invite questions from particular students, raise issues and ask for comments or ask open questions of their own.

Information Hunt

The simple and uncomfortable truth is, the more you find things out and work things out for yourself, the more it sticks. Hunted information is much more memorable than information received on a plate.

Purposes (what the activity is designed to achieve)	
Thinking	* * * * *
Emotional Intelligence	*
Independence	* * * *
Interdependence	*
Multi-sensation	* * (variable)
Fun	* *
Articulation	

Particulars (what elements the activity contains)	
Individual work	* * * *
Group work	* * (variable)
Moving about	* * * *
Speaking	*
Listening	* *
Reading	* * * *
Writing	* * *
Looking	* * *
Choice	*

Specific room layout
Yes   (No)

How?

1. Students are commissioned to find out information about the topic in hand. Each student is supplied with a Fact Finder sheet.

2. For younger students this could be in the form of a Hunter's Map giving locations in the classroom (and beyond – the further afield the better) where certain types of material can be found. The materials (posters, photographs, books, artefacts, CD-ROMs, people …) enable the students to solve riddles that entitle them to a crack at the "treasure chest key question". It's important that there be a variety of information sources, not all the same type, otherwise the exercise can become tedious. Or, again for younger students, it could be in the form of a nine-, twelve- or sixteen-square bingo grid with questions in the boxes (the aim being to get a line, then a full house). For older students the sheet would be a more regular matrix to fill in or a standard question-and-answer sheet.

3. Whatever the style, the idea is to find accurate and complete information against the clock. Students have to organise themselves.

4. At any point in the proceedings students can come to the teacher to check how they are doing. The teacher will tell them which answers are acceptable and which need more detail or need to be redone. Of course, checking with the teacher takes precious time, especially if there's a queue. So the decision to check or not to check adds a bit of tension to the exercise.

5. As soon as someone has a full set of answers/has opened the treasure chest/has a full house, or as soon as time is up, the activity stops and the teacher and class go over the questions together.

Applications

- Any subject as long as the teacher can organise a sufficient range of resources.
- **Modern foreign languages**: the exercise is conducted entirely in target language.
- **Science**: the resource stations can be mini-experiments to carry out.
- **ICT**: conducted entirely on line to help students master the Internet.

Why do it?

- It is designed to practise a number of independent learning skills: working to a deadline; using a range of resources; identifying key points within a resource; recording information quickly; answering questions precisely; having confidence in your own judgment; working with others (where that option is taken).
- It has a kinaesthetic element, moving around, which is important to some students and keeps them on board.
- It demonstrates that learning is more fun and more effective, and that the information is remembered far better, when resources are tackled actively, rather than passively received.

Variations

1. Students work in pairs or small teams rather than individually. This practises the added dimensions of group organisation and interdependence.
2. Instead of managing the operation, the teacher can be one of the resources, perhaps operating in role.
3. The information sources are other students. Everyone has a bingo grid where the boxes contain prompts such as "Find someone who can show you how to …", "Find someone who can explain …", "Find someone who has done …", "Find someone who knows about …" and so on. Students write the information and the student's name in the box so that cross-checks can be made by the teacher. The rule is: you can't have the same name more than once. This "human bingo" works well in **modern languages**, where the questions and responses are entirely in target language.
4. Number the sources of information. Students have to tackle them in order but all start with a different number to avoid congestion. This cuts down the independence of the exercise, and also the teacher's stress levels.
5. Students work in small groups. Each group receives a pack containing a range of source materials. In this variation students don't have to go and consult the materials: the materials have come to them. From the materials, groups have to answer a set of questions or fulfil a more open-ended brief, such as: "Find out as much as you can about French weddings", or "What can you find out about employment in North Wales?"

Mantle of the Expert

Everybody likes to show off every now and again. This is a golden opportunity to show what you know.

Purposes (what the activity is designed to achieve)	
Thinking	* * * *
Emotional Intelligence	* *
Independence	* * * * (expert)
Interdependence	* * (audience)
Multi-sensation	
Fun	* *
Articulation	* * * (expert)

Particulars (what elements the activity contains)	
Individual work	* * * * * (expert)
Group work	* * (audience)
Moving about	
Speaking	* * * * (expert)
Listening	* * * * (audience)
Reading	
Writing	
Looking	* * (audience)
Choice	* * *

Specific room layout	
Yes (No)	

How?

1. Explain that a new topic is to be tackled. Give the learning objectives, offer an outline of the content and connect to the bigger picture of the syllabus or scheme of work (good practice at the start of any new topic, of course).
2. Ask people to jot down what they already know, or can do, regarding *any* aspects of the topic. You might ask them to exchange these details in pairs, so they gain a bit of confidence.
3. Ask for a volunteer to come out to the front, *wear the mantle of the expert* and tell the class what she knows or can do. It's usually effective to have a shawl or scarf for the student to wear – with younger students this can be hammed up into their having magical powers by using a wizard's cloak, for instance.
4. The class can ask questions, the expert has the right to say "pass" if she's not sure of the answer and the teacher can add comments.
5. Another volunteer is sought – "Who can add to what Sharon has just told us?" – and the process continues.

Application

At the start of any topic.

Why do it?

- It provides a student-centred starting point. It enables you to plan (or adjust your plans) based on what students know, rather than press ahead with the idea of covering the curriculum or getting through the book regardless.
- It hooks students in. It says, "This learning is going to be relevant to you."
- Students who don't know much at the beginning will already have learned a lot from the experts' descriptions or demonstrations – it tends to have an equalising effect.

Variations

1. Use it to assess learning at the end of a lesson or topic (see also "Spotlight", page 154).

2. As experts show and tell what they know to the class, the teacher notes key points to come back to – inaccurate information, half-explained ideas, misconceptions, missing bits … These can be tackled straightaway so students don't form the wrong impression, or they can form the basis of a revised teaching plan for the next few lessons.

3. Don't limit "Mantle of the Expert" to facts, what about **skills**? Students can be invited to demonstrate a technique in **PE**, a procedure in **technology**, how to draw a box-and-whisker graph in **maths**, a movement in **dance**, a convention in **drama**, the conduct of an experiment in **science** … You can even prime a couple of students by giving them warning and a bit of coaching the lesson before.

Marketplace

Commerce in the classroom? In the information trade, a little hustle and bustle is a small price to pay for getting the goods.

How?

This exercise is conducted through a series of strictly timed stages. The number of stages, and the timing of each, will vary according to the topic, the complexity of the material and the readiness of the students. Here's a typical example.

Students work in groups of three (fours are too big for this). Allocate a subdivision of the topic to each group and give them resource material on their subdivision only (one copy per person). The material should be mainly text. Also give each group a large piece of sugar paper (or flipchart paper) and three or four differently coloured thick felt pens.

Four or five subdivisions of the topic usually work well. In a regular class there will be ten or more groups, so give out each subdivision twice, to different groups in different parts of the room.

Write up the sequence and timing of stages on the board or overhead projector so that students can follow the exercise easily.

Have a gong or bell or buzzer to signal the start and end of each stage. Occasionally during the Stages, let the students know how much time is left.

Stage 1 (1 minute)

Show the students the learning objectives and the test that they will take later. It's a good idea to use an overhead projector for this. Give them just a minute to read through the test, then switch off. They are not allowed to take notes. Make sure they understand that they will sit this test under exam conditions, without reference to any materials, or anybody, at Stage 5.

Purposes (what the activity is designed to achieve)	
Thinking	* * * * *
Emotional Intelligence	* * *
Independence	* * * * *
Interdependence	* * * * *
Multi-sensation	* * * *
Fun	* * *
Articulation	* * * *

Particulars (what elements the activity contains)	
Individual work	* *
Group work	* * * * *
Moving about	* * * * *
Speaking	* * * * *
Listening	* * * * *
Reading	* * * *
Writing	* * * *
Looking	* * * *
Choice	* *

Specific room layout (Yes) No

Stage 2 (15 minutes)

Each group converts the resource material for its subdivision into a visual display, a "poster", using the large paper and pens. The poster must be designed for visitors to view and understand (at Stage 3). The poster can have *up to ten words and no more* (adjust according to the material, but don't let them have too many words or the activity will be spoiled). The group is encouraged to use as many numbers, diagrams, symbols, pictures, graphs, cartoons, sketches and initial letters as it wishes, but not more than ten words. Abbreviations (e.g. "co-op" for "cooperative") count as whole words. The group collaborates on this, making sure that everyone in the group understands the material and contributes to the "poster". If necessary, give each member of the group a different colour of felt pen and expect to see all three colours in the final product.

Towards the end of this stage, issue each group with its *minimum requirements*. These are the precise details to be included on the poster that will ensure that visitors get access to the right information for the test. The minimum requirements can simply be questions taken from the test that are relevant to each group's material. For example: "As a minimum make sure that your poster gives the answer to these questions …"

Stage 3 (10 minutes)

By now each group has only a fraction of the information needed for success in the test. So groups have to learn from each other. In preparation, each group has to decide which one of its members will stay home and be its "stallholder". The others will go out into the "marketplace" to gather information. The stallholder touts for business by calling out the title of his group's subdivision, so customers can find their way around. The stallholder explains the poster to visitors, but is allowed *to answer only questions asked by visitors*. The researchers who go out into the marketplace will need to visit all the other subdivisions of the topic. They have to organise themselves to get the job done within the time limit, so they might decide to divide up the labour and operate individually. They should all take notes so that they can teach their group effectively at Stage 4. Their job is to look at other groups' posters, try to work out the ideas and information portrayed and ask the stallholders questions for clarification, explanation and expansion. If they have enough time, they should go to other versions of the same subdivision to cross-check information.

Stage 4 (10 minutes)

Everyone returns to their home base. Those who went into the marketplace to research information should now take turns to teach what they found out. It is an opportunity to clarify understanding. Students can run back to look at posters again or to ask quick questions in order to check details. The aim is for everyone by the end of this stage to be ready for the test. Even though they won't be able to use them in the test, encourage all group members to make notes – seeing and doing, as well as hearing, helps information to stick. During this stage distribute test papers, face down, to each group in preparation for Stage 5.

Stage 5 (10 minutes)

All notes, posters and original source materials are put out of sight. The test is conducted under examination conditions, individually and in silence.

Stage 6 (5 minutes)

In each group, students now put their heads together to see if they can come up with a complete and accurate set of answers between them. It's important that they did *not* know about this stage at the beginning.

Finally, the teacher goes through the test, focusing on questions that groups generally found difficult. For each of these tough questions the teacher asks volunteers to have a go at the answer. Then, as a last resort, the teacher teaches! In this way gaps are filled and holes are plugged.

Applications

Any topic that can be subdivided

- **Business Studies**: different types of business: sole traders; partnerships; joint stock companies; cooperatives; public-sector industries. Different theories of motivation: Herzberg; Maslow; McGregor; Taylor.
- **English**: different stanzas in a poem; different chapters; scenes; novels; characters; parts of speech; writing styles.
- **Technology**: assessing different materials; evaluating different products; comparing designs.
- **Maths**: revising different topics; learning new procedures and methods.
- **History**: examining a range of causes for the French Revolution; studying different interpretations of a character or event; comparing and assessing various primary and secondary sources; assessing various consequences of an event.
- **GNVQ leisure and tourism**: the relative attractions of different European holiday destinations.
- **ICT**: different software programs and applications.
- **Geography**: the causes and/or effects of urbanisation; different cities; different climate and natural vegetation zones.
- **PE**: inventing and sharing different games; demonstrating different warm-ups; different muscle groups; different drugs.
- **Drama and dance**: different interpretations from the same stimulus.
- **Art**: the essential characteristics, with examples, of different movements in the history of art; different artists; different painting techniques.

Why do it?

- By asking students to represent information using limited words, they are forced to understanding the material.
- The exercise works with the "grain of the brain" by asking students to see patterns and make connections. This suits the neocortex down to the ground.
- We know that peer teaching is effective. Students are required to articulate and rearticulate material several times over, by which time it should have gone in!
- The exercise gives students a transferable model for notemaking – identifying key words, using a nonlinear layout and a range of symbols.
- The exercise encourages the use of visual intelligence, which supports those students who do not function well with words, and challenges those who do.
- It builds the skills of independent learning, including: time management; working with and through others; handling a range of resources; selecting information; asking the right questions; verbal and visual presentation techniques; memorising; handling pressure; operating under exam conditions.
- The exercise creates a model of interdependent citizenship.

Variations

1. Use it for revision rather than to learn new material.
2. Instead of a question-and-answer test at the end, there might be a task. For example, to write a report or essay, to make a series of key-word plans, or to make a product.

3. Instead of reprocessing source material given by the teacher, groups might prepare posters to explain their idea for a design, or solution to a problem, or experiment, or research method, or series of movements in dance. At Stage 4, students are not frantically trying to teach each other facts and concepts, but are explaining other groups' ideas and discussing which one they think is best.

4. Instead of allowing students to mill around the marketplace deciding their own route in their own time, use a more structured approach. Move students round in a circus from one stall to another at set intervals.

5. Sustain the activity over a series of lessons. Groups might take two or three lessons to research their material from a range of resources; they might take a whole lesson to prepare their "stall", which will be more than a simple poster but might have an audio recording, photographs, or a laptop PowerPoint presentation. This extended version works well at A level and advanced GNVQ.

6. Students set the questions for their part of the test. These are then checked, and if necessary refined, by the teacher.

Masterminds

Masterminds do it together! Why not try a little collaborative research to spice up your learning life?

Purposes (what the activity is designed to achieve)	
Thinking	* * * *
Emotional Intelligence	*
Independence	* * * *
Interdependence	* * * *
Multi-sensation	*
Fun	* * *
Articulation	* *

Particulars (what elements the activity contains)	
Individual work	* *
Group work	* * * *
Moving about	
Speaking	* * *
Listening	* * *
Reading	* * * *
Writing	* *
Looking	* * (variable)
Choice	* *

Specific room layout	
Yes (No)	

How?

1. Discuss with the class the next topic to be tackled, dividing it up with them into manageable and, as far as possible, equal chunks.
2. Ask class members to organise themselves into small research groups. Some of the options for different types of groupings can be found under "Groups Galore" (page 207). You might suggest that *mixed skill* is likely to be the most appropriate type of grouping for "Masterminds".
3. Each research group takes a different aspect of the topic and is expected to research it thoroughly by a common deadline. Resources both in and out of the classroom can be used. The teacher is on hand to advise on information sources and research methods. Each group is asked to ensure that every member fully understands the material.
4. At the appointed time, groups enter the "Masterminds" competition as experts in their field of research. The rules are those of the TV show of the same name, except that the whole team enters and conferring on all answers is allowed. The questions set by the teacher should reflect the standards of whatever official assessment the students are facing: Key Stage 3 SATs, GNVQ, GCSE, A level …

Applications

- At any age in any subject as long as resources can be found for the learning in hand.
- For example in **modern languages** researching different verb patterns, different parts of speech, the basic vocabulary for various topics (using audio or video as well as text resources).
- Particular successes have been noted at A level and in GNVQ.

Why do it?

- This strategy demands a variety of study skills: information accessing; information selecting and information recording; plus speed reading if tight deadlines are set.

- A range of social skills is also required for successful team work and (if outside resources are being used) for working with adults out of school. Such skills are acquired only by practice, through exercises like this.
- Once the game is over, it will be important to spend some time reflecting on what has been learned about learning to bring out the double benefit: content *and process*.

Variations

1. Groups can put forward just one person to be their "entrant"; the others just applaud and cheer wildly.
2. Instead of being allowed to confer, students must answer questions in turn, individually. This will sharpen the group's resolve to ensure that every member understands all the material.
3. Groups can devise the "Mastermind" questions for other groups. This way they have to research two topics.
4. Give very structured research sheets as opposed to open-ended research briefs, cutting down the degree of independence. This is important when students are only just learning the skills of resource-based learning.
5. Alternatively, have students working in "ability" groups and vary the degree of structure and help given – in other words, differentiation.
6. Rather than being used to start a new topic, "Masterminds" makes an excellent revision strategy using textbooks and students' notes as resources. A limited amount of time can be given for revision in preparation for the competition, say twenty minutes, or it can make a purposeful homework.
7. After the game, the research can be used for peer teaching. Get the students to form mixed groups, one person from each of the original teams, and take it in turns to teach each other.
8. Any unanswered or wrongly answered questions in the game can be cleared up by the teacher afterwards.

Memory Board

A quick and easy game to help students remember technical terms and definitions. No, they won't be bored with "Memory Board"!

How?

1. Write a dozen or more technical terms on the board, taken from the topic just completed or a topic being revised after some time. Better still, write the terms in advance on an overhead transparency.
2. Give the students a minute to remember the list.
3. As soon as the time is up, rub them off, or roll the board round, or switch off the overhead projector.
4. The students have to write out not the terms themselves, but their *definitions*, remembering as many as they can, again in a specified length of time.
5. Go over the terms and discuss the different ways in which students have defined them.

Purposes (what the activity is designed to achieve)	
Thinking	* * * * *
Emotional Intelligence	
Independence	* * * *
Interdependence	(variable)
Multi-sensation	
Fun	* *
Articulation	* * * *

Particulars (what elements the activity contains)	
Individual work	* * * *
Group work	(variable)
Moving about	
Speaking	
Listening	
Reading	* * *
Writing	* * * *
Looking	* * *
Choice	

Specific room layout	
Yes (No)	

Applications

- In any subject where knowledge of technical or specialised vocabulary is expected: **science, maths, geography, English, PE** – is there any subject that doesn't qualify?
- In **modern languages**, the game could be used for the straightforward translation of words or phrases.
- In **maths** equivalent fractions could be used. One-quarter could be written as two-eighths for example. Or random numbers are written on the board and students have to write calculations to which the numbers are the answers.

Why do it?

- The exercise requires an active engagement of the mind.
- It teaches memorisation by making two points. First, the conversion of material from one form (technical term) into another (definition) forces understanding. Deep learning can occur only when material is understood. Rote learning is superficial and inefficient. Second, when the brain has a go at something, then compares the attempted version with the accurate version (when the teacher goes over the answers), memorisation occurs naturally.

- If you do Variation 4 below, the exercise teaches a further point about revision – the need to go over material several times in order for it to stick (based on the Ebbinghaus Effect). This is excellent training in basic revision technique.
- Games such as these add spice to otherwise dull learning chores. They make learning, and life, a bit more bearable.

Variations

1. Have students working in pairs rather than on their own.
2. Use pictures or diagrams rather than words on the "Memory Board". For example, stick up flash cards in **modern languages**, photographs in **geography**, diagrams of apparatus in **science**, geometric drawings in **maths**, materials or tools in **technology**. Or show a slide sequence or a quick-fire PowerPoint presentation during which the students are not allowed to write anything down.
3. Make it a cooperative exercise by having so many items to remember in so short a time that no one person could possibly get them all. Students work in groups and organise their strategy in advance for the successful collaborative completion of the task.
4. Use the exercise to teach the importance of revisiting material several times. Imagine you are using an overhead projector. Show the technical terms for a minute. Switch off. The students have half a minute to go over them in their heads. Switch the projector back on for a further minute. Switch off. Again, the students have half a minute to go over them in their heads. Switch back on for the third and final time. Then the students are allowed to write the definitions. Discuss how much clearer and more complete their memories are after the third viewing compared to the first. Relate this to the need for revision.

Multisensory Memories

Memorising makes sense. Senses make memory.

How?

Bring material alive by using colours, patterns, sound and movement.

For example, revising *Macbeth* **by William Shakespeare.** Turn the classroom into the play:

1. Move the desks and create a circle of chairs. Ask the students to position spare chairs in the circle to represent different characters: Lord Macbeth, Lady Macbeth, Macduff, Banquo and so on.
2. Then allocate a colour and a group of students to each character. Give appropriately coloured paper to the groups, who then decide on, write out and cut up key words and quotations for "their" character.
3. Using Blu-Tack, they stick the coloured pieces of paper on "their" character chair in a pattern that makes the connections between ideas clear. Or they can mount more elaborate displays for their character using cardboard, sugar paper, glue – they can even dress the "characters" in bits of costume.
4. The class mill around revising the characters by looking, reading and notemaking.
5. Then, with the class sitting down, the central theme – "evil", for example – is placed on a large piece of paper in the middle of the floor.
6. A student is invited to demonstrate the connections between the theme and the characters by walking the connections, moving the chairs, explaining out loud, using gestures and reading out the key quotations.
7. Discussion follows and other students are invited to make adjustments or give alternative interpretations by moving furniture, walking, gesticulating and speaking out loud. Then another theme or issue is examined in the same interactive way.

Purposes (what the activity is designed to achieve)	
Thinking	* * * *
Emotional Intelligence	* *
Independence	*
Interdependence	* * * *
Multi-sensation	* * * * *
Fun	* * *
Articulation	* * *

Particulars (what elements the activity contains)	
Individual work	*
Group work	* * * *
Movement	* * * * *
Speaking	* * *
Listening	* * *
Reading	* *
Writing	* *
Looking	* * *
Choice	* *

Specific room layout
(Yes)   No

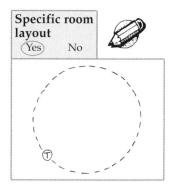

Applications

Endless, for example ...

- **Modern languages**: working in small groups, students set up displays of different tenses – present, perfect, pluperfect, future – with the characteristics, properties and examples of the tense presented in big, bold and colourful ways. Students mill around, using the displays to revise their working knowledge of the four tenses. Then, with the class sitting around in a large circle, a handful of students volunteer to take on characters in a story. They move around the room, with different characters visiting different displays (and using different tenses) at different times as they build up the story out loud entirely in target language. The job of the audience is to spot mistakes. As soon as three mistakes have been made, a new "team" gets up and takes over the story.

- **Maths**: "live" algebra. Volunteer students come out to the front holding large, colourful number, letter and function cards. The class have to balance equations and work out values by directing the students to move in or out of the calculation at different stages. They follow the same routines as if they were doing the work with pen and paper; this is just a large, live, collaborative version of the same process. The teacher can prompt, suggest, question and assess, and can alter the difficulty of the challenges set.

- **English** and **modern languages**: kinaesthetic spelling test. Students form three teams of ten, each standing against a wall of the classroom. Each team is issued with a pack of twenty letters, each on a separate A4 card. The letters are distributed, two per person. No one can give or take letters. When the teacher announces a word the teams race against each other to spell the word correctly, by players getting into position and holding their cards in front of them. (If both a student's letters are required, then a bit of contortion is necessary – it all adds to the fun.) The first team to spell the word correctly from the teacher's point of view gets a point. More words follow and it's the first team to five. Obviously, the teacher varies the number of letters to suit the test.

- **Technical terms in any subject**: train students to memorise the meaning of technical terms. Get students to say each word or phrase out loud, while looking at a cartoon or symbol of the word and simultaneously adding gestures to demonstrate its meaning.

Why do it?

- The overriding purpose of this technique is to aid memorisation, particularly of technical material such as the spelling and meaning of technical terms, the rules of grammar or mathematics, difficult names, quotations and so on. Multisensory experiences are remembered longer and in more detail than events that engage just one or two senses. They are also recalled more readily.
- Students who do not learn well through traditionally academic methods can find success and gain confidence through physical and visual learning.
- Consequently, examination results will improve!
- The technique is fun, and its informality helps to create relaxed working relationships among students and between the teacher and the class.

Variations

1. Students can be encouraged to use multisensory approaches in their revision at home. For example, they can turn the lounge into the play *Macbeth*. The settee becomes Lord Macbeth, the television is Lady Macbeth, the sideboard is Banquo and so on. In which case Post-it notes will be more acceptable than Blu-Tack! They may need to have the technique modelled for them in the classroom first.

2. In the privacy of their own homes, students can also use the "simultaneously speak out loud plus look at a symbol plus do gestures" method of learning technical vocabulary.

3. Also, encourage students to talk to themselves! Apart from being the first sign of madness (or so they say), explaining something to yourself in the mirror, or conducting a role-play where you switch between characters (ideal for **modern languages**), is an excellent way to consolidate learning in private.

On Tour

A chance for students to get out and about. They all get there in the end, but the route has many twists, turns and stops along the way.

Purposes (what the activity is designed to achieve)	
Thinking	* * * * *
Emotional Intelligence	*
Independence	* * *
Interdependence	* * * *
Multi-sensation	
Fun	*
Articulation	* * * * *

Particulars (what elements the activity contains)	
Individual work	
Group work	* * * *
Moving about	* * * * *
Speaking	* * *
Listening	* *
Reading	* * *
Writing	* * * *
Looking	*
Choice	* * *

Specific room layout	
Yes ~~No~~	

How?

1. Decide on a series of challenging questions that require long, detailed answers. These could be genuine exam questions from past papers.

2. Each question is written at the top of a large sheet of sugar paper or flipchart paper and the sheets are put out on desks around the room. There have to be more question sheets than there are pairs of students, to avoid congestion.

3. Explain to students the overall aim: to ensure that all the questions are answered as fully and accurately as possible within a given time limit. The class has collective responsibility for this, and everyone is asked to keep going until satisfied that all the answers are as good as can be.

4. Students work in pairs. At the word "go" each pair make a start on the question nearest to them. They are allowed to work at it for a few minutes, then the teacher shouts, "Move." From here on, pairs move freely around the class, deciding which questions to tackle in which order.

5. Pairs are encouraged to add, delete and redraft in the collective attempt to create a set of perfect answers. The only rules are: only one pair at a question at a time; and you can spend no more than five minutes at a question. Of course, they also have to keep their eyes on the clock.

6. When time is up, pairs return to their original questions and mark them. You will need to explain the assessment criteria and mark schemes first. Alternatively, each pair writes up a polished version of the answer, these are collected, photocopied and distributed to everyone. A third option is for you to collect in all the large sheets, go through some of them with the class and bring out key teaching points, both about the content and about exam technique.

Applications

Any subject that can be tested through long answers, even **maths**, with long complex calculations.

Why do it?

- Exam technique: the exercise trains students to answer questions precisely and fully, and it simulates the pressure of an exam in presenting a number of diverse questions to be answered within a set time.
- It contains peer teaching at two levels. First, the two students in each pair are pooling their expertise, discussing and making decisions together. Secondly, they are learning from the work of others as they move from paper to paper scrutinising contributions.
- The corporate and ultimately anonymous nature of the exercise makes it inclusive.
- It provides a diagnostic assessment for you, enabling you to work on aspects of content and exam technique that emerge as weak.

Variations

1. Instead of allowing free movement around the questions, move pairs on at set times (say every five minutes), and perhaps in a set order.
2. Reverse the management of the exercise. Instead of having students move, the question papers move. You decide when to take a paper away from a pair and which pair to give it to next. This enables you to build in fairly precise levels of differentiation and challenge.
3. To begin the exercise, pairs are allowed a substantial amount of time to answer "their" initial question as accurately and fully as possible. The rest of the time is spent moving round and marking, not adding to, answers. Each pair could be responsible for a particular assessment criterion or aspect, for example: content, spelling, grammar, paragraphing, use of tense and voice ... This is ideal for **modern languages** and **English**, or subjects that have particular writing conventions such as describing experiments in **science**.

One-to-One

The simpler the better – and when it comes to peer teaching, you can't get simpler than "One-to-One".

Purposes (what the activity is designed to achieve)	
Thinking	* * * *
Emotional Intelligence	*
Independence	* * *
Interdependence	* * * *
Multi-sensation	
Fun	*
Articulation	* * * *

Particulars (what elements the activity contains)	
Individual work	* * *
Group work	* * *
Moving about	*
Speaking	* * *
Listening	* * *
Reading	* * * *
Writing	* * * *
Looking	* *
Choice	

Specific room layout
Yes (No)

How?

1. Divide the class into halves.
2. Divide the topic under study into halves. For example, the Native Americans' perspective on the colonisation of the American Midwest, and the settlers' perspective. Or series circuits and parallel circuits. Give one subtopic to one half of the class and the other one to the other half, along with appropriate study materials.
3. Give a reasonable deadline, by the end of which every student must have mastered their topic and produced a teaching aid to use at the next stage. During this initial study period, students can work individually or in pairs. They can seek help from others in their "half" or, as a last resort, from the teacher. The teaching aid should be on A3 paper; use a range of colours and a mixture of words and images.
4. Pair students up across the halves, either randomly, or by taking account of learning styles, reading and writing abilities, personalities, levels of confidence. Students move to sit by each other in their new pairs. Alternatively you can pair up the first two students to finish, then the next two and so on. This means you can then set differentiated extension tasks to the faster workers while the rest catch up.
5. Pairs now teach each other using the teaching aids they prepared earlier. Reasonable deadlines are given. The teacher moves around monitoring, supporting and providing input where students are stuck or inaccurate.

Applications

Any subject that can be divided into two subsections, for example …
- Ideal for exploring two halves of a debate, two interpretations, or two horns of a dilemma in **history, religious education, PSHE, citizenship.**
- **English**: two key characters in a novel, or two quite different interpretations of a character.

- **Art**: critical studies – the life and work of two artists, the characteristics and significance of two art movements or two examples of an artist's work to be studied in detail.
- Excellent for **revision** in any subject.

Why do it?

- It requires everyone to learn. In order to teach something, you have to understand it. If you understand something, you remember it. Also, research suggests that students learn more efficiently from peers than from teachers.
- It requires everyone to take responsibility and therefore trains students in independent and interdependent learning.
- It's easy to set up and manage.
- It prepares students for the more advanced forms of peer teaching such as "Ambassadors" (page 65), "Corporate Identity" (page 89), "Delegation" (page 91), "Marketplace" (page 122), "Scrambled Groups" (page 150).

Variations

1. After the paired peer teaching, a test can be given under exam conditions. Students sit the test without reference to notes or to each other. The pair's marks are added together and divided by two, giving each the same mark. This reflects the quality of their teaching as well as their learning.
2. Before the test, there can be an opportunity to check understanding with the rest of the class and the teacher in an open forum for five to ten minutes.
3. Instead of just teaching each other the material, pairs have to do something with it. For example, they have to compare the properties of two materials (in **technology**) and decide which one will be best for the job. Or they have to rank all the causes (in **history**), or decide which of two experimental methods to use (in **science**), or choose which settlement site to vote for (in **geography**), or write a business plan once all the factors are known (in **business studies**).

Pairs to Fours

This is a classic active learning strategy – simple, effective and collaborative.

Purposes (what the activity is designed to achieve)	
Thinking	* * * * *
Emotional Intelligence	* *
Independence	* * *
Interdependence	* * * *
Multi-sensation	
Fun	* *
Articulation	* * * * *

Particulars (what elements the activity contains)	
Individual work	*
Group work	* * * *
Moving about	*
Speaking	* * * * *
Listening	* * * * *
Reading	* *
Writing	
Looking	
Choice	

Specific room layout Yes (No)	

How?

1. The students form pairs.
2. Each pair has a task to complete, involving the need to discuss and make decisions together. For example, a ranking exercise, choosing which mock business plan to accept, sequencing a narrative, creating headings for paragraphs in a text, proposing the design of an experiment, deciding on captions for a series of photographs, putting forward a proposal for a drama, deciding the order in which topics will be covered.
3. As pairs finish (or after a set time) they come together into fours. That is, two pairs join up, just by turning their chairs, and each pair shares the results of its labours with the other. The four then enter into further debate in order to arrive at an agreed version, which will then be shared with the whole class.
4. It's important that any one of the four is able to explain and defend the decisions made by their group. The teacher may want to "drop on" any of the four to do this, rather than have the group decide who the spokesperson will be. Just to keep everyone on their toes.
5. Debrief the content, and debrief the process, focusing on the nature of decision making and on the pros and cons of consensus, compromise and voting.

Applications

Endless, wherever tasks can be devised that require debate and decision. For example:
- "Here are five possibilities. Which one will be the most efficient?"
- "Work out how these two sets of cards match up."
- "You are such-and-such a group. If you had only this much time/money/material, how would you use it?"
- "Predict the declension of this verb you have not come across before."
- "Put these quotations in order of significance."

- "What do you think will happen if I mix these two materials/turn on the power/add this component?"
- "Given what we know about the stated beliefs of this person, which of his actions was most hypocritical/characteristic/expedient?"
- "Which observation and recording techniques will be appropriate for the field trip?"
- "To what extent was Margaret Thatcher a good prime minister?"

Why do it?

- Deep learning occurs when the brain sorts things out for itself. The process of creating a personal construct is powerfully aided by discussion. The more a learner talks and listens, the more ideas are settled in the mind.
- The technique promotes cooperation, practises oral and listening skills, rehearses debating and decision-making skills. Together, these strengthen interpersonal, linguistic and logical intelligences. They are also among the subskills of independence.
- Presenting and defending a position, arguing and compromising, exercising cabinet responsibility – these are all key citizenship skills.

Variation

If numbers (and nerves) will stand it, the fours could move into eights and so on until a whole-class decision had been reached.

Pass the Buck

Why not pass the buck and let someone else do the work? But, to mix metaphors, when the buck stops, all your chickens come home to roost.

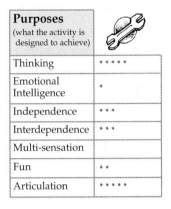

Purposes (what the activity is designed to achieve)	
Thinking	* * * * *
Emotional Intelligence	*
Independence	* * *
Interdependence	* * *
Multi-sensation	
Fun	* *
Articulation	* * * * *

Particulars (what elements the activity contains)	
Individual work	
Group work	* * * *
Moving about	
Speaking	* * *
Listening	* * *
Reading	* * *
Writing	* * * * *
Looking	
Choice	

Specific room layout Yes (No)

How?

1. Students work in pairs and have five minutes to begin a draft answer to a difficult question. It's best if they work on large sugar paper or flipchart paper with felt pens.
2. As soon as time is up, they pass their partial answer to the pair behind them and receive the work of the pair in front.
3. They now have five minutes to continue, not their own answer, but the received answer from the pair in front, picking up from wherever it was left. They are encouraged not just to add, but to cross out bits they don't agree with and redraft others.
4. Again, when time is up, papers are passed on.
5. The newly received answer is continued for a further five minutes.
6. And so on until the process has served its purpose.
7. Papers are then returned to their original authors, who, use the several contributions to draft the final polished version of the answer.

Applications

● **Exam preparation**: pairs tackle SATs or GCSE questions to show how much precision and detail can be achieved in exam answers when they really think about it.
● **English**: to bring out the difference between rushing an essay and planning an essay; extended creative writing; writing about the same subject for different audiences.
● **MFL**: translations; writing open-ended stories; writing a story in target language from a storyboard.
● **Technology**: generating or evaluating different designs to given specifications.
● **Maths**: solving substantial problems; carrying out investigations.
● **Art**: developing drawings and paintings in the style of a variety of artists (with longer times).
● **Revision**: in any subject, ideal for getting students to recall material already taught.

- **Processing ideas**: such as "What shall we do about bullying?"; "How shall we organise ourselves?"; "What are the priorities for school council expenditure?"; "What are the arguments for ... ?"; "How should the classroom rules be revised?"

Why do it?

- This activity trains students in crucial exam technique, particularly the art of writing precise and full answers.
- It promotes a more conscious approach to writing, including planning, accuracy, attention to time and speed, awareness of audience.
- Even though the material might be heavy and serious, the activity itself is light. No one gets too bogged down. The pace and the passing make it sparky and fun.

Variations

1. There are so many variables in this activity, for example ...
   - Vary the time for each round. Give four minutes for the first round, five for the second, six for the third and so on to allow enough reading and thinking time as the answers become fuller.
   - Vary the length and complexity of the tasks. Differentiation can be built in.
   - Vary the questions, so each pair starts with a different question – this really keeps people on their toes. Students have to switch their thinking to a new subject every round. This simulates the pressure of an exam.
2. In the first round give people enough time to write a complete answer. Then, the pair behind don't *continue* it: they *redraft* it.
3. Or, the pair behind *mark* the answer to set criteria. This is particularly powerful if exam criteria are used. Students will need to know beforehand how an examiner approaches a script.
4. As work is passed on, different pairs mark different features: one pair marks spelling, the next marks grammar and syntax, the next content, the next style, (in **MFL** you could have tense, voice, gender ...).

Question Generator

Question the teacher? What is the classroom coming to? This approach will easily generate lots of learning.

Purposes (what the activity is designed to achieve)	
Thinking	* * * *
Emotional Intelligence	*
Independence	* * * (variable)
Interdependence	* * * (variable)
Multi-sensation	
Fun	*
Articulation	* * *

Particulars (what the activity contains)	
Individual work	* * * (variable)
Group work	* * * * (variable)
Moving about	
Speaking	* * *
Listening	* * *
Reading	*
Writing	* *
Looking	
Choice	* * *

Specific room layout	
Yes (No)	

How?

1. Describe the topic to be studied.
2. Ask students to generate as many questions as they can about the topic. This can be done as a whole-class brainstorm, as an individual list or in pairs or small groups.
3. The questions then need to be sorted. If the generation was done by individuals, pairs or small groups they simply rank the items, putting the questions they are most interested in at the top. If the generation was by whole-class brainstorm, ask a student to propose a question they are interested in, then gauge general interest by using "Thumbometer" (page 161), "Calling Cards" (page 181) or just a show of hands. Then another question is proposed and soon a rough ranking is established.
4. The teacher then builds the teaching inputs and materials around the questions, beginning with the most popular. The first few questions might last for a couple of lessons. Later, minority-interest questions can be dealt with on the quiet with individuals or small groups while the rest of the class are working.

Applications

- Use where the students have enough general knowledge to frame intelligent questions about the topic, so it may not be appropriate for highly technical material of which they have no prior experience.
- Ideal for addressing meaty chunks of the syllabus that could be rather dry, for example in **humanities** and **social science** subjects at GCSE and A level.
- Perfect for practical and vocational courses, where students need to know how to carry out certain procedures accurately, for example **child care**, **catering**, **business studies**, **technology**.
- In **PE** and **ICT**, where students are keen to get on and do.

Why do it?

- It increases students' interest in, and curiosity about, the topic – this raises their level of motivation and opens their reticular activating systems.
- Information that students are asking for enters the memory more readily than material that comes out of the blue.
- The brain is self-rectifying. If it receives information that doesn't confirm but challenges its preconceptions and prior knowledge, it will naturally adjust. Learning feels easier to the student, and to the teacher!
- It gives students practice in an important study skill: framing appropriate questions.

Variations

1. Lucky Dip

Instead of answering the questions yourself, have the students do so. Generated questions are written on small cards – one question per card. All the cards are collected in a box. The box is passed round, each student taking a card until no cards are left. Students are then called on to offer answers, which are checked with the whole class, and/or by the teacher.

If appropriate, students can be given research time before answering begins. They could refer to books and each other. They could work in small groups to share questions and answers before "going public". The exercise could be extended into a substantial piece of research, especially if it is an entirely new topic.

2. Scrambled Groups

The students are divided into groups of, say, five. Only the top few questions are taken, each is given to a different group. The groups are expected to research their question to a common deadline. The teacher can inject supplementary or extension questions from the list if necessary. Each student is expected to have a clear understanding of their group's question and to have prepared a teaching aid by the deadline. Groups are then rescrambled and students teach each other. See "Scrambled Groups" (page 150) for instructions.

Question Time

Curiosity may have killed the cat, but it generally keeps motivation alive. Questioning the teacher is a particularly curious business.

Purposes (what the activity is designed to achieve)	
Thinking	* * * * *
Emotional Intelligence	
Independence	* * * *
Interdependence	* *
Multi-sensation	* *
Fun	* *
Articulation	* * *

Particulars (what elements the activity contains)	
Individual work	* *
Group work	* * * *
Moving about	* * * *
Speaking	* * * *
Listening	* * * *
Reading	
Writing	* *
Looking	* * * *
Choice	* *

Specific room layout	
Yes (No)	

How?

1. Place a good number of resources around the room relevant to the topic in hand. They should be nontext or low-text resources: for example, pictures, artefacts, photographs, diagrams, posters, maps. Make sure that there are more resources than there are pairs of students.

2. Students work in pairs and go round examining the resources. For each resource, they define one question raised by the resource about the topic in hand.

3. The pairs write down their questions, perhaps on a preprinted sheet. Each student should keep their own record.

4. Pairs move freely from one resource to another ensuring that there are never too many people at any one station at any one time. They spend as long as they need at each resource, knowing that they are working to a final deadline. The pair must agree that the question they write down is, as far as they can tell, the most significant question raised by the resource.

5. Once time is up the pairs go back to their places or form a circle. The teacher leads a discussion about each resource in turn, based on the students' questions. The quality of the questions is discussed and the key questions are identified. The teacher provides the "input" to the lesson by answering the key questions.

6. Individual students can note down the "answers" during the process, or at the end, or the teacher can supply a photocopied summary sheet.

Applications

- **A-level sociology**: the hidden curriculum's effect on gender role formation in primary schools by using a Development Education Centre photopack called "Behind the Scenes".
- **Physics**: circuit boards set up to show different electrical functions and effects.
- **Biology**: a series of photographs from under an electron microscope showing various types of cell behaviour.

- **Religious education**: sacred objects.
- **Business studies**: roles within a company shown through a series of photographs of different people at work.
- **Technology**: equipment, machinery and tools positioned around the workshop.
- **Maths**: a series of problems – pairs have to identify the key question that will unlock each problem.
- **Geography**: photographs of international migration – different examples from different times and different countries.
- **History**: photographs of the Holocaust.

Why do it?

- Being curious and asking questions are the natural function of the brain's neocortex. So, the activity is likely to be motivating.
- Students are usually more receptive to information that answers questions they themselves have asked.
- Those students with kinaesthetic urges can move around the room legitimately!
- Finally, the process trains students in an essential study skill: asking the right question.

Variations

1. Instead of having the students organise themselves, move them round the resources in an orderly fashion at set intervals.
2. Provide one single piece of stimulus material that all the class can see easily. The bigger and more colourful the better (e.g. a large map of a medieval village in **history**, a picture of a distorted face of a cat looking through a goldfish bowl for **science**, a life-size drawing of Pan Ku for **religious education**). In pairs, students pose a maximum of three questions they want to ask about the picture. The questions are collected and written on the blackboard so that similar questions can be grouped together. If there's time, discuss the relative merits of the questions and how the same question can be posed in different ways. Then allocate questions to pairs of students to research, or allow students to choose which ones they want to do, or just get on with answering them yourself!

Quick on the Draw

A research activity with a built-in incentive for team work and speed.

Purposes (what the activity is designed to achieve)	
Thinking	* * * *
Emotional Intelligence	*
Independence	* * * *
Interdependence	* * *
Multi-sensation	* *
Fun	* * * *
Articulation	* *

Particulars (what elements the activity contains)	
Individual work	*
Group work	* * * * *
Moving about	* * *
Speaking	* * *
Listening	* *
Reading	* * * *
Writing	* * *
Looking	* *
Choice	

Specific room layout
Yes   No

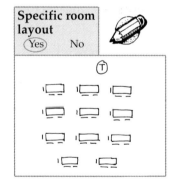

How?

This is a straightforward race between groups. The aim is to be the first group to work its way through a set of questions.

1. Prepare a set of, say, ten questions about the topic in hand. Copy enough sets for each group to have its own. Each question needs to be on a separate card. Each set of questions needs to be in a distinctive colour. Put the sets out on the teacher's desk, numbers facing up with number 1 on top.
2. Divide the class into groups of three (fours if necessary, although this invites passengers). Allocate a colour to each group so they can identify their set of questions on the teacher's desk.
3. Give each group source material that contains the answers to all the questions – one copy per student. This could simply be selected pages from the regular textbook. The answers shouldn't be too obvious: the idea is for students to have to search the text.
4. At the word "go", one person from each group "runs" to the teacher's desk, takes the first question only of their colour and runs back with it to the group.
5. Using the source material, the group finds and writes down the answer on a separate piece of paper.
6. This is taken to the teacher by the second person. The teacher checks the answer. If it is accurate and complete, the second question from their colour pile is collected … and so on. If any answer is inaccurate or incomplete, the teacher sends the runner back to the group to try again. Writers and runners should rotate.
7. While one student is "running" the others should be scanning the resource and familiarising themselves with its contents so they can answer future questions more efficiently. It's a good idea to make the first couple of question fairly easy and short, just to get momentum going.

8. The first group to complete all their questions "wins".
9. You then go over all the answers with the class and written records are made.

Applications

- Endless from Year 7 onwards. The depth and complexity of questions can be varied to suit many different contexts. At A level, for example, run it over a week with questions that demand out-of-classroom research.
- **Science**: in addition to straightforward questions on text, run it with apparatus! Groups can collect their next piece of equipment only when they have got the earlier bits set up correctly.
- **Maths**: each card can be a separate problem, or each card can be one step in a series that leads to the completion of a more complex task. This trains students to check that each stage of a process is correct before moving on to the next.
- **English, humanities, PSHE, business studies**: the source could be text, pictures, artefacts.
- **Modern foreign language**: the source material could be a text such as a story, making the activity a straightforward comprehension exercise. Or the material (or the questions) could be pictorial. Or it could be an exercise in sentence construction, matching one half with the other, or simply an exercise in collecting new vocabulary.
- **Study skills**: debrief the range of skills used in the exercise, including skim-reading, scanning, close reading, key-word identification, collaboration; and the ways in which students can organise more effective resource-based learning in future.
- "Quick on the Draw" is ideal for **revision**.

Why do it?

- The activity encourages team work – the more efficient the team work, the faster the progress. Groups learn that dividing labour is more productive than duplicating labour.
- It gives experience of a variety of reading skills, driven by the pace of the activity, plus a host of other independent learning and examination skills – reading the question carefully, answering the question precisely, distinguishing between crucial and the peripheral material …
- The exercise helps to get students used to basing their learning on resources other than the teacher.
- Suits learners with a kinaesthetic disposition who can't sit still for more than two minutes!

Variations

1. Can be played as a race against the clock, rather than against other groups.
2. Alternatively, the activity does not have to be competitive at all – groups can check answers with each other to ensure detail and thoroughness.
3. Groups can collect visual pieces to build up a finished picture. For example, in GCSE PE, pieces of skeleton can be collected to build up a whole body. Each of the pieces must be named and a question about its function or vulnerability in sport answered correctly before the next piece can be collected.
4. A short cut: instead of copying a set of questions on card for each group, the teacher whispers the question to each runner as they come out.
5. The questions could be graded: the first ones deal with essential information (*must*), the next few embellish or deepen understanding (*should*), the final ones "extend" understanding (*could*).
6. Rather than all groups having the same questions, each group could have its own. If the groups are carefully composed by the teacher, this enables learning to be differentiated to a very precise degree.

7. Alternatively, different groups could have questions on different aspects of the topic. Afterwards, this would lead to peer teaching.
8. Once all the answers have been gathered, discussed and consolidated, a written record could be made by each student.

Ranking

An activity that ranks high in anyone's list of active learning strategies. As the saying goes, it requires engaging the brain while putting the mouth into motion.

Purposes (what the activity is designed to achieve)	
Thinking	* * * * *
Emotional Intelligence	*
Independence	* * *
Interdependence	* *
Multi-sensation	* *
Fun	*
Articulation	* * * *

Particulars (what elements the activity contains)	
Individual work	
Group work	* * * *
Moving about	
Speaking	* * * * *
Listening	* * * *
Reading	* *
Writing	
Looking	* (variable)
Choice	

Specific room layout	
Yes (No)	

How?

1. The class needs to work in pairs or small groups.
2. Pieces of information or ideas or pictures or statements – whatever is appropriate to the learning in hand – are presented to each group as a collection of separate items, perhaps on cards. For example, the causes of World War Two, the paintings of Van Gogh, the evidence for global warming, the sayings of Jesus or scientific discoveries of the twentieth century.
3. The criterion for distinguishing between the items is explained (for example, "How controversial would these sayings of Jesus have seemed at the time?" or "With hindsight, how significant were these discoveries?" or "Which are the most convincing ...?"). The group is asked to debate the relative merits of the items and place them in rank order according to the criterion. This is most easily done if the items can be moved around on the desktop or floor.
4. Once the exercise is complete, the results can be compared and discussed with the whole class.

Applications

- Any subject that requires judgments to be made between different options.
- Ranking is a decision-making process; it can be used to decide between differing proposals at a meeting: for example, where to go for a field trip. It is a positive alternative to voting.

Why do it?

- Ranking is an *academic* exercise; through the exchange of opinion thinking is exercised and personal understanding is achieved of key issues and concepts. This results in deep rather than shallow learning.

- Ranking is also a *democratic* exercise that encourages debate, listening, compromise and consensus.

Variations

The ranking brief can vary, for example ...

1. Produce a straight run of all the items from most favoured to least favoured.
2. Just the top three in order.
3. Just the top two and the bottom two.
4. Pyramid ranking could be produced (one at the top, two on the next row, three on the third row and so on), or a diamond shape.
5. Once the original pairs have completed their rank order, use "Pairs to Fours" (page 137).

Scrambled Groups

The groups may be scrambled, but brains are only fried as each person in the class gets a chance to hear and discuss everyone else's contribution.

Purposes (what the activity is designed to achieve)	
Thinking	* * * *
Emotional Intelligence	* *
Independence	* * *
Interdependence	* * * * *
Multi-sensation	*
Fun	* *
Articulation	* * * * *

Particulars (what elements the activity contains)	
Individual work	* *
Group work	* * * *
Moving about	*
Speaking	* * * *
Listening	* * * *
Reading	* * *
Writing	* * *
Looking	* * (variable)
Choice	

Specific room layout	
Yes No	

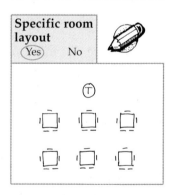

How?

1. Explain the learning objectives and the whole "Scrambled Groups" process to the students before you begin. The exercise is then conducted over two stages.

2. At the beginning of Stage One the class is divided into groups of, say, five. Each group is given a research or discussion brief that specifies the learning objective for the group, the required outcome, the deadline and step-by-step guidelines if necessary. Each brief is different. Each concerns a particular aspect of the topic in hand (for example, different types of business: sole traders; partnerships; private limited companies; cooperatives and so on). The briefs are like pieces of a jigsaw; together they make the whole picture.

3. The groups conduct their specified research or discussion, all working to a common deadline.

4. During the process, each person is responsible for understanding (they ask others in the group for clarification if necessary) and recording the main points or essential research information. Each student must then prepare a teaching aid to use at the next stage (this can make for very productive homework if the exercise runs over two lessons). Teaching aids are best on A3 or A2 paper, so they are easy to see. Encourage a range of colours and graphic devices.

5. Towards the end of Stage One, the teacher gives each person a letter, A–E in each group. This determines which new group each student will move into.

6. At the beginning of Stage Two, the groups are rescrambled. All the As form a group, all the Bs form a group, all the Cs and so on. This means that each of the new groups has one member from all the original groups.

7. In these new groups, people take it in turns to report on their previous group's discussion, or to teach the research using their teaching aids, being careful to relay all the key points. Everyone should take notes; ideas and facts are more likely to sink in that way. Also, each student can do a bit of personal revision before the test (if the test option is chosen by the teacher, see below).

8. Once all the reports have been heard, the group holds a final discussion designed to ensure that everyone understands all the material.

9. In theory, at the end of the process any one person in the class should be able to sum up the whole range of opinion or information. A formal test may be set to check this. To make matters "worse", you could award the average test mark of the rescrambled group to each of its members. This reflects the quality of their teaching as well as the quality of their learning.

Applications

In any subject where separate elements can be researched or discussed, for example:

- **English**: different stanzas of a poem, different characters or scenes in a play.
- **Science**: different types of molecule, different separation techniques.
- **Geography**: different urban problems and solutions; different data collection techniques; different types of volcano; different flood-management programmes; different fieldwork techniques in preparation for coursework.
- **Modern languages**: different parts of speech; different verb patterns.
- **History**: different key figures; different sources; different cause, interpretations or consequences; different themes within a topic (for instance twentieth-century culture: music, food, fashion, furniture, stereotypes, media).
- **Maths**: different problems demanding the same technique; different techniques for the same problem.

Why do it?

- To reinforce listening skills and acceptance of other people's ideas; it is inclusive and collaborative.
- To demonstrate that in good group work there are no passengers, everyone is involved all the time. In this exercise students' participation is forced, but the experience helps to establish the expectation and habit of getting stuck in.
- To reinforce the idea that learning involves asking questions and checking understanding. It is an active process.
- To practise the study skills of key-point identification, note taking, summarising and presenting.
- To encourage students to work productively in random groupings – so they get used to it – and experience a high level of interdependence.
- To guarantee that learning actually takes place. Given the number of times the material is explained and re-explained, it certainly should do!

Variations

1. Naturally, group numbers will need to be altered according to the size of the class. For a small class of twelve, for example, three groups of four will rescramble into four groups of three (or vice versa). So, don't forget your calculator!

2. Differentiation can be built in. *Either*, you can deliberately create mixed-ability groups in the first place – this means that those who struggle with text or concepts can be supported by those who don't – *or* the first-phase groups can be created according to "ability". The more able groups will receive more demanding briefs and resources. Second-phase groups will then automatically be mixed.

Silent Sentences

Classrooms are usually noisy places. This is one way for students and teacher alike to get an unusual bit of peace and quiet.

Purposes (what the activity is designed to achieve)	
Thinking	* * * * *
Emotional Intelligence	* * *
Independence	
Interdependence	* * * * *
Multi-sensation	* *
Fun	* * *
Articulation	

Particulars (what elements the activity contains)	
Individual work	
Group work	* * * * *
Moving about	
Speaking	
Listening	
Reading	* * * *
Writing	
Looking	* * * * *
Choice	

Specific room layout	
(Yes) No	

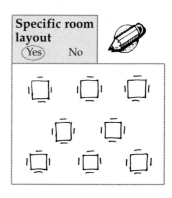

How?

1. Students work in groups of four.
2. Each group has a set of envelopes – one envelope per person. Each envelope contains a different selection of words or phrases on bits of paper or card. The selections are such that no one can make correct, sensible sentences from their own bits. They need other people's and other people need theirs.
3. The challenge is for each player to have complete, grammatically accurate and meaningful sentences in front of them within the given deadline.
4. The rules are:

   - total silence: no one may speak or use sign language
   - players may only give, they cannot take, nor may they beckon for others to give them cards
   - if a card is offered it cannot be refused
   - stay on your seat

5. The exercise gets under way. Students look to see who might need a card and they offer it. There's no need to take turns because there isn't time – groups are working against the clock.
6. When a student has a set of finished sentences, they have not necessarily finished. They might have the wrong solution – they might hold cards still needed by other players and so must remain actively involved.
7. The exercise is complete only when everyone has an accurate set of sensible sentences. The activity works best when there is only one solution, only one correct permutation.

Applications

- **English**: sentences must be grammatically correct, make logical sense and contain specified parts of speech. Give clear instructions as to which parts of speech must be included in all sentences.

- **Modern foreign languages**: as above, but in target language. Variables can include gender, singular and plural endings, tenses and voices.
- **Science** and **maths**: make balanced equations.
- **Maths**: shapes instead of sentences. For example, each person has to make a square equal in dimensions to everyone else's from various cut up bits.
- **Science**: circuit boards and components – working circuits have to be made to certain specifications.
- **Art**: "jigsaws" of paintings, perhaps in different styles, to train students in looking closely.

Why do it?

- With speaking eliminated, observation and mental processes are heightened.
- Those with dominant interpersonal and spatial intelligences and those with Concrete Sequential Mind Styles or visual learning styles are in their element.
- Students' understanding is put to the test. By wandering around the room, it's easy for the teacher to see where confusions and uncertainties occur. The exercise offers informal formative assessment.
- It provides a strong lesson in true group work, cooperation and, above all, self-discipline.

Variations

1. Vary the number of "sentences" per person. For older or more able groups lots of sentences each will be needed to ensure enough complexity.
2. At a simple level coloured cards can be used. For example, all the verbs are on red card, all the nouns on blue and so on. Then debrief the patterns with the students: "What do we notice about the colours in every sentence? Why are they like this? What would happen to the sentence if we …?"
3. Can be played in groups of varying sizes.
4. Each player can have a different specification to meet. For example, circuit boards – each player has to make a specific circuit to do a specific job. In this case, the various specifications need to be known by all players.
5. Debrief with students at two levels: the *content* of the material – misconceptions and confusions that were exposed; and the *discipline* of the exercise – learning about group work, collaboration, citizenship … and silence.

Spotlight

When you're caught in the spotlight, all is revealed. This is one way for everyone to shine.

Purposes (what the activity is designed to achieve)	
Thinking	* * * * *
Emotional Intelligence	
Independence	*
Interdependence	
Multi-sensation	
Fun	* *
Articulation	* * * (volunteer) * (class)

Particulars (what elements the activity contains)	
Individual work	* * * * *
Group work	
Moving about	*
Speaking	* * * (volunteer)
Listening	* * * * (class)
Reading	
Writing	*
Looking	
Choice	

Specific room layout	
Yes No	

How?

1. A volunteer student comes to the front of the class and stands "in the spotlight". This means standing on a special spot, or sitting on a celebrity chair, or wearing a scarf denoting the "mantle of the expert".

2. All the other students turn to the backs of their books, or use scrap paper, and list numbers 1–10 ready to respond to questions.

3. The teacher asks ten questions of the spotlight volunteer about the topic just covered. The student answers each one in turn out loud. After each answer, the rest of the students individually decide whether the response was right, or wrong, or if they weren't sure.

4. If they think the answer was right, they put a tick against the number; if wrong, they put a cross. If they weren't sure (or the spotlight volunteer couldn't answer it), they put a question mark.

5. To conclude, the "spotlight student" is applauded and the teacher goes over the responses. For each question, the teacher asks how many people gave which response. This gives feedback to the teacher about who has learned what. It also gives precise feedback to individual students about the issues they need to work on further.

Applications

- Ideal as an end-of-lesson check on learning in almost any subject.
- Conduct a more substantial version at the end of a topic or scheme of work.
- Use it for predictions, in **science**, for example: "What do you think will happen when …?"
- Use it to gather whole-class opinions quickly. Students mark whether they agree with the spotlight volunteer's views and suggestions, whether they disagree or have no strong feelings either way.
- Use it to make whole-class decisions.

Why do it?

- It's a novel way of doing diagnostic assessment. The teacher can then plan further learning in the light of what is revealed.
- It's immediate – the teacher and students get instant feedback. The brain is a self-rectifying organ, thrives on immediate feedback, and automatically makes adjustments when it knows what it should have thought.
- It gives show-offs a chance to show-off constructively.

Variations

1. Vary the number of questions, vary the number of volunteers.
2. Instead of writing ticks, crosses and question marks on paper, students can hold up one of three response cards as soon as an answer is given. The cards give an immediate visual impression of who understands what. (See "Calling Cards" on page 81.)
3. Questions can be put by members of the class, not just by the teacher.

Stepping Stones

One step at a time. That's the safest and surest way to make progress.

Purposes (what the activity is designed to achieve)	
Thinking	* * * * *
Emotional Intelligence	*
Independence	*
Interdependence	* *
Multi-sensation	* * *
Fun	* * *
Articulation	* * * (volunteer)

Particulars (what elements the activity contains)	
Individual work	* * * * (volunteer)
Group work	* * * * (variable)
Moving about	* *
Speaking	* * * * * (volunteer)
Listening	* * * * (class)
Reading	
Writing	
Looking	* * *
Choice	* *

Specific room layout (Yes)   No

How?

1. Clear the desks and sit the class in a circle.
2. In the centre place several sheets of sugar paper or flipchart paper and a thick felt pen.
3. Discuss with the class the number of steps in the process under discussion. For example, a procedure (carrying out an experiment or making a recipe), or the stages of a physical phenomenon (the water cycle, for example), or the logical steps of a thinking process (the calculation of quadratic equations, or the identification of a piece of rock).
4. Number the pieces of paper and set them out in sequence across the circle to represent the stages of the process. These are the stepping stones. If necessary, add key words to each one. For example, for the water cycle, "evaporation", "condensation", "precipitation" and so on.
5. Ask for a volunteer who thinks they can get right across the circle on the stepping stones. They stand on the first "stone" and explain the step accurately and fully. If the teacher is satisfied they move to number two, attempt to explain the second step to the teacher's satisfaction and so on.
6. The successful student is applauded loudly. If a student gives an incomplete or inaccurate answer, they've fallen off, sit back down and another volunteer takes up the challenge.

Applications

- Excellent as a **revision** exercise – several different processes can be covered at one sitting.
- **Technology**: the design-and-make process – students become clear about what they have to do before they go off and do it.
- **Science**: endless applications from simple experiments to chain reactions involving complex formulae and molecular structures.
- **Maths**: the conventional ways to carry out a whole range of calculations.
- **Dance**: revise a sequence of movements.

- **Gymnastics**: the step-by-step conventions of particular movements.
- **Geography**: the water cycle, the processes of glaciation, settlement growth, industrialisation.
- **History**: any sequence of events such as the Norman Conquest of England, various causes and effects.
- **Business studies**: cycles of economic growth and depression.

Why do it?

- It's a novel and fun way of dealing with potentially dry material.
- It's multisensory using auditory, visual and (for volunteers) kinaesthetic learning channels.
- It requires students to articulate and clarify their understanding, either verbally as they cross the stones, or in their heads as they compare what the volunteer is saying with their own thoughts.

Variations

1. Let the class rather than the teacher judge whether steps have been explained accurately and fully.
2. Have rules to speed up and spice up proceedings: no repetition, hesitation or deviation. If the volunteer does any of these, they're off!
3. To keep everyone on their toes, you can pick on people (or pull names from a hat) to come and repeat a successful crossing.
4. Instead of using it to consolidate or revise material, use it to introduce material. Ask students to have a go – use prior learning, bits of general knowledge, logical thinking and guesswork.
5. Use it as an arena for teaching. The teacher moves from stone to stone explaining the concepts involved. This gives a strong visual impression to complement the verbal exposition.
6. Students can make written notes once the fun and games are over.
7. The students can divide into teams and each team put forward a "champion" to have a go. The list of stepping-stone "challenges" can be described in advance by the teacher and allocated randomly to teams. Each team can then coach their champion before the competition begins.

Still Image

A visual and involving way of understanding concepts. Seeing is believing, they say.

Purposes (what the activity is designed to achieve)	
Thinking	* * * * *
Emotional Intelligence	* * * * *
Independence	* * *
Interdependence	* * * * *
Multi-sensation	* * * *
Fun	* * *
Articulation	* * * *

Particulars (what elements the activity contains)	
Individual work	*
Group work	* * * * *
Moving about	* * * * *
Speaking	* * * *
Listening	* * * *
Reading	* * (variable)
Writing	
Looking	* * * *
Choice	* * * *

Specific room layout (Yes)   No

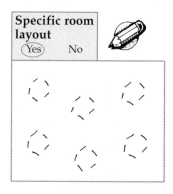

How?

Students work in small groups, the exact number depending on the type of image to be presented.

1. Explain that a still image is like a photograph or a freeze-frame on a video. It captures action, but is silent and motionless. It is a "tableau", like a scene at the waxworks. Players use position, levels, body posture and facial expression to portray an incident or an idea. Still images can be *realistic* (for example, "Leaving Home" – young evacuees waving goodbye as they set off for the countryside) or *symbolic* (for example, "Revolution" – a depiction of the meaning of revolution involving joined hands and fists breaking through imaginary chains). Either way, the image must have significance: it should capture a crucial or poignant moment, or an essential idea. It will then have sufficient interest for the participants and the audience.

2. Explain the learning objectives. These determine the content, preparation method and stimuli needed for the images. For example, imagine the students are about to start "international migration" as part of GCSE geography. The syllabus says that they must "be able to explain the causes and consequences of international migration … present a case study which shows the perception of opportunity to migrate, the push and pull factors involved, and the consequences at local and national levels in both the home and host countries."

3. To get the groups going on their image you provide a photograph of a migrant family arriving dishevelled and bewildered at a foreign port. Groups can re-create the photograph as a still image, inventing the names and life histories of the characters or, if they don't want to be tied to the picture, they can just use it as a prompt and make up their own image based directly on the learning objectives.

4. In some cases, still images can be created completely from imagination (for instance, in RE: portray a moral dilemma faced by a Sikh family), in others they can arise from text (for example, a moment from a set play in English in order to study a theme or a character in more depth), in others technical knowledge is required which has to be researched (for instance in science: the vaccination of a small boy by Edward Jenner, or the control room of a hydroelectric power station).

5. Groups have time to prepare. This will vary from, say, ten to thirty minutes, depending on the learning objectives and method of preparation – research-based or spontaneous. Then the images are presented in turn to the class. Ground rules will be needed to make sure that the images are not mocked, for example: don't ask questions that are designed to get a laugh.

6. Each frozen image is sustained long enough, perhaps half a minute, for the audience to work out what it is portraying. Then the players can relax their positions a little without losing the overall shape of the picture. To bring out the meaning and learning of the image, either of two procedures can be followed. (1) Members of the audience, including the teacher, ask questions. It's best if questions are directed to specific characters, calling them by role name rather than real name. It's often helpful to allow only those questions that relate directly to the learning objectives. (2) The teacher takes the lead initially, tapping players on the shoulder in turn. When tapped, the player says what they are thinking and feeling. This is technically known as *thought tracking*. It can, of course, then lead to questions from the audience.

Applications

- To portray and study significant moments in **history**, **religious** ceremonies, **business** life, a **novel**, a **poem**, a **play**, a **biological** process.
- To bring to life a **photograph**, **drawing** or **painting**.
- To freeze and examine movements in **dance** or **sport**.
- To provide a human angle on **technical knowledge**: for example, a physiotherapist treating a specific injury.
- As a starting point for a piece of creative **writing**, in which case the image could be made up from a simple prompt – an empty chair, for example.
- To portray **chemical** reactions, **mathematical** truths, the laws of **physics**, or abstract ideas symbolically.
- To explore **moral** dilemmas and **social** issues: for example an image entitled "To accept the offer or not?"
- Still image is a powerful literacy tool. It supports extended writing, particularly in subjects such as RE and history, where people's motives and feelings are explored. Even poor writers tend to put detail and depth into writing that has been stimulated by a still image; they seem to have so much to write about. Feeling chuffed with themselves, they can then usually be persuaded to improve the technical aspects of their work.

Why do it?

- Still images, like other dramatic devices, strengthen visual and creative forms of intelligence.
- They are also ideal for Abstract Random and "activist" learning styles and give such learners a rare chance to thrive.
- Reading and writing abilities are not required by the process, though still images may create the motivation to read or write. The strategy is relatively inclusive.
- Many students gain easier access to sophisticated ideas once they are set in a human context. These days most students live in a soap-opera world: they watch fictional lives playing out fictional scenes all the time and they are remarkably nosy about people's actions, motives and relationships (think of the popular programme, *Big Brother*!). Still images fit this teenage culture perfectly.

- Clearly, many aspects of emotional intelligence are both required and developed by still images, as are independent and interdependent learning.
- Dramatic, bold activities that people take part in, or simply watch, engage the emotions and are therefore well remembered.

Variations

1. Still images may naturally lead to "Hot-Seating" (page 116) or "Forum Theatre" (page 105).
2. Still images may stimulate a period of research because they have aroused curiosity and raised unanswered questions.
3. Two or three still images could be presented in sequence to show, for example, the progress of a scientific reaction, or significant moments in the build up to the Jarrow March, or the plot of a story.
4. Still images might be prepared at the start of a new topic, for example, "The Plague". The teacher gives various scenes to be prepared (a doctor is attempting to cure a rich young man, a priest is fetched by distraught parents to pray for their young sick child). The questions that can't be answered by students form the teacher's agenda for the next couple of lessons.
5. Still images may be prepared *after* a period of substantial research. They can be the culmination, the means of expressing the learning. To return to an earlier example, international migration, students could initially consult textbooks, maps, employment statistics, facsimiles of adverts published by the British government in West Indian newspapers, extracts from the log of *SS Windrush*, personal reminiscences … and then prepare an image of very high quality. The period of research could be extended over a number of lessons and homework assignments.

Thumbometer

What are they thinking? How much do they understand? Are they awake? It's easy to gauge the situation - just take a reading with the "Thumbometer".

Purposes (what the activity is designed to achieve)	
Thinking	* * * *
Emotional Intelligence	* *
Independence	* * *
Interdependence	
Multi-sensation	*
Fun	* *
Articulation	* *

Particulars (what the activity contains)	
Individual work	* * * * *
Group work	
Moving about	
Speaking	
Listening	* * *
Reading	
Writing	
Looking	*
Choice	* * * *

Specific room layout Yes (No)

How?

1. Demonstrate how to present the Thumbometer: arm out, fist clenched, thumb up.
2. Show how to use the Thumbometer to indicate a personal response. Thumb straight down is a downright negative, thumb straight up is a maximum positive, with all positions in between.
3. Whenever you want to gauge whole class understanding, thinking, feeling or opinion, ask them to get their thumbs out!

Applications

- To **check** how well an instruction or concept has been understood: for example, "How confident are you that you've understood what I've said?" or "How well would you be able to explain this to someone else?"
- To **test** knowledge: for example, "How sure are you about the following statements ...?" or "Are the following statements true, or false, or don't you know?"
- To **gauge** feelings: for example, "How are your concentration levels?" or "How interested are you in this new topic?" or "How prepared are you to have a go at this new learning technique?"
- To **gather** opinions: for example, "How much do you support the idea that we ...?" or "To what extent do you agree with ...?"

Why do it?

- It gives you immediate feedback, so you can tailor your plans accordingly.
- It gives students a genuine sense of participation.
- It requires all students to be on the ball - there's no hiding place.
- It promotes the notion of shared responsibility and demonstrates democracy.
- It includes those who can't speak, or who are shy and feel awkward about speaking in public.

Variations

1. If peer-group pressure is a problem, ask students to close their eyes during "Thumbometer".

2. Have "Thumbometer" ongoing during the lesson. Students can indicate the points at which their understanding or concentration wanes They can silently tell you which bits they understand clearly so you can move on, and which bits you need to spend more time on. They can indicate when they can't take any more and when it's time to change activity.

3. Instead of using their thumbs, students can indicate the strength of their response by showing a number of fingers on a scale of one to five. Make sure that their palms, not the backs of their hands, are facing you!

Value Continuum

This rather technical-sounding term describes a strategy that encourages people to express their views in complete emotional comfort.

Purposes (what the activity is designed to achieve)	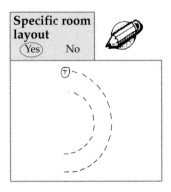
Thinking	* * * * *
Emotional Intelligence	* * * *
Independence	* * *
Interdependence	* *
Multi-sensation	* *
Fun	*
Articulation	* * * * *

Particulars (what the activity contains)	
Individual work	* * *
Group work	* *
Moving about	* * *
Speaking	* * *
Listening	* * * * *
Reading	
Writing	
Looking	* * * *
Choice	* * * *

Specific room layout (Yes)   No

How?

1. Clear the desks and arrange the class in a semicircle.
2. Across the open end of the semicircle ask people to imagine a line (or use chalk, masking tape or a rope) and place a chair at each end.
3. Introduce the issue to be discussed (e.g. vegetarianism) and outline the two opposite positions. Do this by sitting on one chair and speaking as if you held this extreme view: "I never eat meat. Meat eating is an abomination – unhealthy, unnatural and uneconomic. I campaign day in and day out to persuade others to give up this immoral habit. A law should be passed banning the eating of meat, on pain of death." Then sit on the other chair: "I am a devotee of meat ..."
4. Ensure that the two views are *extreme* and *balanced* – one is not obviously more right (in the teacher's eyes) than the other. Explain that everyone's view will fall somewhere on the sliding scale between the two chairs.
5. Explain the rules: "You choose whether to participate or not. The person who is on the line is guaranteed that her view will be listened to. There will be no agreeing or disagreeing (there will be time for that later) – no reaction, verbal or otherwise from the audience. Honesty is expected."
6. The teacher sits down in the semicircle and anyone may begin by taking her chair and sitting in a position on the continuum that represents their view. The volunteer is expected to say a few words to the class about her position and then stays in her chosen spot.
7. The process is repeated, with volunteers going out and speaking, one after another. If one person's view is identical to that of an earlier speaker, she can sit in front of him. (Alternatively, of course, you might have students standing instead of sitting.)
8. If, after the first few brave souls, the rest of the students are reluctant to take part, then you might use two softer strategies: "Come and stand on the line, but you don't have to say

anything." If there is further reluctance you can say, "Stay where you are and just point to your position on the line." This way everyone makes a "statement" of some kind. These options might be needed with shy or fearful students initially, but the aim is to encourage bolder participation in future, which is why protective ground rules are so important.

9. The process is likely to come to a natural end.

Applications

● To discuss any issue about which there can be polarised, but equally plausible, views. **RE, personal, social and health education** and **citizenship** are obvious contexts.

● **Science**: ethical dilemmas such as genetic engineering, nuclear energy, animal experiments.

● **History**: questions of judgment: for example, "Was Catherine the Great an enlightened despot?" Students have to defend their positions with evidence.

● **English**: character studies, for example, Curly's wife in the novel *Of Mice and Men*: total tart to the most complex and tragic character in the story. To introduce nonfiction text about an issue such as animal rights. Once initial positions on the line have been established, students read the arguments for and against, then reposition themselves with increased awareness.

● In any subject, to assess **what people know** about a topic before it is begun. From "I know absolutely everything there is to know about this topic" to "I know nothing at all about it."

● To assess **how much support** there is for a proposal.

● In any subject, to **evaluate learning**. From "This was the best possible way to solve the problem/fulfil the brief/conduct the experiment/learn the topic" to "This method was completely useless, it had no merit at all."

● Try conducting the exercise in a **modern foreign language** at a senior level.

● Use it to establish a **timeline**, in which case each student will be given a card with an event/invention/breakthrough/character/clue.

● **Maths**: set up a line of probability from nought to one. Distribute cards with possible events written on such as "Stoke City Football Club will be in the Premiership within the next three years." Students take turns to come out and position their event on the line. Once several students are on the line, adjustments to some positions will be inevitable as relative probability is debated.

Why do it?

● It's good training in self-discipline, group cooperation and courage! It therefore promotes both independent and interdependent learning.

● The activity develops listening skills as well as patience, tolerating differences of opinion, managing feelings and other aspects of emotional intelligence.

● "Value Continuum" raises self-esteem when conducted in strict accordance with the rules, as each student receives the full attention of the class. This usually translates into increased confidence to speak and participate in future.

● It asks people to consider a range of opinions and is excellent preparation for the art of debate, essential for all active citizens

● It requires and practises a range of thinking skills as students interpret, compare and contrast positions.

Variations

1. A **two-dimensional continuum** might be used to explore two related issues at once. In this case students will need to sit in a circle and a cross is marked on the floor using chalk, masking tape or string. For example:

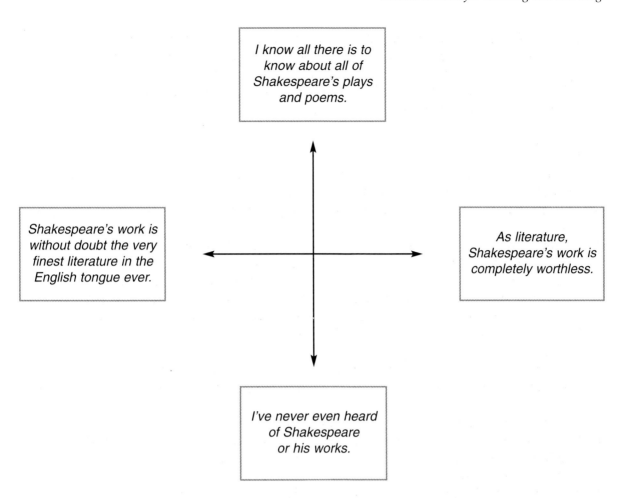

2. When all or most people are on the line, or at least have made their mark by pointing, you can "break" the line in half and make **two debating teams**. The teams face each other (as in Parliament) and take turns to make points. It might be helpful to give each team an object, a pencil and a felt pen, for example, with the rule that students can speak only if they are holding it. The same person cannot make two consecutive contributions. The aim is to persuade people to change sides and the team with more converts at the end "wins" the debate. In the process of course, the finer points of the arguments should emerge. Partway through, teams could go off and research their arguments in more depth and detail.

3. The *Value Continuum* could initiate, or could be the culmination of, an extended **period of research** about an issue.

Verbal Football

Physical skills are replaced by mental in this action-packed, high-tempo game of two halves.

Purposes (what the activity is designed to achieve)	
Thinking	* * * *
Emotional Intelligence	*
Independence	* * *
Interdependence	* * * *
Multi-sensation	*
Fun	* * * * *
Articulation	* * *

Particulars (what the activity contains)	
Individual work	* *
Group work	* * * *
Moving about	*
Speaking	* * * *
Listening	* * * *
Reading	* * * *
Writing	*
Looking	*
Choice	* *

Specific room layout
Yes (No)

How?

1. Explain that the aim of the game is to test knowledge and understanding. Divide the class into two teams. Each team should appoint a captain.
2. Explain that success in the match will depend on serious training. Training involves the team going over a given topic, checking facts and understanding with each other and memorising details ready to answer the teacher's questions.
3. When the training period is over, all books and notes have to be put away, the captains are called together, a coin is tossed to see who has kick-off and the game begins.
4. The team with kick-off receives a question from the teacher. Anyone can answer within five seconds. If they answer correctly, they retain possession. Another question is asked by the teacher. Again, if someone on the team answers correctly within five seconds, the ball has been passed successfully and possession has been retained. Put together a string of three correct answers (= three passes), and it's a goal! Once a person has answered a question, they cannot answer again until everyone else on the team has had a go. It's up to players, and especially the captain, to monitor who has and who hasn't taken part.
5. If a player answers incorrectly, that's a tackle and possession moves to the opposition. So the teacher starts to ask them the questions. If no one answers within five seconds, that's a loose ball. If the opposition can answer within a further five seconds, they pick up possession and begin to receive questions.
6. Fouls are committed for shouting out answers when it's not your team's turn, for answering when you're ineligible, and especially for arguing with the referee! The referee is encouraged to use yellow and red cards.
7. The winning team is the one with more goals at the end of the session.

Applications

- Consolidation at the end of a topic or revision later on.
- To introduce a new topic. "Verbal Football" enables you to check how much is already known.
- To conduct informal diagnostic assessment partway through a topic – the exercise roughly reveals how much has been understood and how much detail has been retained so far. This enables you to adjust plans for following lessons.

Why do it?

- It's fun and adds variety into the teaching and learning diet. Students hardly notice that they are being tested.
- The "training" phase encourages students to look back at the work in some detail. This establishes the notion that long-term memorisation requires material to be revisited again and again. The exercise demonstrates the value of revision.
- There is an incentive for the stronger students to ensure that the weaker members of their team have mastered the information and concepts.
- It appeals to students who don't settle well to concentrated desk work.

Variations

1. During training each player prepares several questions to ask the opposition. During the game, instead of the teacher asking the questions, students ask each other. A student cannot ask a second question until everyone else in the team has contributed. In this case, fouls are committed for asking incomprehensible questions and for not knowing the answer yourself! Captains organise the order in which players ask questions.
2. Teams can either be given the same topic in training, or be given different topics.
3. Instead of using it for consolidation or revision, use it to introduce a topic. In this case, the training involves research, either open-ended if the class have the skills, or structured. Both teams will need to research, and prepare questions on, the same material.
4. Instead of football, use netball, cricket, hockey …

Verbal Tennis

Love, sets and matches. They're all part of school life. Make them a productive part of learning with a quick bit of banter.

Purposes (what the activity is designed to achieve)	
Thinking	* * * * *
Emotional Intelligence	
Independence	*
Interdependence	*
Multi-sensation	*
Fun	* * * *
Articulation	* * * *

Particulars (what the activity contains)	
Individual work	*
Group work	* * *
Moving about	
Speaking	* * * * *
Listening	* * * * *
Reading	
Writing	
Looking	
Choice	

Specific room layout Yes (No)	

How?

1. Students sit facing each other in pairs. No books or notes are allowed.
2. A topic is set by the teacher. Each pair tosses a coin to see who "serves" first. The server begins by saying a word or phrase associated with the topic, the partner immediately gives a second word or phrase, the server gives a third and so on backwards and forwards in rapid succession. It has the pace and feel of a word-association game.
3. When a student hesitates, or gets stuck, or repeats a word or phrase already given by either player, or makes a contribution off the topic, or gives an inaccurate contribution, their partner gains a point. The scoring follows the rules of tennis.
4. Some topics can be sustained for a number of games, even a whole set, because they are sufficiently wide. Otherwise, write a list of topics on the board and ask students to change to a new topic at the start of each game.

Applications

- Ideal for **revision** in any subject: names of twentieth-century artists; safety procedures in the workshop, key moments in the French Revolution; chemical formulae; words associated with *The Crucible*; numbers divisible by nine ...
- Makes a perfect lesson starter.
- Can be done as an informal "test".
- **Modern foreign languages**: adjectives, sports and hobbies, pluperfect constructions, shop names and goods.
- Exchange creative ideas, such as: possible ingredients in a healthy snack; ways of finding information about an assignment; where to go on the school trip; ways of spending the school council budget. Can be preparation for a whole-class brainstorm.

Why do it?

- Students often need to "warm up" before they are ready to take part in open discussion. This exercise is structured and non-exposing.
- It raises energy levels in a flagging class.
- It focuses attention on the topic in hand at the beginning of a lesson, especially after a break or lunchtime.
- It switches the brain on and gets creative and lateral thinking going.
- It's fun and helps to create a conducive learning environment.

Variation

Play to squash or racquet-ball rules instead of tennis.

Wheel of Fortune

It won't tell your fortune; it won't make your fortune. But, for those who are fortunate, it will make you take part.

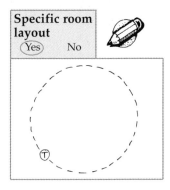

Purposes (what the activity is designed to achieve)	
Thinking	* * * *
Emotional Intelligence	
Independence	*
Interdependence	* *
Multi-sensation	* *
Fun	* * *
Articulation	* * * *

Particulars (what the activity contains)	
Individual work	* * * (variable)
Group work	* * * (variable)
Moving about	* *
Speaking	* * * *
Listening	* * *
Reading	*
Writing	
Looking	*
Choice	

Specific room layout

(Yes)   No

How?

1. Make a set of large cards with prompts or questions on one side and numbers on the back.
2. Make a "Wheel of Fortune" out of card. Divide it into as many sectors as there are question cards and number the sectors. Make a spinner using a cardboard arrow and a brass paper fastener. The finished product should look like a "Twister" wheel.
3. The students sit in one large circle. The cards are spread face down covering most of the floor space with the numbers clearly visible.
4. A volunteer begins, takes the wheel and spins it. A number is shown. The student gets up, picks up the card corresponding to the number on the wheel and responds to the prompt or question.
5. A brief discussion takes place between the teacher and the whole class. If they judge that the student has responded fully and accurately, the card is placed back on the floor face up. That number is now void. If the answer is incomplete or inaccurate the card is placed back face down for someone else to try their luck.
6. The wheel passes to the next person. As time goes by more and more cards are turned face up. Whenever a void number is spun, the player simply passes the wheel to the next student – they were off the hook. So, the game speeds up.

Applications

- **Revision** in any subject. The cards can have very demanding questions, GCSE or A level, with strict marking schemes that the students have to pass before the card can be turned over.

- **Modern languages**: the cards are pictures that have to be described accurately in target language; phrases to be translated.
- **English**: stanzas from poems in the GCSE anthology – students have to give the poem and poet, the context, imagery, symbolism and meaning of key words.
- **Maths**: calculations to be conducted on the board; name the rule or procedure to be applied to such-and-such a problem.
- **History**: dates; give the details of an event; give the main achievements of such-and-such a character.
- **Technology** and **science**: name the equipment, procedures and safety regulations for various processes; the meaning of technical terms, with examples.
- **Defining technical terms**: any subject.

Why do it?

- It encourages reluctant students to take part – they tend to accept the random selection of the wheel.
- It is a game with a challenging edge, like many TV game shows. This is a familiar and motivating genre for most students.
- At an advanced level, it is excellent preparation for an exam.
- It practises recall and speed of thought.

Variations

1. Reverse it. Take the question cards in sequence and let the wheel decide which student is going to answer next. For this, the room need not be reorganised: simply number the students.
2. Playing with a large class can be tedious. Instead, break into three or four groups each with their own set of cards and wheel. Or stay as a whole group and divide the students into teams. When the team turns a question up, they have to decide quickly which of their members is going to answer. Each team member can have only two goes.
3. Beat the clock – each player has only thirty seconds to give the answer.
4. The cards on the floor are roles. The student has to answer questions from the class in character for one minute. For example, roles within a company in **business studies**, characters in a novel or play in **English**, key players in a military or political engagement in **history**, famous designers or artists in **art/design/technology**.

Where There's a Will ...

... there's a way.

Working with individual students who appear to have learning difficulties involves finding personally appropriate strategies. Here are a few to keep up your sleeve.

These ideas are particularly designed for learning assistants and support teachers, but you should find them useful in any situation where you have one or two individual students who need individual attention and individual strategies.

At the start of the lesson

1. Convert your instructions or lesson plan into a

   - flowchart
   - series of pictures or diagrams
   - list of key words
   - timeline
   - time circle (like a clock face)
   - series of coloured cards placed in sequence on the desk.

2. Have the instructions recorded on audio tape – the student can listen (using a personal stereo such as a Walkman) as often as necessary.

3. Ask the student to explain to *you* what to do before starting.

4. Ask the student to explain to another student, or to find out from another student, what to do.

5. Go through the instructions again, adding gestures and actions.

6. Mime the instructions and get the student to tell you what you are doing.

During the lesson

1. Set short deadlines for (or with) the student for specific tasks – turn these into challenges.

2. Let the student hot-seat you to find out information.

3. Give the student the "mantle of the expert" (use a scarf or shawl) and hot-seat the student for information.

4. Have audio cassettes to hand with various types of "mood music" for the student to work to (using a personal stereo or MP3 player).

5. Cut up the worksheet/information sheet and move the pieces around on the desk to reinforce the connections or the order.

6. Ask the student to reassemble cut-up material.

7. Give the student a few minutes "time-out" – make sure that the time limit and the rules (not to disturb other students) are understood first.

8. Go with the student to watch another student doing the task – observe, then ask the student to explain to you how the other person did it.

9. You demonstrate the task to your student – then ask her or him to close their eyes and tell you what you did step by step.

10. You do the task (badly) asking the student to stop you whenever you do something wrong.

11. Ask the student how she would explain this to a good friend, or a close member of the family, or an alien (which you can pretend to be!).

12. Enlarge text on the photocopier.

13. Use coloured pens or crayons to underline or highlight photocopied text.

14. Use coloured paper to distinguish different tasks, or points, or steps, or aspects of the topic.

15. Read the text to the student and make deliberate mistakes, then swap over – make it into a game. Try to catch each other out by slipping a mistake past the other person without their noticing it.

16. Explain using mime – no words.

17. Find objects in the classroom and arrange them on the desktop to simulate or "model" a point or a process or a relationship – or ask the student to do it.

18. Ask the student to predict what you are going to say next.

19. Turn an abstract ideas into a mind map, or key-word plan, or flowchart, or storyboard.

20. Use spontaneous role play with the student – act out the concept, the connection, the meaning, the cause-and-effect, the equation …

Section 3

Tools for Managing Group Work, Behaviour and Personal Responsibility

Introduction

Everyone is concerned about behaviour. Naturally. We all know how our best-laid plans can be wrecked by one or two disruptive students. What puts many teachers off using innovative and interactive classroom techniques? Discipline.

Even when they are convinced by the theory and can see that the practical idea is a good one, most teachers will still refuse to try a technique if they suspect that discipline and control will be undermined. The reasons for this are understandable. First, there is a biological explanation. Whenever a person perceives threat – physical, emotional or psychological – the blood supply to the ancient, instinctive bits of the brain is dramatically increased. Survival behaviours are instantly and automatically activated and rationality goes out of the window. The brain's job, first and foremost, is to ensure survival. It will go for the safest option, the tried and tested solution. When the chips are down, when it is fearful, the brain will instinctively protect itself, its reputation, its job!

Second, we live in a culture in which there is little acceptance of personal responsibility. On the whole parents, the media, inspectors, school managers, and certainly most pupils, think that it is the teacher's job to control the class. Any teacher's reputation hangs of falls by their ability to master difficult groups of students. There is little belief in self-discipline. Otherwise we wouldn't be so dependant on rewards and punishments, which perpetuate students' reliance on extrinsic behavioural motivators (for further discussion of this point, Alfie Kohn's book *Punished by Rewards*[1] is excellent). The role models portrayed in most walks of real and televised life suggest that getting away with it if you can and blaming someone, or something, else is normal. The job of reversing these norms appears enormous.

However, this section bravely tries to do just that. It draws on humanistic rather than behaviouristic psychology and presents a series of strategies that attempt to transform your average classroom into a self-regulating mini-society. Given the forces at work, though, the section also offers a number of fallback positions and pragmatic techniques that may not be ideal, but at least help us make progress.

The goals are:

- to create sufficient self-discipline for teachers to feel confident about using active and interactive learning strategies

- for students to feel that they can take part enthusiastically in whole-class and small-group activities without fear of negative consequences from their peers

The reptilian response of the brain, described above in the case of fearful teachers, applies to fearful students, too. They also tend to play safe when they sense ridicule or marginalisation. Acceptance by the peer group is all-important to most secondary school students and they will not sacrifice their standing with their mates for the sake of the teacher's fancy classroom techniques. So, basic work has to be done on attitudes to learning, to each other and to the teacher. "Murder Hunt" (page 179), "Framed" (page 182), "Observer Servers" (page 185),

"Learning Listening" (page 187), "Sabotage" (page 190) and "Games" (page 192) are all designed to begin the process of creating new behavioural norms through direct experiential means. "Maintenance" (page 195) and "Assertiveness" (page 199) suggest ways of maintaining momentum towards the new order.

Apart from creating the conditions in which "risky" learning strategies are most likely to work, there are three further and noble reasons for investing time and effort in these matters.

First, **inclusion**. Enabling *all* learners to be physically present in a classroom is only the first step towards inclusion. Full participation in learning occurs only when each student is genuinely accepted, and *knows* that she or he is genuinely accepted, by the whole group. This requires students to behave towards each other in an acceptant and inclusive manner. In concrete terms this involves:

- letting each other speak without background sniggers and witty remarks
- listening
- inviting
- encouraging
- most fundamentally, *eliminating all types of put-down*

Such behaviours are reassuring, encourage participation and build self-esteem, which increases confidence. These are the deep-seated needs of all students, not just those with identified "special needs".

Second, **citizenship**. These inclusive behaviours are also the foundation stones of democracy. People are allowed – no, *encouraged* – to have their say. Everyone is heard. Opinions are respected. These are the preconditions of open debate. Beyond this, every student is asked to accept responsibility for their own and for the group's behaviour. Crucially, the society of the classroom is of the students' making. The teacher does not allow the class to cop out by shovelling all responsibility on to the one person with the positional power, whom they can then resist, fight and blame.

Third, **emotional intelligence**. Daniel Goleman's internationally renowned work has once more brought to prominence the importance of personal and social development. Being able to identify, name, describe and manage one's own feelings, being able to read and accommodate the emotions of others and developing key personal qualities such as perseverance and self-restraint are all hallmarks of an emotionally intelligent person. Such intelligence can be developed; it can be "taught". It will be easy to see how such learning can occur through the activities in this section.

All in all, then, the campaign for self-discipline and collective responsibility is well worth the effort.

Murder Hunt

It's a mystery. What kind of ground rules will the group create? The plot thickens ...

How?

This exercise is a version of "Broken Pieces" (page 78). It follows exactly the same instructions and rules. Explain to the class that a murder has been committed and it is their responsibility to solve the mystery. The answers to these six questions have to be found within the next fifteen minutes (adjust the time to suit the class):

1. Who was murdered?
2. Who committed the murder?
3. When?
4. Where?
5. What was the weapon?
6. Why?

The class sits round in one large circle and every student is given a clue card. The teacher explains the rules: "You have to keep your own card – you can't give or show your card to anyone; only one person in the group is allowed to write; you can't leave your places. When, as a group, you think you have all six answers, let me know and I'll tell you how many you've got right and wrong, not which ones. If you don't get them all right within fifteen minutes, I win!" From this point on the teacher doesn't intervene, no matter how badly the group does, unless violence is about to be committed! The teacher acts merely as timekeeper and gives the students a reminder halfway through.

These are the thirty clues that should be printed onto small cards:

- Only one bullet had been fired from Mr Azir's gun.
- Clare Smith saw Jamil go to Mr Azir's block of flats at 11.55 p.m.
- The workman had been with the company for years and was regarded as completely truthful and trustworthy.
- The workman said that he often saw Jamil's sister walking down the road with Andrew Scott.
- The workman reported to the police that he saw Jamil with no injuries at 11.50 p.m.
- Jamil had destroyed Mr Azir's business by stealing all his customers.
- Jamil's sister disappeared after the murder.
- The workman saw Jamil's sister go to Andrew Scott's house at 11.30 p.m.
- It was clear that Jamil's body had been dragged a long way.
- Clare Smith worked at the same school as Andrew Scott.
- Jamil's bloodstains were found in Andrew Scott's car.
- When he was found dead, Jamil had a bullet hole in his leg and a knife wound in his back.
- Andrew Scott's ex-wife was regarded as a very jealous woman.
- Mr Azir disappeared after the murder.
- Clare Smith often followed Jamil.
- Jamil's body was found in the park.
- The police were unable to find Andrew Scott after the murder.
- The workman saw Jamil go to Andrew Scott's house at 12.25 a.m.
- Mr Azir had told Jamil that he was going to kill him.
- Andrew Scott was a teacher who was very keen on outdoor pursuits.

- When the workman saw Jamil just after midnight, Jamil was bleeding but did not seem very badly hurt.
- Mr Azir shot at an "intruder" in his block of flats at midnight.
- Jamil had been dead for an hour when his body was found, the police doctor said.
- A knife with Andrew Scott's fingerprints on it was found in Clare Smith's garden.
- Jamil's bloodstains were found on the carpet outside Mr Azir's flat.
- Jamil's body was found at 1.30 a.m.
- In the local community Mr Azir was regarded as a cheerful and kind man.
- The bullet taken from Jamil's leg matched the gun owned by Mr Azir.
- The workman said that nobody left Andrew Scott's house between 12.25 a.m. and 12.45 a.m.
- Jamil had very strong religious beliefs.

Make up more clues if you need them. Consider asking one or two members of the class to be "Observer Servers" (page 185). The job of observers is to note, and report back to the class, helpful and unhelpful behaviours during the exercise. Whether you use observers or not, "Murder Hunt" is designed to lead into a discussion about group behaviour, and then to the formation of ground rules.

The answers

1. Victim: Jamil
2. Murderer: Andrew Scott
3. When: 12.30 a.m.
4. Where: Andrew Scott's house
5. Weapon: Knife
6. Why: It seems as though Jamil interfered in a relationship between his sister and Andrew Scott. Presumably they did him in so they could carry on undisturbed. (This question, by its very nature, cannot be answered with the same degree of certainty as the others.)

Application

This is a classic way to get students to appreciate the need for basic rules and procedures. More often than not, when its teacher's controlling hand is removed, a class behaves in a disorganised way. Left to their own devices, students generally have little understanding of how to give and take leadership, how to organise discussion, how to include everyone, how to process information collectively, how to make decisions, how to manage time. At worst, the group disintegrates – some people withdraw, others shout, others argue. Mocking, name calling, and wisecracking rise to the surface.

Therefore, the experience is likely to be frustrating for the students (and very frustrating for the watching teacher). However, this is the intention. The exercise creates the motivation to identify the current behavioural norms of the class, and to propose the changes needed if group work and interactive learning are to be successful in the future. A discussion with the students about these issues can now be precise and concrete – it is about a common experience that just happened.

"Framed" (page 182) and "Observer Servers" (page 185) can help with this debriefing process. The intention is to arrive at a new set of behaviours that everyone agrees to uphold. They might include:

- we will take turns
- we will let people finish what they are saying
- we will be quiet when people are speaking
- we will look at the person who is speaking

- we will cut out rude comments and gestures
- we will not make fun of anyone
- each of us will be able to sum up what other people have said

Sometimes, though, the students never get this far. They strongly resist the idea that they should take this amount of responsibility for their own behaviour. They fiercely cling to the belief that it's the teacher's job to make them behave. At this point, you will need to judge whether you have the skill and strength to persevere, or whether a combination of the students' upbringing, the culture of their local society, the modus operandi of your colleagues, the behaviour policy of the school … simply make it too hard a task.

It may be that back-pedalling is required and a number of preliminary steps need to be taken, such as increasing your own assertiveness (page 199), changing classroom language (page 307), campaigning to raise students' self-esteem (page 289). Beyond this it will be important to raise self-discipline as a whole-school issue and seek agreement across the staff about "new" approaches to behaviour management.

Ultimately, "Murder Hunt" is daring because it allows the truth about students' behaviour to surface. It confronts students with the challenge to be self-disciplined, and it takes away their usual dependency on carrots and sticks, which means asking some of them to change the habits of a lifetime.

Why do it?

- The overriding purpose of "Murder Hunt" is to establish agreed behaviours that support self-esteem and collaboration. It confronts students with the idea that they should accept both personal and corporate responsibility, self-discipline and the creation of a self-regulating classroom society. Such learning can occur only experientially.
- Secondarily, the activity exercises a wide range of thinking skills, especially as only one person is allowed to write and so much has to be held and processed in the mind.

Variations

1. Instead of leaving the students to conduct the exercise on their own, and probably do a bad job of it, lead it for them. Take the "chair", demonstrating the processes of good group leadership and getting them to adopt the desired behaviours such as taking turns, listening, inviting contributions, summing up, building on each other's suggestions, giving way, being persistent, keeping their eye on time, checking that all information has been gathered. Give them a good and positive experience. Then, ask them to adopt the behaviours that worked well, and to take responsibility for ensuring that they happen even when the teacher isn't in charge.
2. Instead of running "Murder Hunt" as a whole-class exercise, do it in small groups. In this case each student will have a number of cards that they hold close to their chest, just like a hand of playing cards.

Framed

It's not very comfortable being framed. But sometimes you just have to face up to what you have, or haven't, done. Still, you can always do it better next time.

How?

1. Have the students carry out a **collaborative** exercise. This may be a genuine learning activity about the topic in hand using "Delegation" (page 91), "Scrambled Groups" (page 150), "Corporate Identity" (page 89), "Ambassadors" (page 65), "Quick on the Draw" (page 145) or "Still Image" (page 158), for instance. Or it could be an artificial exercise designed to test cooperative behaviours. "Murder Hunt" (page 179) is ideal for this.

2. Then ask the students to reflect on the experience and examine their behaviours. The first step is for them to recall what happened. This might be done by hearing feedback from "Observer Servers" (page 185), or by watching a video recording of the lesson (ideal: there's no argument, the camera doesn't lie), or by listening to an audio recording of themselves. Otherwise students' and teacher's memories will have to be relied upon.

3. Whatever recall device is used, ask students individually to record their own and other students' helpful and unhelpful behaviours in this simple frame. The rule is: name behaviours, don't name names.

What I did that helped the group	What I did that hindered the group
What other people did that helped	**What other people did that hindered**

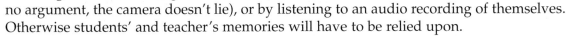

4. Discussion follows. It is crucial that no one be criticised. Don't focus on the past (What should we have done?), but on the future (What should we do differently from now on?). Be tough. Don't let students play down the damaging effect of behaviours. Insist that improvements will be identified and agreed on. Explain why. It's best to tackle *whole-group* issues first, looking to secure everyone's commitment to a few general changes. For example: "Everyone will speak one at a time."

5. Individuals can then be encouraged to make *personal* changes: for example, "I will ask people what they think more often" or "I will not interrupt".

6. The new whole-group "rules" should be immediately written large and posted on the classroom wall, so they are in the students' faces for the foreseeable future.

7. Both the corporate and the personal agreements can be recorded by everyone on their "team action plan" and, after a few more lessons, an assessment of progress can be carried out. To do this, set up another cooperative whole-class or small-group exercise. After discussion everyone marks with a cross on the right-hand side of the sheet the progress made – or not.

TEAM ACTION PLAN

Progress

As a whole group we agree to . . .

	No different than before	We've kept the agreement completely

_____   ⌊_____⌋

_____   ⌊_____⌋

_____   ⌊_____⌋

_____   ⌊_____⌋

Personally I agree to . . .

_____   ⌊_____⌋

_____   ⌊_____⌋

_____   ⌊_____⌋

_____   ⌊_____⌋

Name: _____

Signed: _____   **Date:** _____

Application

Vital foundation work with any class in any subject.

Why do it?

- It's pragmatic. A great deal of time is often wasted during group work – students not taking part, annoying each other, being marginalised, retaliating. Likewise, whole-class activities are often sabotaged by unthinking, clumsy or malicious behaviour. It is more efficient to tackle these issues up front, in advance, than it is to fight a running battle during lessons.

- Students keep their heads down and play safe if they suspect that they might be "got" for taking part. Few students admit this, but brain scans show that the blood flow to the ancient instinctive parts of the brain is automatically and instantly increased when a person feels threatened. This tends to trigger survival (fight, flight, freeze and flock) behaviours and reduces rational thought. So, to maximise participation and therefore learning, it is vital that students regard the classroom to be emotionally and psychologically safe – they know that they will be protected from each other's hostility. They are confident that they will not be ignored, name-called, mocked, belittled, laughed at or joked about for having an idea, or attempting an answer, or volunteering, or being keen. Until these norms are proven (and students will test them!), the teacher is likely to struggle to get widespread participation, which means that a lot of *Toolkit*-type ideas will collapse.

- Making a big deal about interpersonal behaviours and their effect on feelings raises the status of emotional intelligence. This whole aspect of being human is hugely underplayed in most schools these days, where pursuit of narrow attainment still tends to dominate proceedings. Only if they are able to recognise and manage emotions can students be fully successful within themselves and with other people. This is most likely to happen if the key concepts of emotional intelligence are explained and *lived* in classrooms.

- Social inclusion can become a reality only if hostile and excluding behaviours are eliminated.

Variation

Instead of students recording helpful and unhelpful behaviours in the "frame" individually, ask them to call them out and you build up a whole class record on the blackboard, whiteboard or overhead projector.

Observer Servers

Out of sight, out of mind. It's easy for everyone to slip back into old ways, unless, that is, you have an Observer Server.

How?

1. Set the students a collaborative task, either in small groups or as a whole class. It's important that they have to work together. It's best if this is a genuine task, a natural development of the ongoing topic, though an artificial task will do: make a bridge out of a few sheets of newspaper, some straws and a length of string; or drop an egg from a second-floor window with a device that will enable it to land without breaking, for example. Ask for one or two volunteers to opt out of the task and be "Observer Servers". Explain that this involves watching what goes on during the activity and reporting back to everyone at the end.

2. The observers look at how well the students work together. They might be given an open brief: "Write down everything you see and hear that helps the group to get the job done and everything you see and hear that undermines and spoils their efforts." The rule is: just name the behaviours, don't name the people.

3. Or they might have more structured questions to answer such as:

- Did you notice any of the following behaviours (and, if so, what effect did they have)?

  - interrupting
  - inviting someone to contribute
  - shouting out
  - ignoring
  - making fun
  - adding to someone else's idea
  - contradicting
  - asking someone a question
  - summing up
  - congratulating
  - being rude
  - withdrawing
  - giving way to someone else
  - standing up for yourself

- What were people doing apart from the job they were supposed to be doing?
- Were there any leaders? What did they do?
- How did they become leaders?
- How equally did people take part? What effect did this have on getting the job done?
- What did the teacher do to help or hinder the group?
- What advice would you give to the class and the teacher for next time?

4. Ensure that there is enough time left at the end for the observers to feed back to the class and for discussion about lessons learned. It is easy for this to be done badly as many students are not used to giving and receiving feedback constructively. If you have time, train them; if not, try one or two rules that might help:

    -   Observers do not name students, they just describe behaviours.
    -   Observers simply say what they saw and heard.
    -   To avoid any hint of accusation, feedback sentences begin with "I" (for example, "I saw …", "I noticed …", "I observed …", "I heard …"), not "You" ("You did such-and-such" or "You didn't do …").
    -   If observers give an opinion or advice, the sentence begins with "I think …" or "In my opinion …" rather than "You should …"
    -   In fact, observers never use "should", "ought", "must", "have to".
    -   The class and the teacher do not interrupt the observers – there will be time for discussion later.
    -   In any discussion that follows, speakers begin all sentences with "*I*" (for example, "I disagree …" or "I'd like to add …" or "I saw something different …")
    -   Actually, there's no need to persuade anybody. If you don't agree with some of the feedback from the observers, just put it in your mental dustbin.

5. To make best use of the feedback, play "Stop-Start-Continue". Ask each student to decide on one behaviour they will stop, one they will start and one they will continue doing. These can be written in personal journals or at the back of their diaries.
6. You could end with a "Round" (page 196) of "What I personally intend to improve next time is …"

Applications

-   Any class, any subject. Observers provide a mirror for the class. Use the strategy to create ground rules by highlighting what needs to be done differently.
-   Refresh ground rules by pointing out the difference between what was previously agreed and what is actually happening now.

Why do it?

-   With so much pressure to cover content these days, it is easy to neglect the process of learning in general and the quality of group interactions in particular. However, we know that for optimum learning to occur the brain requires a sense of security, wellbeing and the absence of threat – emotional, psychological and physical.
-   The "Observer Server" strategy promotes the habits of self-appraisal and personal reflection. These are lifelong learning skills.
-   The technique also helps to establish the skills of giving and receiving feedback. As students grow older they will discover that these life skills are crucial to the health of all substantial personal and professional relationships.

Variations

1. Use a video recording of the activity to feed back to the class rather than human observers.
2. Swap observers partway through the activity or lesson, so you get more people involved and more perspectives.
3. Make the role of observer server a high-status one: to undertake the role, you must be willing to catch up with the classwork later! It's not a cop out.

Learning Listening

This is an effective and fun way to get people to listen. I said, this is an effective and fun way to get people to listen.

How?

This activity is conducted over four rounds. Organise people to sit in pairs facing each other. Ask each pair to decide who is A and who is B.

Round One

As and Bs are to speak to each other simultaneously, without hesitation, repetition or deviation, nonstop, for two minutes. Ask the class for a topic or give a suggestion (e.g. favourite TV programmes, music, places, holidays, food, clothes, sports ...). While talking nonstop, each partner also has to listen to what the other is saying!

Debrief. How did you get on? How did you feel? How successful were you at listening and speaking simultaneously? How often does this occur in real life? When do you see people talking *at* each other rather than listening *to* each other?

Round Two

The As speak for two minutes about a new topic (e.g. family and friends or what I'd do with £10,000), while Bs turn to stone, showing no movement or response of any kind, not even in the eyes. Before they begin, ask the statues to get comfortable and look just past their partner's face at a point on the other side of the room.

Debrief the feelings of being completely ignored, the effect this has (for example, drying up, wanting to thump the statue ...) and the occasions when this kind of thing happens in everyday life.

Round Three

Bs now have their turn to speak for two minutes (e.g. people, places, events and things that matter to me or my favourite memories) while As use subtle behaviours to show that they are not really paying attention (e.g. glance at watch, yawn, make eyes glaze over, look over speaker's shoulder). Alternatively you can ask As to try and steal the show and take over the conversation with comments like "Oh yes, of course that happened to me ..." and "Yes, I know, that reminds me of ..."

Debrief, focusing on the feelings of not being *really* heard. How can you tell? What did you do about it? When does it happen, both in and out of school, that people are being polite, but not really attentive?

Interval

Based on the first three rounds of poor listening, ask the class to list the hallmarks of quality listening. What do good listeners do? For example:

- maintain eye contact
- respond nonverbally as appropriate using nods, frowns, smiles, quizzical looks … (this is technically known as mirroring)
- use grunts, yups, ahas and other verbals to signal their continued attention
- at intervals, sum up and feed back what has been said (this is the acid test of listening)

Active listening does not involve asking questions, except for clarification.

Round Four

Pairs practise active listening of this quality with topics that are fairly serious and personal (e.g. what I'd like to do with my life or what I worry about or what I think about God, education, ghosts, politics, aliens, life after death …). It is important that both A and B get a chance to speak and listen and have enough time to do the job well, say seven or eight minutes each. At the end of each turn, the listener sums up what their partner said, but they were not allowed to make notes as they went along! This really brings home to students the degree of concentration needed to listen properly and take in what people say. This last round also gives students experience of the feel-good factor, the feeling of worth, the boost to self-esteem, generated by someone paying them exclusive and total attention.

Debrief. Ask about successes and difficulties. What were the feelings? When is it important to listen properly – with friends, family, in class? Finally, ask students to consider making quality listening a feature of every lesson. Ask them to commit themselves to making it the "rule".

Applications

- Use it to make or refresh **ground rules** with a class. This is the main purpose of the activity.
- Use it to open up discussion or to conduct **revision** in any subject – the topics talked about would be relevant to the syllabus.
- Vital as a foundation for **PSHE** and **tutorial** work, central to citizenship and crucial to group-based and interactive learning in any subject.
- Teach listening as part of a conflict resolution strategy, such **as peer mediation**. Most arguments are resolved by first asking students to listen to each other and feed back to each other what they have said.
- At an advanced level the exercise could be conducted in a **modern foreign language**.

Why do it?

- Listening has an immediate and positive impact on self-esteem. People who are genuinely heard universally say that they feel valued and respected. Self-esteem cannot be raised superficially through smiley faces and the like, but by allowing people to feel that they matter enough to be listened to.
- Listening is the basis of quality discussion, negotiation, conflict resolution, peer assessment, decision making and the tutoring process.

- Listening is therefore the feature of classroom life most generally required for nondidactic methods to work. Many teachers feel confident about trying more adventurous techniques only once self-discipline (through firm ground rules based on listening) has been established. Likewise, most students want to feel the protection of firm ground rules before they will participate in "risky" learning activities.
- Listening is the life skill, at the core of all personal, professional and civic relationships. If you value achievement beyond exam success, teach and model listening.

Variation

Begin the Interval stage by asking for a volunteer to help you demonstrate active listening. They talk, you listen. Show how to give total attention, putting everything else out of your mind, and demonstrate all the verbal and nonverbal behaviours. Ask the rest of the class to watch and then list the skills you use.

Sabotage

Poor behaviour wrecks learning. Here's a nifty way to sabotage the sabotage.

How?

1. Write the word "sabotage" on the board and ask the students what it means. Provide dictionaries if necessary and hold a discussion to ensure that everyone gets the idea of subtly wrecking, spoiling or undermining.

2. Ask the students in pairs to list all the ways in which learning is being (or could be) sabotaged by members of this class. They may need some encouragement to be honest and should not write students' names – just list the behaviours.

3. Students then take turns to call out behaviours from their lists and you write them on the board.

4. Now be open about how difficult it is for the teacher to control all these. In some cases they're difficult to pin on anyone, sometimes they're behind the teacher's back, under the desk, outside the classroom … Therefore it's up to the students to decide: do they want to carry on these behaviours and spoil their own and other people's learning or cut out these behaviours and do well? The responsibility is actually theirs. Discuss the consequences of this decision and give the upbeat message that you want them all to succeed and that you bet they all want to too, secretly. Allow some discussion. Resist their attempts to shovel all the responsibility back onto you.

5. Ask which of the listed behaviours do most damage. Select the top two or three. Challenge the class to tackle these first. Suggest that they agree with each other to cut these out from now on.

6. If agreement can be reached, write up the new "expectations" (avoid the word "rules" if you can) and display them large in the classroom. Resist the idea of punishments, even though the class might want them. Instead, establish the idea that it is the joint responsibility of teacher and students to remind and challenge each other.

7. If agreement cannot be reached easily, suggest that the class try cutting out specified behaviours for a trial period, after which the effects of the experiment will be reviewed.

Application

To create workable ground rules directly and quickly with any class, in any subject.

Why do it?

● It locates the responsibility for students' behaviour where it actually belongs – with the students.

● It makes sharp points about personal and collective responsibility which are the stuff of citizenship.

● It makes equally strong points about life being a series of choices and consequences, that no one can escape responsibility for their own actions. It uncompromisingly points out the immaturity of looking for people to rescue others from their actions (expecting the teacher to hand out punishments, for example). Consequently, it deals with some tough aspects of emotional intelligence.

- The teacher's openness and honesty usually result in more respect for the teacher and a more wholesome relationship with the class.
- If it works, it reduces the teacher's stress as she is no longer having to control the class single-handedly.

Variation

Give students behaviours on cards to rank, rather than expect them to come up with their own lists from scratch.

Games

Life's a funny thing. Well, it could be. Here's a way of creating some serious rules with some serious fun.

Classroom games are currently out of fashion, which is a pity. So much potential benefit is lost. Well-chosen games can:

- create more flexible working relationships between students
- break the ice between students and teacher
- raise or lower energy levels
- refocus attention
- practise a range of thinking skills painlessly

But the particular use of games described here is their ability to create an acceptance of basic ground rules. The following four games are just examples (many more can be found in collections such as the *Gamesters' Handbooks 1, 2* and *3*,[2] Tim Bond's *Games for Social and Life Skills*,[3] *Serious Fun*[4] by Dynamix and Mary Hohenstein's *A Compact Encyclopedia of Games for People of all Ages*[5]). Such games effectively alter the dynamics of the classroom and usually create a greater willingness to learn and behave. These benefits can be increased substantially if time is taken to debrief the experience with the class. There are two levels of debrief:

Level 1

Debrief the **effects of the experience**. Prompts might include:

- Why do you think I chose this game?
- What have we learned from it?
- What real-life issues are mirrored in this game?
- How can games like this affect the way you feel about being in this classroom?
- How can games like this alter our relationships with each other/the way we see each other?
- What might be the benefits of playing such games in the future?

Level 2

Debrief the **workings of the game** and their transferability to regular classroom life. Prompts might include:

- How did the game work?
- What can it teach us about the way we operate in this classroom?
- What part did rules play in the success and enjoyment of the game?
- What effect would/did people breaking the rules have on the game?
- How could the rules be improved?
- How could we improve our rules to make sure that our classroom is purposeful and fun at the same time?

Tick Tock

1. All sit in a circle, including the teacher, who holds two objects (for example, a felt pen and a ruler), one in each hand.
2. The teacher turns to the student on her right (Student 1) and offers the object in her right hand saying, "This is a Tick". Student 1 says, "A what?" and the teacher repeats, "A Tick". Only then may Student 1 take the object.
3. Student 1 then immediately turns to Student 2, saying, "This is a Tick". Student 2 asks, "A what?" to Student 1, who repeats the question to the teacher. The teacher answers, "A Tick" to Student 1, who in turn says, "A Tick" to Student 2. Only then may Student 2 take the object.
4. Student 2 offers the Tick in the same way to Student 3 and so on round the circle. Each time, the question "A what?" must pass from student to student back to the teacher and each time the answer "A Tick" must go out from the teacher along the chain.
5. Once the group has had a practice, the teacher explains the challenge: "The idea is to pass the Tick right round the circle at the same time as passing the Tock right round the circle the other way. Eventually I should get them both back."
6. So, the game starts for real. The teacher sends the Tick out to the right and the Tock straightaway to the left. If all goes well, the teacher sits there sounding like a clock while the crossover point really throws a spanner in the works!

This game can be a bit slow to get going with a large class, so explain to two students how to lead it, divide the class into two circles, have two separate games going and you supervise.

Key debrief points might include: team work; everyone playing their part; sticking to rules and routines; supporting each other when stuck; having fun but avoiding the temptation to make fun of others. In addition, this is an example of mental exercise, stimulates concentration and prepares the mind for further learning.

Giants, Dwarfs and Wizards

1. The teacher divides the class into two equal(ish) teams a couple of metres apart, perhaps separated by a length of rope or masking tape or a chalk line.
2. The teacher explains: "You live in a world inhabited by warring giants, dwarfs and wizards. Giants always beat dwarfs by stamping on them. Wizards naturally beat giants by casting spells, and dwarfs beat wizards by, I'm told, tickling their legs. You're about to do battle with each other. Your team must decide, collectively, which of three beings you are. Everyone in your team must agree to be the same and you must keep your joint decision secret – whatever you do, don't let the other team know!"
3. The teams huddle together to make their decisions, then line up and face each other.
4. The teacher continues: "On the count of three you will all display what you've decided to become. Giants will stand on tiptoes with their hands stretched above their heads. Dwarfs will crouch down and wizards will step forward with their spell-casting hands outstretched."
5. The teacher counts, the teams display their characters and points are awarded: two for a win, one each for a draw. Further rounds follow and the first team to ten points wins.

The debrief can include a discussion about competition versus cooperation (both elements are present in the game), making and upholding group decisions, inclusion, exclusion and the various us-and-them divisions in the classroom.

Caterpillar

1. Everyone sits in a tight circle with the sides of their chairs touching. One person volunteers to be "on" and stands in the middle, leaving her chair free.
2. At the word "go", everyone shuffles round clockwise with their bottoms sliding from chair to chair as fast as possible. While the person in the middle desperately tries to sit back down on any seat, the rest keep the motion going, so there's never a chair free.
3. If the circle is too slow moving, try two spare chairs instead of one. Become adventurous and have two people in the middle, then go for three people with three spare chairs. Upgrade to four as the game builds momentum.
4. If a person who's "on" does manage to sit down, then someone else takes their place in the middle.
5. To add spice, whenever the teacher claps her hand, the movement changes direction.

Lots of debrief potential here about being left out, ganging up, in-crowds and out-crowds, humiliation and the potential escalation of conflict.

Control Tower

1. Clear the desks and chairs. Ask for two volunteers, one to be the control tower, the other to be the aeroplane.
2. The control tower stands on a chair in one corner of the classroom and the plane, blindfolded, stands in the opposite corner awaiting instructions.
3. The rest of the class clutter the runway (the rest of the classroom) by standing one arm's length away from one another with their arms by their sides and feet together in total silence so they don't give their position away.
4. The control tower's job is to give oral instructions to guide the plane down the runway to the tower without its hitting any human obstacle. "Right a bit, stop, two steps forward ..." and so on. One penalty point for each obstacle touched. Three penalty points and the plane crashes.
5. After the first go, new volunteers are sought. Each time there's a new control tower and aeroplane, all the obstacles change position.

As for debrief, this game works because one person is allowed to speak and everyone else is quiet. An obvious lead into listening, taking turns and other classroom ground rules.

Maintenance

Maintain your sanity with these six and a half easy-to-use techniques for reinforcing listening skills and maintaining ground rules.

Even when classroom rules have been successfully created with a class through experiential means, behavioural norms are not significantly changed without continued effort. Agreeing ground rules with students is only the start of the process. In secondary schools, when you see a class at intervals and sometimes only once a week, it is hard to build momentum. Changes secured in one lesson will often be reversed in the interim and behaviours will then be back to square one next time. This sounds depressing, but with determined optimism and the skilful use of some pragmatic techniques it is possible to create in just one classroom norms that might not apply elsewhere in the school.

Use whatever means you can to support the cause. For example, in addition to modelling the key behaviours yourself, pay attention to seating arrangements. Are students looking at the back of one another's head? Setting desks out so they form three sides of a square creates a common arena for speaking and listening. Alternatively, pushing desks to the sides of the classroom means that students can turn their chairs inwards for inputs, discussion and activities and can turn their chairs to the desks facing the walls for individual work. Another standard layout would be to have desks pushed together in blocks to form working groups of four, six or eight students.

Naturally, it's important to arrange the space to suit the activities. This will often mean moving the furniture several times a week, a day, or even within one lesson! Students can help and are often willing to come in a few minutes before the end of break or lunchtime. An outgoing class can quickly rearrange desks and chairs for the next group in the final couple of minutes before the bell. Or an incoming class can be challenged to get the furniture reorganised within two minutes, following a plan you've drawn on the board.

Now that the rearrangement of furniture is an established principle, use pragmatic techniques that encourage, or even require, the new behaviours. Here are some suggestions.

Circle

This refers to an open circle of chairs with everyone, including the teacher, taking part.

The aim is for the circle to be a place where people can speak freely, ask and answer questions, express opinions, suggest solutions, share feelings and contribute ideas – or not – without fear of ridicule, marginalisation or punishment. It is an ancient and universal meeting format. There are several reasons for using a circle:

- It is a powerful statement in itself about making the group feel united: "We are each responsible for this group's learning and behaviour. We are in this together."
- It shows that the teacher is flexible enough to adopt different roles – in a circle the teacher is more of a supporter and tutor than a deliverer and controller.
- A circle is open, even exposing, and it consequently challenges students to be more relaxed and confident with each other.
- A circle encourages participation from the whole group – there's no hiding place.
- A circle is practical. It creates an open space for games, for drama and for many of the learning activities described in *The Teacher's Toolkit*.

One or two practicalities. Bags and coats should be left outside the circle, perhaps on the desks that have been pushed to the side of the room. Naturally, students will immediately want to sit with their friends. Initially, this might not be a bad idea as it provides familiarity in an unfamiliar setting. Before long, though, mix them up. This can be done randomly by giving out shuffled playing cards, one per person, then asking students to sort themselves into runs, flushes, suits … Or by playing games such as "Fruit Bowl", "Move to the Left" and "The Sun Shines On", that appear in *Gamesters' Handbooks 1, 2* and *3, A Guide to Student-Centred Learning*[6] or *The Student-Centred School.*[7] Often in a cramped space students get left outside the circle, or the circle takes on an amoeba shape around science benches, for example, with people in odd nooks and crannies. It's better to have two concentric circles with everyone involved than to have a few students marginalised. Finally, some students, out of nervousness or devilment, may deliberately push their chairs out of the circle. They should be challenged to come back in before proceedings continue.

The circle is an ideal way to begin a lesson – to conduct a learning review, the explanation of learning objectives, connecting the lesson with previous and forthcoming learning experiences, re-establishing the big picture. It is also an ideal way to end a lesson – to conduct a plenary and a check on progress.

Round

This is a time when everyone in the circle has an opportunity to speak, in turn, without being forced to do so.

Explain the **rules**: "Anyone may start, then each person will have a chance to speak in turn round the circle. No one may comment, verbally or nonverbally, negatively or, positively on what anyone says; no one may interrupt. Anyone can say 'pass' when it's their turn." Explain the **spirit**: "This is an opportunity to listen to each other. Discussion can come later." Decide whether the Round will go clockwise or anticlockwise and ask for someone to begin.

The Round provides a structured and calm way of encouraging students to speak to each other and the teacher. No one has to fight for "airtime", because everyone is guaranteed a fair share. It encourages participation by removing the fear of being ridiculed or ignored; everyone will be heard. It challenges shy and retiring students to speak by momentarily putting them in the spotlight and presenting the expectation that they will have something to say. The Round acknowledges that everyone has an equally valid and valuable contribution to make. Thereby, it contributes to raising self-esteem. Use it to find out what students know about a topic in advance, or what they have learned afterwards. Use it to get students' opinions, thoughts and feelings into the open. Use it to generate ideas, to air grievances or to make decisions. This is of course the basis of "Circle Time", which has become a successful and important feature of many British primary schools.

Variation: Paper Round

Useful when class members are not confident enough to express personal opinions in public, perhaps because the material is sensitive or because the students are very shy.

1. Give everyone a piece of paper and a pencil.
2. Ask for contributions to be written individually and privately but not named.
3. Papers are folded, collected in a container and shaken.
4. Pass the container round the circle, each person taking out one piece of paper.
5. Take turns to read the papers out loud, each person reading the comment as if it were his or her own.

Conch

Choose an object (a felt pen, small box, ruler, ball …) to use as a conch (the idea of "Conch" is taken from the novel, *Lord of the Flies*). Explain that a person can speak only when they are holding the conch. When a speaker has finished, she passes the conch directly to the next person who wants to speak.

This usually brings order to a discussion. It's amazing how much authority the innocent object can have! A single conch can be used in whole-class discussions, two conches used in formal debates (one for each side) or several conches used for several small groups. With younger students, use a "magic microphone".

Tokenism

Give everyone three tokens (buttons, counters, pieces of card …). Each time a person makes a constructive contribution to the discussion by making a point or asking a question he surrenders a token, putting it in a box in the middle of the circle. Vary the number of tokens per person according to the size of the group and nature of the discussion.

This simple device starts to equalise participation, to limit the garrulous and encourage the shy. If someone is out of tokens and desperate to speak, they can buy back a token by summing up the main points of the discussion so far.

Sum Up and Speak Up

When a person wants to contribute to a discussion, he must first sum up what the previous speaker said and then given his own opinion: "So-and-so said …"; "I think …". Every so often the teacher shouts, "Sum up and speak up" – whereupon someone volunteers to sum up the main points of the discussion so far, drawing applause from the whole group.

Randomiser

The teacher prepares two identical sets of cards (playing cards or handmade numbered cards). One set is shuffled and distributed to the class, one per person. The other is retained by the teacher, shuffled publicly and "cut" by a student. The teacher turns the top card, revealing who is to speak first. When the first speaker is finished, the next card is turned. This second person must sum up what the first speaker said and then make her own contribution. The student with the third card must sum up what the second speaker said before adding his own comments, and so on. As no one knows who's next, everyone must listen.

Those who have gone first might be tempted to breathe a sigh of relief and sit back, believing they've done their job. However, turned cards are placed at the bottom of the pack and the teacher continually shuffles the deck – just to keep everyone on their toes!

Although tough, this process is usually accepted as totally fair. It works particularly well when a sequence of ideas (such as steps in an experiment, or historical events, or a story) is being created or recalled. It is also good for opening discussion of sensitive issues (for example, in religious education or personal, social and health education), when students might be reluctant to speak out. It is also an excellent way of checking understanding towards the end of a lesson or of conducting revision.

All the above techniques, then, are designed to train students to behave civilly towards each other. They are essential to the teaching of citizenship. they are also fundamental to the creation of a genuinely inclusive classroom.

For some students, however, and for some entire classes, these strategies are not enough. The behavioural habits and attitudes they bring into the classroom require other skills of the teacher. Maintenance techniques help, but work only if the students recognise that the teacher is sufficiently strong. Strength is demonstrated through assertiveness (page 199). It is sometimes tempting to resort to threats and punishments, but these serve only to undermine the cause of self-discipline in the end. Assertiveness is rooted in the teacher's unshakable self-certainty and perpetually optimistic belief that students can change their behaviour. It does not depend on the ultimately diminishing effects of behaviourism.

Assertiveness

When the going gets tough, the tough get assertive.

Even with well-made ground rules, a teacher determined to uphold them and a range of "maintenance" devices in place, there will still times when students are naughty. Then what does the teacher do? Given sufficient will and skill, both low-level disruption and more serious disturbances can be countered with assertiveness.

In the face of naughty behaviour, it is tempting for any teacher immediately to threaten punishment: "If I catch you doing that one more time, I'll …" This reaction is understandable given that most of us have been brought up with popularised behaviourism. The problem is that punishments, *and rewards* for that matter, keep students dependent on external motivators. Whenever they are used, long-term losses are traded for short-term gains. The development of self-awareness and self-discipline is sacrificed for the sake of immediate compliance. This is expedient, but not ultimately beneficial to the students, their future relationships or society in general.

In any society, behaviours have consequences and students need to learn the dynamics of social cause and effect. This, after all, is a fundamental part of citizenship. However, negative consequences imposed quickly by the teacher actually take away the need for the student to face the issue, address the behaviour, make choices and take personal responsibility for actions. The endurance of the punishment is often regarded, by students and teachers alike, as absolving the student. Punishments do not generally change behaviour at depth.

What's more, punishments can contribute to the widening of a gulf between teacher and students. In some schools, the us-and-them culture reaches a point where there's a big payoff for being punished – students are cheered and applauded by their peers as they are sent out of the classroom, for instance.

The more productive path is that of assertiveness. The teacher uses a set of skills to confront students and challenge them strongly to change their behaviour. This approach has a double benefit: it deals effectively with the behaviour and role-models a crucial set of life skills to students (especially if the teacher takes some time to debrief encounters with students). In the cut and thrust of regular classroom and corridor life, quick-fire assertiveness is often required – there's no time for lengthy discussion. Wherever possible, though, it is desirable for the teacher to look for opportunities to address the situation or issue fully. This is particularly important where misbehaviour is persistent or repeated.

Quick-fire, **regular** and **full-length** versions of assertiveness are modelled below.

Such skills do not come easily. They can be learned, but carry conviction only if they are rooted in two inner qualities: first, the teacher's self-belief, in other words her certainty that she possesses sufficient personal power to handle difficult situations; and, second, her fundamental desire only to change the student's behaviour, not to humiliate the student. In a *truly* assertive approach, students' behaviour is dealt with by teachers' *skills*, not by a system. Individual teachers take high levels of responsibility for resolving conflict, settling disruption, keeping students on task, managing strong feelings and maintaining safety. They rely entirely on their assertiveness, conflict-resolution and mediation skills.

Understandably, many teachers feel uncomfortable with this. They feel inadequate and vulnerable. So it is helpful to envisage a plan of campaign in which there are fallback positions. What if the teacher's attempts at assertiveness do not work, owing to lack of experience, or lack of confidence, or the student's downright determination to be difficult? Warnings and consequences then perhaps do have their place, *after* assertive efforts have been exhausted. This creates the prospect of a three-zone approach: the teacher takes the misbehaving student through an Assertive Zone, followed by a Warning Zone, and finally a Consequence Zone. This should provide a sufficiently strong framework to support less experienced teachers, but give enough room to manoeuvre to the more experienced. The overall picture looks something like this:

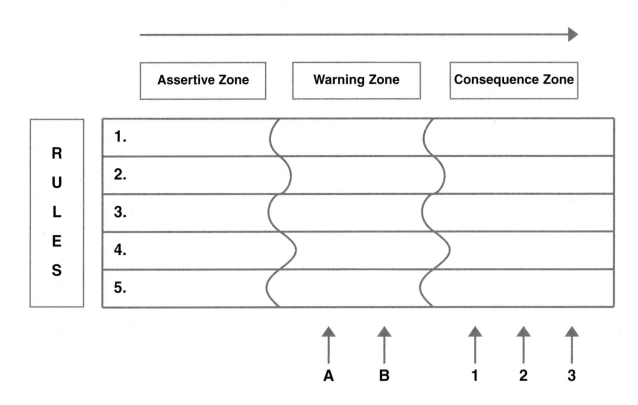

All successful behaviour management depends on a few positively stated, crystal-clear rules. They work least well where they are imposed, and best where their benefit has been understood and accepted by the class. Some of the methods for achieving this are described earlier in this section: "Murder Hunt", "Framed", "Observer Servers", "Learning Listening", "Sabotage" and "Games". In the above diagram, the rules are the rows. They run through the whole plan. They are consistent. Five is about the most people can concentrate on at any one time, beyond this the plan starts to feel overwhelming. They can of course be changed later. As some behaviours are improved, others can be brought into the frame. The word "rules" isn't ideal, though it is often the students' favourite – perhaps "standards" or "expectations" would be better. Also, for best results, make sure that the students understand the whole plan of campaign. Let them know the 'big picture' of your approach. Explain the zones. Tell them how you will operate, what they can expect and in what order. Make sure that the rules, the warning system and the scale of consequences are written up large on the classroom wall.

The first base in tackling behaviour that is contrary to the rules is to be **assertive**. The skills are described below. The attitude that you bring to this is crucial. Intend to resolve the issue by assertiveness, intend to stay in the **Assertive Zone** as long as possible. Believe that your strength and skills will be sufficient.

However, if the behaviour is not modified through assertiveness, then reluctantly move into the **Warning Zone**. This is the second base, where you warn the student that consequences will be applied if the behaviour continues. It is often helpful to have two levels of warning, such as yellow and red cards, or name noted, then ticked. It's vital that you let the student know when they are in the Warning Zone and exactly where they stand in the sequence of events. Only then can they be expected to make choices. You don't have to make a song and dance about the warnings. They can be done discreetly by catching a student's eye and showing a card or jotting their name on a piece of paper without interrupting the flow of teaching. The key is to keep offering choices: "This is what will happen next, to avoid it you must …"; "At this moment you have a choice, you can …, in which case this will happen, or you can …"

If the behaviour persists, the third base is the application of **consequences**. At this point it is important that consequences be scaled. If a major consequence is applied too early, there's nowhere left for you to go. First consequences might include a five-minute discussion with the teacher about the work or the behaviour at break or after school (long thumb-twiddling detentions are usually counterproductive), or a piece of learning to be done overnight for a personal verbal test next day. Beyond this, schools normally have their own procedures for referral, contacting parents – and worse! If a consequence has been "deserved", don't back-track later in the lesson. Don't let students off for subsequently behaving well – this will make it much more difficult to be assertive next time. The students will know that you don't really mean it.

The other side of the coin – rewarding students for good behaviour – does not feature in this plan. Such bribery has no place in the development of personal responsibility. Instead, good behaviour is regarded as the norm, it is expected. The positive reasons for behaving sociably are frequently explained and the incentives for behaving well are simply the feelings of personal and social wellbeing and the conducive learning conditions that are created. In addition, students are given lots of acknowledgment and recognition from the teacher for a whole range of learning achievements.

Having located assertiveness within a supportive behaviour plan, let's have a closer look at the skills involved, as, with trepidation, we enter the Assertive Zone.

Quick-fire assertiveness

This short version of assertiveness is designed for situations that have to be tackled quickly because of safety, or because the moment will be lost, or because disruption has to be minimised, or because the teacher is in a hurry.

Step 1: Take an assertive stance

This is crucial. Body language and tone of voice are much stronger communicators of inner strength and intentions than the actual words you use.

- Stand upright, face the class or individual and make eye contact.
- Do not invade the student's personal space, it is likely to invite a "reptilian response".
- Do not look furious or outraged. Do not say, "How dare you …?" or "You've done it this time!"
- Do not appear to lose your temper. Do not say, "I'm fed up with you" or "I've had enough" or "Right, that's it!"

201

- Do not threaten. Do not say, "If you don't pack it in, I'll …" or "If you do that once more, I'll …"
- Believe yourself to be in total control.

Step 2: State the change

- Firmly state what you want the student to do or to stop doing.
- If the situation allows it, begin with the phrase "I want …" Add urgency by concluding with "*now*".
- Make the request specific. For example, "I want you to stop running – *now*" or "I want you to put your gum in the bin – *now*" or "I want you to stand here *right now* and don't move".

Step 3: Repeat and strengthen the change

- Restate what you want the student to do or stop doing, but escalate the level of instruction.
- Replace "I want you to stand here" with "I am telling you to stand here".
- Beyond this, replace "I am telling you to stand here" with a command: "Stand here. Do it *now!*"
- A teacher who moves too quickly to the command level, who overstates the command or who seems to have lost her temper can appear weak in the eyes of the students. At this point a student might take you on.
- There's no way back once you've got to the command level. The student either obeys you or defies you. Compliance or confrontation are the only outcomes. Use command only if you are sure that your force of personality will win through, or your status in the student's eyes is high, or you are willing to go through with the consequences of being defied.

Step 4: Divert discussion

If the student challenges you or answers back, say, "I'm not prepared to discuss it now. Do as I say". You may wish to add, "We'll discuss it at the end of the lesson or with your head of year at the end of school …"

Step 5: Confront with choice

- The final step in the Assertive Zone before you cross into the Warning Zone is to confront the student with a choice. For example, "I've told you twice to stand here. Now you have a choice. You can either do as I ask or I'll show you a yellow card/note your name/fill in a consequence form. Make your choice now".
- It is crucial that the student immediately experiences the predicted consequence of the choice that he or she makes.

Regular assertiveness

This more amplified version of assertiveness is designed for use in run-of-the-mill classroom, corridor and playground situations.

Step 1: Take an assertive stance

Same as above.

Step 2: State the change

- Firmly state what you want the student to do differently.
- Begin with the phrase "I want …"
- Be specific – state only those changes that can be observed. For example, instead of "I want you to listen to me" say "I want you to put your pen down and look at me now". Instead

of "Get on", say "I want you to pick up your pen and write the answers to questions one and two by half past ten".

- Do not generalise. Do not use "always" or "never". Do not say "Never in all my teaching days have I ever met anyone as lazy as you …"
- Do not start sentences with "You", it invites confrontation. Do not say, "You, yes, *you* …" or "You're late, you're *always* late" or "*You* again?" or "You're not paying attention".

Step 3: Acknowledge the student

Acknowledge the student's position. For example, "I can see that you're angry …" or "I know you feel it's unfair …" or "I realise that he hit you first …" or "I know you feel bored …"

Step 4: Restate the change

- Simply restate, calmly and firmly, the behaviour change you require. Follow again the guidelines under Step 2 above.
- Avoid the temptation to stick the knife in or be sarcastic. Do not say, "I'm not surprised you don't know what to do: you weren't listening, were you?" or "You're bored, are you? Perhaps you'd prefer an interesting day sitting outside Mr Batty's office".
- Avoid the temptation to ask why. Do not say, "Why haven't you done your homework?" or "Why aren't you listening?" or "Why are you pushing?"
- Avoid the temptation to use "but". Instead of "but" use "and". Do not say, "I know you don't see the point of doing French, but just get on with it". Instead, say, "I know you don't see the point of doing French, and I want you to do the next exercise in the next ten minutes". Do not say, "I realise you didn't start the argument, but you retaliated". Instead, say, "I know you didn't start the argument, and I saw you retaliate".
- Keep your remarks factual. Say what you saw and heard, not what you think about it. Do not say, "I would have thought that a boy of your age would have known better …"

Step 5: Hear the pupil

If the student challenges or argues back, listen to them. Letting the student know that you have heard their point of view does not mean that you are agreeing or colluding with them. There is no need to disagree. Avoid arguing with the student. Avoid attempting to persuade the student. For example, do not say, "I don't care what you think, I'm telling you to do it". Do not say, "Look, if you don't do this you'll do badly in the test next week".

Step 6: Restate the change

Once you have heard the student's point of view, calmly and firmly restate the behaviour change you require. Follow the guidelines under Step 2 above. For example, "I know that Jason nudged you as he went past and spoiled your diagram. I'm going to speak to him next. What I want you to do is to draw the diagram again". (This continual restatement is known as "broken record".)

Step 7: Confront with choice

The final step in the Assertive Zone before you cross into the Warning Zone is to confront the student with a choice. For example, "I've asked you three times to keep all four legs of your chair on the floor. Now you have a choice. You can do as I ask or you can carry on rocking and I will note your name/show you a yellow card/fill in a situation slip. The choice is yours." It is crucial that the student should experience the predicted consequence of the choice he or she makes.

Full-length assertiveness

This full-scale assertive approach, based on humanistic psychology, is designed to tackle poor behaviour rigorously while preserving the self-esteem of both student and teacher. It aims to achieve an outcome that is acceptable to both. Teachers often find themselves dealing with students whose self-esteem is very low. Such students are likely to kick and fight or be completely unresponsive, making the assertive approach difficult to sustain. The behaviouristic alternatives are tempting, but remember: while they may appear to achieve short-term success they make medium- and long-term problems worse.

What is described here can be used only when you have set aside quality time to work on a behaviour issue with a student, perhaps after school or at lunchtime. This full version draws on some basic counselling skills and is similar to the recognised procedures of mediation technique. Students themselves can learn these skills and use them with each other informally or as part of a peer mediation programme of the kind that is very successful in many primary schools.

Step 1: Personal preparation

- If a difficult incident has just occurred, calm down. Assertiveness works only when you are in charge of your feelings. It is never helpful to *react* to a student's poor behaviour. Instead, *choose* to deal with it assertively. This may mean putting some distance between yourself and the incident.
- Remind yourself of *your* personal rights and the *student's* personal rights. For example, you both have the right to be heard, to disagree, to ask for more information, to ask for time to think, to speak honestly, to avoid aggressive behaviour.
- Gather whatever information you need – be well informed about the facts of the matter.
- Feel intent on achieving a win–win outcome. This includes feeling prepared to accept a compromise on the *nature* of the solution, not on the *need* for a solution.
- You are looking to create an adult–adult conversation (in Transactional Analysis terms).
- Be prepared to listen, genuinely and fully.
- Choose an appropriate time and place.

Step 2: State your position

A. **Come to the point quickly.** Announce that you have something to say that you want the student to listen to and discuss: "I want to talk about your homework."
B. **Describe the behaviour you want the student to address.** Tell the truth, directly, without beating about the bush. Don't try to "butter up" the pupil by telling them how good they are at other things or how pleased you are with them for something else.

  - As far as possible use "I" statements to describe the behaviours that you want the pupil to address: "I saw you copying …"; "I didn't receive your homework …"; "I heard you …"; "I've been counting and this is the third time that …"; "I noticed in the register that you've been absent."
  - If the behaviours are reported by another person, say so: "So-and-so tells me that …"; "Your report card says …"; "I have a note from so-and-so that says …" Keep it factual. Don't agree or disagree with the reported facts. Concentrate only on describing the behaviours to be challenged.

C. **Declare your genuine feelings about the student's behaviour**, again using "I" statements: "I feel very angry when you …"; "I am worried about …"; "I feel frustrated …"; "I am concerned …"; "I was surprised when I saw …"; "I'm afraid of losing my patience …"

  - It is important to begin as many sentences as you can with "I". This way you "own" your response to the student's behaviour and confrontation is reduced.

- Avoid labelling and accusing. Don't begin sentences with "You" and don't use words like "never" and "always". These invite defensive or counterattacking responses from the student.
- It is neither accurate nor constructive to say, "You make me feel/do such and such".

D. **Say what you want the student to do differently.** Make your requests specific and precise. Describe observable behaviours rather than general qualities. So, rather than "I want you to be more punctual", say "I want you to be in the classroom by 8.45 a.m. every day". It is usually helpful actually to use the word "want".

Step 3: Ask for the pupil's feelings and perceptions

- For example, "I want you to tell me how you feel about what I have said" or "I want you to tell me how you see it".
- Listen and **reflect back** what the student says.
- Let the student know that you understand their perspective and feelings and that you accept them as theirs.
- If you don't understand, say so and ask for more details.
- You are neither agreeing nor disagreeing with the student at this stage. You are just listening.

Step 4: Restate your position

- Follow again the guidelines under Step 2 above.
- This restatement is known as "broken record". "I understand that you feel ..."; "The way you see things is differently from the way I see them: I feel ... and I want you to ..." Steps 3 and 4 may need to be repeated several times.
- If you feel that you have not been heard, ask the student to feed back what you have said to them. If they can't do this, it shows that they haven't in fact been listening! In this case restate your position again and again until they can summarise it back to you.

Step 5 Stuck?

- When each person states their position and the other person hears it, this sometimes results in an automatic solution.
- If it doesn't in this case, there are several strategies you can try. Whatever you do, you *do not* compromise on the core issue or behaviour to be addressed. You may compromise on the type of solution, but you do not compromise on the *need* for a solution.
- So, if you're stuck, you could swap roles (it helps to swap places physically, too) and talk to each other in reverse. This is a powerful strategy that increases empathy, but it's not one with which many students or teachers feel comfortable.
- You could ask how a third person might see the conversation from an objective point of view – a neighbour, a youth club leader, a friend's mother. Put yourselves in such a person's shoes and share your perceptions.
- You could list all the options you each have so that you might move on to make choices.
- You could agree to try one option for a limited period of time and then review it. This makes the decision less intense because it's not once and for all.
- The difficulties may be with language. For example, ask the student to change "but" to "and". For example, in the sentence, "I'd like to be on time, but the bus doesn't arrive until 8.55", if "and" replaces "but" the inevitability is taken out of the situation and the idea of catching an earlier bus becomes an option.

- Similarly, drop the word "try", change "can't" to "won't" and never ask the question "why?" All these language modifications are designed to heighten a sense of personal responsibility and can often break a deadlock.
- If all else fails and a solution is not urgent, it may help to leave it for a while and come back to it in a couple of days, or go to "arbitration".

Step 6: Reach a win–win conclusion

- When you have reached a position where a solution seems possible, keep talking until the final outcome is *genuinely* agreed by both parties.
- This will usually mean a degree of compromise on both sides. For example, "You're agreeing to do one hour's homework each night as soon as you get in from school and I'm agreeing to see your geography and maths teachers about the kind of homework they set."
- Creative thinking may be needed to find solutions that give both parties as much as possible of what they each want.
- It is often helpful to agree to try a solution for a while and then review it.

Step 7: Make a firm agreement

- Make and, if it seems helpful, write a contract.
- An oral agreement should, as a minimum, leave both parties in no doubt about their future actions.
- A written contract or note is preferable because it can contain specific behaviours and deadlines, the types of support to be provided and reviews to be undertaken.

It is easy to see how the teacher needs a large dose of emotional intelligence to make this work. Identifying, naming, explaining and managing emotions go with this territory. The experience should also help to develop the emotional intelligence of the student, partly through the teacher's model and partly through the demands made by the process on the student. Listening, empathy, self-control, articulation of feelings, perseverance and a willingness to compromise are all required.

Finally, try these approaches to assertiveness with family and friends. They won't know what's hit 'em!

Groups Galore

Teachers often ask what kind of small groups work best. There are many options. They serve different purposes. So, it's horses for courses - or groups for hoops.

There are at least eight types of group. Ask yourself:

- Which type will work best for this activity?
- Which will work best given the current state of the class?
- Which type will move them on socially?
- Which haven't we used for a while?

1. Random groups

These are composed by chance. For example, you can:

- pull names out of a hat
- stick a pin in the register
- number round the class
- give out differently coloured cards as the students come in

2. Friendship groups

Students get together with their mates.

3. Interest groups

Students get together because they want to work on the same topic, or use the same approach.

4. Skill groups

Students with the same skills form groups. For example, all the readers, all the speakers, all the drawers, all the dramatists.

5. Mixed-skill groups

Students with *different* skills get together, so every group has a mixture. For example, an organiser, a confident speaker, a fast reader, a motivator, a creative writer.

6. Learning-style groups

Students with the same learning style get together. For example discussion group, role-play group, reading and note-taking group, worksheet group, trial-and-error group.

7. Support groups

Students who know they can do something well get together with people who need some help. For example, good readers get together with poor readers and help them, or experienced interviewers work with people who've never conducted an interview before.

8. Performance groups

Students with similar levels of current performance in the subject get together. This enables them to work at a common level and pace. It allows the teacher to differentiate the tasks and challenges.

What about ability groups?

Ability? Is there such a thing? The answer is probably no, not in a crude sense. In the past we tended to think of ability as fixed and consequently used it to define students. We now know that intelligence is fluid – it can be increased, students can become cleverer. Intelligence also comes in all shapes and sizes – nowadays we recognise and value a whole range of abilities.

Therefore, a student who is poor at reading and writing, but highly skilled interpersonally, might still be regarded as "able". As we saw earlier, *Mensa Magazine* of March 2000[8] dared to suggest that the footballer David Beckham is as bright as Albert Einstein! With our current knowledge of the brain, it is neither easy nor desirable to define and measure ability in the way we once did.

A further problem with labelling students as "more" or "less" able is the effect of the message on performance. Since Rosenthal and Jacobson's *Pygmalion in the Classroom*,[9] we have known that teachers' internalised expectations of students impact directly on the quality of their learning. Students tend to live up or down to expectations. Finally, labels tend to stick. Most students regarded as "less able" at school continue to think of themselves as less able throughout life. The hold that categorisation has on self-image and therefore on self-esteem is sometimes unshakable.

So there are many problems with the idea of ability groups. A positive way forward is to replace the word "ability" with the phrase "current performance" or "current competence". These terms suggest, even invite, improvement. They also refer to particular skill sets, rather than make generalised judgments. A student's current performance in algebra might be quite different from their current performance in geometry, and this might reflect their different levels of logical and spatial intelligence. Therefore, "performance groups" might be created only in relation to the subject matter and particular task in hand.

What about group size?

Does size matter? The answer is definitely yes! Obviously it depends on the nature of the activity. In *The Teacher's Toolkit* different sizes of groups are required for different exercises. For general purposes, though, when you just want students to discuss, read, brainstorm, think, plan, define or decide something together, it seems that fours are too big, pairs are too small and threes are just right.

How to avoid creating "passengers"

If the group is supposed to produce some sort of flipchart presentation or poster, give each of the students a differently coloured felt pen, which they are not allowed to swap. As you move round the room, you will be able to see who is contributing what by the colours on the paper.

Let the class know that at the end of the group activity you will ask each student secretly and anonymously to submit effort percentages for all group members. See "Proportional Representation" on page 216.

Let the class know that during the group work you will be moving round, dropping on individual students at any time and asking them to explain what has been discussed. If they can't do it, the group is in big trouble!

Step On It

Managing individual or group projects can be a slow and painful process. Students some-
times meander and take the most tortuous route or leave the beaten track completely. If
it's all too slow, get them to step on it.

How?

The basic idea is to help students to identify the short steps they need to take in advance and
always to keep ahead of themselves.

1. Prepare a "Step On It" recording sheet, like this.

Date and time written	Steps to be taken	How long the step should take	How long it actually took

2. Each student has their own A4 copy. The student decides what they have to do first. The step should be small and specific: for example, "Use the history-of-art CD-ROM and draw a timeline of Picasso's life" or "Write and post a letter to the Welsh Tourist Board asking for leaflets on the top ten attractions in West Wales" or "Select the three most useful books on this topic from the school library" or "Read the information sheet from the teacher and turn it into a flow diagram".

3. The date and time of writing the step are recorded in the first column and an estimate of how long it will take is entered in the third column. This should be a challenging deadline that doesn't give the opportunity to mess about. Then, afterwards, the time the job actually took is entered in the final column. This sometimes gives students an incentive to beat their prediction. If, however, it ended up taking longer than estimated, this invites a debrief with the student. Was there a subskill to master, such as knowing how to write a business letter or knowing how to make notes? Or were the resources inadequate – students were queuing for the only CD-ROM, for instance? Or was it lack of motivation or distractions, or … At this point you are operating as a tutor rather than teacher.

4. For "Step On It" to work properly, though, defining and doing a single step at a time is not enough. Students are asked always to be at least one step ahead of themselves. So, when they have written the first step, they decide on and record the second step *before* they actually do the first. Likewise, before they get on with the second step, they think through and record the third step and maybe the fourth as well. This helps them to stay on track and keep their momentum up. They are always looking beyond the immediate; there's always something else to do. Also, as you move round the classroom, you can see where each of them is going. This enables you to anticipate problems, select resources, organise equipment and prepare teaching inputs on particular facts, concepts or skills. No one is caught out.

5. The predictive nature of "Step On It" also allows you to adjust steps with certain students and even write steps for others. Some members of the class can get on with little help. They know what to do and how to do it. You can trust them to write realistic steps and be self-directing. Others need more support. You may want to rewrite vague steps such as "Find out about the Crusades" or "Investigate ingredients" or "Carry on with the book". You may need to sharpen time scales. Or you may need to delete some of the steps ahead because they would take the student off at an unproductive tangent. At  the other end of the scale with highly motivated and capable students, you may want to make their steps more complex, long-term and challenging. Finally, you may wish to suggest alternative ways of doing a step, to bring it more in line with the student's learning style. For example, "Find out about the Crusades by watching the first twenty minutes of such-and-such a video" or "... by talking to me about it", rather than "... by reading a book", which is what the student originally wrote. So the process allows for a high degree of differentiation in regard to detail and depth, pace and style of learning.

6. The "Step On It" sheets are out on the desks always available and the students follow continual cycles of plan-do-review with your tailor-made support.

Applications

*   This can be used in any situation where students are expected to sustain a piece of learning over a long period of time: a research project; GCSE coursework; GNVQ assignment, for example.
*   It is also a very useful way of managing group work (see "Variations" below).

Why do it?

*   It's pragmatic. In the hurly-burly of a busy classroom with a million different things going on at once it helps to keep things on track and on time.
*   It's educational. Many students find individual or group research difficult, usually because they haven't done much of it before. "Step On It" trains them in some of the basic procedures of self-management and personal or group organisation.
*   It's idealistic. The procedure helps to develop personal responsibility for learning, one of our long-term goals.

Variations

1. If the class are working in small groups, the "Step On It" sheet might look something like this:

Date and time written	Name of group member	**Steps to be taken**	How long the step should take	How long it actually took

This central record sheet is kept by the group leader or manager who liaises with the teacher. From time to time the group meet to decide on the next round of steps, remembering always to keep at least one round ahead.

2. Alternatively, this recording device might be filled in each time the group meet:

Date and time of meeting	Next step	Time	Then	Time	Then	Time
Name		Estimate Actual		Estimate Actual		Estimate Actual
Name		Estimate Actual		Estimate Actual		Estimate Actual
Name		Estimate Actual		Estimate Actual		Estimate Actual
Name		Estimate Actual		Estimate Actual		Estimate Actual

The group will meet again on .... **at** ....

211

Help! How Do We Hold A Group Discussion?

Talking? People do it all the time, even when they shouldn't! This advice is designed to bring a little order and calm to small-group proceedings.

In all group discussions, rules are important:

- they encourage people to take part
- they stop arguments
- they make sure time is used well

Here's some advice for students. It could be given to them as a handout:

Get organised

Most groups find these two "golden rules" helpful:

- we will give our complete attention to the person who is speaking
- we will respect other people's opinions even when they are different from our own

Instead of adopting these, you might want to make your own. If you do, make sure that they say what people should do, not what they shouldn't do. The rules should enable you to have organised discussions and should make sure that no one's feelings get hurt. Don't have punishments. Write the group rules on a piece of paper or card large enough for everyone to see. Make sure they are displayed every time the group meets together.

If a member of the group breaks the rules, simply remind them of what has been agreed. Help them get into new habits.

Now what's the best way to organise your discussion? Here are **five possibilities**:

1. Sit properly

Everyone needs to see and hear each other easily. So make sure you are sitting in a circle or round a desk. Sitting in a line along a desk or bench doesn't work.

2. Appoint a chairperson

Signal to the chairperson that you want to speak. The chairperson will call on you when it is your turn.

3. Use a round

This means taking turns, one after another, round the group. You can speak only when it is your turn – this eliminates interruptions and witty comments. If you don't want to make a contribution when your turn comes, just say, "Pass". You can go round and round the group as many times as necessary.

4. Use tokens

At the start give everyone five tokens: for example, buttons, pieces of paper, counters. Every time a person speaks, they give up a token. When people have no tokens left, they can't say any more.

5. Use a "microphone"

Choose an item to be a "microphone": for example, a pen, a ruler, a box, a book. You can speak only when you are holding the "microphone". When you have finished speaking pass the "microphone" on to the person who wants to speak next.

Other useful tips

- Face the person who is speaking.
- When you are speaking, make eye contact with the other members of the group.
- From time to time sum up what other people are saying. This lets them know that their contributions have been heard.
- If you don't understand someone's comment, ask for it to be explained.
- If you don't feel that *you* have been understood, ask someone else in the group to sum up your point of view. If no one can do it, you will need to try to make your point again in a different way.

Civilised discussion and debate lie at the heart of the political process, so the guidelines above make a significant contribution **to citizenship education**. They give students a taste of the dynamics of debate and will stand them in good stead. Apart from political applications, the guidelines apply equally to family, social and business discussions.

What's more, the national drive for **inclusive education** must come down to this: attention to detail. Simply allocating a student to a group does not guarantee inclusion within that group. The procedures above are designed to make inclusion a genuine rather than a superficial experience.

Help! How Do We Make Decisions?

Give this advice to small groups when they are struggling to agree. Or before! After all, prevention is better than cure.

Groups often face questions such as:

- What shall we do and how shall we do it?
- Who's going to do what?
- How can we make sure that everyone is happy with the decision?

These steps will help students answer such questions efficiently:

Step 1

Make sure that everyone in the group understands the question or problem. Try writing it down large enough for the whole group to see. Use the blackboard, white board, flip chart or large piece of paper. Check that everyone understands by asking them to explain it in their own words.

Step 2

List all the possible answers or solutions. Brainstorming is a good way of doing this. Alternatively, use a round. Again, write down all the possibilities for everyone to see.

Step 3

Now you have to choose one solution from your list. Aim for everyone to agree (this is called consensus). Give yourselves a time limit for discussion, perhaps five or ten minutes. If you all agree at the end of this time, then congratulate yourselves. If you don't all agree, then move on to Step 4.

Step 4

Now try for a compromise. This involves some "give and take". Look at the two or three most popular solutions and ask yourselves:

- What changes would we have to make to one of these solutions for everyone to accept it? **or**
- Which one of these would we all be willing to try for a short time only – then we'll review it?

Again, give yourselves a time limit. If you are still stuck, go to Step 5.

Step 5

It's now time for the last resort: voting. You could go for a straight vote with a show of hands, or a secret ballot in which everyone writes anonymously on a piece of paper. You'll have to decide beforehand what percentage is needed for the vote to be carried. The snag with both of these is that they create "winners" and "losers". There is another way of doing it …

1. label the different solutions A, B, C, D, E ...
2. go round the group asking each person in turn for their "top three"
3. someone tallies the marks
4. the solution with the highest number of "hits", is accepted; second and third choices will also emerge

This method should give you the favoured solutions without splitting the group.

Collective decision-making is a large part of **citizenship**. The steps above explore ways of doing this and train students in good practice.

Proportional Representation

Groups are notorious for carrying passengers and tolerating pillion riders. But beware. The proportion of your representation will be represented proportionally.

How?

1. Let the students know that at the end of the group work each group member will be expected to judge the percentage contribution of all the others. Show them the sheet that they will have to fill in:

Name of group member	Their % of the total group effort
Name	
Name	
Name	
Self	
	= 100%

2. As soon as the group work is finished, ask each student to complete the form secretly and anonymously. They are being asked to judge the relative contribution of each member over the whole period of group work. For example, a student who shone at the end because they are a confident and engaging presenter would still be given a low percentage if they did little of the initial thinking and research – and vice versa. Remind students to include themselves in the equation and that the percentages should total 100.

3. You collect the forms and look for patterns within groups. If people have been honest, it will enable you to see who's contributed what. Dishonesty will usually show as discrepancies between students' returns. Either way, the information will give you a lot to talk about with the class about how to handle group work in future.

Applications

- Do this whenever you suspect that students are not pulling their weight in group work.
- Do it anyway, just to keep everyone on their toes.
- Do it to strengthen people's resolve to challenge their lazy peers. The exercise brings the issues out into the open, it breaks the ice and gives people an agenda to talk about more candidly.

Why do it?

- It makes group work more productive by encouraging everyone to do a fair share of the work. Few students want to be exposed as lazy and anti-social.
- It contributes to your campaign for everyone to accept personal responsibility for their behaviour. It's not possible to hide behind the group.
- It encourages corporate responsibility by making very explicit the idea that "we are all in this together".
- On a practical note, it helps you to allocate marks, grades or comments to individuals when group work has been used for some kind of assessment.

Variations

1 Don't do it anonymously. Ask students to "own" their judgments by putting their names on the forms. This really does promote the concept of personal responsibility and explores conflicting loyalties between individual mates and the group.
2 Students don't fill in the form individually, but as a group. Each small group discusses and agrees on an accurate distribution of points.

Triple Check

If at first you don't succeed, check and check again.

Here are three checklists for quality small-group work in the classroom, lab, workshop – even studio or gym, perhaps.

Be explicit with the students about the quality of group work you want to achieve, perhaps by showing them and explaining these checklists. Make spot checks – or stop the lesson and ask students to carry out spot checks – on the quality of group work. Every now and again spend a few minutes before the end of a lesson asking how much group-working progress has been made. Set new targets for quality group work: for example. "By the end of next week, let's make sure that we're all brave enough to ask for something to be explained again if we haven't understood it first time."

When a group is working well ...

- The group sits so that each group member can see and hear all the others easily.
- One person at a time speaks during discussion.
- Everyone turns to face the person who is speaking.
- Individual group members remind others if they break agreed ground rules.
- Any member at any time is able to explain:
  - ❖ what she is doing
  - ❖ how this contributes to the overall group task
  - ❖ what other group members are doing and why
  - ❖ what the next step will be
- The group always works to agreed and explicit deadlines – each member should be able to answer the question, "When will this be finished?"
- A group member who finishes a task early offers to help others, or negotiates the next step with the group manager.
- Everyone contributes equally to looking after resources, to clearing up and to moving furniture.

If group work isn't going well, check that ...

- time has been given to creating ground rules and making clear the behaviour expected of everyone within a group
- there is a designated leader, or manager, for each group
- there are clear procedures for discussion (see "Help! How Do We Hold a Group Discussion?" on page 212)
- the manager is the main channel of communication between the teacher and the group
- over a long period of group work (a technology project, for example) there are group meetings at intervals, chaired by the manager, at which agreements are made about division of labour, deadlines and use of resources

- apart from very short-term tasks, notes are kept of who should be doing what by when

- the teacher is unbending about the keeping of agreed ground rules

- the group has procedures for making decisions and solving problems (see "Help! How Do We Make Decisions?" on page 214)

Still problems? Check ...

Classroom layout: Is the furniture arrangement conducive to group work?

Resources: Are they appropriate for the task (content, readability)? Are they sufficient for the numbers? And do the students know where to get them and how to use them?

Time: Has enough time been invested in setting up group work properly in the first place, in the belief that it will be recouped later? Do you need to go back a step or two?

Trust: Is it believed that students will, in the end, handle group work well and use it to achieve great things? Do the students know your high expectations of them?

Safety: Are safety requirements, where they exist, built into the ground rules?

Tasks: Have the tasks been designed and structured for collaboration so that they cannot be achieved by any individual alone?

Ground rules: Do they need revisiting, or even re-creating?

Skills: Do the students need to acquire certain subskills, for example, scan reading or note making?

Teacher: Do you need to learn how to operate differently, for example, getting round the groups and always being there to check on deadlines when you said you would?

Think About It

The more students are asked to do for themselves, the more they need a reflective attitude and reflective skills. They'll acquire them only if you encourage them to think for themselves over a long period of time. So here are some habits to get into:

1. Get into the habit of **asking open-ended questions**: for example, "What if ...?"; "Why do you think ...?"; "How many ways ...?"; "Have you got any ideas about ...?"; "Why not ...?".

2. Ask students to **explain things** to the class on your behalf: for example, "Can anyone tell us how ...?"; "Who can predict what I'm going to say next ...?"; "Who can improve what I just said ...?".

3. Ask students to **ask you questions** – informally or through techniques such as "Hot-Seating" (page 116) or "Paper Round" (page 196).

4. Teach students the difference between **open** and **closed questions** – and leading, probing, rhetorical and cheeky ones!

5. Get students to **test you** on the topic in hand, through an informal quiz, written test or "Beat the Teacher" (page 71).

6. **Redirect questions** asked of you to be answered instead by other students. "Who can help us with that question?" Use "Calling Cards" (page 81) to make sure everyone is mentally involved.

7. When you ask a question to the class, give everyone a minute's **"think time"** before you ask for responses. Or, give them two minutes' **"talk time"** in pairs.

8. Spend five minutes at the end of each lesson considering the extent to which the learning objectives have been met and the extent to which progress is being made towards **longer-term goals** (getting to the end of the topic or syllabus by a particular date).

9. Keep adding to a **public word bank** of technical terms (large wall chart or key words displayed on cards around the room) and insist on their use in all question-and-answer sessions and discussions. Challenge sloppy language by asking the student to say it again using the precise vocabulary. Test the students regularly on technical terms: use "Bingo" (page 73), "Memory Board" (page 128) or "Verbal Tennis" (page 168).

10. Model the use of technical language yourself. **Build key words** into your regular talk.

11. Check the **overall balance** between teacher-talk and student-talk. Is there anything you said that a student could have said just as well: for instance, key points, instructions, next task, homework routine, summary of the learning ...?

12. Model the use of **reflection and self-assessment** yourself. Publicly evaluate the quality of your teaching in front of, or with, the students.

13. Get students to **mark model answers** that you have written or other students' anonymous work. They can do this on their own or in pairs.

14. Get students to **work out assessment criteria** with you before work is marked. Relate these to national curriculum levels and exam grades. Ask, "So what will I/the examiner be looking for?"

15. Give out several pieces of work and ask students (individually or in small groups) to rank them according to their **fulfilment of the assessment criteria**.

16. **Assess a piece of work** in public. Put the work onto an overhead projector, or use broadcaster software, so that everyone can see and show students how you mark it. Give a commentary, explaining what goes on in your head as you tackle the assessment.

17. Get students regularly to **set test questions** for each other. Organise tests in pairs/groups/whole class or use "Verbal Football" (page 166) or "Masterminds" (page 126).

18. Divide the class into small groups and give each one a different **assessment criterion**. Give the same piece of work to each group and ask them to evaluate it against their criterion only. Then have an open discussion or do "Scrambled Groups" (page 150) to bring the complete assessment together and to discuss what is meant by standards and rigour.

19. In your one-to-one conversations around the classroom, make sure that you **prompt reflection** (by using open-ended questions) and rigour (by referring to technical language and assessment criteria).

20. Use "reflection pro formas" at intervals during a sequence of lessons. At the end of each learning step, students have to **reflect on, and record, what they have learned** about the topic and what they have learned about learning. Students have to complete these to the teacher's satisfaction before they can move on to the next stage.

21. At the end of a piece of work **use self-assessment sheets** with an emphasis on "Next time I will …".

22. Use **visual devices** for reflecting on performance and quality, and for setting next personal targets, such as line graphs, scales, metres, mountain peaks, concentric-circle targets, dartboard.

23. Use "Value Continuum" (page 163) or "Centre of the Universe" (page 83) to get students into the habit of making **personal judgments** and speaking their minds in public.

24. Get students to **identify the choices they made** (and consequences they therefore created) in the lesson or assignment. Get them to draw it out as a timeline or flowchart with branches that show alternative courses of action. Establish the idea that life is a series of moment-by-moment choices and that old patterns of behaviour and work can be broken.

Settled Starts

The first few minutes of a lesson are crucial. They set the tone for what is to come. Here are ten tasty tips for getting off to a smooth start:

1. Act as "gatekeeper" – stand at the door, letting pupils in one at a time. You can smile, frown, have a quiet word, give a warning, hold a pupil back, separate pupils, direct pupils to particular seats, instead of letting them come in en masse with all their "baggage".

2. Have a simple task for everyone to get on with as soon as they enter the room – expect everyone to settle immediately. This gives you a chance to deal with individuals and get your head together. Introduce the lesson only when you are ready.

3. Have learning objectives that are expressed in the form: "By the end of this lesson you will be able to …" This suggests to pupils that the lesson is purposeful and that they will have experienced success by the end. Have them written up on the board or on a handout before the students come in.

4. Link the learning objectives to the "big picture" of their learning – what's gone before and what's coming after and how it all adds up to success in the forthcoming assessment. This helps students to see the relevance of the current work and to open their reticular activating systems!

5. Have learning objectives that are *differentiated*, using, for example, the must-should-could model (see "Upwardly Mobile" on page 234). This lets pupils know that they will be able to achieve, and it encourages them to aspire.

6. Have the lesson plan written up on the board or on an OHT as a flowchart, timeline or time circle (like a clock face), showing the time scale. Talk through the plan with students and ask them to help you keep to time.

7. Instead of standing at the front, position yourself near to the potential troublemakers and introduce the lesson from there.

8. Ask one or two pupils to explain to you (and therefore to the whole class) what everyone has to do before anyone is allowed to start.

9. Give a tight deadline for the first task. This creates a sense of pace and a sense that the teacher is firmly in charge. Make sure you've got a clearly visible clock in the room!

10. Give upbeat messages about the students' abilities and the learning planned for the lesson. Say things like, "I know today's work is challenging, and I also know we can all master it, so let's get cracking" and, "I've designed some exercises that will stretch you, but once they're done you'll feel really good about what you've achieved". Don't give the impression that you are reluctantly accepting learning that is being forced on the class from above: "Oh well, if I had my way we wouldn't be doing this …". Instead, let the students know that you are in charge and have reworked national curriculum or GCSE obligations, designing tailor-made activities just for them.

Tricks of the Trade

Dealing with low-level disruption can be tricky. Here are thirteen (unlucky for some) ways of outsmarting the smart-Alecs.

1. **Set deadlines for specific tasks** – create a sense of urgency. Public, whole-class deadlines can be written up on the board. Individual deadlines can be jotted down in the margin of the pupil's exercise book or on the teacher's clipboard. Break the learning into short steps and challenge reluctant pupils to complete the next step within a tight timescale: "I think you can do questions 2 and 3 within the next ten minutes. I'm jotting that down and I'll be back to check at 2.25 p.m." See "Dreadlines" on page 103.

2. **Use traffic lights** – have red, green and orange cards. Stick the green card on the board when you are happy for students to chitchat as long as they are getting on with their work. Stick the orange one up to signal that silence will be expected in one minute. Naturally, red indicates total silence. Red and orange together mean only one more minute of silence before chitchat will be allowed again.

3. **Use tokens** – everyone starts off with three tokens each (buttons, counters, small cards). Each time a person speaks when they shouldn't, they surrender a token. They can win tokens back for particularly impressive contributions. The aim is for students to make sure that they are never without a token. For the reverse of this idea see "Tokenism" on page 197.

4. **Rearrange the room** – make sure it promotes the kind of listening you require. For example, having tables in groups with some students' backs to the teacher is not a good idea until self-discipline has been firmly established.

5. **Have a sit-out area** – pupils who have been reminded once or twice are given a choice: *either* settle down and pay attention *or* go to the sit-out area (a designated area at the back of the room), where straightforward work is already laid out for them to get on with. They can come back into the main learning activity as soon as they are prepared to behave.

6. **Never talk over chatter** – wait until you have complete silence.

7. **Play "eye-eye"** – require everyone to turn and look at the person who is speaking, whether it's the teacher or a pupil.

8. **Have a "chatterbox"** – have a sealed shoebox with a slit in it (like a ballot box) on the teacher's desk. Each time a person disrupts, jot their name down and pop it into the chatterbox. Open the box each month and names that appear more than five times are in *big trouble*.

9. **Ask other pupils to remind talkers** – have rotating "talk police". Choose a couple of people each lesson to be on the lookout for low-level disruption and to issue reminders. People can be "booked" for more serious offences.

10. **Play the waiting game** – stop and wait for silence. Don't say anything. Some teachers have a signal, for example, raising a hand or holding a pen, to show that they are waiting. It's important not to look bored, angry or frustrated – this only gives the unsettled pupils the incentive to carry on being unsettled.

11. **Record instructions or passages on tape** – curiously, pupils will often settle to a *recording* of the teacher's voice more than a live performance. The recording also frees you to watch the class while they listen.

12. **Don't stand at the front** – go and stand next to likely interrupters when you are addressing the whole class. Move round, making sure that you make eye contact with potential disrupters.

13. **Don't raise your voice** – lower it.

Section 4

Operating Tools

Introduction

This section presents six operating systems, in other words six fundamentally different ways of managing learning. Each describes a workable set of guidelines for planning and delivering learning experiences designed to accommodate students' individual learning needs. They are not the only six available – you may know of others – but they are a representative sample. Also, you may know them by other names – these are just my nicknames, for convenience. Largely, they are not my inventions: all I've done is to refine them in the light of experience and present each of them as a coherent, self-contained modus operandi – I hope.

These operating systems vary in complexity from "Overtime", the simplest, to "Blank Cheque", the most intricate. They deliver increasing degrees of differentiation and student responsibility, and consequently demand increasingly sophisticated skills of the teacher. They also become more and more compatible with the way the brain naturally learns, so in a strange way the more demanding they are, the easier they are, as students become more motivated, less troublesome and learn more efficiently. In fact, the six systems can be set out on a continuum.

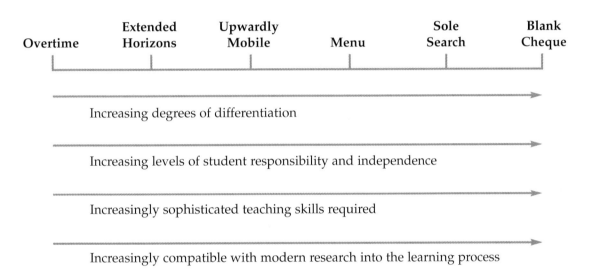

The most "extreme" method, "Blank Cheque", delivers highest levels of learning and the widest range of simultaneous outcomes. However, many teachers feel uneasy about the degree of negotiation involved, either because of their own or their students' lack of experience. It is perhaps helpful to imagine this continuum of systems as a swimming pool. There's no point jumping in the deep end if you can't swim. On the other hand, it's not much fun spending the rest of your life in the shallows. So judge your point of entry, but intend to master the depths in time.

The first two, "Overtime" and "Extended Horizons", are commonplace. Many teachers find these operating systems comfortable, do them naturally and apply them extensively. So, they are described only briefly. In my work around the country I find that the other four are less established, so they are presented in more detail.

Overtime

"Overtime" has nothing to do with working extra hours, you'll be pleased to know. Rather, it's a positive attempt to make learning personally appropriate for students. In fact, it is a teacher's minimum response to the truth about learning styles: that we all have them, that they are diverse and that in any class at any age in any subject there will be a variety of styles to accommodate.

The "Overtime" operating system is simple. You plan to use a variety of teaching and learning techniques with the same class over a period of time – perhaps a month, a half-term, a scheme of work. You commit yourself to ensuring that a mix of styles is accommodated over that period by using different techniques one after another. For example, a series of three lessons might begin with a **kinaesthetic** "Quick on the Draw" introduction to the basic facts, then move into worksheet-based research (**Abstract Sequential**), followed by small group discussions (**auditory**), then **Abstract Random** "Still Images" to articulate understanding, and conclude with individual mind-mapping (**visual**) of the subject to create a record of learning for future reference.

Of course, it's not possible to cram all styles into a short sequence – lessons would be far too bitty. Instead, the teacher monitors provision over a longer period and sees to it that everyone gets a fair deal within reasonable bounds. In the above example the teacher would make sure that Concrete Sequential and Concrete Random styles, missing this time round, are featured in the next topic. The teacher remains in total control, making all the usual decisions about timings, groupings, movement, resources and tasks. The pupils all do the same thing at the same time. There is no choice, no negotiation.

To help with monitoring and planning "Overtime" provision, why not use a recognised learning-styles model (for further information see page 34)? This applies to individual teachers planning on their own and to departments planning together. In fact, it may be worth considering the inclusion of a learning-styles column in the format of your scheme of work. Here's a part-complete example from a science department with a Year 7 topic on states of matter. They have chosen to use Anthony Gregorc's Mind Styles analysis as their guide.

Lesson focus	Learning objective	Learning activities	Learning styles check	
Understanding the characteristics of solids, liquids and gases.	To be able to categorise common materials accurately as solids, liquids or gases.	In pairs, sort picture cards of different materials into solid, liquid, gas groups. Then "Pairs to Fours" to check agreement.	CS	
		Individually complete worksheet, which explains and checks understanding of the differences between solids, liquids and gases.	AS	
	To be able to explain the difference between solids, liquids and gasses physically and at the molecular level.	In small groups design three easy-to-draw symbols to express the physical characteristics of solids, liquids and gases. You will then use these symbols in the margin of your exercise book in coming weeks.	AR	
		In the same groups, devise a way of showing the class the difference in molecular structure between solids, liquids and gases, by using yourselves as molecules.	CR	

In most instances the learning-styles column is a simple but powerful addition to existing documentation, as in the case of this example from a geography department.

Unit Title:

Class	How this Unit fits into the Big Year 7 Picture
Number of weeks	
Number of lessons	
Lead Teacher	

Coverage
H = Hit directly V = Also visited

Levels	1	2	3	4	5	6	7	8
Places								
Patterns & Processes								
Environmental Relationships								
Geographical Enquiry & Skills								

Assessment by
C = Classwork   H = Homework
A = Assessment task   I = Informal

1	2	3	4	5	6	7	8

Differentiated objectives. By the end of this Unit pupils . . .

MUST be able to

SHOULD be able to

COULD be able to

Lesson number	Key facts, concepts, skills	Key words	Teaching and learning methods	Learning-style category	Homework	Assessment
1						
2						
3						
4						
5						

Naturally, the head of department has a responsibility to check that a sufficient range of styles is being genuinely accommodated over a reasonable period of time – that promises are being kept. This means popping into classes to see what's going on, getting feedback from colleagues and students, looking at examples of students' work – in other words, using all the usual monitoring techniques. But it's bound also to raise professional development issues as some colleagues may feel that they don't have the skills or confidence to try all the ideas that they are expected to use. At this point, turn to page 318 for a number of possible strategies to support them.

Extended Horizons

This is an even more positive strategy that begins to build in differentiation, not just variety. It is well known and well used by many teachers, so doesn't need to be described in detail here. Core tasks are designed that all students are expected to do. For the "more able", extension work is devised with more challenging tasks and more demanding materials. This approach can be quite motivating; indeed, for some students getting to the extension material is a goal in itself and delivers a strong feel-good payoff. Also, the faster workers are not held back and can go on to tackle the more sophisticated aspects of the topic when they're ready.

It's important for the teacher to get the tone right. Encourage students to push themselves and go for the higher-level learning – we know how powerful expectations are – but make sure the message is clear: the extensions are luxury items. Mastering each of the core tasks is a sound and important achievement in itself, which should be celebrated genuinely.

The character of the tasks is also crucial. It usually works best if the first few core items are relatively easy, so everyone builds momentum. But the core tasks can't all be simple, otherwise students feel dumbed down by them. The extensions should be different from the core both in depth and character. In fact, the "Extended Horizons" operating system provides the opportunity to introduce variety twice over:

1. by varying the **core** tasks over the series of lessons
2. by making sure that the **extension** tasks are quite different in style from the core tasks

However, it's not all good news. Despite its simplicity and popularity, there are three potential snags with this operating system:

1. The core tasks can end up being pretty standard – worksheets, for example – so it's only those with a particular sort of learning style who ever get on to the more interesting extensions.
2. When the extension tasks are too similar to the core tasks students can quickly become disheartened. They've worked hard only to get more of the same and feel cheated. Extension tasks need to be more interesting, more fun, more rewarding. Otherwise, the incentive that they normally provide is removed.
3. The third snag is common to all explicit differentiation methods. Students who never get on to the extension work start to feel like second-class failures. To avert this you could:

    *   make differentiation covert: for example, by giving certain tasks to some people and different tasks to others discreetly as you move around the room; or preferably
    *   change the style of the core tasks so they suit different types of learners at different times: for example, if you required drama-based rather than written evidence of understanding, the hierarchy of students would immediately reshuffle itself.

So, given what we've said, what do you think of this genuine worksheet from a geography department? How would you improve it?

Nairobi Year 10

Nairobi is the largest city in Kenya, a less developed country in East Africa.

Nairobi is growing rapidly (urbanisation). Many people are migrating into the city from the countryside (rural–urban migration). This causes problems for people, but there are ways of making life better.

You are going to learn about Nairobi by working through a series of tasks. Everyone must do the main tasks, but if you are aiming for A or B at GCSE you should do the extension tasks as well.

The tasks are based on pages 48–53 of *People, Cities and Countryside*.

1. On an outline map of the world, locate Nairobi and Kenya. Shade Kenya in a bright colour and mark and label Nairobi.

2. On graph paper make a line graph of the increase in the total population of Nairobi from 1960–1980 (see table D on p. 49).

    Extension: devise a way of putting a line on the same graph for the increase in the population of the four shanty towns over the same time. This lets you compare the rates of growth.

3. Describe what your graph shows.

4. Use source C p. 48. Make a timeline showing the growth of Nairobi. Events should be simplified e.g. 1960–1970 business grew, money made, people began to move to the city and live in shanty towns in poor conditions.

5. Illustrate each part of the timeline e.g. a train to show that it began as a railway town.

    Extension: look carefully at Source C. Describe where you think the planners for the city were short-sighted or failed to do enough. Which were the good decisions and plans that were made?

    (The series of main and extension tasks continues ...)

What kind of activities make good extensions? Here are a few ideas:

1. Play *"Beat the Teacher"* (page 71):
    *   prepare a written test or challenge for the teacher, who will sit and do it; or
    *   pit your wits against the teacher to see if you can do something faster or more skilfully than she; or
    *   see if you can find all the teacher's deliberate mistakes.

2. Prepare a presentation that you will give at home, after which the lucky members of your family will be tested on what they have learned from you.

3. Make a model *or* prepare some visual aids *or* write a passage to explain such-and-such. You choose.

4. Prepare to be hot-seated next lesson in role as ... (page 116).

5. Mark an anonymous piece of work by someone in a set, or year, above.

6. Three or four of you get together and prepare a series of "Still Images" (page 158) to present to the class which shows such-and-such a process, or event, or meaning, or ...

7. Go to the library and ...

8. Prepare the materials to be used in next lesson's "Scrambled Groups" (page 150) exercise.

9. "Ranking" (page 148) individually, in pairs or better still, "Pairs to Fours" (page 137).

10. Make a short video that will be used in "Ambassadors" (page 65) next week.

11. Start a "Sole Search" project (page 253), complete with a personal learning plan, that will deepen and broaden your understanding and will be ongoing as extension work for a number of weeks.

12. Prepare to be in the "Spotlight" (page 154) at the end of this lesson or the beginning of the next.

13. Organise yourselves to run "Marketplace" (page 122) or "Verbal Football" (page 166) (or any other learning activity) in two lessons' time.

14. Look at what's coming up in the syllabus in a couple of weeks and decide how we should learn it.

15. Do "Conversion" (page 87). Consolidate your learning by turning different aspects of the material into different formats. You choose the formats for yourself.

16. Draw a mind-map summary of the whole topic, or a mind map of how this topic fits into the whole syllabus.

17. Here's the syllabus. Find the more advanced bits that I haven't covered with the whole class and have a go at them – I'll give you the necessary resources if you like, or you can do independent research.

18. Here is a set of answers. Work out the questions.

19. Here is one answer. Work out as many questions as you can for it.

20. Give each of these drawings/photographs/cartoons a caption that expresses the essential point.

21. Here are some captions. Draw a sketch or cartoon that faithfully portrays each of them.

Upwardly Mobile

This is a more sophisticated approach that enables each student to achieve to her or his own highest level. As the name suggests, it encourages learners to better themselves by climbing the ladder of achievement. On the way, they encounter a fair degree of differentiation and a variety of learning styles, and beyond first base they are asked to work independently of the teacher.

The design and delivery of this operating system depend on clear learning objectives differentiated to three levels. In her planning the teacher first decides on the *minimum* learning needed for the *essentials* of the subject. This becomes the *must* target, which all pupils are expected to achieve. The teacher then decides on two further levels of sophistication: the *should* (most pupils) and *could* (some pupils) targets.

The intention is to create a structure that *invites* students to aim high. Some teachers fear that if you tell students what the minimum is – this is all you *have* to do – then that's all they *will* do. My experience is that if you tell students what the maximum is, that's what they want to go for. Peer pressure may hold them back (see Section 3 for ways to change classroom norms), but inside, among their secret thoughts and feelings, almost all students want to be very successful.

For each of these three levels, pupils are offered:

- **a learning activity**: these vary in style across the three targets
- **a proof activity**: a way of showing that the learning has been acquired
- **a loop activity**: to have a go at the same learning in a different style if it wasn't grasped the first time
- **a second proof activity**: in a different style to the first

This structure provides the opportunity for students to rise to a high level of achievement, but the teacher has to provide the encouragement and support and, if necessary, the challenge. As with all the ideas in *The Teacher's Toolkit*, the procedures create only the skeleton: the life blood comes from the teacher's high expectations and sense of enthusiasm.

Here's an "Upwardly Mobile" planning template:

ALL STUDENTS MUST	ALL STUDENTS SHOULD	ALL STUDENTS COULD
Learning objective 1	Learning objective 2	Learning objective 3 ....
....	....	....
....	....	....
Learning Activity	Learning Activity	Learning Activity
Proof Activity	Proof Activity	Proof Activity
Loop Activity	Loop Activity	Loop Activity
Reproof Activity	Reproof Activity	Reproof Activity

The "Upwardly Mobile" method operates most powerfully if the learning objectives are expressed as "be able to" statements. These give students a clear and concrete vision of what they're aiming to achieve, which helps them stay focused and motivated. The more an objective is presented as a do-able activity, the more inviting it is. Also, such objectives provide observable and measurable success criteria, making self-assessment and teacher assessment relatively easy.

An example: Year 8 science

When we first sat down to plan I asked the teacher, Sue, what we'd be doing over the next couple of lessons. "Vaccination", she said.

"What will the students be learning?" I enquired.
"Well, they'll be learning about vaccination."
"What exactly about vaccination?"
"You know, how vaccines work."
"What's the absolute minimum that you want all students to leave the lesson having understood?"

Silence. Sue wasn't used to thinking like this. In fact, she normally just did the next double spread in *Spotlight Science*, which she eagerly opened for me to see. Sue was used to planning from the resource, rather than from learning objectives. She seemed to feel that the textbook had done the planning for her and that all she had to do was follow it. I gently suggested that we close the book, define what we wanted the students to learn and then see whether any bits of the book were going to be a helpful to us. So, we started with a blank piece of paper.

The need to have three learning objectives, each at a different level and each beginning with the phrase "be able to" forced some hard and detailed thinking. Before long the *must* and *should* targets were defined:

- *All* students *must* be able to describe how a vaccine is given and what basic effect it has.
- *Most* students *should* be able to explain that both disease and vaccination involve microbes entering the body.

Then we got stuck. Sue felt sure that the students wouldn't be able to grasp any more than this. So we talked a bit about the potential of the brain and the power of expectations and then decided that *some* students *could* be able to explain the effect of vaccination on the body's immune system.

With the differentiated learning targets in place, we could now decide how they would be achieved and assessed. Sue's immediate thought, again, was to turn to *Spotlight Science* for guidance, but we resisted the temptation and instead reminded ourselves of students' learning-style differences and the need for variety. Before long this is what we'd come up with.

Aim: to understand how vaccines work.

ALL MUST	MOST SHOULD	SOME COULD
be able to describe how a vaccine is given and what basic effect it has.	**be able to explain that both disease and vaccination involve microbes entering the body.**	**be able to explain the effect of vaccination on the body's immune system.**
Teacher hot-seated in role as a doctor	Read and digest an information sheet	Work out key questions and conduct a library search
Draw a six-frame storyboard of a child's vaccination against measles and what happens during an outbreak	Construct a labelled diagram from the above text	Prepare (alone or in pairs) a 2–3-minute presentation to the whole class, including visuals aids or "acting out"
Match sentence halves	Teacher explanation to individuals and small groups	Work from the CD-ROM
Put the completed sentences in chronological order	Label a pre-drawn diagram	Make a bench-top model of the effect of vaccination on the immune system using ordinary items from around the room

The learning begins with a whole-class activity: hot-seating. At this point the teacher is both the leader of the activity and the main source of information. As soon as the exercise is finished, everyone attempts to prove, both to themselves and the teacher, that they've achieved the first learning objective. If they can draw the six-frame storyboard accurately and in suffi-cient detail, without any help, it proves that they have "got it" and they move directly on to the next level. If they need help, from a peer or the teacher, that's OK: it just shows where the misunderstandings or gaps are, so they can be rectified. These students have another go at the basic learning objective but use a different strategy – matching sentence halves. Then they make another attempt to prove that they've grasped the idea by sequencing events in chronological order.

Meanwhile, some students have read and digested the information sheet for the *should* level and are now trying to prove their understanding by turning it into a diagram. As time goes on the students become more strung out, working at different paces with different degrees of success. The teacher moves round offering help where it's most needed, checking the completed proof activities and if necessary double-checking student's understanding orally – students have to be OK'd by the teacher before they can move to the next level. This is how rigour is maintained.

There are several points to note. The first is that, as you look across the whole page you see evidence of *different learning styles and intelligences*. For instance, hot-seating is fairly Abstract Random; reading and digesting an information sheet is Abstract Sequential; matching sentence halves and putting sentences in chronological order are Concrete Sequential; and making a bench-top model to explain a process is pretty Concrete Random. There's *visual* (diagrams and text), *auditory* (hot-seating and the teacher's explanations to individuals and small groups) and *kinaesthetic* (making a model, moving bits of card). Multiple intelligences are also in evidence. For example, working out key questions and sequencing (*logical*), matching sentences and reading an information sheet (*linguistic*), storyboard (*visual*), working in pairs and presenting to the class (*interpersonal*).

I'm not suggesting that it's possible or desirable to pack all the styles under the sun into a short series of lessons. However, it is important to honour students by building in variety, even within a single lesson, and the different models on offer simply help to stretch our thinking in different directions.

The second point to note is that, beyond the first learning activity, after everyone has done hot-seating, *learning is relatively independent*. Students move at different paces, will therefore be at different points at different times and cannot be collectively led by the teacher. Students clearly need to have a number of basic independent learning skills and attitudes in place, otherwise the teacher will be torn to shreds as she tries to be everywhere at once. On the one hand, "Upwardly Mobile" is good training for the more advanced independent qualities demanded by the "Menu", "Sole Search" and "Blank Cheque" operating systems. On the other hand, there's no use pursuing this method if the students are not ready – it only leads to a sense of frustration and a rejection of the approach.

Thirdly, so that everyone can keep their learning on track, it's important to give each student a copy of the planning sheet. The way it's presented above looks rather like a snakes-and-ladders game, which is appealing, but the layout and graphics really need to be more student-friendly. At best such a sheet should *provide students with a route map* of their learning. Learners should be able to see clearly where they are, where they're going, what the destination's like, what represents achievement at each level and what the various options are.

Pragmatically, giving the route map to students and taking time to explain it at the beginning of the topic takes pressure off the teacher. It cuts out the "I've finished – what do I do now?" syndrome. Psychologically, seeing the big picture helps to open students' reticular activating systems and is particularly important for right-brain, holistic learners. It supports students' motivation, focus and perseverance.

So, here are two further real examples, both from art, of upwardly mobile route maps. They don't look like the planning template above, nor should they. The idea, as we've said time and again in *The Teacher's Toolkit*, is for you to customise rather than copy the ideas presented.

Pop-up Card Project

Overview
- You are required to make a pop-up card to celebrate an occasion.
- The card must be A5 size.
- Photomontage must be used to create the images on the front and inside.
- Computer-generated lettering must be used for any message.

Homework
Homework will consist of collecting images and card examples as well as the DOCUMENTATION.

The deadline for Realisation and Documentation is:

Investigating and collecting

start here

You must

Investigate some examples of pop-up mechanisms by studying the samples and making your own paper working models.

Collect examples of cards for any occasion.

Collect images from magazines and newspapers for use as a photomontage.

Use one of the computer programs to generate examples of lettering to use with your design.

You should

Draw some of your collected images

Make some drawings of different letter shapes.

You could

Make some coloured drawings of imaginary monsters which could be used as part of the design.

Draw things from direct observation to include in your design

The deadline for investigating and collecting is:

Experimenting

You must

Make some photomontage images for the front cover of the card based on your collected images.

Make some photomontage images for the inside of the card based on your collected images.

Make a working mock-up of the card in paper, using blank vignettes of the proposed layout to make sure the mechanism works.

You should

Make some alternative mock-up designs showing different layouts and mechanisms.

Try to make some working designs using multiple pop-up mechanisms.

You could

Try to design a 3-dimensional pop-up card to be presented in a box.

The deadline for experimenting is:

Realisation

You must

Make a pop-up card using photomontage to celebrate a special occasion based on your investigations and experiments. Colour and pattern must be used for the pop-up image.

You should

Draw out some pop-up ideas immediately after you have finished the final piece.

You could

Make a second, improved, version of the card.

Documentation

Record by drawing and writing all the changes made during the whole process.

Write, in rough, a comparison between the best and worst designs of your collection of card examples.

Write an evaluation of the whole project considering these points. 1) Did it end up as you meant it to? If not, why not? 2) Why you chose the images you did and were they appropriate to the celebration? 3) Any problems you experienced and how you solved them. 4) Use of the key words.

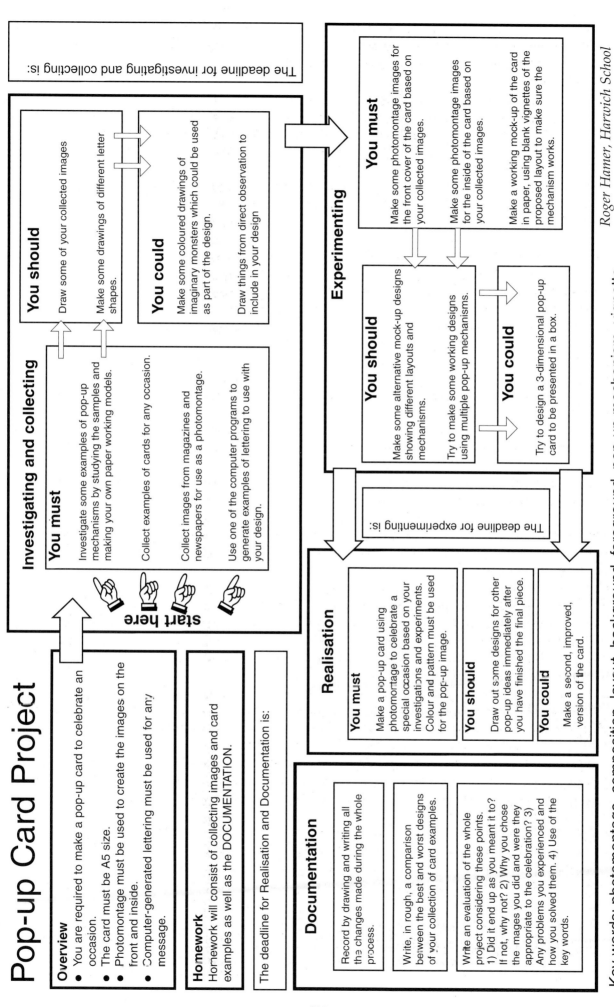

Roger Hamer, Harwich School

Key words: photomontage, composition, layout, background, foreground, pop-up mechanism, vignette

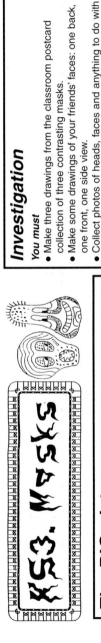

KS3. MASKS

The BIG picture

You are required to make a mask out of either clay or card based on observations of other masks, collections of images of heads and drawings of heads.

Marking ★★★

When you finish any of the tasks:
1/ mark it yourself, using pencil, referring to the Assessment Grid.
2/ bring it to the teacher for a final mark.
3/ if you have time, make some improvements and have it re-marked.

Homework ★★★

Apart from the work done in your homework book every other week, you will be expected to set your own homework to finish this project:
This can be:
1/ making improvements to your drawings.
2/ recording changes to your final piece.
3/ finishing your final piece by coming in to school at the end of the day.

Timing

Keep an eye on the times so that you finish by the deadline. This should help you decide when you need to do some extra homework.

DON'T FORGET THAT YOU CAN COME IN MOST EVENINGS TO CONTINUE YOUR WORK.

Investigation

You must
- Make three drawings from the classroom postcard collection of three contrasting masks.
- Make some drawings of your friends' faces: one back, one front, one side view.
- Collect photos of heads, faces and anything to do with heads like hats, armour etc.
- Look at the examples of ceramic and card masks to pick up ideas.

You should
- Make some detailed drawings of your eyes, nose or mouth. Make each drawing big enough to fit on an A5 page.
- Make drawings from comics of really expressive faces.

You could
- Write about the masks you chose to draw, explaining why you thought they contrasted.
- Do some research on masks in the Resources Centre. Find out where different masks come from, why they are made and why they differ in style.

Deadline for investigation is:

Experimentation

You must
- Make three drawings which include features from your investigations.
- Look at the worksheets on "How to Make" clay and card masks.
- Make some simple drawings of how you will construct your chosen idea in your chosen media.

You should
- Write a short piece about your intentions: what expression and feeling you want the mask to have.
- Write how you plan to use line, pattern, texture, colour and form in achieving this expression.

You could
- Make some more drawings of one of your ideas showing what it would look like with a costume.

Deadline for experimentation is:

Realisation

You must
- Make a mask.

You should
- Record all your changes made during the making process by quick drawings and notes.

You could
- Make a second mask using different materials, if you have time.

- Have a good look at the Help Sheets to guide you in the building process.
- *Remember that you get points for **quality**, not for speed.*
- As you progress you may want to change your ideas to improve the design. Do not worry that you are not making it the same as your original ideas because this is how ideas develop.

Group														
week	*1*	*2*	*3*	*4*	*5*	*6*	*7*	*8*	*9*	*10*	*11*	*12*	*13*	*14*
1st period							Half term							
2nd period														

Roger Hamer, Harwich School

240

"Upwardly Mobile" can be connected to official standards of attainment: for example, SATs levels and GCSE grades. A science teacher who was used to teaching his Year 10 middle set formally as a whole class decided to change tack. He prepared a "route map" for the topic of plant hormones and auxins, set out all the necessary resources on the side bench and explained that after the initial activity they would be asked to work at their own pace, taking their learning to the highest level of their ability and aspiration. At each stage they would know exactly what they were achieving in exam terms.

EXAM LEVEL	TARGETS	LEARNING ACTIVITY	PROOF
E	◆ Know that plant hormones are chemicals ◆ Know that hormones control the growth of shoots and roots ◆ Know that plant hormones control flowering and ripening of fruits ◆ Know that shoots grow towards the light	◆ Information race in which you answer questions as quickly as you can	1. Completion of check sheet with questions about the targets 2. Exam questions at Grade E level
C	◆ Know that plant hormones are called auxins ◆ Know that auxins move through the plant in solution ◆ Know what phototropism and geotropism are ◆ Know that auxins are involved in phototropism and geotropism ◆ Be able to relate the action of plant hormones to their use as weed killers, rooting powders and fruit ripeners	◆ Comprehension exercise in which you research the answers to key questions ◆ A modelling exercise in which you act out how phototropism and geotropism work	1. Word and meaning matching 2. Sentence completion 3. Exam questions at Grade C level
A	◆ Be able to interpret data from experiment results about the action of auxins ◆ Be able to explain *how* auxins make shoots curve ◆ Be able to evaluate the economic benefits of hormone use in agriculture	◆ Data interpretation sheets on the use of plant auxins	1. Exam questions at Grade A level

Paul Stewart, Willingsworth High School

The teacher set the students off by going through the E-grade targets (top left box) and leading the "Quick on the Draw" (page 145) information race (top middle box). After that they were on their own. Some got their heads down immediately and worked fervently, others formed pairs and some did nothing. Partway through the next lesson the usual group of troublesome boys were still waiting to be told to get on with their work. This to them was a doss. Then it began to dawn on them that the teacher wasn't going to be drawn into the usual game of "make me if you can", that they were actually staring serious failure in the face, and they began to settle down. By this time one or two other students were already tackling the A-grade material. The teacher spent most of his time by the side bench administering the resources, checking attempts at the proof exercises and giving guidance where pupils were stuck.

Afterwards, he said it was hard, managing the classroom in a totally different way, and particularly holding back enough for students to get the message that they were truly responsible for their own levels of achievement. At the end of the "experiment" he said, remarkably, that he could now see how he had previously held back many of the students by his lock-step teaching. He had not realised how quickly and rigorously many of them could work as lessons were normally slowed down by constant interruptions from those who needed to be told off or have things repeated.

Here's an example of a technology department using "Upwardly Mobile" to structure its thinking about a whole scheme of work: Year 7 toy making. We join them partway through the planning process:

	Planning	Assembly	Evaluation	Research	Solutions
MUST NC Levels 2/3	Be able to choose appropriately from a list of materials and equipment.		Be able to write a personal judgment by completing sentence prompts.	Be able, after looking at three toys, to determine the one most suited to the early-years child. Be able to give a prompted reason for the choice.	
SHOULD NC Levels 4/5	Be able to choose, without prompts, correct materials techniques and equipment and say why. Be able to present a step-by-step plan in a form that suits the pupil.		Be able to identify the similarities and differences between the original design and the finished product. Be able to make and explain changes during and/or at the end of the process.	Be able to come to a conclusion about the most suitable toy from a wider range of sources (e.g. survey, Early Years Learning Centre catalogue, visit to a toy shop).	
COULD NC Levels 5/6	Be able to produce a timed plan independently which is adapted according to ongoing requirements.			Be able to present the research data using ICT (e.g. word-processed report, graphics, PowerPoint). Be able to put the research into the context of early-years development theory.	

When their planning is finished and all the learning objectives have been mapped out, the department will be in a position to devise the route map for students. It's easy to see how everything falls into place once differentiated "be able to" objectives have been thought through carefully.

Sometimes learning has to follow a predetermined sequence. For example, making a "steady hand game" in technology. The teacher wants to introduce certain concepts and procedures at certain times to the whole class. In fact, health-and-safety regulations require that he do so – the explanation and demonstration of the Perspex heat former, for instance. So there are definite points where the whole class need to come back together in order to move on to the next stage. Therefore, there's a limit to how far individual students can race ahead.

In such cases, "Upwardly Mobile" might look like this. Students can extend their learning at each separate stage, taking it as far as they can before having to come back down to earth for the collective start of the next stage.

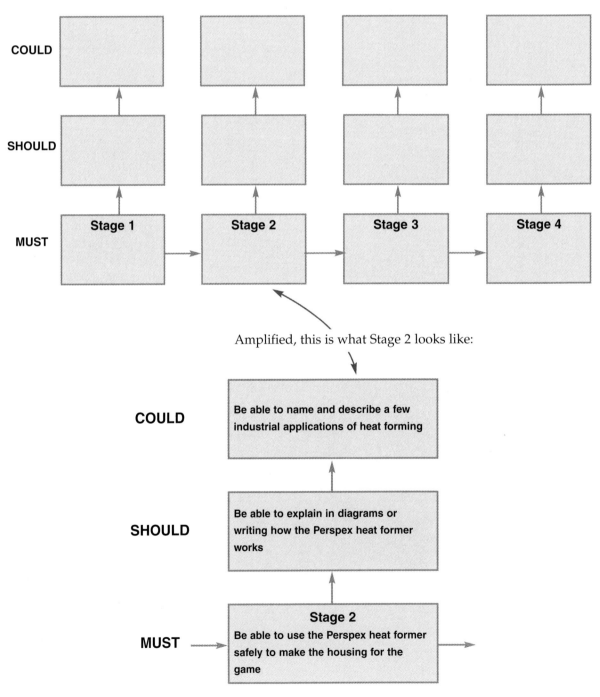

Amplified, this is what Stage 2 looks like:

In conclusion

The language of *must, could, should* is only one way of describing the different levels. *All, most, some* is another. If you don't like either of these, try *bronze, silver, gold*, which suggests a challenge, an invitation for students to stretch themselves, to go as far or as fast as they can, to beat their personal best. Everyone gets a medal; all achievement is valued. This sort of language appeals to some students, but not all, so use different nomenclatures at different times.

Also, there's no need to limit the approach to just three levels – have as many as you like!

The "Upwardly Mobile" operating system takes more time to prepare than "Overtime" and "Extended Horizons" and it demands more independent tasks and resources. However, once the structure is in place, it is designed to be self-sufficient for several lessons. What's more, three types of differentiation are achieved: with regard to pace; with regard to the sophistication and complexity of the learning; and with regard to learning style. Gains in pupils' motivation and achievement usually result in teachers feeling that it was well worth the effort.

Menu

This method takes independent learning one stage further, by offering pupils a choice of learning strategy. It also allows for a more tailor-made delivery of learning-style differences.

The teacher designs a number of learning strategies based on different learning styles. Students will work at the same topic, but in different ways. They will travel to the same destination, but by different routes. So the end point, the learning objectives, needs to be made clear to students at the beginning. As we've said before, objectives are best expressed as "be able to" statements: for example, "By the end of this lesson you will be able to tell the difference between series and parallel circuits". Objectives expressed in such concrete, doable terms leave students in no doubt about what they have to aim for. Students will know when they've arrived. By offering measurable success criteria, they make achievement real.

It's important to spend enough time explaining and generating enthusiasm for these objectives. They will drive the learning. The more independent the learning, the more students need the guiding lights of internalised learning objectives. So, don't just write them on the board: be excited about them; give demos of what students will be able to do when they've achieved them; explain how this learning will open doors to further possibilities; show how far the learning objectives will take them towards exam success; encourage them to ask you questions about the objectives and their assessment. Only then will reticular activating systems actually activate.

The next step is to provide a basic introduction to the topic, giving whatever minimal information is needed to orientate the students. They will benefit from knowing some of the key technical terms, basic facts and main features of the material. Then offer the options. Here's an example. As part of their GCSE coursework Year 10 students have to present a piece of work in the style of the American pop-artist Roy Lichtenstein. The teacher explains the learning objective: "to be able to paint in the style of Roy Lichtenstein". The students then gather round the art room PC to watch a PowerPoint presentation about Lichtenstein, giving examples of his work and highlighting the main features of his style.

The final screen of the twenty-slide presentation offers the students four ways into their project:

For the detectives!

Find out more about Lichtenstein and his methods before you begin painting. Go to the school library, use books and the CD-ROM, *Major Artists of the Western World*, to find out about his life and times. Work out Lichtenstein's place in the history of art. Then come back to the art room and make a start on your practical piece.

For the team players!

Get together with a few others, bounce some ideas around, brainstorm, do some draft doodling, compare ideas. When you've got your creative juices flowing, break away and start your individual work.

For the alchemists!

Get paint and paper and make a start straightaway. Just have a go. It doesn't have to be perfect first time: you can experiment and rework your ideas. After a while you come to me, or I'll come to you, and we'll discuss how you're getting on.

For the busy bees!

If you want to get going straightaway but you're not sure exactly what to do, then click this button. You will receive a set of step-by-step on-screen instructions.

Alan Cadman, Thistley Hough High School

Students then make their individual choices and get going. The teacher moves around the classroom supporting, encouraging, challenging, micro-teaching – exactly as normal. He's already had a word with the school librarian and she's happy to oversee the "detectives" during their initial period of research.

One issue that often arises when students are asked to make this kind of choice is peer pressure: some students just go with the crowd, choosing what their mates choose. One way of overcoming this is to ask students to indicate their choices by closing their eyes and putting their hands up. Another way is to ask everyone to hold up a choice card simultaneously, or to write their choice secretly on a piece of paper and hand it in. Of course, students can find ways round these and if they really are intent on copying others then they probably aren't ready for the "Menu" approach.

Incidentally, you may have noticed that the four Lichtenstein choices are based on Dr Anthony Gregorc's analysis of learning styles:

Detectives = Abstract Sequential   **Team players** = Abstract Random
Alchemists = Concrete Random   **Busy bees** = Concrete Sequential

Here's another example. A technology department has realised that it doesn't have to continue its habit of getting all the students to do the same things in the same way. Instead it now asks teachers to offer four choices to students, again based on Gregorc's model, for each stage of design.

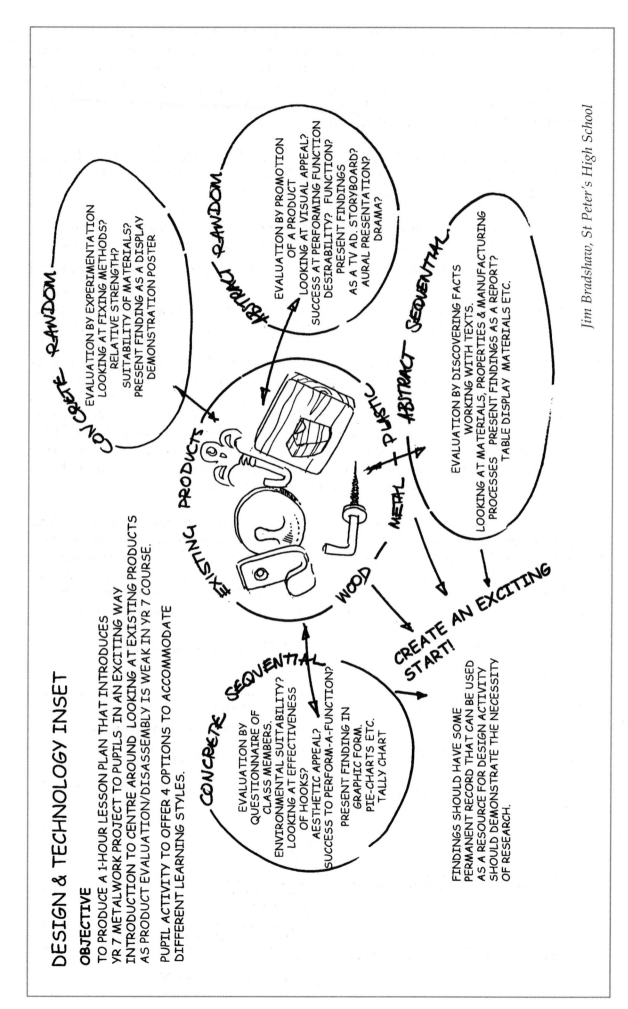

DESIGN & TECHNOLOGY INSET

OBJECTIVE

TO PRODUCE A 1-HOUR LESSON PLAN THAT INTRODUCES
YR 7 METALWORK PROJECT TO PUPILS IN AN EXCITING WAY
INTRODUCTION TO CENTRE AROUND LOOKING AT EXISTING PRODUCTS
AS PRODUCT EVALUATION/DISASSEMBLY IS WEAK IN YR 7 COURSE.

PUPIL ACTIVITY TO OFFER 4 OPTIONS TO ACCOMMODATE
DIFFERENT LEARNING STYLES.

CONCRETE RANDOM

EVALUATION BY EXPERIMENTATION
LOOKING AT FIXING METHODS?
RELATIVE STRENGTH?
SUITABILITY OF MATERIALS?
PRESENT FINDING AS A DISPLAY
DEMONSTRATION POSTER

ABSTRACT RANDOM

EVALUATION BY PROMOTION
OF A PRODUCT
LOOKING AT VISUAL APPEAL?
SUCCESS AT PERFORMING FUNCTION
DESIRABILITY? FUNCTION?
PRESENT FINDINGS
AS A TV AD. STORYBOARD?
AURAL PRESENTATION?
DRAMA?

ABSTRACT SEQUENTIAL

EVALUATION BY DISCOVERING FACTS
WORKING WITH TEXTS.
LOOKING AT MATERIALS, PROPERTIES & MANUFACTURING
PROCESSES PRESENT FINDINGS AS A REPORT?
TABLE DISPLAY MATERIALS ETC.

EXISTING PRODUCTS

WOOD — PLASTIC
METAL

CREATE AN EXCITING
START!

CONCRETE SEQUENTIAL

EVALUATION BY
QUESTIONNAIRE OF
CLASS MEMBERS.
ENVIRONMENTAL SUITABILITY?
LOOKING AT EFFECTIVENESS
OF HOOKS?
AESTHETIC APPEAL?
SUCCESS TO PERFORM-A-FUNCTION?
PRESENT FINDING IN
GRAPHIC FORM.
PIE-CHARTS ETC.
TALLY CHART

FINDINGS SHOULD HAVE SOME
PERMANENT RECORD THAT CAN BE USED
AS A RESOURCE FOR DESIGN ACTIVITY
SHOULD DEMONSTRATE THE NECESSITY
OF RESEARCH.

Jim Bradshaw, St Peter's High School

The department has already introduced the idea of learning-style differences to this Year 7 class, which makes the choosing a bit more serious and deliberate. As the work gets under way, the teachers begin to operate as personal tutors and not just technology experts. They discuss students' choices with them, helping each learner to judge whether the choice they made was a good one and whether they would choose similarly or differently next time. This of course begins to increase students' self-awareness and confidence.

In another school, a food technology teacher applied the "Menu" method to pizza making. As soon as the students came into the room she gave them the learning objective – "to be able to make a successful pizza base" – and three choices:

1. You can read about how to make a pizza base and follow written instructions. Come over to this side of the room, where I've put out a number of books, pictures and recipes.

2. You can watch me do a demonstration, then go off and copy what I did. Gather round the front bench.

3. Then there's trial and error – work it out for yourself! Bring your ingredients over here, where I've put out all the equipment you'll need.

The class were taken by surprise: they'd never had options like this before. Choices were made spontaneously as the teacher urged the students to be quick; there was hustle and bustle for a few minutes, then the students settled down and got on. After a while a couple of lads who'd initially chosen trial and error drifted over to the teacher's demo and two others went across to read some recipes. Once the demo was over, the teacher moved busily round the classroom performing her usual teacherly duties. At the end of the lesson, in the calm after the storm, she reported that the more difficult students had been much more on-task and achieved better results than normal. A risk worth taking, as it turned out.

Here is a maths example. A young teacher is tackling decimals with a mid-set Year 7 class. They don't enjoy the subject on the whole and struggle with most concepts. Formal teaching of the whole class is not producing good results. So, he tries the "Menu" approach and puts together a Argos-type catalogue of 25 different activities and exercises for learning and practising decimals. The contents are a mixture of home-made handwritten pages and photocopiable extracts from commercial resources. The cover page gives the learning targets:

Objectives By the end of the next 7 lessons you must ...	Explanations and examples
be able to describe the decimal system	Explain that it is based on the number 10. Explain that the decimal point separates whole numbers from fractions.
be able to give the value of a digit in any number	31.67 – What do these digits stand for?
be able to recognise and read decimals in common usage	Read and explain: £17.52 36.4°C 5.17 metres 16.3 secs 29.25 kilograms 0.33 litres
be able to measure accurately using various units	What is 346p in £s? Height of the filing cabinet in m. Body temperature in °C. 50m run in secs Weight of a shoe in kilos Capacity of a milk bottle in litres
be able to add and subtract decimals to 2 decimal places	Calculate a) 16.35 + 23.17 b) 38.52 – 19.67

The activities, each one described on a separate page of the catalogue, include:

- Bunny hopping in the playground
- Shuttle running
- Shuttlecock throwing
- Measuring stones using a Eureka can
- Weighing parcels on a pair of scales
- Making a "Decibeast", a large drawing of a fantasy animal to given proportions
- Playing hopscotch with counters
- A variety of games to be played with other students or with family at home
- Number-crunching worksheets
- A couple of investigations
- Cutting-and-sticking exercises
- Charts to fill in
- Straightforward explanations of concepts and techniques with examples
- Practice sheets
- Simulated shopping

Of course, students are not expected to work their way through the entire catalogue – there's not enough time. Rather, they are asked to select the methods that will work most efficiently for them. The teacher has already spent time gathering all the resources – from the science, geography, art and PE departments mainly – and organised open-access storage on shelves and in the main cupboard. He is fortunate in having a downstairs classroom overlooking the playground, so he can keep an eye on the fun and games outside.

Different areas of the classroom are designated for different types of activity. There is a quiet area with desks separated for individual work, a messy area for the water, paint and glue types of activities and an area for group work. When it's wet, the physical activities take place in the hall rather than outside.

The students keep choosing and rechoosing activities as they go along, supported and challenged by the teacher. Some are so keen that they do all the activities anyway, coming in at lunchtime to continue and doing the less complicated exercises at home. Others need more support from the teacher, who sometimes pulls several students together to explain a crucial point.

The options in the catalogue are not based on Gregorc – in fact they are not based on any one learning styles model but have been influenced by several. There are visual, auditory and kinaesthetic options, several Gardnerian intelligences are represented and there are pragmatist, theorist, activist and reflective options based on Honey and Mumford's construct.

Let's look at a final example from the area of religious education. Year 8 are about to begin Buddhism and a variation of the "Menu" method, the "Set Menu" method, is seen by the teacher as a way of easing them into more independent ways. Last lesson the teacher explained about learning styles, used the questionnaire on page 283 and asked each student to hand in their colour preference written on a bit of paper. For this lesson, the room has been divided into three areas and the teacher has put a name tag on every desk. All the yellow students are in one area, all the blue in another, and the rest (red and green combined) are across the back.

The teacher explains that different groups will tackle different aspects of the topic in different ways:

1. The **yellow** group will find out about the life of the Buddha using a research guide and the trolley of books on loan from the school library. You can work in pairs or alone, but each person has to end up with their own written report on the Buddha's life. Everyone will then read theirs to a small group of students from the other colour groups.

2. The **blue** group will invite a couple of Buddhist monks from the local temple in Birmingham into school. You will need to make all the arrangements, provide hospitality, conduct interviews and then present "The Life of a Buddhist Monk" through hot-seating and a series of still images to the whole class.

3. The **red** and **green** groups combined will study the architecture, symbolism and key features of Buddhist temples, particularly contrasting ancient with modern styles. You will visit the local Birmingham temple, decide for yourselves how to record what you see, then make labelled cardboard models to bring out the key points. When they're finished, the rest of us will move round the classroom viewing your models while you provide commentaries.

Once this work had been completed, several lessons later, the whole experience was debriefed. Students were asked to compare their initial questionnaire results with their experience of their preferred style in action. This led to heightened self-awareness, a more serious attitude to learning styles and, most crucially, the ability to make wise choices when the teacher provided a menu of choices for the next topic.

To conclude, there are five further points to be made:

1. In all these examples, the learning objectives are not explicitly differentiated. The teacher does provide high levels of individual, and therefore differentiated, support to individual students, though. Even so, the upfront learning objectives *could* be differentiated. In the maths example, there could have been *must*, *could* and *should* levels with activities in the catalogue dedicated to each category. in the art and first technology examples, the objectives could have been differentiated because the four options were broad enough to allow for different levels of learning to be achieved.

2. This brings us to a further application of the "Menu" operating system. Particularly with a mixed-ability class, it may be beneficial to offer options based not so much on different learning styles, but on different levels of current ability in the topic being studied. Just to remind you, it's not helpful to talk of a student's generic "ability" – it doesn't exist. All students have a *range of abilities* linked in some way to their multiple-intelligence profiles (page 46). Also, as Professor Tim Brighouse once said, "A teacher knows nothing about a student's ability – only what he or she has achieved so far". Ability is ever changing, suddenly a penny drops and a leap forward is made after weeks in which the idea has not sunk in. This is consistent with the notion of constructivism and the pattern-making function of the neocortex (page 18–19). So our judgments of students must be continually updated. The ultimate aim is to help a student move from where they are now to a point beyond.

3. As a topic progresses, it's important for the teacher not only to check the quality of learning, but also to debrief learning styles with students so that their future choice making might be precise and productive. It's inevitable that, as students accumulate more and more experience of making choices and working with different styles, the wiser they become. However, this natural process can be accelerated by the teacher debriefing with individual students *during* the learning process and with the whole class at the end. In my view this is a vital aspect of what Abbott and Ryan call "intellectual weaning".[1]

4. The "Menu" method allows individual styles to be accommodated fairly precisely. The more choices made available to students, the more chances there are of accommodating individual preferences. There's a limit, though, governed by a combination of the teacher's energy, creativity, time and available resources. In the preparation of the various options, most teachers find it helpful to use a learning-styles model to prompt their thinking and ensure that all angles are covered. There are many on the market. See page 34 and Appendix B for an overview of options.

5. There's a trap. Students might continually choose the same sort of option. At first this might not be a problem, as it's important for them to have lots of success in order to feel confident and capable as learners. In time, though, you might want to encourage students to take on nonpreferred options in order to broaden their experience and skills base. Again, we see how important it is for the subject teacher to operate as a tutor.

Sole Search

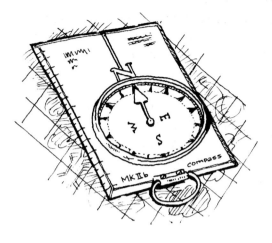

In this approach, as its name suggests, students work independently – they are on their own. This doesn't mean that they necessarily work individually. Some may, because that suits their style. Others will work in pairs or small groups. The point is that they are not being taught by the teacher: they are finding things out and working things out for themselves. This requires them to exercise a greater degree of responsibility than any of the operating systems presented so far.

Students are guided by the teacher to prepare a tailor-made learning strategy, which is recorded in their personal learning plan. Details of the student's learning objectives or research questions, their timescale, their learning methods, their co-conspirators (if they are working in a small group), the means of evidencing and assessing their learning are all recorded. The plan also contains the student's "Stepometer", a device for keeping their learning rigorous and focused so that achievement is maximised.

After an initial introductory lesson, the teacher provides very little input of content. Her job is to operate as a tutor and manager. Students learn by using appropriate resources: books, videos, people, places, CD-ROMs, Internet, audio tapes, worksheets … Resources and learning method will vary from student to student, depending on their learning style, prior knowledge and current ability in the area of study. Inevitably, success will depend on the range and quality of resources available, which means that the teacher may need to invest time in preparing materials to complement commercial items.

The learning targets are usually fixed for everyone; it's the means of reaching them that differs from student to student. This is the simplest version. However, a more differentiated application of "Sole Search" is to vary the targets for each student to suit individual needs.

Let's have a look at the approach in more detail. First, the personal learning plan. Here's a typical example with all the essential components. Please don't use it slavishly: you are encouraged to design your own version to suit your own circumstances.

Personal Learning Plan

Name_____ When this plan starts_____

This is what I am setting out to learn *or* **These are the questions I will answer**

1 _____

2 _____

3 _____

4 _____

5 _____

I have to have this learning finished by _____

This is how I will carry out my learning

With	By	Using
_____	_____	_____
_____	_____	_____
_____	_____	_____
_____	_____	_____

This is how I will *teach other people* what I have learned

_____

_____

I will do this on _____ **(date)**

This is how I will *present* my learning for assessment

_____

_____

I will present it on _____ **(date)**

Assessment arrangements_____

_____

Here are some ways to carry out your learning. Mix and match from the three columns.

With

- Yourself – work on your own
- A partner
- Others in a small group

By

- Reading
- Notemaking
- Testing a hypothesis
- Following instructions
- Collecting and analysing data
- Observing
- Peer teaching
- Watching
- Making
- Debating
- Modelling
- Listening
- Questioning
- Thinking
- Imitating
- Visiting
- Imagining
- Dancing
- Interviewing
- Exploring
- Meeting
- Dramatising
- Trialling
- Surveying
- Reflecting
- Evaluating
- Discussing
- Corresponding

Using

- TV
- Books
- Magazines
- Internet
- Photographs
- Family
- Your teacher
- Video tapes
- Journals
- Telephone
- Online course
- Experience
- Your own imagination
- Visitors
- Newspapers
- CD-ROMs
- Audio tapes
- School library
- Distance-learning materials
- Radio
- Friends
- Video conferencing
- Visits
- Public library
- Other teachers
- Neighbours
- Primary source documents
- The mail
- Other pupils' work
- Objects
- Pictures
- Computer
- Experts
- Models
- Pamphlets
- Study guides
- Your environment
- Worksheets
- Museum

Here are some ways of presenting your learning. Make choices based on what best suits the nature of what you've learned, your own learning style, and the assessment requirements.

Newspaper	Lead a discussion or debate	Teach a lesson
Illustrated booklet	Posters or wallcharts	Diagrams
Project	Essay	Radio show
Lecture	Exhibition	Flowchart
Seminar	Puppetry	Key-word plan
Video recording	Song	Storyboard
Audio recording	Overhead projector presentation	Lead a visit or field trip
Mime	Game	TV show
Hot seat	Contribute to discussion or a	Interview
Still images	debate	Poem
Dance	Model	PowerPoint presentation

STEPOMETER

Date and time when this step was written	This is the small step I need to take next	This is how long it should take … and how long it actually took

The plan is designed to be used after an introductory lesson and continues for the whole of the research period. It fits into the sequence of lessons as follows:

Define 'first steps' for each student

```
┌─────────────┐    ┌──────────────────────┐   ┌─────────────┐   ┌──────────────┐
│ Introductory│───▶│ Research according to│──▶│ Tidy up,    │──▶│ Assessment   │
│ lesson      │    │ the Personal Learning│   │ clarify and │   │ against the  │
│             │    │ Plan                 │   │ consolidate │   │ original     │
│             │    │                      │   │ the learning│   │ questions    │
└─────────────┘    └──────────────────────┘   └─────────────┘   └──────────────┘
```

Each student fills in the Plan

Resources: classroom materials, library resources and others

Stage One

Provide an introductory lesson, which should:

Give an overview of the topic to be studied. This could be presented both orally and visually, perhaps as a mind map. Students will need to find their way around the topic as they conduct their independent research, so it's important that they can see the whole territory, the important connections and the blind alleys in advance.

Introduce the learning objectives. These are most inviting if presented as questions to be answered. You might have two or (maximum) three questions that everyone has to tackle. These would relate to core learning objectives. You might then suggest different additional targets to different students, some simple, some complex depending on individual students' prior knowledge and current abilities in the given area of study. You might ask students to add their own questions instead, so that their personal interests and curiosities are built in and their motivation harnessed. You might even have completely different questions for different students if you want to go for a fully differentiated approach. The questions will be tackled in order, so make sure that students have got the sequence right.

Explain the resources available and the constraints that apply. This means what students can and can't use, where they can and can't go, how long they've got, what choices they have about the way their learning is finally presented and the way in which their learning will be assessed. Explain that assessment will be conducted against the original questions.

Explain the learning-style choices recommended for this topic. Students are asked to select their personal strategy from the lists on the second page of the plan. They mix and match from the three columns. However, it's rare that there will be an entirely free choice, since most topics lend themselves to only certain styles of enquiry. The teacher's job is to suggest as wide a set of combinations as possible, realising that motivation will be lost if too many options are eliminated. This is where personal learning styles are accommodated, so a good variety of possibilities is essential. Once students have used "Sole Search" a few times, have become more familiar with independent research and more self-aware, they will be able to work out the options for themselves. Be careful that you don't provide guidance beyond the point at which it's needed. The intention is to wean students off the teacher's wisdom onto their own.

Before the end of this introductory lesson, students fill in their personal plans and hand them in to the teacher.

Stage Two

Before the next lesson the teacher goes through all the learning plans making modifications and adding comments where necessary. The most important job is to write the first couple of steps in each student's Stepometer. The Stepometer is a simple device:

Short next steps are written in advance. It's important for students always to be at least one whole step ahead. So, when the first step has been carried out, the third step is written in before the second step is undertaken.

The date and time of writing each step are recorded, so that the pace of learning can be monitored by the student and the teacher.

The predicted time to be taken for each step is also written in, so that learning is not allowed to meander slowly, as is sometimes the case with project work.

The *actual* time taken is also recorded, so that discrepancies can be discussed. If a step takes much longer than anticipated the reasons need to be uncovered – was it laziness or a genuine difficulty? This might prompt the teacher to offer micro-teaching of particular skills or concepts. On the other hand, if the step was finished early, was it just a bad estimate or was the work carried out superficially?

The Stepometer is totally flexible. For some students, those who are relatively new to independent learning or who have little prior knowledge of the area of study, the steps need to be short and precise. For others, those who have a good track record of independent learning, the steps can be bigger and take longer. These students can be expected to sustain their endeavours with less intervention from the teacher.

Students can be expected to decide on the steps themselves. Once the research is under way this will certainly be the case (see below), but initially many students will benefit from having the teacher set them off on the right track. The teacher knows the resources and the pitfalls. Many independent research projects get stuck in the early stages because students have only vague ideas, such as "Write to such-and-such an organisation for information" or "Go to the library and look for something on …" They soon get bored because there's no early sense of achievement and this puts the teacher under enormous pressure, having to redirect too many disgruntled and aimless students at once.

This said, if you want to stretch your students, then they should propose the first couple of steps in their Stepometer before they hand their plans in at the end of the first lesson. You then go through them and simply make modifications where necessary.

The other great benefit of scrutinising the plans at this stage is that you will be able to prepare the resources needed for the first research lesson. You will also know which students to target at the start of the lesson, the ones who have the most ambitious plans, or those who are likely to need encouragement or a firm word.

For further details about the use of the Stepometer, see "Step On It" on page 209.

Stage Three

At the start of the second lesson give out the learning plans and ask students to get on with their first steps. Make a beeline for the students you had targeted, then spend your time moving round the room guiding, challenging, suggesting, and, if necessary, rewriting steps for students who are struggling.

Students should always write a new step into their Stepometer as soon an old step has been completed. This way, they are always thinking at least one step ahead, which means they never get stuck. They always have an "approved" step to get on with while they are waiting for you to come round and look at the next step they've just written. Your job is to check these proposed steps, validate them if they're OK or suggest, even insist on, modifications to the content or timings. This is how rigour (through the nature of the steps) and pace (through the timing of the steps) is monitored and maintained by the teacher. In extreme cases, where a student doesn't have the will or the skill to propose their own steps, you can dictate them. But remember that the overall aim of "Sole Search" is to increase and improve the quality of students' independent learning skills, so you would resort to such measures only if all else fails!

Students are expected to work out of class time. Homework and classwork are regarded as a seamless robe of research, so steps have to be written that will be undertaken *between* lessons. These need to be written into homework diaries before the end of the lesson.

If students are working in pairs or small groups, it's not good enough for one person to write steps on behalf of the others, for three reasons. First, there's always the risk of passengers. This approach is designed to promote personal responsibility, so there shouldn't be an easy way out. Second, everyone needs to get used to keeping their own documentation – it's a good habit to get into for GCSE coursework, GNVQ assignments and the like. Finally, if a pair or group is functioning properly, each student will have different steps to undertake – work should be delegated – so they need their own record.

Stage Four

Personal learning plans are handed back to the teacher at the end of each lesson. Between lessons the teacher again goes through them, checking proposed steps, monitoring progress, suggesting strategies, tightening timings, ordering and preparing resources, making a note of pupils to target. The aim is for all students to be able to make immediate progress at the start of the next lesson. This replaces marking books.

This cycle is repeated throughout the period of research.

"Sole Search" can put great strains on the teacher. Managing resources, answering questions, keeping track of time, giving personal tuition, checking steps, writing permission slips to go to the library, rummaging in the stockroom for a key resource, organising photocopying – all these can result in a serious bout of dizziness. The cure is to share the management of time and resources with the students: expect *them* to take responsibility for locating and booking resources, storing their work, monitoring time and so on. For practical ways of doing this see page 268.

One idea, though, that should be discussed here is **help sheets**. These provide tutorial support on paper. Each sheet explains a concept or describes a process. Help sheets do the job of the teacher by repeating ideas and skills that have been previously taught. The sheets are on open access, to be consulted by any student at any time. However, there's often an irritating initial stage to work through where enquiring students still come to the teacher for help, simply out of habit. Once the teacher has redirected them to the help sheets a few times, they get the hang of it.

For example, an art class making clay animal plaques has access to help sheets that remind them how to

- draw an animal's head
- draw an animal's body
- make a clay animal plaque

These are printed on A3 sheets and stored in plastic pockets in a large ring binder. The department is building up quite a collection with different members of staff providing sheets on different topics. Instead of using lo-tech paper, the help sheets could be available on a home-made or commercial CD-ROM, or on the school computer network. For some topics explanations could be provided on audio cassettes or as MP3, wav or midi files. Video clips could be made available via media players on the classroom PC. In this day and age it's easy to get help to students without the teacher having to provide it herself. For further suggestions and examples, see "Double Take" (page 101).

Stage Five

Once the research period has ended, it's time for learning to be reviewed and consolidated. "Rounds" (page 196) or mini-presentations could be used to let students know what each other has done. The teacher will already have a shrewd idea, as progress will have been closely monitored at every step. More thorough exchanges could be achieved through "Marketplace" (page 122).

If students have worked to a common set of questions, "Spotlight" (page 154), "Calling Cards" (page 81), "Beat the Teacher" (page 161), "Thumbometer" (page 161) or "Randomiser" (page 197) could be used with the whole class to get a rough indication of what has and has not been understood. The teacher can then prepare a consolidation lesson, based on this diagnostic assessment, designed to plug gaps, iron out misconceptions and mop up details. All this is in readiness for a more formal assessment – the dreaded Stage Six!

Stage Six

The final assessment will be carried out against the original research questions – after all, these expressed the learning objectives. The assessment is likely to have a number of common tasks to cover the common questions, plus additional tasks to test the differentiated questions pursued by individual students or groups.

The whole escapade will conclude with an evaluation of the method itself. How successful was it as a way of learning the topic and of promoting independence? What should we do differently next time? For one or two ways of conducting such a review, see page 269 ("Blank Cheque", Step 10, "Review").

Blank Cheque

This is a truly student-centred approach, based on the best traditions of humanistic psychology, traditions that have largely been affirmed in recent years by the brain scientists. It is often perceived as the most risky path to tread, perhaps because it demands great skill on the part of the teacher and because in the early stages it appears to take longer than other methods. However, the rewards are great in terms of student engagement and multilayered achievement. Once the approach gets going, learning accelerates, owing to the deep understanding and ownership achieved by students during the initial process of negotiation.

Why have I called it "Blank Cheque"? Because some details of the teaching and learning process are already written in (learning objectives and timescales are nationally determined these days): the cheque has been signed, dated and made out to a recipient, as it were. Yet the amount, the learning strategy, is still to be determined by the person who will benefit – the learner.

The ten steps below attempt to describe in detail a process that should be dynamic. They offer a set of guidelines that should be modified to suit your circumstances. Use them flexibly, find your own ways of proceeding while holding true to the intentions to promote personal responsibility, collective responsibility, self-esteem and success for each and every student.

This approach has to be sustained for a number of lessons, so it is ideal for a topic or project that will take, say, six weeks, for GCSE coursework and for long-term homework assignments, and it is compatible with most vocational course structures.

All that I know about student-centred learning can be traced to the great Dr Donna Brandes, originally of Chicago and now based in Australia, with whom I worked closely for a number of years when I was a much younger teacher and trainer. Together we wrote *A Guide to Student-Centred Learning*[2] and *The Student-Centred School*,[3] books that will give you much more insight into the principles and practice of this most humane, democratic and brain-compatible of all teaching styles.

Step 1: Establish self-regulation

Successful "Blank Cheque" learning requires students to be self-disciplined. In regular classrooms up and down the UK teachers sometimes resort to controlling students' behaviour by imposing non-negotiable tasks and strict deadlines. They give students work that will keep them quiet and in their seats. In the "Blank Cheque" approach this is not an option: decisions about learning strategy are made jointly with students. Students quickly sense that this creates a vacuum of authority and it's usual for some of them to attempt to exploit the situation by messing about. They tease the teacher, knowing that she cannot resort to old control strategies *and* remain true to the spirit of the new approach. They might even feel that they have the upper hand, that they will not be punished no matter what they do and that the teacher has therefore lost control. While other students join in the mischievous fun, some become angry at the waste of time and withdraw, leaving the rest to beg the teacher to tell the troublemakers off. This is what gives the student-centred approach a bad name.

The root of the problem is the students' collective and firm belief that it is the teacher's job, and the teacher's job alone, to control the class. They have been brought up to believe this. What's more, current policies in education reinforce the notion with schools being held totally and publicly responsible for students' behaviour (even outside of school), every aspect of their achievement (think of the lengths that some teachers go to drag coursework out of students) and even their attendance (when the causes of nonattendance are well outside the school's control). The "Blank Cheque" approach is founded on a different set of premises, belongs to a different world-view and is frankly out of step with our dominant culture of semi-benevolent despotism.

It is therefore necessary for the teacher to work hard, against the current trend, to reorientate students. This is done by taking time to establish, and agree procedures for upholding, a new set of behavioural norms. There are several ways of achieving this.

Method 1

The safest, yet in some ways the most direct, method is for **the teacher to be up front and insistent about one or two behaviours** that she knows will strike at the heart of self-discipline. Without discussion she announces a couple of new "rules": for example,

- Each of us will give our complete attention to whoever is speaking.
- We will support each other's self-esteem. This means that we will not put each other down.

The teacher takes the lead in establishing a new classroom order. She sets out her stall, explains why she is insisting on these new rules and comes across as fiercely determined to see them established. She writes them large on wall posters; she reminds students when they are not being upheld; she often stops proceedings and make a fuss about behaviour issues; she frequently explains why they are important; she takes students to one side and talks to them privately; she uses behaviour contracts in certain cases; she involves parents where necessary. All without resorting to rewards and punishments. Assertiveness, optimism and determination are the hallmarks of the strategy, underpinned by the teacher's fundamental belief in her ability to assert control if necessary.

All this is done initially while "regular" teaching approaches are being used. It is a low-risk option that leaves the teacher in the driving seat. Then, as the new behaviours gradually become internalised, the teacher begins to use increasingly student-centred processes to test and consolidate the gains. "Scrambled Groups" (page 150) would be a good starting point; likewise, discussions could be held in a "Circle" (page 195) using a "Round" (page 196). Over time, maybe weeks, maybe months, personal and collective responsibility will become sufficiently established for the teacher to let go of decision making and start sharing it with students. The transition from authoritarianism to democracy can occur smoothly because the preconditions are in place.

Method 2

Bring behavioural issues to the surface for discussion by using one or two contrived exercises such as "Murder Hunt" (page 179), along with "Framed" (page 182) and the more general strategy of "Observer Servers" (page 185). These allow teacher and students to examine the changes required and to agree new norms together. Full details are given in Section 3.

Method 3

Give students an experience of new behaviours and then ask them to make a comparison with old habits. For instance, challenge the class to let people finish what they are saying without interruption for a whole lesson, or to bite their lips instead of making witty or rude comments. Then discuss the benefits of operating like this and see if a commitment to an extended "trial" period can be secured. For a more structured approach to this method try "Learning Listening" (page 187).

Method 4

Confront students' irresponsibility directly. Follow the steps described in "Sabotage" (page 190). An initial reorientation of students' attitudes and an initial agreement about new ways of behaving are important achievements, but will be short-lived unless four further steps are taken:

1. Frequently use strategies to maintain self-disciplined behaviours (see "Maintenance" on page 195 and "Tricks of the Trade" on page 223).
2. Model desirable behaviours consistently yourself.
3. Expect all members of the class to *remind each other* of the ground rules. This might mean sometimes holding back and waiting for students to do something about undesirable behaviour rather than intervening immediately yourself. Or it might mean having a quiet word with a couple of the more confident students, asking them to deal with a situation. With younger students use "Talk Police" (page 223). If you can get students to start tackling, independently and spontaneously, behaviours that break the agreed rules, then self-regulation is becoming a reality in your classroom and you are well on the way to reaping the rich harvest that "Blank Cheque" can deliver.

4. After an initial period, perhaps a couple of months, open up the ground rules for renegotiation. This keeps them fresh and alive.

Step 2: Bring out students' feelings

Students are often expected to be interested in topics that have absolutely no connection with their experience, aspirations or curiosity. Teachers get angry with students for not appearing to be interested; students resent this and retaliate with a range of guerrilla tactics. It doesn't have to be this way. It is possible to soften the harsh imposition of nationally dictated subjects by giving students a chance to say how they feel, and to have those feelings acknowledged. We know that learning is an emotional business (page 25) and that if negative feelings are not dealt with, they will continually get in the way, so time spent on this step is repaid over and over.

First, announce the new topic to be studied, but don't go into too much detail. Students should know just enough about it to be able to feel an emotional response. The detail can come later, at the next step. You could then hold an open discussion: "How do you feel about studying X?" However, unless the group is very experienced at self-regulation, it will probably be better to use a "Round" (page 196) or, if the topic is delicate or the students are shy, a "Paper Round" (page 196). To give students a chance to talk over what they want to say before going public, use "Pairs to Fours" (page 137) or "Scrambled Groups" (page 150) or "Discussion Carousel" (page 95). To bring the range of responses out into the open visually as well as orally, use "Centre of the Universe" (page 83), "Thumbometer" (page 161) or "Value Continuum" (page 163).

Encourage students to express honest feelings. At first they may be reluctant to do this because it's a reversal of most school procedures. Your response to the first few comments (which might be quite extreme, just to test you out) will be crucial. Throughout the exercise it is essential that you do not censor students' comments, or reinterpret them, or ask students to explain why they feel like they do, or try to persuade them to feel differently. Just accept what they say as being true for them. You don't have to agree with it to accept it. Explain all this to the students before you begin and agree rules about language if you feel that's necessary. During the exercise the most important responses for you to make are:

- to feed back to students a brief summary capturing the spirit of what they said
- to ask students who don't say much if they want to say more
- to explain that any issues for explanation or discussion (e.g. "Why do we have to study this anyway?") can be dealt with later

When everyone has had their say, you might want to return to matters arising. If students are asking why the topic has to be covered at all, give straightforward factual information such as "It's on the syllabus and may well come up in the exam" or "It's part of the national curriculum and I have to teach it by law". Don't try to persuade them to change their feelings. However, let them know that you hope they will come to enjoy the topic eventually and that the aim is to find a way of studying it that will suit everyone.

This step, which seems radical to some teachers, makes the group's emotional starting point explicit. The truth is out. Consequently, levels of both enthusiasm and resistance can now be discussed in a grown-up way rather than have a hidden agenda, and often an underground war, between students and teacher. Interestingly, when negative feelings are aired and acknowledged, they often dissipate.

Insights gained at this point will inform decisions made at Step 7.

Step 3: Make the learning requirements clear

Give the students a chance to get their heads round what they have to learn, how long they've got, what the requirements and constraints are and what significance the topic has within the big picture of the course. Let them in on the kind of information that you need when you plan lessons.

There are many ways to do this. For example:

- Ask students to work in threes and reassemble cut-up and jumbled copies of the syllabus/scheme of work/project requirements (see the "Big Picture" application of "Assembly" on page 67) so they are forced to understand how it all fits together.
- Give students time to study the requirements in pairs, then ask for volunteers to take part in "Hot-Seating" (page 116), in role, as experts in the matter.
- Give different sections of the syllabus to different groups and then play "Masterminds" (page 126).
- Conduct a straightforward question-and-answer session – students questioning the teacher, that is! See "Beat the Teacher" (page 71).
- Use "Scrambled Groups" (page 150) with different component parts of the syllabus, so that everyone eventually ends up with a grasp of the whole lot.

This step is different from just writing the learning objectives up on the board: it requires students to understand and internalise longer-term requirements. Learners are not able to be involved in any decisions about learning strategy (Step 7) unless they fully appreciate the challenge that faces them. So, again, time invested in explaining technical terms in the syllabus or having students look them up in the dictionary, in helping them to see connections with past and future learning, in checking their comprehension of the details, is time that will be handsomely repaid.

Step 4: Bring out prior knowledge

Ask students what they already know about the topic, and what they can already do. If students still fear put-downs from their peers, use silent options such as "Thumbometer" (page 161) or "Calling Cards" (page 81) in response to probing questions you put to the class. Or give out a series of continua or targets on paper so that students can make individual "mark-with-a-cross" responses. If students are ready for more explicit expressions of their prior knowledge then "Centre of the Universe" (page 83) and "Value Continuum" (page 163) are ideal. Use paired discussions or "Discussion Carousel" (page 95) to help people prepare their public responses. A two-dimensional continuum (page 164) allows this step to be combined with Step 2 above: you assess interest and prior knowledge at the same time. Students can place card markers with their names on if they are reluctant to speak in front of their peers.

The more backward the students are at coming forward, the longer Steps 2, 4 and 5 take. There's a dilemma here for the conscientious teacher. Do you take time to develop students' confidence and articulation knowing that it will be good for them personally and for the pace and quality of learning later on? Or do you get too nervous about the time it takes when you have a syllabus to get through, abandon the plan and go back to a teacher-led style? Let's assume you have faith and want to continue.

Whatever process is used for making prior knowledge and skills explicit, a record needs to be made so that learning can be celebrated later on. For instance, students can make individual notes in written or diagrammatic form, or "Value Continuum" or "Centre of the Universe" can be photographed or hastily drawn (students can take turns to do this).

If a more precise assessment of prior knowledge is required, then issue a set of tasks that become increasingly difficult. As students get stuck they ask the teacher for help. Through the subsequent short discussions with individual students the teacher uncovers their levels of understanding and misunderstandings, their abilities and weaknesses in the given area.

Apart from laying down a marker against which further learning can be measured, there are a couple of other benefits to spending time on prior knowledge. It reassures those who have already learned aspects of the material that they won't have to go over the same ground again, and it prepares for the negotiation of individually precise learning tasks at Step 8.

Step 5: Generate possibilities

Now ask the crucial open question, "What are all the ways you can think of that will help us to learn what we have to learn?" At this point creative and lateral thinking are required so brainstorming is the ideal method.

Brainstorming is often done badly. There are strict procedures and rules to follow. For example, do not wait to be asked – as soon as you have an idea, say it. No one may comment (not even with a grunt or a gesture) on any contribution until the brainstorm is over. Everything that is said is written up in the contributor's words. The record should be visible to everyone (so use large flipchart paper and thick pens, or overhead projector, or interactive white board). Silence is OK. If two or three people speak at once and contributions get lost, say them again – take responsibility for getting your idea recorded. The group will need to regulate the flow of ideas to suit the speed of the recorder (pick a fast writer as recorder, do it yourself or have two recorders).

As teacher, you too can contribute, adding all sorts of methods of your own. Even if some of the ideas put forward seem likely to be time-consuming or completely off the wall, don't censor them at this stage. You don't know what fruit an unusual idea might eventually yield.

If the class is not practised at brainstorming, do a couple of trial runs with neutral topics such as "Alternative uses for our school building" or "What you could do with an old shoe on a desert island". If only a few people are contributing to the brainstorm, stop and check the reasons. Maybe the ground rules need revisiting because people are still scared of appearing too keen or of saying the wrong thing; maybe students need a bit of time to think quietly on their own first, or talk with a partner for a few moments to clarify their suggestions; maybe they need reassuring that it's OK to break the hands-up habit.

And don't forget, there are other ways of generating learning strategies apart from brainstorming:

- Run a "**Marketplace**" (page 122). Actually, this is best done once resources and constraints have been explained, so the order of Steps 5 and 6 have to be swapped. Divide the students into small groups and ask each group to come up with a favoured learning strategy. One member of the group then stays behind as stallholder to explain the strategy to prospective "buyers". The other members of the group go round the stalls, as prospective buyers, to hear the ideas being presented by the stallholders of other groups. They make notes so they can report back. Once all the stalls have been visited, everyone goes back to their original groups to explain and discuss the various suggestions. They could then go on to decide as a group which of the proposed strategies they prefer (this is the equivalent of Step 7 below). I did say that the guidelines are supposed to be used flexibly!
- Run a "**Discussion Carousel**" (page 95), but don't give long for each exchange and keep it going for at least four rounds. Students are allowed to modify their original ideas or add new ones as their thinking is extended by other people's creativity. Once the carousel is over, all the ideas are listed on the board for all to see.
- Make **lists in small groups**, rather like mini-brainstorms, then put them all together.
- Use "**Pass the Buck**" (page 139).

Step 6: Assess resources and edit the possibilities

Set the brainstorm aside for a moment and discuss with students the resources that are available and the constraints that apply. Resources include people, places, artefacts and events as well as books and hi-tech wizardry both in and out of school. Encourage students to see their own experience, intuition, imagination and creativity as resources, too. They have each other. Explain the extent to which you will be a resource for them.

Constraints might include: time; quantity or accessibility of information resources (including books, software, Internet sites, CD-ROMs); availability of consumable resources; school regulations about movement around or beyond the site; availability of hardware (such as computers, video recorders, television sets, audio tape recorders, cameras); availability of spaces other than the classroom for learning activity; externally decreed assessments; the school's homework policy; health and safety precautions. Don't promise anything that you can't deliver, tempting though it is, because students start to get enthusiastic and want to know if they can have this, use that and go there …

The brainstormed list of ideas is now scrutinised in the light of these constraints. Ask the students whether any ideas now seem unworkable and should be abandoned. Cross them off. Make sure that you are left with only workable ideas.

Step 7: Decide on learning strategy

With all this information about students' motivation and prior knowledge and all the workable possibilities to hand, at long last, it is time to decide on learning strategy. There are so many variables at this point. Individual or group work? Nature and size of groups? Method of learning? Pace of learning? Location of learning? Means of providing evidence of learning?

These decisions are normally made by the teacher. In the "Blank Cheque" approach, they are made by the students with the teacher. Using the edited brainstorm as a prompt, there are several ways of proceeding:

- Have an open discussion and attempt to come to a consensus. This is the most grown-up and "citizenship" way of doing it, but demands high-level skills and the will to compromise.
- Allocate a letter to each of the ideas on the brainstorm: A, B, C, D and so on. Give each student three choices – they decide which three ideas they could go with (the "votes" must be spread across three different ideas). Go round the class asking each student in turn to shout out their three letters. The scores are tallied and a group preference emerges. Second and third choices also emerge, indicating which two or three strategies should be pursued simultaneously within the class. It's important to avoid having winners and losers, which is the problem with straightforward majority voting.
- Ask each student to write their first choice secretly on a piece of paper. Everyone then declares what they've put, groups form and pursue their chosen strategies. If there are mutually exclusive ideas such as a whole-class lecture and "Scrambled Groups", then compromises have to be found. For example, the whole-group lecture could become a lecture to the small interest group, while "Scrambled Groups" would be scaled down to the number of students who want to do it – perhaps three groups of three – or is changed to "One-to-One" (page 135) (same idea of peer teaching, different format).
- Students do "Ranking" (page 148) in small groups, then compare results. A consensus might emerge, or further whole-class discussion will create one, or different groups could pursue their different chosen strategies.

The overall aim of this step is to give each student, as far as possible, the chance to pursue the most appropriate strategy: the one they are keenest on, which will automatically be the one that suits their learning style or the one that they have the intrinsic motivation to see through even if it is outside their normal comfort zone. The first key to success is motivation. If a student has the will to persevere, to go the extra mile in their learning, to overcome obstacles in pursuit of their goal, they will achieve more with a rough learning strategy than they will achieve by slavishly following the teacher's fancy plans, however well constructed. Such will arises from deep intrinsic motivation and is achieved only through having the student create their own strategy and make genuine choices. This process opens the student's reticular activating system and inevitably takes time. Every short cut in the process reduces the degree of ownership and therefore the level of motivation.

This step results in every student having a learning strategy to follow, perhaps as an individual, perhaps as a member of a small group, perhaps as part of a whole-class strategy. Now this has to be turned into a personal learning plan or contract.

Step 8: Write personal learning plans

A personal learning plan is written by each student specifying their learning targets, learning strategy, resources required, timescale, form of evidence and method of assessment. They express firm and detailed intentions and formalise the student's commitment to learn. They keep the student on track and provide a kick up the backside if motivation wanes.

Such plans also provide a focus for the tutoring process. They enable the teacher and student to monitor progress and to reappraise and modify short-term targets and strategies as time goes by.

An example of such a plan can be found on page 254.

Step 9: Share the management of learning

Once learning plans have been written, learning activity begins. Life can suddenly become very hectic. Students want such-and-such a resource, they need help with this, advice with that and permission for the other. There are several ways of sharing the management of learning with the students:

- Give each group or individual some storage space. This might be a cardboard box, a length of shelf, a box file, a locker. This is where ongoing work will be kept. Students are responsible for their own material – they get it out and put it away. This way they can easily get to it between lessons if they want to continue their work out of hours.
- Have all the resources that you normally control – textbooks, paper, videos, pens, overhead acetates, audio cassettes – on open access to students. This might simply mean tidying the stockroom, cataloguing its contents and leaving the door open. If necessary have a sign-out/sign-in system or rotating resource monitors.
- Have large wall charts for booking the teacher's time, for booking hardware resources, for booking library time and for booking visits to learning locations out of school. Students fill these in themselves, relieving the teacher of administrative responsibilities and leaving her free to get on with the tutoring process. If the teacher wants to address the whole class, she can book time like everyone else. For example:

Resources	Dates of lessons							
	March 1st	March 8th	March 21st					
Overhead projector								
Video camera								
TV and VCR								
Cassette recorder								
Classroom computer								
Using IT facilities in Room 47								
Using the library								
Out of school visiting the . . .								

Teacher's time	Dates of lessons							
	April 1st	April 29th	May 7th	May 19th				
Start of lesson								
5 mins								
10 mins								
15 mins								
20 mins								
25 mins								
30 mins								
35 mins								
40 mins								
45 mins								
50 mins								
End of lesson								

- Have a pile of pre-signed permission slips for the school library. Trust students to use them responsibly in conjunction with the booking chart.
- Prepare a Students' Toolkit, a ring-binder file with information on how to write a letter requesting information, how to look for a book in the library, how to scan a text for main points, how to make notes, how to write a report, how to invite and receive a visitor, how to conduct an interview, how to conduct a survey, how to prepare a questionnaire and so on. Students can consult this instead of going to the teacher for advice.
- Have a large calendar or timeline on the wall on which students write agreed deadlines and note progress made.
- Have key teaching points on audio or video cassettes that you have recorded in advance. Students can listen to or watch these whenever they need to instead of bothering the teacher. See "Double Take" (page 101) or use the help sheets mentioned there.
- Have a pile of reprographics request slips and a box to receive the materials to be photocopied. Make arrangements for students to use the photocopier themselves. Give them a photocopying budget which they have to manage themselves.
- Have request forms printed so that students can fill in at the end of a lesson what they will need for the next lesson – a piece of advice, a particular resource, a point to be explained by the teacher, feedback on an idea or a draft piece of work.
- If you use personal learning plans with the Stepometer attached, this won't apply. If not, then consider having a index file box on your desk with a card for each student. Students are expected to take their personal card out at the beginning of the lesson, and at the end of the lesson note what they have done in that session, what they intend to do *before* the next lesson and what they plan to do *during* the next lesson. On the way out they put the card back in the box. This gives you a chance to monitor progress, target particular students to see next lesson and if necessary write notes which students pick up at the beginning of the next lesson.

Step 10: Review

From time to time it will be important to get the whole class together, preferably in a "Circle" (page 195), for a formative review of progress. This might involve:

- asking each individual or group to say how they are getting on and what they have learned so far

- identifying and solving problems raised by students or by the teacher, to do with behaviour, working arrangements or difficult concepts in the learning
- reviewing ground rules

At the end of the whole cycle an evaluation of the outcomes and processes of learning will be required. With regard to learning outcomes, a test of some kind might be used, especially if there are exam standards to meet. The results will tell the students and the teacher if anything needs to be gone over again. This is where the teacher plugs the gaps.

"Rounds" (page 196) of "positives" and "improvements needed" are the simplest way to review the learning strategies used. Alternatively, cut up two colours of card into playing-card-size pieces and give everyone a few of each. One colour is "positives" and the other is "improvements". Students have a few minutes to write separate points on separate cards, then, when everyone is ready, students offer their points, reading out what they've written and placing the cards in two piles in the middle of the circle. This builds a visual impression of the balance of "good" and "bad" and also provides a handy written record.

The results of this evaluation will set the next learning cycle in motion.

Conclusion

The student-centred "Blank Cheque" process described above is clearly time-consuming and, in the high-pressure, factory-farming approach to learning found in today's schools, most teachers simply won't go for it. But, before the approach is dismissed out of hand, consider four major returns on the initial investment of time:

1. Later learning is accelerated. Students become used to the process so it doesn't take so long in future. Also, the degree of motivation generated by student ownership usually results in lots of spontaneous out-of-class effort – at home, at lunchtime, after school. Finally, less time is spent fighting battles. The "Blank Cheque" approach always results in a sweeter relationship between students and teacher, better behaviour and a more willing attitude to learning in general.
2. Students learn how to learn. This is an automatic outcome. Consider how much time is spent on study skills in PSHE or specialist courses, time that is often wasted because students don't transfer the learning because it was delivered out of context.
3. Students' personal and social development takes huge leaps forward. They learn about individual and collective responsibility and something about all five areas of emotional intelligence.
4. Core citizenship skills and attitudes are powerfully delivered, including debate, democratic decision-making, conflict resolution, navigating the tension between individualism and collectivism and resource management.

Looked at this way, "Blank Cheque" appears very efficient. It covers chunks of content and delivers a range of additional, often elusive, outcomes simultaneously. The benefits are eloquently described by a sixth-former who experienced the approach for the first time under the guidance of Lesley Browne at Park Hall School on the edge of Birmingham:

> The relative success of the group in external examination results, despite seeming to mean "everything" at the time, is actually secondary. The real success of the democratic learning cooperative lies in how much it instilled key notions of cooperation, mutual support and tolerance in a group of 16–18 year olds. These are skills which reach far beyond the short term goals of A-level exams and university graduation. Coupled with the confidence developed through the DLC's reliance on public speech, teaching and discussion with others, I believe our experiences equipped us with essential transferable skills.[4]

Section 5

Audit Tools

Introduction

I wasn't sure whether to call this section "Audit Tools" or "Tools for Guidance". The items are a mixture of the two. You will find checklists, suggestions, questions, tips and recommendations, all designed to bring a number of key issues down to earth. The aim as ever is to be concrete and practical, even with the more nebulous concepts such as self-esteem.

You may use the tools genuinely as audit instruments, in which case you will allow them to ask stiff questions of your current practice as an individual or institution. This testing process will identify very precise practical steps that you could then take to enhance provision. On the other hand, you don't have to be so rigorous and systematic. Just use the tools informally to guide and stimulate your thinking about the seven issues – read through them, you may disagree with some of the stronger suggestions but at least you'll be thinking about practical manifestations and implications rather than leaving matters vague.

Remember, it's only when people know exactly what to do and how to do it that change ever takes root. Working out the practical details of big ideas is the change agent's job, whether you're changing yourself, your department, your school or just the whole world!

Check Your Lesson Plans

This audit tool has two purposes:

1. to summarise all the thinking behind *The Teacher's Toolkit* – in other words, to present current ideas about learning in a way that readily translate into the design of lessons and schemes of work
2. to put the *Toolkit*'s individual practical ideas into context so that they don't appear to be just one-off ways to spice up a lesson; the purpose and potential of the individual techniques are understood only once it's clear how they fit into a whole

Bearing these in mind, this section presents the sort of questions that might run through your head when you're planning a series of lessons. The questions are divided into five sequential parts:

- learning objectives
- learning method
- learning environment
- assessment
- recording

You can use this tool to:

- audit existing lessons and schemes of work
- design new lessons
- observe other people's lessons and give constructive feedback

This checklist is intended to be organic. Delete things, modify some, add others. In other words, use it just to get you going, then customise the list to represent your own understanding of quality teaching.

Part 1: Learning objectives

1. Are the learning objectives expressed as "learners will be able to …"?
For example: By the end of this lesson you will be able to …

- recognise series and parallel circuits on circuit boards and in diagrams
- predict the brightness of bulbs in one circuit compared to another
- connect an ammeter into a circuit correctly
- explain the effect of changing the resistance in a circuit

2. Are the learning objectives clearly related to the big picture?
In other words, are they connected to the syllabus as a whole, what has been covered already, the longer-term learning goals and deadlines? For example, see "Assembly" ("Applications", page 68), "Circus Time" (page 85), "Mantle of the Expert" (page 120), "Upwardly Mobile" (page 234).

3. *Are the learning objectives differentiated?*

Do they have two or three levels of sophistication? For example: By the end of these three lessons you

- *Must* be able to describe Sunday worship in one Christian denomination and explain why it is like it is
- *Should* be able to list the main similarities and differences in Sunday worship between four different denominations
- *Could* be able to explain why these differences exist

4. *How are the learning objectives made clear to the students?*

For example, see "Upwardly Mobile" (page 234, "Sole Search (page 253).

5. *Can the students have an input into defining the learning objectives?*

For example, see "Sole Search" (page 253), and "Blank Cheque" (page 261).

6. *How will individual students' learning be checked against the learning objectives, and when?*

Will this be during the lesson, at the end of the lesson, for homework, at the beginning of the next lesson? For example, see "Beat the Teacher" (page 71), "Bingo" (page 73), "Calling Cards" (page 81), "Centre of the Universe" (page 83), "Dicey Business" (page 93), "Dominoes" (page 99), "Guess Who" (page 109), "Masterminds" (page 126), "Memory Board" (page 128), "Spotlight" (page 154), "Stepping Stones" (page 156), "Thumbometer" (page 161), "Verbal Football" (page 166), "Wheel of Fortune" (page 170) in addition to the more usual types of tests and assessment tasks.

Part 2: Learning Method

1. *How are high expectations communicated?*
- Through the learning objectives?
- Through the teacher's energy and optimism?
- Through the teacher's interaction with individual students?
- Through the nature of the activities?
- Through deadlines?

2. *What account is taken of pupils' prior knowledge, experience and performance?*

For example, see "Calling Cards" (page 81), "Centre of the Universe" (page 83), "Discussion Carousel" (page 95), "Mantle of the Expert" (page 120), "Question Generator" (page 141), "Value Continuum" (page 163), "Upwardly Mobile" (page 234), "Menu" (page 246), "Blank Cheque" (page 261).

3. *What can students work out for themselves during the lesson or topic?*

For example, see "Assembly" (page 67), "Broken Pieces" (page 78), "Conversion" (page 87), "Question Time" (page 143), "Ranking" (page 148), "Silent Sentences" (page 152) .

4. *What are students encouraged to find out for themselves ...*
- from text sources such as books, information sheets, leaflets, newspapers, magazines, letters, journals, other students' work?
- from visual sources such as charts, pictures, photographs, advertisements, slides, posters, exhibitions, demonstration?
- from ICT sources such as CD-ROMs, PowerPoint, Internet, television, video tapes, radio, audio tapes, video conferencing?
- from human sources such as their own experience, each other, the teacher, other adults?
- from physical sources such as places, artefacts?

For example, see "Ambassadors" (page 65), "Delegation" (page 91), "Double Take" (page 101), "Hot-Seating" (page 116), "Information Hunt" (page 118), "Marketplace" (page 122), "One-to-One" (page 135), "Quick on the Draw" (page 145), "Scrambled Groups" (page 150), "Sole Search" (page 253), "Blank Cheque" (page 261).

5. Are the students sufficiently active mentally – and physically?
For example, see "Back-to-Back" (page 69), "Bodily Functions" (page 75), "Calling Cards" (page 81), "Discussion Carousel" (page 95), "Marketplace" (page 122), "Verbal Football" (page 166).

6. Do the students need to consolidate preliminary skills before activities can be successful?
For social skills see the whole of Section 3. For research skills see "Conversion" (page 87), "Distillation" (page 97), "Hierarchies" (page 113), "Information Hunt" (page 118), "Marketplace" (page 122), "Question Generator" (page 141), "Question Time" (page 143), "Scrambled Groups" (page 150) .

7. How is variety provided so that different learning styles are satisfied?
For example, "Overtime" (page 228), a sequence of different styles within the lesson or over a number of lessons, or "Menu" (page 246), different learning strategies operating simultaneously so students have choice. For guidance you could use:

a. sensory model: visual, auditory, kinaesthetic
b. Gregorc's model: Abstract Sequential, Abstract Random, Concrete Sequential, Concrete Random
c. Gardner's model: linguistic, logical-mathematical, spatial, bodily-kinaesthetic, musical, interpersonal, intrapersonal, naturalistic

8. How is learning made multisensory or emotionally strong?
For example, see "Bodily Functions" (page 75), "Forum Theatre" (page 105), "Go Large" (page 107), "Multisensory Memories" (page 130), "Still Image" (page 158).

9. To what extent are students involved in making decisions about learning strategies?
Level 1: teacher adjusts activities as a result of feedback from students
Level 2: students choose between different preset activities ("Menu", page 246)
Level 3: individual students propose and negotiate their personal learning strategy ("Sole Search", page 253)
Level 4: the teacher asks the class the open question: how shall we tackle these learning objectives? ("Blank Cheque", page 261)

10. How are students encouraged to make their own meaning?
For example, see "Conversion" (page 87), "Corporate Identity" (page 89), "Hierarchies" (page 113), "Hot-Seating" (page 116), "Pairs to Fours" (page 137), "Ranking" (page 148), "Stepping Stones" (page 156), Value Continuum" (page 163).

11. How does the lesson develop the students' use of language?
For example, see "Back-to-Back" (page 69), "Distillation" (page 97), "Dominoes" (page 99), "Guess Who" (page 109), "Hide 'n' Seek" (page 111), "Memory Board" (page 128), "On Tour" (page 133), "Pass the Buck" (page 139), "Silent Sentences" (page 152), "Verbal Tennis" (page 168).

12. *How does the lesson support the development of independent learning and thinking?*
For example, see "Beat the Teacher" (page 71), "Calling Cards" (page 81), "Circus Time" (page 85), "Conversion" (page 87), "Double Take" (page 101), "Dreadlines" (page 103), "Guess Who" (page 109), "Marketplace" (page 122), "Upwardly Mobile" (page 234), "Menu" (page 246), "Sole Search" (page 253), "Blank Cheque" (page 261).

Part 3: Learning Environment

1. *What else can be done to make the environment emotionally conducive to learning?*
- ground rules that guarantee listening and no put-downs
- teacher's use of language (see "Check Your Language", page 307)
- use of conflict diffusion and resolution strategies
- humour

2. *What else can be done to make the environment biologically conducive to learning?*
- oxygen
- plants
- temperature
- hydration – access to water
- ioniser

3. *What else can be done to make the environment psychologically conducive to learning?*
- colour
- aesthetics
- aromas
- music
- displays

4. *What else can be done to make the environment physically conducive to learning?*
- room layout appropriate to the learning activities
- clarity of whiteboard and overhead projector, blackout
- sufficiency and accessibility of learning resources

Part 4: Assessment

1. *How do students prove what they have learned?*
Ideas: sit a formal test, write an explanation, conduct an interview, be interviewed, teach someone else, explain to a parent and test them, make a model, devise a quiz, give a demonstration, sequence jumbled information, label a blank diagram, construct a diagram, undertake a challenge against the clock, give a commentary, mime it, spot the deliberate mistakes, predict what will happen if ..., devise questions to given answers, fill in missing key words, write an essay, make a presentation, devise a worksheet, mount an exhibition, be hot-seated, complete an unfinished chart or table or timeline, present a still image, match words with definitions, conduct an experiment, do past exam questions, make a mind map, draw a storyboard, set and mark a test for the teacher ...

2. *How quickly will students get feedback on their progress?*
The sooner the better!

Part 5: Recording

How do students record what they have learned for future reference?

Options include: bullet points, key-word plan, mind map, diagram, storyboard, written questions and answers, flowchart, diary, letter, annotated picture, script, table or chart, list, audio recording, video recording, photographs, flashcards, writing frame, magazine or newspaper article, completed worksheet, photocopy, report, headed paragraphs, timeline, file-card summaries, crossword connections ...

Check Your Students' Learning Styles

Why? Because people are different. They learn in extremely different ways and this has a profound effect on their levels of achievement and self-belief. For more information about learning styles theory and research, see page 33.

So, how can teachers detect students' learning styles so they can operate effectively? There are at least four ways of doing it, though these suggestions come with serious health warnings. See "But is it desirable to try to identify students' learning styles?" at the end of this section.

1. Through observation

Perhaps the most natural, and certainly the least intrusive, way of identifying students' preferences is to watch them at work and play. Notice the frequency of movement, the tendency to be with others, the desire to follow or break with convention, the amount of silence they enjoy or endure, the way they set things out on their desks and on paper, the types of activities they go for when there's choice, when they are most easily distracted, how often they check the time, how carefully they follow instructions, whether they operate from oral instructions or need to see them written down, and so on.

Most teachers say they can get a sense of these things during the natural course of events as one lesson follows another. However, it's not easy to teach and observe at the same time, so the conclusions we come to are often way off the mark. This is partly because we catch only glimpses of behaviour in the cut and thrust of lessons, and prominent incidents stick in our minds and colour our judgment. And it's partly because we are observing without a purpose. Mike Hughes says that "if teachers don't know what they are looking for in a lesson they will have difficulty seeing it".[1] Left to our own devices we tend to "see" the things that bother us, that get our hobbyhorses going (such as when students chew gum, rock back on a chair or shout out instead of putting their hands up) and we miss the essential signs of style. Therefore, prepare an observation schedule based on one of the learning-styles models – it's easy to customise one of the questionnaires mentioned below – and stick to it!

Observing against a schedule is a full-time job, it requires total concentration, so give yourself the opportunity to do it well by:

- videoing some of your lessons and watching them afterwards in the comfort of your own home; or by
- visiting the target class in other people's lessons where you are completely free from the responsibilities of teaching and managing behaviour; or by
- having a colleague come into some of your lessons to operate the schedule – you have to be sure that they are skilled enough to put their own agendas aside, otherwise you'll be letting yourself in for a lot of unwelcome feedback!

Naturally, an accurate picture of students' styles can be built up only over time. A one-off observation won't do: there are too many variables skewing the behaviours that indicate style. However, you can short-circuit the process by deliberately setting your students a series of open tasks that allow for a variety of personal responses. For example:

Explain how to get from school to your house. Some students will draw a map, others will write a series of instructions, others will explain orally with lots of gestures and hand signals.

How would you find out how a battery-operated clock works? Some will want to consult a book, others will want to ask an electronics boffin, others will want to take a clock apart and work it out for themselves, others will want the teacher to explain it with diagrams and components.

Present a proposal for reorganising the classroom. Natural preferences will be revealed at two levels. First, the way they go about it – on their own, with a partner, in a group, drawing rough sketches, closing their eyes and visualising, measuring the space and plotting the furniture on squared paper, conducting a survey of what people want, getting up, walking around and weighing up options, wanting to move the furniture and try it out in different positions. Second, what they come up with – a circle of chairs with desks to the walls, tables blocked into groups, separate desks in rows, cabaret style …

The neurolinguists would have us believe that it's possible to detect auditory, visual and kinaesthetic dominance by noticing students' eye movements and their use of predicates. Details are available in most books about accelerated or brain-compatible learning.

2. *Through structured choices*

Prepare several ways of studying the next topic, each based on a different learning style. Write a briefing sheet and marshal the resources for each option. Introduce the topic to the class, explain the various options and ask the students to make individual choices. It might be a good idea to allocate different parts of the classroom to the different options so that students have to physically move to their chosen areas.

For example, **Buddhism with Year 8**. After a general introduction to the topic, the teacher offers four options (based on Gregorc):

1. Study the life of the Buddha by following a structured research guide that refers to the collection of books on class loan from the public library. You will end up with a written report: "Highlights of the Buddha's life." You will work on your own. (Abstract Sequential.)
2. Invite into school, entertain and interview a couple of Buddhist monks from the local temple, then present "A day in the life of a Buddhist monk" in a series of still images that will be photographed. You will need to add captions and labels. You will work in small groups. (Abstract Random.)
3. Find a way of presenting to us "Buddhist beliefs about life and death". You can use whatever resources and methods you like, but you can't use any spoken words in your presentation. You can choose to work on your own or in a pair or in a small group. (Concrete Random.)
4. Make a model of a Buddhist temple by following the instruction sheet. You will need to bring out the architectural and symbolic features, so different parts of the model will need to be labelled and a tour guide prepared. You can work on your own or in a pair. (Concrete Sequential.)

The teacher explains that, afterwards, everyone will teach each other using "Scrambled Groups" (page 150).

Another example (based on VAK) – **Percentages with Year 7:**

1. You will work outside or in the hall (if it's wet) in pairs. Follow the instructions on the sheets for bunny hopping, shuttlecock throwing and shuttle running. Take all the measurements and then calculate the shortest and slowest as percentages of the longest and fastest. Then you will be asked to hop, throw and run to given percentages. (Whole-body kinaesthetic.)
2. You will work in small groups, push a couple of desks together and follow the detailed instructions for measuring, cutting and assembling different shapes of different relative proportions. (Tactile kinaesthetic.)
3. You will listen to my explanation about percentages and the instructions about what to do on audio cassette. You can listen to the tape, or bits of the tape, as often as you like until you feel sure that you have understood. If you're still stuck, ask each other and, as a final resort, ask me. (Auditory.)
4. You will watch me showing you how to do percentages using diagrams on the board, posters and a variety of objects from around the room. In pairs you will then prepare colourful visual aids for teaching these points to Year 6 children in the primary schools you've just come from. (Visual.)

This is of course the "Menu" method described in more detail on page 246.

If students are not used to making these sorts of choices, their initial decisions might be influenced by peer pressure (they'll choose what their mates are doing) or by sheer laziness – which one will be the biggest doss? To minimise the first problem, students could be asked for a show of hands with their eyes closed, or could be asked to write their names and selections on pieces of paper that are then folded and handed in.

The only way to counter the second problem is probably to let "bad" choices be made, then, once work is under way, challenge students as you move round the classroom. Focus on the learning outcomes and ask students to show you how far they've got; ask them to explain what they've understood so far. If it's clear that not much progress has been made, ask them to rechoose their strategy.

At the end of each unit of work, it's important to debrief the whole experience with the students, focusing on what they've learned about themselves as learners. Discuss how demanding, comfortable, natural, forced, satisfying, boring or motivating the choices felt. Ultimately, ask each student to get a sense of how efficient their chosen strategy turned out to be. How much was achieved with what amount of time and effort? Would they choose it again? This way students become more self-aware and more likely to choose wisely next time. After giving them several opportunities to make choices of this kind, consider asking confident students to stretch themselves by deliberately working in nonpreferred ways at the next opportunity. It's probably a good idea to keep a note of who chose what so that a picture of individuals' styles can be built up over time and you can operate effectively not just as a subject teacher but as a personal tutor.

3. Through a questionnaire

There's a lot of debate about the use of learning-styles questionnaires with students. On the whole, the younger the students, the greater the risks. If questionnaires are to be used, then seven rules that have been borne out of some bitter experiences need to be followed:

1. The person administering the questionnaire must have a *good understanding* of its intentions and underlying rationale. Only then will she be able to explain its purpose to students and answer their questions.

2. The person administering it must also be *committed* to the exercise. If the questionnaire is given out casually as "just another worksheet" to be filled in, students will complete it carelessly and the results will be invalid. It's important that the reasons for doing the questionnaire, and the uses it will be put to, be fully explained.

3. The instructions given to the students must *keep faith with the instrument*. For example, is a gut reaction required to each prompt, or a carefully considered response?

4. The model must *not be used for illegitimate purposes*. All models are simplifications of reality. They cannot be used to categorise or label students. They are not the last word on someone's character. They don't "sum someone up". They simply provide insights that lead to increased understanding of self and others.

5. Individual results must be *shared with individual students*. It is not OK to take the results away and use them secretly, nor is it OK to share the results publicly with the class, colleagues or parents without students' permission. The prime purpose of the results is to help students understand themselves better so they might become increasingly successful as learners. Their secondary purpose is to help teachers plan learning strategies that will give everyone a good deal.

6. Enough time must be given for *reflection and discussion*. Students benefit from talking with each other and with the teacher about the "results": the extent to which they are accurate, context-specific, changeable. How much of the feedback from the questionnaire is being accepted and how much resisted? Students often want to know what types of learners are best, who will do well in test and exams and what they can do to better their chances. Lots of reassurance is usually needed.

7. Do not administer a test unless you are determined to *do your professional best* to accommodate all learning types in future. It is very damaging to expose the issue of learning differences, to raise students' expectations and then not deliver.

If you are still determined to use a student questionnaire after all this, then have a look at the options in Appendix B.

Finally, I have developed a questionnaire based on insights derived from information-processing models. I hesitate to use it for reasons that will be discussed in a moment, but I have found that it can be illuminating for students and teachers if administered in accordance with the rules above. Here it is.

Learning-styles Questionnaire

1. In each row (A-F), rank the 4 statements. The statement that fits you best gets a score of 4, next best 3, next best 2 and the one that fits you least gets a score of 1. You cannot use half-marks.

2. Add the scores down in each column. Put the total at the bottom.

3. Plot your scores on the Learning Styles Profile. You will end up with a kite shape. Inside your kite shape is your area of preference.

4. Compare your kite shape to those of other people.

		score		score		score		score
A	I like to be given problems to solve.		I like to talk things through with other people.		I like to do practical work.		I like reading.	
B	I like to work out answers for myself.		I use my imagination a lot.		I like to be told exactly what to do.		I am happy to work alone.	
C	I have a lot of ideas.		I understand how people feel.		I like to take things one step at a time.		I like to find things out from books and other sources.	
D	I like to try my ideas out even if people think they are odd.		I like to use drama, art and music.		I like to be organised.		I weigh up different ideas.	
E	I like to find out how things work.		I like my work to be fun.		I pay attention to detail.		I am keen to do written work.	
F	I like to have something to show for my efforts.		I like my work to be about people.		I like to get things right.		I organise my studies carefully.	
	Red		**Blue**		**Green**		**Yellow**	

The rationale for these four categories arises from the work of Kolb, McCarthy, Butler and Gregorc (Gregorc himself is firmly opposed to student questionnaires, perhaps rightly). These researchers share the basic idea that there are two mental processes involved in learning, one concerned with *acquiring* and the other with *sorting and storing* new data. They agree that there are big natural differences between people on both counts and therefore the two processes can be seen as continua with extremes at each end and shades in between. In my model, acquiring runs from highly *physical and sensate* to highly *abstract and reflective*. The sorting-and-storing continuum runs from extremely *structured and linear* to extremely *random and diverse*. If these two continua are set at right angles to each other, four possible learning modes are created. Therefore …

Red	physical, hands-on, unstructured, open-ended, practical, investigative
Blue	having lots of ideas, unstructured, open, reflective, arty, human
Green	structured, practical, guided, doing, precise
Yellow	thinking, structured, academic, reasonable, likes research

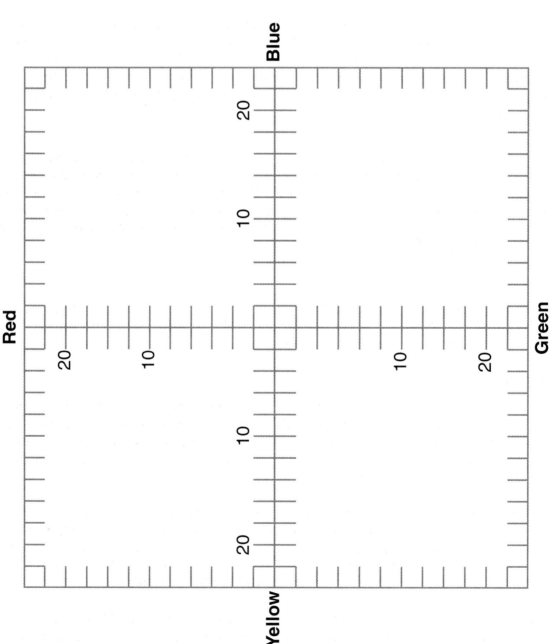

4. Through reflection on multiple activities

This approach requires you to set up a number of diverse learning activities, which all students do. Once they've been through them all, you lead a reflection in which students identify their preferences. The diverse learning activities need to be designed against a learning styles model, so decide this first. You might use VAK (in which case I recommend that you design four activities: visual, auditory, tactile and whole-body kinaesthetic) or Gregorc (in which case you will design four activities: Abstract Sequential, Concrete Sequential, Abstract Random and Concrete Random) or Gardner (in which case you will design eight activities: linguistic, logical-mathematical, spatial, musical, kinaesthetic, interpersonal, intrapersonal and naturalistic).

There are four formats in which this approach can be delivered:

Format 1

Take a series of lessons and make each one different. Follow your usual curriculum, but deliver it in diverse ways. For example, the first lesson will be auditory, the second visual and so on. The advantage of this format is that each learning style is sustained over a whole lesson, giving all students chance to feel genuine reactions. The disadvantage is that you have to find a section of the curriculum that lends itself to delivery through different styles.

Format 2

Change learning-style activities within a lesson. There might be an auditory exposition and discussion, a visual development (PowerPoint, for example) and a kinaesthetic reinforcement (a "Bodily Functions" enactment, for instance). The advantage of this format is that no one gets bored. The disadvantage is that no one has to put up with a distasteful style for long enough to feel the incompatibility. Therefore, run several "varied" lessons of this type before moving on to the reflection.

Format 3

This is a circus. Set out the varied activities around the room and have students move among them, either randomly (individuals are responsible for getting through all the activities, in any order, before the bell) or orchestrated by you.

Format 4

This final format is more ambitious. Collapse the timetable for a year group for a day and run a "learning-styles experience". During the day students work in their form groups and go through a series of activities, each in a different style. At the end of the day the final lesson is given over to reflection led by the form tutors. Clearly this requires a good deal of organisation and the cooperation of many colleagues.

A school in Greater Manchester recently organised such a day around the theme of "Healthy Living for Healthy Learning" with Year 9. The event began with the whole-year group in the school hall for an Abstract Sequential lecture and worksheet from a visiting dietician, then form groups went on a circus: Concrete Random creative cooking; Abstract Random forum theatre to explore temptation; and Concrete Sequential fitness planning.

A school in Pembrokeshire in West Wales ran a similar day with Year 7 based on "Pirates". There was a fact-finding lesson involving a research guide and several in-class texts (AS), an empathetic small-group exercise exploring piratical encounters and tensions through still images (AR), an outdoor orienteering exercise around a fictional treasure island (CS) and a communications problem – work out a way, without using spoken words, of getting messages to the group across the room that no other people would be able to understand (CR).

Reflection

Whichever format you use, the reflection needs plenty of time, probably a minimum of 45 minutes. One tried and tested way of doing it is to clear the desks, arrange the chairs in a circle, and make a cross with masking tape on the floor with the two axes stretching right across the circle. This gives four sectors (vary depending on which learning-styles model you are using and how many categories it has). In each sector of the circle place a large A1-size card with details of each style written big in students' language. For example, if you are using my four categories as presented in the questionnaire above, then the cards would read

Yellow

- You like reading
- You are happy to work alone
- You like to find things out from books, from talks and from other sources
- You weigh up different ideas
- You are keen to do written work
- You organise your studies carefully

Green

- You like to do practical work
- You like to be told exactly what to do
- You like to tackle things one step at a time
- You like to be organised
- You pay attention to detail
- You like to get things right

Red

- You like to be given problems to solve
- You like to work out answers for yourself
- You have lots of ideas
- You like to try your ideas out even if other people think they are odd
- You like to find out how things work
- You like to have something to show for your efforts

Blue

- You like to talk things through with other people
- You use your imagination a lot
- You understand how people feel
- You like to use drama, art and music
- You like your work to be fun
- You like your work to be about people

It is best if these are each written in their different colours for ease of reference.

Students first discuss which of the day's activities belong to which sectors, and paper or card markers are placed on the floor to show where each lesson is located on the learning-styles map. The nuances are important. For example, was the lesson entirely such-and-such a style or did it tend towards or cross over into another? How extreme was it (towards the outer edge of the circle), or how mild a version of the style (towards the middle)? This discussion should be allowed to continue until sufficient understanding has been created for the next step.

Now students are given three pieces of card and they write their names on each. Then time is given to quiet personal reflection prompted by a series of questions that you might write on the board, have prewritten on an overhead transparency or just talk through, for example:

- During today's lessons, when did you feel most comfortable?
- Where did you feel you were learning most naturally?
- What did you find hard to understand?
- What did you enjoy?
- Which bits of the day were a struggle?
- Where did you feel you achieved most?
- What seemed to come naturally to you?
- Which activities were you keen to do?
- What would you choose again if you had the chance?
- What would you avoid again if you had the chance?

After a few minutes of individual thought, students are asked to place their cards. They can put all three in one sector if they feel strongly that this is their single dominant style, or they can spread them two and one, or three ones. There is a quicker and cruder version of this self-assessment step: instead of cards, students simply stand up, move around and sit down in the sector that represents their dominant style.

Records can then be made. Students write down their individual preferences in their planners, and the whole-class distribution is recorded by taking a photograph or by plotting the positions on a large wall chart.

Finally, time should be given to discussing the teaching implications of the findings. What needs to change? How feasible are such changes given our curriculum and resources? What can students do for themselves to use their preferred styles at home? What changes do students need to make to behaviour and attitudes if a wider range of teaching styles is to be used?

But is it desirable to try to identify students' learning styles?

There are serious concerns about both the validity and potential side effects of "testing" for students' styles.

First, in questionnaires and self-confessions (like the third and fourth strategies described above), students might not tell the truth – for understandable reasons. Many tend to give answers that will please the teacher, or demonstrate their conformity to institutional expectations, or answers that are acceptable to the peer group, or that arise from an illusory view of themselves.

Second, in questionnaires and self-confessions the prompts often have to be too simple to be of much use. The kind of abstract and general terms often found in adult questionnaires are too unfamiliar, and younger students haven't had sufficient life experience to be able to give accurate responses. This means that the prompts have to describe context-specific situations that don't necessarily give insight into the all-important generalities of the mindsets that underlie the styles. In fact, in the end they might only report preferred behaviours in particular circumstances, not styles at all. The students' liking for the subject, their relationship with the teacher, a mood swing, a fall-out with friends – all these can affect the results. Which means that on a different day a different set of preferences might emerge for the same student. The best way to counter these first two difficulties is to go for skilled observation (the first two strategies above), rather than questionnaires.

Third, the human tendency is to categorise and label. This applies to both teachers and students. Although it is true that no one is ever entirely one style, once a student's dominant score is revealed, that's the category that sticks. Students start to talk of themselves as being that type of learner or, worse still, that type of person. Teachers quickly pigeon-hole and label students, usually with the good intention of providing appropriate support. Some schools and colleges offer self-help booklets, *For The Visual Learner*, *For The Kinaesthetic Learner* and so on containing tips for mastering material personally, no matter how it's presented by the teacher. Such resources are well intentioned and are in many cases helpful, but they do reinforce the idea that students are either one thing or the other.

So, the discerning teacher is left with a tough decision – to test or not to test?

Check Your Impact On Students' Self-Esteem

Self-esteem is notoriously difficult to define. It can't be reduced to glib terms such as "self-confidence" or "feeling good about yourself". According to Tony Humphreys, "There are two central dimensions to self-esteem: the feeling of being lovable and the feeling of being capable".[2]

The *Student's Dictionary of Psychology* describes self-esteem as "The personal evaluation that an individual makes of her or himself; their sense of their own worth or capabilities".[3]

So we see that self-esteem is a personal *judgment* – a gut feeling about how worthy I am, how happy I am to be me – based on the extent to which I feel lovable and capable. Clearly, the conclusion I come to will be fed by the extent to which I am *actually* loved and am *actually* able to do things. The judgment can, of course, shift either way over time.

What about self-image?

> "The internal picture that an individual has of her or himself, a kind of internal description, which is built up through interaction with the environment and feedback from other people."[4]

Moment by moment we get feedback about ourselves. Some comes from other people, who react to what we say and do, or who tell us what they think of us. Some feedback is in the form of results – were we successful or did we fail or were we somewhere in between? Feedback comes from looking in the mirror, from comparing ourselves to and with other people, real and fictional, from reflecting on our lives, from undertaking formal assessments, from noting how our plans work out, from trying something new and seeing what happens (for example, attending a voice workshop for the first time to discover "Oh, I never knew I could sing like that!"). The countless messages we receive about ourselves are woven into a *picture*: this is the person I am.

And self-concept?

> The sum total of the ways in which the individual sees herself or himself. Self-concept is often considered to have two major dimensions: a descriptive component (known as self-image) and an evaluative component (known as self-esteem).[5]

Therefore, in crude but helpful terms: self-image + self-esteem = self-concept. In other words, the kind of person I see myself as being, plus the extent to which I feel it's OK to be like that, equals what I really think about myself. Clearly this is an oversimplification, but a constructive one, I hope.

Consequently, we have a challenge on our hands. The *images* that students build up of themselves are the result of the feedback they get, over time, from sources we can't control, such as family, friends and neighbours, and sources we can, such as ourselves and other students. The subtle messages we give through tone of voice, body language, being available and having a laugh are as powerful as the explicit messages we give through encouragement, assessment comments, reprimands and acknowledgments. They all tell students what we think of them. Imagine, for example, the effect of saying, "You're not like your older sister, are you? She didn't need things repeating umpteen times". Likewise, imagine the positive effect of smiling at a student every time you see them in the corridor.

Messages from other students come through all sorts of situations. Imagine as a student the positive experience of classmates wanting you to be part of their group, listening while you speak, not making fun, asking your opinion, congratulating you on your achievement, letting you go first, and so on.

In developing a healthy *self-image*, students also benefit from receiving accurate information about their learning progress, their learning potential and their learning styles. Their images can remain positive if they receive the constant message that each of them is, in fact, a potentially successful learner. To believe this they will need many experiences of actual success, mixed in among the moments of mistake, struggle and relative failure.

Artificial success is no good. Giving students watered-down tasks that a donkey could do, or praising them for work that is clearly substandard because you feel it will boost their confidence, is actually counterproductive. For a start, most students see through it. Also, it builds a dangerously shaky foundation for the future by giving students a false impression of their capabilities. Later in life, when the shattering truth becomes clear, the blow is bitter. This has implications for the way we design learning experiences. Differentiation and variety are minimum requirements. Differentiation provides all learners with stretching but achievable learning activities so that *genuine* success can be experienced. Variety ensures that different learning styles are provided for, so success is more likely.

In regard to *self-esteem*, students' value of themselves is largely a product of how much they *feel* valued by others. Consequently, it's important to create an acceptant, inclusive classroom with firm ground rules that eliminate put-downs and guarantee listening. Likewise, as teachers, we can signal unconditional regard by remaining upbeat with students even when there are some serious behaviours and learning skills to be improved. Don't allow behaviour and performance to define the student. No one is "bad", "stupid", "unteachable", "lazy" or "no good at maths", at least not entirely! Remain optimistic about the person and their potential for learning. This fundamental orientation will come through in all your dealings with them. Similarly, students are expert at detecting truthfulness and integrity – it's impossible to pull the wool over their eyes. When we treat them as adults, being willing to let them know when we feel stuck, giving them the real reasons for a change to the plan, for instance, they grow taller inwardly.

Asking students for their opinions, asking them to make choices, asking them to negotiate and arrive at decisions with you, rather than just follow the decisions you have made for them, all signal that you trust and value their judgments. Being prepared to break the icy barrier that often exists between students and teacher – by chatting informally, sharing a joke, listening to their music and playing a game – again signals acceptance. Equally, it's important that students are not let off the hook, that they understand how certain actions bring certain consequences. This is all part of their learning about personal responsibility, personal style and choice, which in turn enables each student increasingly to shape their life.

Naïvely, schools tend to assume that self-esteem can be raised by awarding merit marks, stickers, prizes, medals and even financial incentives. Nothing could be further from the truth. In fact, when self-esteem is taken seriously, the issues to be addressed strike at the heart of school routines and organisation, and at the delicate area of teachers' personal style.

Bettie B. Youngs lists the "six vital ingredients that can empower or detract from the vitality of our lives".[6] Self-esteem is fed by all of them:

1. **Physical safety**: freedom from physical harm
2. **Emotional safety**: the absence of intimidation and fears
3. **Identity**: the "who am I?" question
4. **Affiliation**: a sense of belonging
5. **Competence**: a sense of feeling capable
6. **Mission**: the feeling that one's life has meaning and direction

How many of these do schools deliver? Some would argue that typical British secondary schools, as institutions, are anti-self-esteem. On the whole they are built like factories and, according to Charles Handy, run like prisons. What messages does your organisation give? If we go down this path, we quickly arrive at the need for schools to reconstruct themselves utterly. While there are many American examples of schools doing just that (Ted Sizer's Coalition of Effective Schools, for example) and a few British ones (mainly outside "the system"), the current political climate in the UK will not tolerate such a fundamental rethink. For a fuller discussion of these points see the many publications of *Education Now*; see also Section 1 of *The Teacher's Toolkit* under the heading "Why?" (page 3); and the subheading "Everyone needs to feel emotionally secure and psychologically safe" (page 25).

So it's time for an honest assessment. Translating desired esteem-raising qualities into hard behaviours and procedures is not easy, but let's have a go. Take an honest look at yourself, your department or team and your school. Use this inventory on the one hand to identify areas you need to strengthen and on the other to spot behaviours and procedures you need to drop. There are five domains to scrutinise.

The items listed below are interrelated. Some of them may seem extreme or impossible, and in isolation they probably are. For example, "Do away with threats and bribes" – in fact, most schools depend on them. Yet with several other strands in place – such as "Teach students how and when to be assertive with each other", "Create and maintain classroom ground rules", "Train and use peer mediators" and "Always follow through the consequence that has been described" – doing away with threats and bribes becomes a realistic prospect.

Enhancing self-esteem is like weaving a spider's web. Every strand is individually strong and important, but only when many strands are interconnected will the web do its job. This takes time, but then spiders are remarkably patient creatures.

Decide on the subjects of the audit. For example A = yourself, B = your department or team, C = the year team, D = the school. Then use a five-point scale to give an honest and accurate assessment of each skill or quality: 5 means "perfectly" or "totally in place" or "always"; 1 means "not at all".	A	B	C	D
I. Underlying issues – what goes on inside your head				
1. Believe that all your students are capable. Have high expectations of students based on modern notions of intelligence and potential, rooted in a scientific understanding of the brain's capacity. Realise that your expectations of students influence their expectations of themselves.				
2. Reflect on the psychology and philosophy underpinning your teaching. Rarely operate from expediency. Consistently work to humanistic and democratic principles, rather than behaviouristic and authoritarian. Keep long-term aims in mind.				
3. Retain a generally positive approach to teaching and nourish it with an understanding of recent brain research. Consequently, bring energy and optimism into the classroom, and learn how to work with, rather than against, "the grain of the brain".				
4. See students as individuals. Accept that each human brain is as unique as a fingerprint. Understand and use at least one learning-styles model.				
5. Open yourself to self-reflection and self-examination. Model the learning process yourself, which means be prepared to experiment, take risks and learn from disappointments and mistakes.				
6. Be aware that your demeanour has a profound impact on students. Work to demonstrate genuineness, empathy and unconditional positive regard – the classic and well-researched Rogerian attitudes. The minimum is basically to like students and have a warm disposition towards them.				
7. Believe that every student has the right to be included in a success culture and has the right to achieve to the highest levels of which they are currently capable.				
Totals				

II. Teachers' personal skills and behaviours – the way you come across to students	A	B	C	D
1. Eliminate sarcasm and all other forms of put-down, even in fun, from your communications with students.				
2. Challenge damaging talk about students by colleagues, in the staffroom, for example. It's easy to perpetuate a culture of negativity. This needs to be reversed.				
3. Use the "language of responsibility" with students – there are particular skills involved (see "Check Your Language" on page 307)				
4. Be aware that when students feel wrong they feel small – use alternative means of challenging students who have inaccurate or incomplete ideas. For example, ask students to prove their answer, or ask them to check with other students, or go back to the book and rethink. Turn mistakes into learning points.				
5. Strive for "adult–adult" interactions with students, to use a term from *Transactional Analysis.* This means approaching students as grown-ups. Use reason and expect reason. Tell the truth, remain calm, listen. Model these behaviours to students. Show how a crisis can be dealt with without turning it into a drama.				
6. Approach students in an "I'm OK, you're OK" frame of mind. Clear your mental slate of anything that's gone on before. Make each lesson a new start. Expect things to go well.				
7. Listen actively to students, especially when there is a difference of opinion, a conflict or strong emotion involved. At a busy moment, let them know that you realise they have something important to say and that you'll catch them later – during or after the lesson. Don't make promises you can't keep.				
8. Use assertiveness with students as an alternative to behaviourist techniques. Do not use rewards and punishments, bribes and threats. Instead be clear about rules, explain and offer choices. Speak of consequences, rather than rewards and punishments. Always follow through the consequence that has been described.				
9. Acknowledge students often, both in private and in public. Let students know that you have noticed their achievement and their efforts. Thank students. Do not use artificial praise.				
10. Avoid communicating judgments that run the risk of labelling students. Especially risky are throw-away comments such as "You'll never make a musician", "You're not like your older brother", "Well, that's a surprise coming from someone who … "				
11. Use the skills of giving and receiving feedback. Be willing to receive constructive feedback from students about your teaching and style. Model how to give positive and negative feedback in the way you assess and comment on students' learning.				
12. Bring energy and optimism into the classroom. Be lively. Use humour, but never at anyone's expense.				
13. Make it a priority to learn and use all students' first names.				
14. Teach students how to use self-affirming language. Use affirmations yourself: for example, "I have all the skills I need to be an excellent teacher".				
15. Seek the students' opinions as often as possible about the order in which things should be tackled, about learning strategies, timescales, assessment procedures, problems they're facing, solutions, improvements to the classroom, behaviour issues, conflicting priorities …				
Totals				

III. Classroom environment – what it's like to be in your lessons	A	B	C	D
1. Teach students to listen actively to each other and expect it of them in class. Challenge students who don't listen. Ask students who have not been heard properly to repeat what they are saying and ask someone else to feed back a summary.				
2. Create and maintain ground rules that eliminate put-downs and guarantee emotional "safety". These need to be made with each class. Review these rules every now and again with students.				
3. Teach students how and when to be assertive with each other. Expect assertiveness instead of aggression and weakness.				
4. Play esteem-enhancing and cooperative games. These can be done at registration, during form period, in PSHE or at the start or end of lessons.				
5. Make the classroom aesthetically pleasing. Attend to colour, display, carpet, plants and aroma, as well as the basics of oxygen and temperature.				
6. Make resources available. Teach students where to get, and how to use economically, consumable resources such as sugar paper, felt pens, glue, card, crayons, paper clips, stapler. Ensure that text and reference books, CD-ROMs, worksheets and tapes are openly available in the classroom or stockroom, or that students know where they are located in the school resource centre.				
7. Play varieties of music. Perhaps at the beginning and end of the lesson, and sometimes during. Value different tastes.				
8. Give students access to quality drinking water. Ideally have a chilled-water dispenser in the classroom.				
9. Welcome students to the lesson, preferably by greeting them at the door.				
Totals				

IV. Learning strategies – the teaching techniques you use	A	B	C	D
1. Let students in on your thinking about learning objectives, learning strategies and progress. Keep reminding them of the "big picture" of their learning. Have timescales, deadlines and progress charts on the wall. As a minimum share lesson objectives with students.				
2. Challenge yourself to share more responsibility for learning with students. Offer choices, negotiate, make decisions democratically. Discuss and decide with students the learning strategies, deadlines, means of recording and assessing outcomes. Plan *with* them rather than *for* them.				
3. Organise learning activities to take account of a full range of learning styles. The minimum is to vary teaching techniques so that all learning styles are honoured over, say, four lessons. Beyond this, offer different ways of doing things simultaneously.				
4. Monitor learning tasks to ensure that they are sufficiently stretching. No one should be "dumbed down" by colouring in, doing word searches or copying out. On the other hand, tasks should be achievable even though they will require effort, thought and perhaps support from peers or the teacher.				
5. Give prompt and regular feedback about learning progress. Give lots of on-the-spot feedback. Supplement marks and grades with constructive and practical tips for improvement. Suggest personalised targets. Do not use norm-referencing. Criterion-referenced and ipsitive assessment only.				
6. Teach students how to assess their learning realistically, how to use criteria and look for evidence. Teach them how to set their own targets for improvement.				
7. Acknowledge, celebrate, and display all relative success. Frequently hold pieces of work up for everyone to see and explain the achievement. Never hold work up for ridicule. Do not select only the best work for display. Have plenty of space for work to be pinned up casually for short periods of time. Teach students how to mount work for longer-lasting displays.				
Totals	A	B	C	D

V. Whole-school issues – things to think about with your colleagues	A	B	C	D
1. Develop the student council so that it functions effectively within the school's communication and decision-making structure. Ensure that it "talks to" the senior staff meeting, the whole-staff meeting, the governors' meeting, various subcommittees.				
2. Devolve a sizable budget to the student council.				
3. Create frequent opportunities for individual, and groups of, students to be heard. Ask them for feedback on teaching, consult them on major policy decisions, have a complaints procedure, have a suggestions box with updates to students in assembly.				
4. Seek to give groups of students their own physical space. If space permits, give each year group a common room. Don't lock students out.				
5. Attend to the aesthetics, safety and comfort of the physical environment. Carpets are essential, lots of plants and art, good ventilation and lighting. Use colour and use fabrics to soften the utilitarian nature of most school interiors.				
6. Check that the students' toilets are dignifying and have paper. Minimise queuing times at lunch. Make sure there's plenty of healthy food and lots of choice. Take students' advice on how to improve these facilities.				
7. Reappraise the behaviour policy from a nonbehaviourist point of view. Do away with threats and bribes. Abandon behaviourist psychology. Negotiate a set of clear rules with students. Agree positive and negative consequences with students. Place a premium on assertiveness. Offer choices. Emphasise personal responsibility. Use trained counsellors. Train and use peer mediators. Make nonpunitive contracts with students about changes to their behaviour.				
8. Allow students to move around the building without permission slips – to use the resource centre, for example, during lesson time.				
9. Group students in a way that supports self-esteem. Hold discussions with students, parents and staff about mixed ability versus streaming and setting. Make self-esteem the deciding criterion. Take account of teacher's ability to differentiate. Make a joint decision.				
10. Consult with students, staff and parents to create a whole-school policy on self-esteem. Uphold the policy through reminders, through modelling the behaviours, through challenging inappropriate behaviours.				
11. Make the enhancement of self-esteem a major plank of the school's mission statement and development plan. Explain what self-esteem is and why it's so important. Encourage reading, have a book review each month, hold seminars and training events. Talk about self-esteem openly. Seek to achieve a common understanding and common priority.				
Totals				
Grand Totals				

Check Your Delivery of Independent Learning Skills

It's no wonder that thinking skills and independent learning are major national agendas. Students need the attitudes and skills of independence for long-term success. GCSE coursework, GNVQ assignments, homework and revision all require qualities such as perseverance and a willingness to defer gratification along with planning, time-management and research skills, plus summarising, memorising and presentation techniques. Together, these create the foundation stones of life-long learning. In this day and age people can expect to change jobs and have to retrain several times within a working lifetime. Increased leisure time for many people means more interests to explore and skills to learn – under their own steam.

John Dewey, the "father" of experiential learning often said, "Children don't do what they learn, they learn what they do". If he was right, the skills and attitudes of independence can be acquired only *experientially*. They can be introduced, but not internalised through dedicated study-skills courses. To stick, they have to be practised and rehearsed many times. In fact, psychologists tell us that behaviours become habits only after *forty or so repetitions*, which suggests the need for cross-curricular delivery. Clearly, no one teacher or department can make it happen single-handedly. Such learning requires all teachers to accept a share of the responsibility and play their part in delivering the messages, otherwise the desired outcomes will fall through the cracks of the curriculum.

Ironically, independence that is built in many primary schools during Key Stages 1 and 2 is dismantled in many secondary schools during Key Stage 3, only to be required again at Key Stage 4 when it's too late because most students are set in their ways! The natural place to focus attention, therefore, is Key Stage 3. And a natural way to begin the process of development is to look at what happens at Key Stage 2 and plan for continuity and progression with Key Stage 2 teachers.

To give an insight into what may be happening in your local primary school, have a look at this attempt to map the systematic delivery of a particular group of learning skills from nursery to Year 6.

An incremental and developmental framework for paired, collaborative and group work

The following skills will be taught to the majority of children in the suggested order and within the appropriate year group. There will obviously be some children who are at a higher or lower developmental stage, and for whom skills should be selected from an appropriate year group programme.

Foundation Stage	Y1	Y2	Y3	Y4	Y5	Y6
Sit properly. Take turns.	Collaborate in pairs.	Respond to other adults/teachers.	Paired talk, A/B. Discussion in 2s to 4s.	Paired talk, A/B. Discussion in 2s to 4s.	Collaborate as pairs to plan/do/review.	Recognise and use social dynamics and learning styles.
Listen to peers/teachers.	Collaborate in 2s to 4s to share findings with others.	Discuss in pairs and 2s to 4s across classes.	Swap texts to read their partners'.	Regular use of envoying approaches and styles, hot-seating, jigsawing, eavesdropping.	Collaborate as a group to plan/do/review.	Present work and ideas confidently as reviews or plenaries using a range of techniques.
Make contributions to discussions.	Understand the concept of "A/B" talk and feedback.	Listen and evaluate, rather than just waiting to talk.	Collaborative discussions and presenting work to their own groups.		Take turns to lead discussions within groups.	
In family groups, tell friends what they did.	Know and use the response strategies of: hands up/think, think/talk.	Know that to listen they need to put all their equipment down and face the speaker.	Following and giving instructions.	Take part in group presentations to the class.	Regular use of "experts" and presenting to other groups.	Develop presentations using suitable visual aids and ICT.
Understand the meaning of purposeful and paired talk.	Work independently for 20 minutes.	Read own text to peers and adults.	Self-review of own work.	Working towards becoming "experts".	Share tasks for extended periods.	Be able to organise discussions to include all parties.
Work independently for 15 minutes.		Envoying.		Self-review of own work.	Develop ideas on learning styles.	Be able to summarise discussions and presentations of others.
		Work independently for 25 minutes.		Review of peers' work.		

Children start to create their own notes to support their work

Cape Primary School, Sandwell and John Peatfield, Education Development Unit, St Martin's College

What would you do in Key Stage 3 to build on this? If students were coming to your school with this experience, what skills would you consolidate, what would you extend and what new skills would you introduce in Years 7, 8 and 9? Then come at the question from the other direction. What skills and attitudes do our students currently lack at Key Stage 4? What, therefore, do we need to do in Key Stage 3 to make sure that those qualities are developed before it's too late?

To get you going, here's an example from a secondary school that commissioned a small cross-curricular working party to answer such questions. This is what they came up with. "At Key Stage 3 we must teach the following ..."

Listening	Problem Solving	Evaluation	Planning	Memorising
listening to instructions practising listening skills interpreting discussing	recognising patterns decision-making research skimming scanning making deductions testing a hypothesis presenting information in different forms and registers as required applying information practical skills ICT	self-evaluation target setting restructuring data making deductions evaluating data	action planning finding information brainstorming working in groups time management questioning techniques note taking/key points constructing a hypothesis applying information organising work (prioritising) ICT exam revision	note taking recalling information restructuring data exam revision

Harwich School

Now look more closely at Key Stage 4 and concentrate on the skills and attitudes required both *during* GCSE and vocational courses, and in the *run-up* to the final exams. The chart below presents them as a series of messages to get across to students. What do you think? This is only for starters. Add your own messages and bullet points.

Message	Implications for teachers	Implications for students
1. Don't just sit there Learning requires the brain to be active – engage it	• Use active learning techniques • Don't give "ready-made information" such as dictation, copying, duplicated notes • Require students to find things out/work things out via research, problem solving, peer teaching, hypothesis testing … • Require them to ask you rather than expect you to tell them • When students ask for help, structure their thinking by asking them questions and giving them prompts so they work it out for themselves	• Keep asking questions of yourself – how does this fit with …? • Don't just passively read text – annotate, highlight, mind-map • Keep comparing what's new with what you know already: "What have I learned today?" • Keep testing yourself • Keep connecting with the exam – where does this fit in the syllabus, what kind of questions on this topic have come up in the past? • Check your understanding with the teacher
2. Get it sorted There is no short cut: your brain learns by sorting things out for itself – give it a chance	• Ask open questions – how, what if, why …? • Ask students to make connections – how is this different from …? • Set tasks that involve translating material from one format into another – list into pie chart, text into key-word plan, storyboard into bullet points … • Ask students to summarise often – draw mind maps of whole topics, make personal summary cards • Require students to articulate their learning to others – peers, parents, a tape recorder • Require students to keep moving in their heads from whole to parts and from parts to whole: What's this an example of? What's the principle behind this? • Get the students to signal to you the moment they don't understand what you are saying	• Turn the given material into another format – your own words, mind map, flow diagram, key-word plan, bullet points, storyboard … • Don't pretend that you understand if you don't – ask the teacher for clarification • Accept the difference between "doing the work" and actually learning the material – don't con yourself into thinking that you will have learned something just because you have completed the exercise – check your understanding • When you read text, ask yourself "What does this mean?" or "What is this saying?" • Explain what you have learned to someone else – if they can understand it, it proves that you have!

Message	Implications for teachers	Implications for students
3. I can't do this, it's too hard The natural response to stress is to close down – use techniques to minimise the problem	• Teach and use self-affirming language: "I have all the skills I need to do well in this exam", "I can get all the knowledge I need to pass, my past is not my potential …" • Teach relaxation techniques – diaphragmatic breathing, muscle relaxation, use of music, colour, aromas • Teach visioning – "In ten years' time I see myself running my own small business", "I see myself in the exam feeling calm and thinking clearly", "I see myself at university" • Teach about the potential and functioning of the brain – students have all the brainpower they need • Avoid threats and punishments such as "If you …" • Enhance self-esteem and therefore raise the reptilian threshold – give lots of acknowledgment, recognition and encouragement • Take time to talk with, and especially listen to, students	• Recognise reptilian behaviour – that is when you feel panic and want to give up and run away – and take time out • Use relaxation techniques • Use self-affirmations: talk to yourself! • Remind yourself of your long-term goals • Break learning into small steps • Record your achievements step by step and feel proud of what you achieve – a bit at a time • Focus on what you have done, not what you have still got to do – the glass is half full, not half empty • Keep talking to people who will encourage you • Get away from your work – take breaks often enough, phone a friend, listen to music, watch TV, go for a walk, read a book
4. It's not my fault Yes, it is – you've only got yourself to blame	• Get students into the habit of making choices – about learning method, deadlines, resources, assessment, modes of recording • Ask students to set their own goals and deadlines • Let students face consequences and encourage them to recognise the options they had • Ask students to come up with learning methods for themselves • Debrief the learning process with students on a regular basis • Support them with a "pupils' toolkit" that gives lots of guidelines for working independently • Model the "language of responsibility" (page 307) • Show students the "big picture" often, so they know where they stand in relation to the coursework and exam requirements • Support them with adequate resources • Avoid using rewards – they keep people dependent on external motivators	• Make sure you know the syllabus and the requirements of the exam, always check what you are doing against the "big picture" – have a clear idea of what you have done and what you have got to do • Own the syllabus – it's yours not your teacher's, it's up to you to master it • Reflect on missed deadlines and targets – ask yourself what you will do differently next time • Remember, in the exam you can use only what's in your head • Remember, only you can put stuff in there in advance • Remember everything you do (and don't do) is a choice • There are no excuses, only choices • Remember that you are doing this for yourself, not for your parents or the school

Message	Implications for teachers	Implications for students
5. What's the difference? All brains are wired up differently – do it your way	• Use lots of varied teaching and learning methods and debrief them with students • Offer a menu of different tasks to suit different styles and ask students to make choices • Be explicit about learning styles with students – explain them, demonstrate them, use learning-styles terminology with students • Ask students to accept increasing responsibility for learning, enable them to study, record and present learning in their own way • Over time, require students to build up a bank of personal learning techniques and encourage them to reflect on the suitability of various methods for their natural style	• Understand about learning styles and recognise your own natural ways of learning • Have a go at lots of different study techniques so you can find the ones that suit you best • Use your preferred methods, practise them so they become easy and natural • Be willing to try new ways – you never know …
6. Take note! Learn to make notes – make notes to learn	• Teach speed reading, scanning and skimming techniques • Teach the idea of hierarchies in text, ranging from headlines to details (most explicit in newspapers, but present in all nonfiction text) – this is the basis of note making • Teach key-point identification • Teach key-word identification • Teach note-making and summarising formats such as key-word plans, tables, mind maps, timelines, storyboards, flow diagrams, concentric circles, target notes, bullet points … • Set note-making homeworks • Build identification of key points and succinct presentation into your assessment policy • As time goes on, ask students to summarise summaries	• Force yourself *not* to copy • Cut down reading time – practise scanning text for the relevant bits • Cut down reading time – practise skimming for the key points • See if you can write points down in the fewest possible words • Use sketches, diagrams, cartoons and symbols instead of words • Try lots of different note-making techniques so you know which ones suit you best • Use colours • Get into the habit of highlighting notes in your exercise book or files – even in textbooks if you own them • Get into the habit of making notes of the work you are covering, even if your teacher doesn't ask you to • As you approach a test or exam, summarise your summaries

Message	Implications for teachers	Implications for students
7. The long and short of it You've got two types of memory – learn how to store things long-term	• Make learning multisensory – discuss the effects with students and teach them how to do multisensory learning at home, for example "Multisensory Memories" (page 130) • Teach about short- and long-term memory • Teach the Ebbinghaus Effect – that retention fades over time unless material is revisited frequently • Revisit and review previous learning as part of ordinary lessons • Set summarising homeworks • Set lots of mini-tests • Have mind-map summaries of topics on the classroom walls – encourage students to do the same at home • Teach memorising techniques, such as "Hide 'n' Seek" (page 111)	• Accept the importance of revisiting previous learning • Make lots and lots of summaries • Use "Hide 'n' Seek" (page 111) – a basic technique • Use physical memory methods – use gestures, put key points on cards, place them around the room and walk around • Listen to the sound of your own voice to aid memory – speak out loud, make tape recordings • Use mnemonics, number words, recordings, listings, Post-it notes, posters • Prove what you know – test yourself or get others to test you
8. Do yourself a favour Your brain works best under certain conditions – give it what it needs	• Make sure your classroom models favourable learning conditions: light; oxygen; colour; peripherals • Encourage students to drink plenty of pure, chilled water instead of cola, tea and coffee • Change learning activities often in lessons • Teach about concentration span, that it is usually chronological age plus two years (up to 14!) in minutes • Teach that it's important to break learning into small chunks to fit concentration span, and to have short breaks between chunks • Model this in the classroom	• Drink lots of water – avoid cola and other fizzy drinks • Eat small and often • Make sure you've got enough fresh air in the room and enough light • Take frequent short breaks • Eliminate distractions – have the discipline to get away from the TV and ask your family not to disturb you • Make the most of peripheral learning: put key points on large paper and stick them around the house – behind the toilet door, for example

303

Message

9. There's plenty of time

Yes, there is plenty of time to learn everything – as long as you manage it well

Implications for teachers

- Give plenty of practice at working to non-negotiable deadlines
- Give plenty of practice at setting realistic deadlines
- Keep referring to different timescales for learning: short-, medium- and long-term – have charts and calendars on the wall
- Have a large clock in the classroom and keep drawing attention to the pace of learning
- Model good time management – let the students know the plan you made for the lesson/course/marking/project work, and the replanning you do as you go along
- Give enough time for students to use their planners to record homework and deadlines and to identify potential clashes
- Remind students that every action, every word, is a choice, every moment of every day – challenge students when they try to blame other people or external factors for choices they have made

Implications for students

- Accept that life is a series of choices – you manage time, it does not manage you
- Make choices in advance, plan ahead – get a wall chart/planner
- Set short- and medium-term targets to guide your choices
- Put "things to do" in different categories to help you make choices: what I have to do; what I'm asked to do; what I want to do
- Involve your family – negotiate study time and ask them to support you by protecting the time
- When planning, follow the rules about reviewing – build in time to go back over things
- When planning, follow the rules about concentration spans – take account of the need for breaks
- Replan when things don't go according to plan
- Do the worst first!

So, I'm arguing that it's possible to see the "independent-learning curriculum", or "study-skills curriculum", as a series of crucial messages that need to be repeated time and time again, messages that contain both skills and attitudes. Naturally, they need to be delivered from Year 7 and built up over the years with lots and lots of opportunities to practise skills and internalise attitudes. Remember, we're talking habit formation. The campaign will work best if the messages are made explicit and explained to students up front, so they know the agenda and its rationale. Then they have to be delivered through a range of activities, both in and out of the classroom. For maximum effect, these activities have to be debriefed to make the "learning about learning" outcomes explicit. For example, studying "The Five Ks of Sikhism" through "Scrambled Groups" (page 150) in a Year 8 RE lesson is useful, but spending five minutes afterwards discussing what was learned about note making and the reasons for converting material from one form into another doubles the benefit.

There are many opportunities in school to deliver these messages. Just as the messages have to be repeated time and again, so they have to come from many angles, through many different channels. Use the chart on the next page to plot current practice and plan further coverage for each year group. Don't just tick boxes: write in detail. For instance, exactly how will student planners be used to get across time management (Message 9)? Only when the detail is secure will things start to happen. It's easy to assume that, because planners are being used, time management is being handled. No, it depends on *how* the planners are being used, what coaching students get from their subject teachers and form tutor, and how much fuss the school makes about, and how much it models, good planning.

Learning Skills Delivery Map For Year ?

Opportunities for Delivery

Message	PSHE lessons	Subject teaching	Assembly	Special study-skills events	Registration and form period	Trips	After-school homework club	Mentoring	Behaviour policy	Student planners	?	?
1												
2												
3												
4												
5												
6												
7												
8												
9												
?												
?												

Check Your Language

We know that the language we use has a dramatic effect on other people's thinking. Over time it shapes their view of us, themselves and the world in general. So students who are continually told that they are stupid come to see themselves as stupid, those who are told they are capable come to think of themselves as capable. The remarkable thing is that they then have an optimistic attitude to challenges that face them and actually do achieve great things. However, Neuro-Linguistic Programming has taught us that it's not just words that matter: it's tone of voice and body language, too. In fact, the suggestion is that the impact of a communication is made up of:

- **7% words**
- **38% tonality, volume and tempo**
- **55% nonverbal signals**

Therefore, it's important to be congruent, which means ensuring that the tone of our delivery and associated body language match the words we're using. Imagine that your students are facing a tough assignment. If you say, "I really believe you can do this; the task is challenging, but I've got total faith that everyone in the room will be able to master it in the end" – with your head down, spoken slowly in a voice that gets deeper and deeper with a resigned look on your face like Eeyore in *Winnie the Pooh* – what message will the students receive?

Likewise, think of giving feedback to a colleague whose lesson you've just observed. If you say, "Well, I thought that was really … um … interesting, and … um … professional, really … um … great" with shifting eyes, exaggerated nodding and absolutely no conviction in the voice, it's obvious that they'll think you regarded it as a poor show, which is of course true.

All this is common sense, but there are some tricks of the trade to learn if we want to have particular effects. Two key intentions of our language, I suggest, are to increase students' sense of *personal responsibility* and enhance their *self-esteem*. These two qualities are promoted by, and in some cases required by, the strategies presented in *The Teacher's Toolkit*. Some of the practical ideas simply don't work unless students have sufficient of both. As we've said several times, the teaching and learning techniques themselves cannot deliver these "soft" outcomes, for the greater impact is made by the teacher's demeanour, her internalised belief in students' potential, her understanding of the brain, her ability to work with feelings, therefore the nature of her interventions – in other words, her total communication.

Carl Rogers, the great inventor of client-centred counselling, summarised years of experience and research when he defined the three attitudes required of anyone in a "helping" relationship. These are the qualities, above all, that a counsellor, friend, parent, spouse or teacher will need in order to be effective:

- **empathy** – being able to feel what it's like to be in someone else's shoes
- **unconditional positive regard** – accepting and prizing someone as they are, with all their faults, without wanting to change them
- **congruence** – being yourself, being truthful and honest about your own feelings, abandoning pretence and play-acting in the relationship

He argued that these three always have a powerful "therapeutic" effect on the other person and will automatically come through in the language and behaviour of the "helper" if they are genuinely felt. But it works both ways. Carefully chosen words support and deepen the internalisation of the feelings. If we consciously pick our phrases and sentences to communicate these qualities, then the qualities themselves become more established within our psyches. The more we use the "right" language, the more we alter our patterns of thinking and our perceptions of self and others.

So watch what you say! Here are some random tips for the use of language designed to promote both responsibility and self-esteem. If you try some of the less familiar suggestions, they might seem very wooden at first. It's like learning to drive a car: with lots of practice you move from a stage of conscious competence to unconscious competence, at which point it all feels quite natural. By the way, an excellent guidebook, written for parents but easily adapted to teaching situations, is *How to Talk so Kids will Listen and How to Listen so Kids will Talk*.[7]

1. Stop using the word "work".
Don't talk to students about the *work* they've got to do, how good their *work* is or what you'll do to them if they don't get on with their *work*. All this just reinforces the idea that school is like a factory, that the students' job is to apply themselves to a task, that all they have to do is endure it and complete it. Replace "work" with "learning". This emphasises the real purpose of school, it stresses outcomes, gains, achievements, enhancements and improvements. In other words, it focuses attention on the destination, not the journey, the end, not the means. This reorientation is a necessary prerequisite of the kind of grown-up discussions and negotiations with learners suggested in *The Teacher's Toolkit*.

2. Ditch the word "ability".
Replace it with "abilities" in the plural to remind yourself and your students that everyone has a range of diverse gifts, talents and intelligences, all of which will be valued in this classroom. If you are asked to define a student's ability, speak of their "abilities profile". Replace "ability" with "what you can do in this area of learning at this moment in time", or a less long-winded version if you can think of one! Perhaps "current competence". In other words, get the idea across that "ability" is only a snapshot, a dipstick measurement of current performance, not a definition of a student's intelligence or character. Talk of ability as dynamic, not static.

3. Abandon all put-downs.
They come in many shapes and sizes and always do damage, even when the student appears to laugh them off. What else is he supposed to do? Sarcasm and other barbed comments puncture self-esteem and confidence, but are still used by some teachers to put students in their places, rather like Blackadder with a class of Baldricks. Phrases like these simply have to go:

- Well, I wouldn't have expected that from you of all people ...
- That's a surprise coming from someone who ...
- Managed to connect our two brain cells, have we?
- Surely you're not going to break the habit of a lifetime and answer a question?
- Keep the noise down, everybody – you might wake Simon.
- Don't strain yourself – you might do yourself a mental injury.
- What fascinating nugget of wisdom do you have for us today, Tracey?
- I've never met anyone as ... as you.
- Are you actually as thick as two short planks or just pretending?
- Congratulations, you must be the world's worst ...

Turning your back, waving a student away with your hand, interrupting a student, striking up a conversation with someone else when a student is speaking to you are all infuriating, dismissive behaviours.

Disapproving of a student's clothes, make-up, accent, class, parents' occupation, hobbies, tastes, humour and personal habits are all invasions of privacy designed to create alienation.

Criticising students for not knowing something they don't know or not being able to do something they can't do makes them feel stupid and results in shut-down. So, don't say things such as:

- At your age I'd have thought you'd be able to …
- What is it with students today? Too much television, I suppose. No wonder you can't …
- Haven't you got it yet? How much *more* time do I have to spend on this?
- Any normal person would be able to …
- What's wrong with you? Can't you just …?

Not facilitating disability and specific learning needs is itself a put-down. These are often institutional matters, but they are also about a teacher's forethought and preparation. Some more tips:

4. Don't compare students with one another

One of the cruellest remarks that can be made to a student is, "You're not as bright/tidy/well behaved/skilful/successful as your brother/sister/neighbour/rest of the class/the average student". Negative comparisons immediately diminish self-esteem and, if repeated often enough, have long-lasting effects. We all know adults who are still trying to live up to standards set by someone else.

Positive comparisons are also unhealthy – they invite superiority, which is esteem at someone else's expense – cheap esteem, externally sourced esteem, not self-esteem at all. It gives the idea that getting one over on someone else is OK, that life is a competition and being better than other people is good. This creates stress; some people live the rest of their lives trying to be better than others. They continually measure themselves against the "competition" and feel OK only when they're sure there are enough people who are not as good as they.

There are clear implications for assessment: norm referencing is bad; ipsitive and criterion-referenced assessments are much more healthy. So cut out descriptors such as "average", "below average" and "above average". Also, cut out the practice of announcing test results from the bottom up, or pinning up a list of students in rank order, or writing "Position in the class" on reports.

5. Talk about the future, not the past

If you want a person to move on, don't keep referring to what they used to be like, how they've changed, how sad it is, and why they can't be like they were before. Instead, speak of future possibilities, what they can become, what they can do differently from now on. This is particularly important if you want a student to change their behaviour or tackle a new learning challenge. Start by honouring where the student is now and being forever optimistic about the prospects for growth. See the student's life as a set of choices that are renewed moment by moment.

When managing behaviour, it is rarely helpful to rake over old ground and ask students to explain past actions. Nit-picking analysis belongs to the courtroom and always creates a judicial defend/attack atmosphere that soon leads to accusation and counteraccusation. "Yes, but you said … and then you … I clearly remember telling you to … And what did you do? You did such-and-such because you were being childish, weren't you, *weren't* you?" "No, you're just picking on me."

Teachers often go backwards because what they really want is an apology, an admission of guilt, a confession followed by adequate contrition. They want to be proved right so their authority can be reasserted. Usually, if a student appears sufficiently humbled and the teacher's pride is suitably restored, the teacher will soften and say something like, "Right, well, I hope you've learned your lesson. Now off you go and don't do it again". It is healthy, but hard, for teachers to give up these personal needs and instead focus exclusively on the student's future behaviour. Retrospection might be useful, but only to help the student see the benefit of making a change, not to ram guilt down their throat.

6. Replace the language of permission, approval and compulsion

You replace this sort of language with that of ownership and self-reliance. For example:

- "If you're good, I'll let you …" becomes "Would you like to …?"
- "I couldn't mark your books last night" becomes "I didn't mark …"
- "I couldn't help noticing …" becomes "I noticed …"
- "You've got my permission to …" becomes "I'll support your decision to …"
- "I'll have to say that …" becomes "I want to say …"

Translate the passive into the active voice, it emphasises who's in charge of the action:

- "This always happens to me" becomes "I do this a lot"
- "This won't get done" becomes "I won't do it"
- "I'm always being picked on" becomes "I allow myself to feel picked on"

It's never accurate to suggest that someone has *made* you feel or think or react. Take responsibility for the responses you make to other people's actions:

- "You make me feel …" becomes "I feel …"
- "I couldn't help it, he hit me first …" becomes "He hit me and I …"
- "I suppose I've got no choice, I'll have to …" becomes "Having weighed up the situation, I've decided to …"

7. Try one word instead of another …

Encourage students to substitute "won't" for "can't" in sentences like these and see if it helps to move things forward:

- "I can't be bothered"
- "I can't possibly get up in front of everyone and make a presentation"
- "I can't do this, it's too hard"
- "I can't spend any more time doing …"
- "I can't sing"

8. Change definitive judgments into statements about the here and now

By doing this, you create new possibilities for the future:

- "I'll never be any good at maths" becomes "I'm finding maths difficult at the moment"
- "I'm no good at drawing" becomes "I haven't mastered drawing techniques yet"
- "I'm thick" becomes "I'm not feeling very capable just now"

9. Avoid the question "Why?"

There is rarely an acceptable answer to questions like these:

- "Why are you late?"
- "Why did you do that?"
- "Why haven't you done your homework?"

"Why?" is usually an accusation in disguise and consequently tends to produce a defensive answer, an excuse, a lie or a rude outburst. It doesn't allow the student to take responsibility for their actions because it's not a genuine invitation to discuss the real reasons. Take "Why aren't you listening?" The truth might be "I'm bored to tears by what you're saying" – but few teachers would accept this, so the student usually mumbles, "I dunno." Instead of asking a "Why?" question, make the statement behind the question: "I really want you to listen to this"; "I'm concerned that your homework has not been done again"; "I'd like to talk about your being late so often."

10. Get rid of all those bossy, know-it-all sayings
These involve such words as "should", "must" and "ought". Here are some more potential substitutions:

- "I think you should ..." becomes "Have you thought about ...?"
- "What you must do next is ..." becomes "My suggestion is ..."
- "You really ought not to ..." becomes "I have some advice if you want to hear it"
- "If I were you, I'd ..." becomes "My considered opinion is ..."

Generally, preachy phrases can be replaced by "could". For example:

- "You should take more exercise" becomes "You could take ..."
- "You ought to do your homework as soon as you get in" becomes "You could do your homework as soon as you get in"
- "You must pay more attention if you want better marks" becomes "You could pay more attention, and then you'd be more likely to get better marks"

Such changes shift the locus of responsibility to where it belongs – the person who has to make the decision or take the action. All the language changes proposed in this section are designed to do just that, to heighten the feeling and execution of personal responsibility. Life is, after all, a series of moment-by-moment choices.

11. Confront people when they talk about trying
The word "try" usually expresses a weak intention. People use it to excuse themselves in advance. For example, "I'll try to get it done tomorrow"; "I'll try to give you a call over the weekend"; "I'll try to be on time". "Try" provides a convenient loophole. "I'll try to concentrate harder, miss" sounds like an intention to make a half-hearted effort, and most teachers are content with this. The expression does enough to satisfy both consciences and avoids having to look at the deeper reasons and genuine remedies: "What can I do to help you concentrate harder, Peter?"

"Try" can signal that a person is not accepting full responsibility for their actions and intentions. For example, "I'll try to mark your books tonight" could be replaced by "I've got five jobs to do tonight. Marking is number four on the list. If I don't get that far this evening it will be top priority tomorrow night". Model this kind of language yourself and begin to expect it of your students.

12. Notice the difference between "but" and "and"
This is a small point and it matters. When the first half of a sentence is followed by "but" (or its cousins "however" and "yet"), its value is cancelled out. For example:

- "I'd like to go to lunch with you, but I have to mark these tests."
- "I'm pleased that you've written so much, but it's still not neat enough."
- "I think you've improved a lot, but I'm very disappointed with your behaviour today."
- "I'd like to let you practise at break, but I'm on duty."

Replacing "but" with "and" immediately prompts both parties to think of solutions and alternatives. With "but" the response is usually negative: "Why?"; "What do you mean?"; "That's not fair." With "and" the response is usually positive: "How about ...?"; "Why don't we ...?"; "Can't I just ...?"; "What if ...?" "And" encourages creative thinking and new choices – it removes the inevitability of a deadlocked situation.

13.   *Personalise and own your statements*
Do this by using "I" rather than "you", "we", "one" or "it". Don't say things such as:

- "You know how it feels when ... "; instead say "I want you to know that I feel ..."
- "When your team loses you feel ..." becomes "When my team loses I feel ..."
- "I'm sure we all think ..." becomes "I, for one, think ..."
- "If one has to, then one has to" becomes "I have decided to"

Be brave enough to announce your thoughts and feelings rather than distance them in the good old British manner.

Get into the habit of starting sentences with "I":

- "This is complete waste of time" becomes "I don't feel this is worthwhile"
- "This is boring" becomes "I'm bored with this"

As a general rule, avoid starting sentences with "You". "You" sentences often sound as though they're telling, preaching, accusing or judging. It's safer to begin with "I think" or "I feel", so whatever comes next doesn't sound like a universal truth, just a personal opinion. This is particularly important when resolving conflict or giving feedback.

Finally, here are a few tips for giving feedback to colleagues after a lesson observation (page 274). All the above points apply, so keep them in mind. In addition:

1.   A useful structure for a feedback session is:

A. Explain the structure of the session to your colleague so they know what's coming and can relax

B. Outline the strengths observed in the lesson

C. Give an opportunity for your colleague to add strengths and discuss the ones you've proposed

D. Suggest potential areas for development – not "weaknesses"

E. Give an opportunity to discuss these

F. Offer practical suggestions to support the potential areas for development, if your colleague wants to hear them

G. Agree on the *actual* areas for development that will become the focus of attention and will be written into the colleague's personal professional development plan (page 314).

2.   When outlining *strengths* back them with evidence so they don't sound like flannel: quote what the teacher said; give times; numbers of students; lists of behaviours; examples of progress and the like. Don't make generalised judgments such as "You're obviously committed to developing students' thinking skills", because you have evidence of only one lesson. Rather, open up the issue for discussion at Stage B, when the teacher can provide other examples and you can speak from your general knowledge of her work.

3.   Remember to start sentences with "I". In this case "I saw", "I heard", "I noticed", "I counted", "I timed", "I listed", along with some personal interpretations: "I felt", "I

thought", "I was struck by", "I considered", "I was impressed by", "I admired". Let your colleague know when you are moving from objective factual mode to subjective interpretation mode. Both types of feedback are valid, it's just important to distinguish between the two.

4. Again, when suggesting potential areas for development, refer to hard evidence and examples to avoid having your points dismissed as personal hobbyhorses based on quirky ideas about teaching. This is why an agreed teaching and learning policy, within the department or whole school, is so powerful. It provides the agenda for an observation and raises in advance the practices and standards to be looked for and commented on. As before, it's crucial to begin sentences with "I", and to distinguish between objective and subjective content.

5. Avoid words and phrases like "weakness", "downside" or "negative aspects". No one is expected to be perfect – even the most experienced teachers have something to learn – so don't use the language of failure. Instead, speak optimistically about professional growth. Also, don't give the impression that you are dictating the areas that *must* be developed: rather you are *suggesting*, based on the evidence of only one lesson. Debate and decision come next.

6. During Stages F and G, the skill is to maintain rigour and generate enthusiasm for development at the same time. This can be a bit of a knife edge. You want to encourage your colleague to face genuine issues for development, without losing their goodwill. It's crucial therefore to *offer choices* from the list of potential areas. In the face of resistance, less skilled operators will back off, allow the colleague to explain away the issue and end up with nothing of substance in the development plan. A more robust approach is to be assertive. Although they're not written with this situation in mind, you might find the guidelines on pages 199 to 206 helpful.

Check Your Professional Development

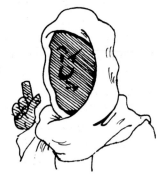

For those of you who have the motivation to develop your craft, two types of awareness are essential. First, an awareness of what's possible in the big wide world of teaching and learning; and, second, an awareness of your own current practice. They are in this order, with future possibilities first, because genuine development is usually pulled forward, not pushed from behind. It's much more exciting and motivating to consider future prospects and improvements than it is to dwell on present realities and limitations.

When a person has a sense of vision, a deeply internalised view of what they want to achieve, development towards that goal tends to happen naturally. The reticular activating system at the top of the brain stem automatically spots opportunities and resources, marshals energies and avoids distractions. This forward-facing approach is quite different from the deficit-based idea of finding fault with current performance first, then identifying remedies. An honest and rigorous assessment of current teaching behaviour is crucial, but it works best when it informs rather than drives the process.

Given this orientation, the process of managing your own professional development divides into six steps. The entire procedure rests on two premises, both of which are true for the vast majority of teachers:

1. That you do not want to stand still as a teacher; you do not have to be persuaded that development is good for you
2. That you are a good and wise judge of your own needs; they do not have to be defined for you by others; as a professional you will seek the best for your students, for yourself and for your school

So this audit tool, or checklist of steps, presents a teacher-centred approach to professional growth that goes against the grain of many current ideas about performance management. In my experience, when the agenda for, or even the process of, development is imposed, people tend to go through the motions; change is therefore superficial and relationships suffer. The performance-management exercise or professional-development activity ends up being nothing more than a ritual, played out to keep everyone happy.

The approach outlined here asks teachers to take responsibility for their development. It is the grown-up version of independent learning, consistent with the underlying intention of *The Teacher's Toolkit* and using the same brain-based principles. Consequently, this approach provides a powerful model to students, it sends strong messages, suggests that everyone is in the same learning boat, and signals that the school is indeed a learning institution.

Compare what happens in your school with the following six-step process.

Step 1: What's possible?

The first stage is to create your own vision for development, not to accept uncritically someone else's definition of what you should be doing. Cast around for ideas, open yourself to new possibilities in teaching and learning, allow your awareness and horizons to be broadened. Don't fix on any particular direction too early.

- Read modern books about teaching and learning. For a comprehensive range of exciting titles visit Crown House Publishing (www.crownhouse.co.uk), the Accelerated Learning

Centre of the Anglo-American Book Company (www.anglo-american.co.uk), and Network Educational Press (www.networkpress.co.uk).

- Go on courses about exciting practical and theoretical ideas.
- Surf the Internet for interesting educational ideas, research findings and innovations. Appendix A has a good selection of starting points.
- Talk to, or watch, practitioners whom you admire.
- Ask colleagues to talk about their own aspirations and adventurous ideas.
- Let the school's or department's teaching and learning policy prompt your thinking.
- Get stuck into a school working party
- Ask a colleague who has a sound overview of good practice to observe you teach and feed back areas that did not feature in the lesson and could be potential areas for development.
- Pick up ideas from meetings – the items for discussion, the throwaway remarks people make, the issues behind the debates.

During this initial stage, allow your existing conceptual framework about teaching and learning to be unsettled, feel your responses to a range of alternatives and then start to generate a sense of excitement about personal possibilities. You will naturally be drawn to some ideas more than others, but the professional response is to view the kaleidoscope of options through your students' eyes, not just your own. What do *they* need, what would *they* benefit from, what do I need to address for *their* sake?

Step 2: What's my goal?

Once you have begun to look forward and identify the kind of practice that suits your wants and your students' needs, you might benefit from a conversation with a trusted and skilled colleague. This could be your line manager, or a chosen mentor, or just a critical friend. Their job is to help you clarify and sharpen your aspiration. At this stage it is important to focus on the destination rather than the journey; where you are going rather than how you're going to get there. Make the goal concrete. Ask yourself, "What will I be doing differently when I've achieved my goal?", "What will I be saying, how will the students be behaving, what would a visitor to my classroom see?" If it helps, close your eyes and play the movie in your head or see it as a series of photographs. This is your vision. Write it down.

It is important not to do this superficially. A personal vision that is clearly formed and internalised *at depth* will hold firm. It will shine through in hectic times when most people default into doing only necessary urgent tasks. Stephen Covey, in his bestseller *The Seven Habits of Highly Effective People*,[8] presents a time-management matrix:

	Urgent	Not Urgent
Important	I	II
Not Important	III	IV

He suggests that everything we do, every day, can be pigeon-holed into one of these four boxes. In the hurly-burly of school life Quadrant I and Quadrant III activities tend to dominate, along with a smattering of Quadrant IV! Quadrant II activities, including professional development, usually go out of the window. This is why an internalised vision is crucial: it keeps the developmental agenda within our field of vision, on our priority list; it nags us to make time for Quadrant II. Many teachers, and many schools, never change because they are always "too busy" for Quadrant II.

Step 3: How am I doing now?

The next step is to define actionable steps towards your goal – how am I going to get there? This is most successful when informed by an honest and rigorous view of what your teaching is like now.

Various sources of information can be drawn on:

- Ask a colleague to observe you teach and to feed back against criteria derived from your vision. You determine the criteria.
- Video yourself teaching and watch the recording at home, comparing what you see to what you want to be.
- Ask students to give you feedback on issues that you identify from your vision.
- Ask colleagues who know you well enough to give you feedback, ask parents, consult performance data that will shed light on your chosen area.
- Consider the school and department/faculty/team development plans – how does your current practice square with these intentions?

Step 4: What steps do I need to take?

Equipped with a clear vision of where you want to be and an equally clear picture of where you are now, you are in a position to size up the professional development task. The "Onion Rings" tool (see below) is designed to help you. It indicates that there are, within every teacher, layers of operation that work together to determine an individual's practice. In order for desired developments to be established, which means they become sustainable, changes in a number of layers are usually required. The "Onion Rings" tool gives you a way of mapping these changes and assessing the strategies, time and resources needed to make them happen.

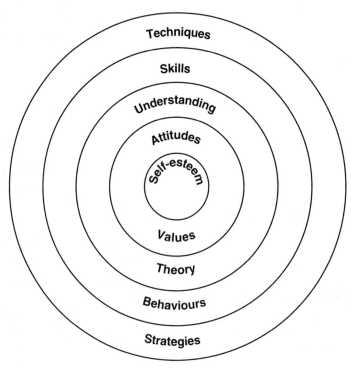

In order to help you appreciate what each layer involves, here's an amplified version. The details in the boxes are not meant to be prescriptive, just to indicate the kind of issues you might need to address.

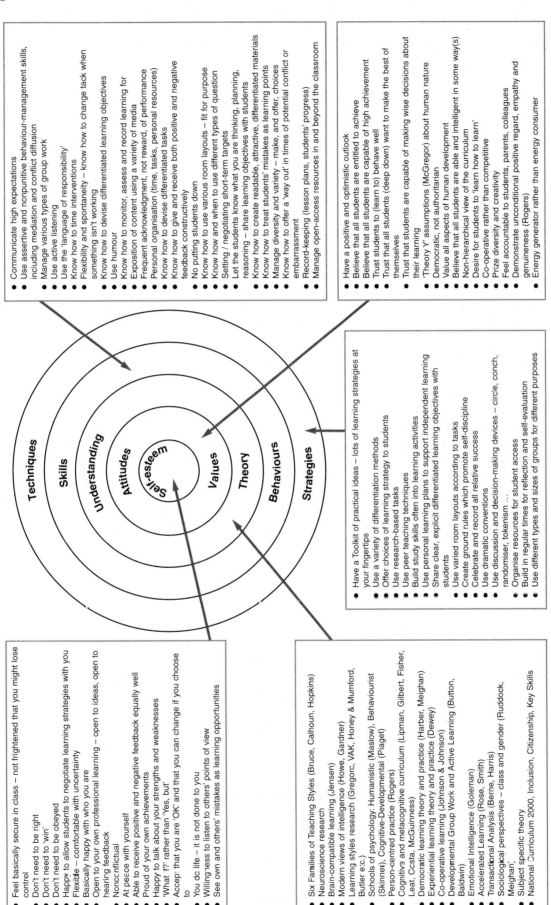

Techniques
- Communicate high expectations
- Use assertive and nonpunitive behaviour-management skills, including mediation and conflict diffusion
- Manage various types of group work
- Use active listening
- Use the 'language of responsibility'
- Know how to time interventions
- Flexibility and spontaneity – know how to change tack when something isn't working
- Know how to devise differentiated learning objectives
- Use humour
- Know how to monitor, assess and record learning for
- Exposition of content using a variety of media
- Frequent acknowledgment, not reward, of performance
- Personal organisation (time, tasks, personal resources)
- Know how to devise differentiated tasks
- Know how to give and receive both positive and negative feedback constructively
- No putting students down
- Know how to use various room layouts – fit for purpose
- Know how and when to use different types of question
- Setting / negotiating short-term targets
- Let the students know what you are thinking, planning, reasoning – share learning objectives with students
- Know how to create readable, attractive, differentiated materials
- Know how to treat students' mistakes as learning points
- Manage diversity and variety – make, and offer, choices
- Know how to offer a 'way out' in times of potential conflict or embarrassment
- Record-keeping (lesson plans, students' progress)
- Manage open-access resources in and beyond the classroom

Values
- Have a positive and optimistic outlook
- Believe that all students are entitled to achieve
- Believe that all students are capable of high achievement
- Trust students to (learn to) behave well
- Trust that all students (deep down) want to make the best of themselves
- Trust that students are capable of making wise decisions about their learning
- 'Theory Y' assumptions (McGregor) about human nature
- Democratic, not authoritarian
- Value all aspects of human development
- Believe that all students are able and intelligent in some way(s)
- Non-hierarchical view of the curriculum
- Desire for students to 'learn how to learn'
- Co-operative rather than competitive
- Prize diversity and creativity
- Feel accountable to students, parents, colleagues
- Demonstrate unconditional positive regard, empathy and genuineness (Rogers)
- Energy generator rather than energy consumer

Strategies
- Have a Toolkit of practical ideas – lots of learning strategies at your fingertips
- Use a variety of differentiation methods
- Offer choices of learning strategy to students
- Use research-based tasks
- Use peer teaching techniques
- Build study skills often into learning activities
- Use personal learning plans to support independent learning
- Share clear, explicit differentiated learning objectives with students
- Use varied room layouts according to tasks
- Create ground rules which promote self-discipline
- Celebrate and record all relative success
- Use discussion and decision-making devices – circle, conch, randomiser, tokenism …
- Use dramatic conventions
- Organise resources for student access
- Build in regular times for reflection and self-evaluation
- Use different types and sizes of groups for different purposes

Attitudes
- Feel basically secure in class – not frightened that you might lose control
- Don't need to be right
- Don't need to 'win'
- Don't need to be obeyed
- Happy to allow students to negotiate learning strategies with you
- Flexible – comfortable with uncertainty
- Basically happy with who you are
- Open to your own professional learning – open to ideas, open to hearing feedback
- Nonconflictual
- At peace with yourself
- Able to receive positive and negative feedback equally well
- Proud of your own achievements
- Happy to talk about your strengths and weaknesses
- 'What if?' rather than 'Yes, but'
- Accept that you are 'OK' and that you can change if you choose to
- You do life – it is not done to you
- Willingness to listen to others' points of view
- See own and others' mistakes as learning opportunities

Theory
- Six Families of Teaching Styles (Bruce, Calhoun, Hopkins)
- Neuroscience research
- Brain-compatible learning (Jensen)
- Modern views of intelligence (Howe, Gardner)
- Learning styles research (Gregorc, VAK, Honey & Mumford, Butler etc.)
- Schools of psychology: Humanistic (Maslow), Behaviourist (Skinner), Cognitive-Developmental (Piaget)
- Person-centred practice (Rogers)
- Cognitive and metacognitive curriculum (Lipman, Gilbert, Fisher, Leat, Ccsta, McGuinness)
- Democratic learning theory and practice (Harber, Meighan)
- Experiential learning theory and practice (Dewey)
- Co-operative learning (Johnson & Johnson)
- Developmental Group Work and Active Learning (Button, Baldwin)
- Emotional Intelligence (Goleman)
- Accelerated Learning (Rose, Smith)
- Transactional Analysis (Berne, Harris)
- Sociological perspectives – class and gender (Ruddock, Meighan,
- Subject specific theory
- National Curriculum 2000, Inclusion, Citizenship, Key Skills

(Circle labels): Techniques, Skills, Understanding, Attitudes, Self-esteem, Values, Theory, Behaviours, Strategies

For example, imagine that your goal is to be meeting students' personal learning needs to a high degree on a daily basis. This might involve learning some new differentiation techniques such as "Upwardly Mobile" (page 234), "Menu" (page 246) and "Sole Search" (page 253). It is also likely to involve new skills such as negotiating short-term targets with students and managing open-access resources. Beyond this, an understanding of learning-styles research and multiple-intelligence theory will be important. In the layer of values and attitudes you may still need to accept that it actually *is* the teacher's job to go to these lengths and that you have a responsibility to maintain high expectations of every student. Finally, in the core of your being you might fear failure and really want to be in total control, which means having the whole class at your beck and call all the time. These are matters of self-esteem.

Generally, if change occurs in only the outer layer – techniques – the development will be short-lived. This is the most attractive and easily penetrated layer, because most teachers are hungry for practical tips. However, if new techniques are not underpinned by sufficient subskills, or by a clear understanding of why they should be used, or by sympathetic attitudes, one of three things will happen. First, the techniques will fail because the teacher is insufficiently skilled; in this case the techniques will be dismissed and the whole idea dropped – "I tried that and it doesn't work." Or, second, the techniques are successful but they run dry. New techniques are required after a while but there's not sufficient understanding to generate new practice, so the development runs out of steam. Or, third, once the novelty's worn off, the teacher reverts to type. Underlying attitudes and values, because they lie deep, exert a powerful influence over behaviour and will tend to pull a person back to their default practice.

It is crucial, therefore, that you take an honest look at what you really need to do, both on and under the surface, to make changes that are sustainable.

Once this agenda has been constructed, once you know what you need to address in order to reach your goal, questions of strategy arise. How will these developments take place? How will you learn new techniques? By reading? If so, which books? By observation? If so, whom will you observe? Or is there a video? How will you develop the skills? Perhaps by discussion with colleagues, followed by trial and error and observation by a trusted friend who has already mastered these things? What about the new understanding? Is there a course? As for attitudes and values, they are harder to shift. Self-talk, discussion, reflection, reading, open-heartedness and will are among the necessary ingredients. Self-esteem is deep stuff; it involves self-acceptance and may require support from someone who has the wisdom and sensitivity of a counsellor. The behaviours of the institution also have a direct impact on your self-esteem, so it may be important to clarify with senior colleagues just how much back-up they will give if you fall flat on your face.

It is easy to see how these layers, or zones of development, interact. New understanding of learning styles, for example, creates new awareness, which will challenge old attitudes. New skills enable new techniques to work successfully, which increases confidence and thereby boosts self-esteem. And so on.

Here's a starter list of possible strategies to support you in pursuit of your identified goal:

- Audio-record yourself teaching, using a personal stereo tucked into your top pocket, or with a microphone clipped to your lapel.
- Plan lessons with a colleague who has different ideas/style/experience.
- Teach lessons with a colleague who has more experience than you in your chosen area.
- Debrief team-taught lessons with your colleague.
- Do the above with a colleague in another school.
- Take part in exchanges of good practice between departments.

- Take part in creative lesson planning sessions between departments.
- Trial and error, followed by lesson observation and feedback.
- Receive consultancy.
- Write new materials, audio-visual or ICT resources that require you to develop new expertise.
- Undertake research on behalf of the school in order to contribute to policy or to make recommendations.
- Observe skilled colleagues in your own or in another school.
- Use a trusted colleague as a mentor.
- Read books on the subject.
- Look at new commercial teaching materials, textbooks, visual aids, packs.
- Look at materials created and used in other schools.
- Go on a course.
- Enrol for accreditation with a higher-education provider.
- Video yourself teaching and debrief with a critical friend.

Once the strategies and resources are in place, simply add deadlines. By when will I have read this book, observed that teacher, tried that method, been on that course …? It is often helpful to plan strategies up to six months ahead, then review and replan.

Step 5: How do I write a development plan for myself?

It will be possible to carry out some of these strategies yourself, without further ado – trial and error, for example, or read a book from the staff-development library. Others will need to be resourced with money (for books, courses, materials, cover), time (to observe, be observed, feedback, discuss, visit, plan) or people (consultant, the right colleague, counsellor, mentor). Such resources are allocated by the institution.

Also, as a member of the institution, you have a responsibility to support the corporate development priorities. These will probably be expressed in the school's, department's and year team's development plans. So the final step is to combine your personal aspirations with these other agendas and prepare a personal development plan. You may find that your personal goal is already in line with the school's next phase of development. If not, you may have to add a second goal and therefore have to devise further strategies.

The person in the best position to help you do this is probably your line manager. They know you and have an understanding of the corporate plans. They are also able to allocate limited funds and can lobby for additional resources on your behalf. The grid below will help you structure such a conversation with your "boss" and record your final thinking. Naturally, the outcome will be a compromise as institutional resources, as well as your time and energy, are limited. This should not be regarded as negative, but realistic. Give-and-take is positive.

The final flourish, of course, is to add monitoring details. How will you, and how will the school, know that you're getting there? There are ways of doing this other than whole-lesson observation. They include:

- Provide brief written progress reports to your line manager or chosen mentor.
- Make mini-presentations to department or whole-staff meetings.
- Make video or audio recordings.
- Have students fill in questionnaires.
- Ask students to be involved in a lunchtime discussion about progress in exchange for a free lunch.
- Ask your line manager or mentor to interview individual or small groups of students.
- Ask your line manager, mentor or critical friend to pop into crucial bits of lessons.

- Hold monthly chats with your line manager or mentor over a working lunch (on the school of course!).

Here's the suggested grid for structuring the conversation with your line manager. It doubles up as a recording framework – just fill in the gaps.

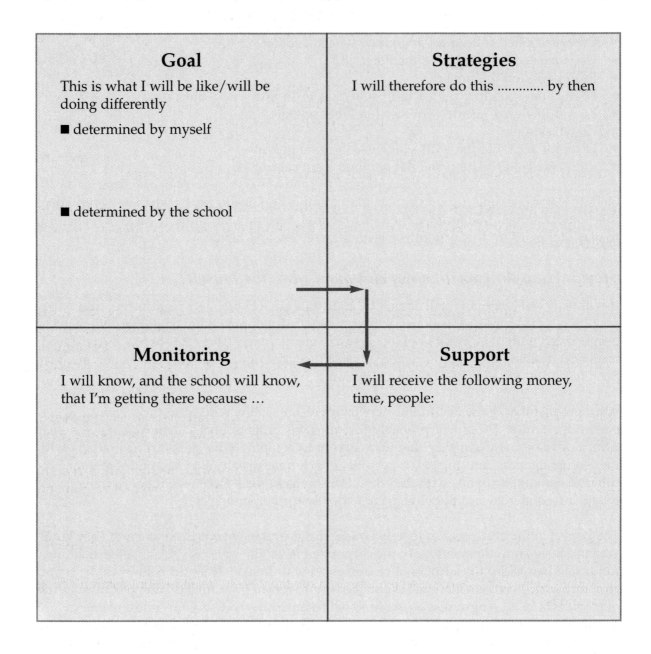

Step 6: Get on with it!

... and good luck.

Check Your Management Of Change

This section is not only for classroom teachers – it's for all who have an interest in, and perhaps a responsibility for, developing the quality of teaching and learning across the school. Consequently, headteachers, deputies, senior teachers, heads of department or faculty and heads of year should find it helpful.

It is not difficult to initiate a process of development. An inspiring training day, an inspection, self-review, a new national policy, a regional initiative, a priority in the school development plan, constant nagging by senior staff – all these can get things going. Sustaining change is harder. Determination and creative thinking seem to be the key ingredients along with a large slice of wisdom. Fortunately, we can learn from other people's experience, distilled here into six strategic planning issues.

The development under discussion is of course the progressive alignment of teaching methods with sound principles of learning which is the underlying intention of the *The Teacher's Toolkit.*

1. Retaining momentum and focus

In our complex and hectic daily lives it is hard to hold the course of change. The pressure is always on to do jobs that are urgent. Consequently, we tend to behave habitually and end up putting lots of effort into activities that simply maintain the status quo. We run fast only to find that we have stood still. Few schools find ways of preserving sufficient time and energy for matters that are not urgent, but important.

Here, however, are 43 ways of doing just that! To achieve the desired effect, several strategies have to operate simultaneously. None of them is sufficiently powerful on its own. So you may wish to use the following ideas as a checklist – how many of these are we already doing? – or as a stimulus to your own inventive thinking. The strategies differ in strength: some are designed to force change, others just to encourage it. All these strategies have been tried and tested in various combinations in schools around the country.

1. Produce, collaboratively, a team, departmental or whole-school learning and teaching policy.

2. Make teaching and learning a standing item on department/team meeting/staff meeting agendas.

3. Make it the first item on the agenda (e.g. What have been the highs and lows of learning this month ... and why? or What has been your most successful teaching technique this month? or What better ways are there of teaching the topic we've just done with Year 8?).

4. Devote some team or department meetings entirely to learning strategies exchange and creation. Deal with administration and business items on paper or through informal chats over coffee and lunch.

5. Revise schemes of work against the teaching and learning policy. This is the main vehicle for bedding in new practice.

6. Open a teaching-and-learning-strategies file (a home-made *Toolkit*) as an ongoing resource in the staffroom – write up and add new ideas week by week. Expect all colleagues to contribute during a term.

7. Have Teaching Idea of the Week on the staffroom or departmental notice board.

8. Make it a mission to collect teaching ideas from other sources – buy, beg and borrow from within and beyond the school. Use morning briefing to draw new resources to everyone's attention. Make them available to borrow.

9. Instead of always meeting in departments, make some curriculum meetings cross-department (e.g. one in every four); focus on practical ideas (e.g. someone put a scheme of work on the table for creative revision).

10. Launch a Variety Club – a voluntary cross-curriculum group meeting after school or lunchtime once a month to support each other in trying and sharing new classroom ideas. Make them "bring-and-buy" sessions – everyone is asked to bring a new idea, and take one away to try.

11. Offer to plan lessons with colleagues.

12. Offer to team-teach with colleagues to help them try new techniques in their classroom.

13. Offer to observe and evaluate lessons with colleagues.

14. Encourage colleagues to come into your classroom to help you to try new ideas.

15. Invite colleagues to conduct observations of your lessons and give you feedback.

16. Insist on one new strategy to be tried per teacher per week – monitor through observation or conversation.

17. Target certain classes or whole-year groups for action research – make it an official project. For example, let's see if we can improve attitudes to learning in Year 9 by giving more choices about learning strategy in lessons.

18. Get class teachers or form tutors to introduce, and then talk regularly with pupils about, learning styles in registration and tutor time.

19. Collapse the Year 7 timetable for a day and do learning styles experientially with the whole-year group. Deliver a circus of contrasting learning experiences and, at the end of the day, form tutors debrief with students using a learning-styles construct (page 34).

20. Work on Key Stages 2–3 transfer. Primary and secondary staff collaborate to produce teaching guidelines that ensure the continuity and progression of students' independent learning skills.

21. Use PSHE or form tutor time to work on ground rules, listening skills, study skills, group work skills, cooperative and team-building games – to support innovative work across the curriculum.

22. As a whole staff agree a set of lesson-observation criteria that reflect brain-based learning principles rather than typical teaching principles.

23. Acknowledge innovative classroom practice through observation or by reading lesson plans, or by inviting colleagues to describe their current best practice. Use the agreed observation criteria to evaluate and feedback.

24. Encourage professional reading – take turns to write and distribute a small book review each month. Likewise, encourage a trawl of teaching and learning websites.

25. Have a professional development library in the staffroom with up-to-date titles about the learning process.

26. Encourage video or audio recordings of classroom teaching for self-analysis or peer analysis.

27. Turn middle managers into managers of learning. This may involve coaching them in the skills of supportive lesson observation, giving feedback and managing the professional development of their team.

28. Encourage departments or year teams or faculties to lead parts of whole staff meetings on a rotational basis to report on their best and innovative practice. They have fifteen minutes to demonstrate or describe what they're doing well.

29. Introduce a personal development plan for each member of staff – ask all colleagues to negotiate and record the professional learning they intend to undertake, by when. Ensure that the support and resources they need are actually delivered (page 314).

30. Organise visits to see, and reflect on, practice in other schools.

31. Invite colleagues from another school to come and see your best practice. Organise this on a subject-by-subject basis.

32. Organise joint training sessions, workshops, peer planning sessions with other schools.

33. Make a public exhibition of quality learning in your department in the school entrance hall. Rotate the responsibility – one department per month.

34. Open a new teaching and learning area of the school's website. Ask every department or team to contribute descriptions, photographs and video clips. Encourage the local education authority to launch a teaching and learning area of its own website and be the first contributors.

35. Invite parents to come into lessons where best or innovative practice is being demonstrated by colleagues.

36. Expect to see learning and teaching as the first heading in departmental development plans. Model this by making it the first heading in the whole-school development plan.

37. Ask departments to review themselves, or to be reviewed, against the school's teaching and learning policy. Then, in time, carry out lesson observations to look specifically at the areas that were weak and are being developed. Expect improvements.

38. Create an official teaching and learning research group commissioned to create teaching and learning guidelines, or design a lesson observation schedule, or produce a "toolkit", or a training event, or a video or CD-ROM of good practice.

39. Devote an in-house training day to teaching and learning, led by key practitioners, departments or teams. Use this time to agree teaching and learning guidelines or a lesson-observation schedule.

40. Devote a staff meeting to a tour of best practice. Two or three departments offer to demonstrate. Staff divide into groups and go on a circus, visiting each department in turn.

41. Colleagues form "innovative pairs" or "buddies", who plan new practice together, teach these new lessons together (if time permits) and evaluate together. The pairs stick together for a term or more, using bits of noncontact time and occasional cover.

42. Take a group of teachers off timetable for a half-day and ask them to help each other plan lessons to be taught in the near future. Working in pairs or threes they take it in turns to table a series of lessons and their colleagues offer creative ideas.

43. Hold themed twilight workshops for colleagues. For example, "Make group work work for your group" or "Perfect peer teaching" or "Independent learning – the possible and the practical". The sessions encourage the exchange of down-to-earth practical strategies.

One of the key messages shining through the list is this: **for development to remain focused and energised, it is helpful to commission a concrete end product to be delivered to an audience by a deadline**. This might be an event, a policy or something material such as a customised "toolkit", a video or a CD-ROM of recommended practice.

2. Using a trainer

If you are investing in the services of an external trainer, in order to secure satisfaction and value for money check the match between your intended outcome and chosen strategy.

Intended Outcome

Strategy	Awareness and knowledge	Acquire techniques	Immediate classroom application	Application to other contexts	Permanent changes to practice
1. Formal or informal talks	✓				
2. Workshop	✓	✓			
3. Trainer-led classroom activity	✓	✓	✓		
4. Teacher and trainer plan, teach and evaluate together	✓	✓	✓	✓	
5. Teacher-led lessons with feedback from trainer	✓	✓	✓	✓	✓

External trainers can do only so much, owing to the limits of school budgets if not the limits of their own expertise! Fortunately, strategies 4 and 5 can be undertaken in-house to great effect. Colleagues can plan lessons together and go on to teach and evaluate them jointly. Likewise, skilled colleagues can observe and give feedback on innovative lessons designed and taught single-handedly by the "trainee". In fact, interested colleagues can pair up as developmental "buddies".

These arrangements work well where a successful training event has started the ball rolling by generating motivation and providing a rationale for new practice. The ongoing need is for the colleagues involved to receive top-ups to their practical and theoretical banks of ideas from time to time.

3. Keeping a balance

According to Stephen Covey, new habits form only when people know *what* to do, *how* to do it and *why* to do it. Therefore, plan to keep all three in continuous balance.

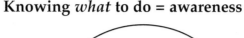

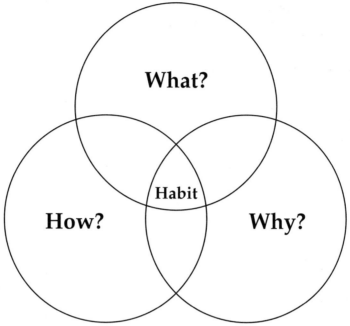

Knowing *how* to do it = skill　　　　**Knowing *why* to do it = motivation**

Ask yourself this:

(a) With regard to "what" ...

Are staff crystal-clear about what they are expected to do differently? When have senior staff made the vision clear? Where can people go to check the vision? How often do they see or hear the vision? Could they describe the vision to visitors, with conviction? Do they know what the vision looks like in practice – for example, "Every lesson will be differentiated to at least three levels" rather than "every pupil will be enabled to fulfil their potential"; or "Every lesson will offer a choice of at least three different learning strategies" rather than "Every student will be respected as an individual"? Is the vision formalised into a policy or a lesson-observation schedule? Do departments have to show how the vision is present in schemes of work? Is the vision written as a set of entitlements to students and parents?

(b) With regard to "how" ...

What training have people already had that equips them to do what they are being asked to do? What do people say they need? What new training will have to be provided, in what form? For instance:

- **workshops** – internal or external practitioner demonstrating techniques
- **visits** – to see practice within or beyond the school
- **coaching** – by internal or external trainer using cycles of plan-do-review
- **seminars** – ideas being explained and discussed
- **books** – read manuals and handbooks

- **consultancy** – one-off sessions with an internal or external expert to support thinking and planning
- **exchanges** – sharing techniques with each other via video recordings, reports, meetings, intranet, websites, video conferencing, within or between schools

(c) With regard to "why" ...

Can staff give coherent reasons for doing things differently? Are there **pragmatic and expedient reasons** – for example, "It's the law" or "Our reputation has to improve if we are to retain our intake" or "It's part of a national initiative and there's money attached"?

Are there **values-based reasons** – for example, "We're doing this because we believe in equal rights and social justice" or "We think it's important that everyone develop a sense of personal responsibility" or "In this school we believe in inclusion"? How many people share the beliefs and values?

Are there **theoretical reasons** – for example, "The neocortex is designed to solve problems and make connections, therefore passive learning is unnatural" or "Under threat the brain defaults into emotion and instinct at the expense of rational thought, therefore it's necessary to create psychologically safe learning environments"?

Do people need to be introduced to, reminded of, or convinced by the rationale – for example, through books, seminars, synopses, thoughts-for-the-day, one-to-one discussions, accredited courses, values-clarification exercises, question-and-answer sessions, debates?

Each month make sure that senior managers look back and identify ways in which the three domains have been promoted over the last few weeks. They can then make adjustments next month to ensure that balance is maintained.

4. Mapping the big picture of change

This tool is created by the juxtaposition of two agendas:

- learning issues
- professional development layers

Section 1 of *The Teacher's Toolkit* suggested that there are a number of learning issues to tackle. These arise from an understanding of how the brain works, along with an acceptance of agendas such as inclusion, lifelong learning and citizenship. In other words, the learning agenda is defined by a combination of neuroscientific research, democratic and humane values, and key socioeconomic considerations. These could be said to boil down to the six issues presented as columns in the diagram on the next page. In my view these could form the main headings of a modern teaching and learning policy that could be used at the department level, the whole-school level or the LEA level.

Meanwhile, the "Onion Rings" model (page 316) describes five layers inside every teacher. These are zones of development, ranging from the most easily penetrated layer, "Techniques", to the deep areas of "Values" and "Self-esteem" that are the product of people's life histories and are therefore difficult to affect.

When set against each other, the issues and the layers create a map of development that can be used to guide the selection of strategies and the allocation of resources. For example, where the issue of **learners' potential** meets the layer of **teachers' skills,** we find questions about expectations. Are your colleagues skilfully communicating high expectations to students? If not, do they need to be challenged, encouraged, or trained? At the slightly deeper level of

teachers' understanding, have they grasped the capacity of the human brain? Do they know how neurons, axons, dendrites and synapses work? At a deeper level still, **teachers' values**, do they really believe that all students are equally entitled to success? Does it really matter when a student underachieves? At the deepest level of all, **teachers' self-esteem**, are they secure enough within themselves to reappraise their attitudes, to consider themselves to be imperfect and willing to do things differently? The answers to these questions guide thinking about what to do next and how much to invest in doing it.

Issues

	Learners have enormous potential	Learners' need to work things out for themselves	Learners' benefit from dramatic, varied, multi-sensory learning	Learners' need to feel emotionally secure and psychologically safe	Learners' desire to have some control over their learning	Learners' diverse styles and intelligences need to be accommodated
Teachers' techniques	e.g. uses "Upwardly Mobile" to plan and deliver positive differentiation					
Teachers' skills	e.g. uses the language of high expectation and knows how and when to intervene					
Teachers' understanding	e.g. knows about neural connections and the brain's biological potential					
Teachers' values	e.g. believes in social justice, inclusion and equalising opportunity					
Teachers' self-esteem	e.g. can tolerate the idea that practice hasn't been perfect up to now					

(Left side label: **Layers**)

Use this chart, or some customised version of it, to:

- audit the current state of play in your school – where are we strong, where are we weak?
- to make strategic decisions – what should we make a fuss about first?
- to allocate resources – which boxes do we need to invest in to generate initial improvements and to lay the foundations for longer-term gains?
- to monitor developments – what do we need to look for?
- to record progress – which bits are getting better?

5. *Involving middle managers*

Team leaders, heads of department and year heads are in the best position to bring about sustained changes to classroom practice and teachers' behaviour. On the one hand, they are close enough to colleagues to influence them through persuasion, personality and role-modelling. They have a range of subtle carrots and sticks at their disposal and can usually get things done by running credit and debit accounts with a mixed economy of favours and goodwill. On the other hand, they have both the clout and the responsibility to progress whole-school agendas.

The modern expectation that middle managers should take responsibility for guaranteeing quality and embedding innovation is actually part of a worldwide trend. Speaking of developments in the global economy, computing and telecommunications, Quinn et al. argue that "these changes have only increased the need to create leaders, at all levels of the organisation".

They go on:

> Regardless of title, more and more, organisations are calling for employees at all levels to take on responsibilities that were previously reserved only for upper-level managers, and this has in turn changed the nature of managerial work.[9]

So, how might middle managers go about the task? There are four steps for them to take:

Step 1: Develop a clear, personal understanding of a modern, brain-based learning agenda. This is the basis of the following steps.

Step 2: Get to know how the members of their teams actually teach. This involves getting into classrooms to see for themselves. Such observation should not be processed against old Ofsted-type lesson criteria, rather against brain-based criteria preferably expressed in a teaching and learning policy. For further guidance see "Check Your Lesson Plans" (page 274).

Step 3: Hold professional development discussions with each colleague. These arise naturally from the lesson observations, but are not conducted like lecturers' lesson crits or inspectors' feedback. They are not conducted in a monitoring spirit, but are for the benefit of the colleague and, though rigorous, have a positive and practical intention and future orientation. Their purpose is to be developmental. In managing the discussion, certain skills, particularly language skills, will be required (see "Check Your Language" page 307).

Step 4: Write a personal professional development plan with each colleague and follow through with the provision of resources and support. See "Check Your Professional Development" (page 319) for details.

To be manageable, this whole process will probably operate on a six-monthly cycle for each colleague. Individuals will be at different points of the cycle at different times, so that there is only ever one member of the team at the forefront (observation-development planning) at any one time. As each moves into the background the line manager will still need to monitor their intended developments by asking how things are going from time to time, by occasionally starting team meetings with a "Round" (page 196) of "where I'm up to with my professional development", and by checking that the agreed resources and support are actually delivered. This process fulfils many aspects of statutory performance management.

6. *Institutionalising the development*

The key theme running through all of the above is the need to institutionalise development. In every school energetic and creative teachers can be found. They make vital contributions, including coming up with ideas, being upbeat, keeping up with current research, going on courses, making resources and talking enthusiastically about their ideas. However, it is unwise to think that they can carry whole-school development.

Change left entirely to a small group of nonsenior enthusiasts will inevitably run out of steam. It is unrealistic, and actually unfair, to expect junior colleagues to innovate, to sustain themselves and in addition to be responsible for persuading other colleagues to convert to the cause.

The answer is to institutionalise the development, which only senior staff can do. There are seven steps for the senior group to take.

Step 1:   Decide the extent to which the proposed change is a necessity, a luxury or somewhere in between. Ask yourselves: are we convinced that we *must*, above all else, change teaching strategies, or do we just *want* to change them, or are we just *toying with* these ideas? Draw a continuum and have all senior colleagues mark their positions. The depth of colleagues' convictions will indicate the levels of energy and determination that will be available to the cause, especially in times of distraction. Also, the answer to this question will determine the strength of the management strategies to be selected: are we going to force people, strongly encourage them, give them a gentle nudge or leave it up to them to do something about it or not?

The rest of the steps assume that the development is regarded as essential, so some fairly tough institutionalising strategies are chosen.

Step 2:   Generate expectations (in line with the answer to 1). These come across most powerfully if expressed as concrete, measurable, observable, doable achievements to be reached by set deadlines. For example, "By the end of next year I want us to be widely known not just for good, but for excellent teaching" or "I'd like us to be holding workshops for parents on learning styles in six months time" or "Can we be running accelerated-learning groups in most subjects by next academic year?".

Step 3:   Establish learning principles. Move towards a fluid teaching and learning policy. This means establishing key principles with the whole staff quite quickly, through a training day with follow-up discussions, or through a working party reporting back and debating the issues collectively, or through a draft being circulated for discussion. It's helpful to suggest to staff that the policy is only based on your corporate understanding at this point in time: "This is where we're at collectively, but I expect our position to change as we learn more, so we will review and redraft the policy in a year's time." The initial policy then becomes the guiding light for a number of activities:

- it shapes lesson-observation criteria
- it determines the use of training days
- it influences the scheduling of priorities on agendas for meetings
- it determines the criteria for recruitment and selection
- it rewrites documentation such as pro formas for schemes of work and lesson plans, and school reports
- it influences the way registration time, tutorial time, personal social and health education time and assemblies are used
- it influences the kind of resources that are bought
- it determines priorities for whole-school expenditure

... and so on. If the policy does not have these sorts of effects, it is not a policy: it's a piece of paper.

Step 4:   Make demands in line with the teaching and learning policy. For example, "All new or revised schemes of work from now on will have a learning-styles column to show how teaching methods in each subject make success accessible to all types of learner" or "In the future, all department meetings should begin with an exchange of teaching ideas – ones that have worked and ones that haven't!" or "Our next training day will be a round-robin exhibition of departments' innovative practice; I'd like everyone to take part" or "I'd like heads of department to monitor homework to check that sufficiently varied tasks are being set; please give me a list of the homeworks set in your subject during the coming month".

Step 5:   Establish procedures. For example: schemes of work will be monitored by link senior managers; minutes of department meetings will be read and issues are picked up with the head of department within a week; a rolling programme of lesson observations will be conducted against the current teaching and learning policy; all Year 7 students will receive an introduction to learning styles and regular tuition in "making the most of your style"; students will give feedback on the quality of teaching through monthly questionnaires and a termly forum; heads of department will be asked to report on progress with teaching and learning to the head every month. Such procedures build momentum; they ensure that the new direction is pursued day by day, week by week. They tell people that the issue will not go away, so they might as well fall in line.

Step 6:   Provide resources and support. For example, training, consultancy, books, visits to other schools, attending courses, time off-timetable to discuss, plan and make resources. Cut down the amount of business and admin required in team meetings. Invite to meetings only people who really need to be there. Do as much business as possible informally, by walking around, and communicate trivial bits of information on paper. Release as much quality time as possible for discussion, planning and resource production.

Step 7:   Follow through. Talk to people who are resisting the change. Listen to them, present the case for change, explain the reasons, offer resources if they are the genuine reason for inertia. Let people know, on an individual basis, what you expect.

Appendix A

Starting Points for Research

Book suppliers

The most interesting and modern titles on teaching and learning can be found at:

Accelerated Learning Centre of the Anglo-American Book Company: www.anglo-american.co.uk

Crown House Publishing: www.crownhouse.co.uk

Network Educational Press: www.networkpress.co.uk

Organisations, networks and projects

21st Century Learning Initiative: www.21learn.org

Alternative Education Resource Organisation: www.educationrevolution.org

Campaign for Learning: www.campaign-for-learning.org.uk

Centre for Studies on Inclusive Education: http://inclusion.uwe.ac.uk

Citizenship Foundation: www.citfou.org.uk

Coalition of Essential Schools: www.essentialschools.org

Creating Learning Communities On-line Resource Centre: www.creatinglearningcommunities.org

Education Now: www.gn.apc.org/educationnow

Human Scale Education: www.hse.org.uk

Project Zero: http://pzweb.harvard.edu

Society for the Advancement of Philosophical Enquiry and Reflection in Education: www.sapere.net

The Co-operative Learning Centre: www.clcrc.com

Society for Effective Affective Learning: www.seal.org.uk

Philosophy for Children: www.p4c.net

Teaching and Learning Research Programme: www.ex.ac.uk/ESRC-TLRP

UK Accelerated Learning Network: www.alite.co.uk

Brain Gym: www.braingym.org

Learning theory and research with lots of links

For synopses of fifty major learning theories: http://tip.psychology.org

Twelve key learning theories summarised: www.funderstanding.com/about_learning.cfm

An introduction to the science of the brain with lots of pathways for further investigation: http://faculty.washington.edu/chudler/neurok.html

Technical stuff about the structure of the brain: www.vh.org/Providers/Textbooks/BrainAnatomy/BrainAnatomy.html

The site of the book *The Learning Revolution* by Dryden & Vos: www.thelearningweb.net

Good starting point for brain-based learning: www.loloville.com/brain_based_learning.htm

An amazing set of links: www.brainresearch.com

A gateway to lots of modern teaching and learning ideas:
http://academic.wsc.edu/redl/classes/tami/braintechwsc.html#other

Another excellent set of links: www.newhorizons.org/blab.html#resources

More interesting links: www.uwsp.edu/education/lwilson/learning

A wide range of topics summarised and linked: www.teach-nology.com/currenttrends

A great catalogue of articles and links: www.emtech.net/brain_based_learning.html

Links to a number of interesting articles: www.middleweb.com/MWLresources/brain1.html

Links to a wide range of theories:
http://dmoz.org/Reference/Education/Methods_and_Theories/Learning_Theories

Lots of links to a range of teaching and learning topics:
http://snow.utoronto.ca/Learn2/resources.html

An impressive bibliography: www.excel-ability.com/Bib/Bib-BrainBasedL.html

Excellent starting point for learning styles research:
www.universaleducator.com/LearnStyle/index.html

Some leading educational lights

Alfie Kohn: www.alfiekohn.org

Anthony Gregorc: www.gregorc.com

Eric Jensen: http://jlcbrain.com

Geoffrey and Renate Caine: www.cainelearning.com

Tony Buzan: www.mind-map.com

Thomas Armstrong: www.thomasarmstrong.com

Nathaniel Branden: www.nathanielbranden.net

Run searches on Howard Gardner, Daniel Goleman, Robert Sylwester, Carl Rogers

In my experience Google is excellent for education searches:
www.google.com (www.google.co.uk now gives you the option of searching UK sites only,
thereby filtering out the rest)

Official views of the territory

Department for Education and Skills: www.dfes.gov.uk

General Teaching Council: www.gtce.org.uk

National Curriculum Online: www.nc.uk.net

National Grid for Learning: www.ngfl.gov.uk

Qualifications and Curriculum Agency: www.qca.org.uk

Teacher Training Agency: www.canteach.gov.uk

Virtual Teacher Centre: http://vtc.ngfl.gov.uk

Appendix B

Learning Styles Analyses

Questionnaires for adults that have to be purchased

Barsch Learning Style Inventory:
www.hcc.hawaii.edu/intranet/committees/FacDevCom/guidebk/teachtip/lernstyl.htm

Creative Learning Company, for an eclectic analysis: www.clc.co.nz/tsa.html

Dunn and Dunn Inventory: www.geocities.com/CollegePark/Union/2106/lsi.html

Gregorc Style Delineator: www.gregorc.com

Herrmann Brain Dominance Instrument:
www.dynamicthinking.com/hbdi.htm or www.hbdi.com

Johnston and Orwig's Learning Type Test:
www.sil.org/lingualinks/languagelearning/otherresources/yorlrnngstylandlngglrnng/
TheLearningTypeTest.htm

Keirsey Character Sorter: www.advisorteam.com/user/kcs.asp

Keirsey Temperament Sorter: www.advisorteam.com/user/ktsintro.asp

Myers-Briggs Type Indicator: www.knowyourtype.com

Questionnaires for adults available free

Honey and Mumford

www.campaign-for-learning.org.uk (Peter Honey's quick questionnaire on the Campaign for Learning site)

www.psi-press.co.uk/lss2.htm (Honey and Mumford's full questionnaire, which you can try for free before deciding whether to buy)

VAK

www.gse.rmit.edu.au/~rsedc/learn.html

www.chaminade.org/inspire/learnstl.htm

www.wiley.com/legacy/college/weygandt5e/32.htm

VARK

www.active-learning-site.com/inventory1.html

Miscellaneous

http://jade.ccccd.edu/harlow/learning.htm (you need to download a bit of software)

www.creativelearningcentre.com/products.asp?page=LSA&lang=&cs=NZ%24&cr=1
(a substantial instrument from the Creative Learning Company, available in junior and senior versions)

www.ewart.org.uk/learning.htm (by a teacher from a Pembrokeshire Secondary School)

www.howtolearn.com/personal.html (from the Centre for New Discoveries in Learning) www.learningstyle.com (the Dunn, Dunn and Price Inventory)

www.learningstyles.net (further Dunn and Dunn questionnaires to purchase)

www.metamath.com//multiple/multiple_choice_questions.cgi (from Diablo Valley College)

www.oswego.edu/~shindler/plsi (the Paragon Learning Style Inventory)

www.ulc.arizona.edu/learning_style_assessment.html (from the University of Arizona)

www2.ncsu.edu/unity/lockers/users/f/felder/public/ILSdir/ilsweb.html
(Soloman and Felder's analysis from NC State University)

Questionnaires for adults in books

Accelerated Learning for the 21st Century by Colin Rose and Malcolm J. Nicholl, page 110:
multiple-intelligence quiz

Accelerate Your Learning (Action Handbook) by Colin Rose and Louise Goll, page 82:
VAK questionnaire

Effective Teaching and Learning in the Primary Classroom by Sara Shaw and Trevor Hawes,
Appendix: hemisphere dominance questionnaire

Effective Teaching and Learning in the Primary Classroom by Sara Shaw and Trevor Hawes,
Appendix: multiple-intelligence profile

Emotional Intelligence in the Classroom by Michael Brearley, page 20:
thinking-styles questionnaire

Learning About Learning by Chris Watkins et al., page 57:
questionnaire based on Honey and Mumford

The Learning Revolution by Dryden and Vos, page 358: an adaptation of Gregorc's analysis

Teaching for Success, The Brain-Friendly Revolution in Action by Mark Fletcher, page 40:
a VAK questionnaire

Questionnaires for students

Some are the following items are free, others have to be bought. They vary enormously in quality and also in the sophistication of the language, the concepts and the contexts they use, so please don't hold me responsible for the choices you make! Check them out, consider their underlying principles and make sure you believe that they will be beneficial before you use them. If you decide to use a students' questionnaire, please consider all the cautions discussed on pages 281–2.

VAK

http://alaike.lcc.hawaii.edu/lrc/lstest.html

http://lookingahead.heinle.com/filing/l-styles.htm

www.clat.psu.edu/gems/Other/LSI/LSI.htm

www.glencoe.com/ps/peak/selfassess/learnstyle

www.ldpride.net/learningstyles.MI.htm#Interactive%20Learning%20Styles%20Test

www.sig.net/~ngayle/sp_style.html

www.usd.edu/trio/tut/ts/style.html

Multiple Intelligences

http://snow.utoronto.ca/Learn2/mod3/miinventory.html

www.colormathpink.com/test_your_skills/learning_styles

www.surfaquarium.com/MIinvent.htm

Right–left hemispheres

http://brain.web-us.com/brain/braindominance.htm

www.mathpower.com/brain.htm

www.mtsu.edu/~devstud/advisor/learn.html

Students' questionnaires in books

Accelerated Learning in the Classroom by Alistair Smith, page 45: VAK prompt chart

Accelerated Learning in Practice by Alistair Smith, page 187: multiple-intelligence questionnaire

Strategies for Closing the Learning Gap by Mike Hughes with Andy Vass, page 126: VAK questionnaire

Also, have a look at the questionnaires designed for adults. Some of them might work with older students and others could possibly be adapted.

Details of all the books can be found in the Bibliography.

References

Section 1: Design Tools

1. Covey, Stephen R. (1989). *The Seven Habits of Highly Effective People,* Simon and Schuster. pp. 47–48.
2. Covey, Stephen R. (1989). *The Seven Habits of Highly Effective People,* Simon and Schuster Audio. Audio cassette of the author explaining the seven habits at a business seminar.
3. Scottish Consultative Council on the Curriculum (1996). *Teaching For Effective Learning.* p. 1. This group now call themselves "Teaching and Learning Scotland" and the second edition of the paper appears under their new name. Visit them at www.LTScotland.com
4. Hughes, Mike (1999). *Closing the Learning Gap,* Network Educational Press.
5. Bowring-Carr, Christopher and John West-Burnham (1997). *Effective Learning in Schools, How to Integrate Learning and Leadership for a Successful School,* Pitman. p. 28.
6. Smith, Alistair (1996). *Accelerated Learning in the Classroom,* Network Educational Press.
7. Smith, Alistair (1998). *Accelerated Learning in Practice, Brain-Based Methods for Accelerating Motivation and Achievement,* Network Educational Press.
8. Smith, Alistair (2002). *The Brain's Behind It,* Network Educational Press.
9. Rose, Colin and Malcolm J. Nicholl (1997). *Accelerated Learning for the 21st Century,* Piatkus.
10. Fogarty, Robin (1997). *Brain Compatible Classrooms,* SkyLight Training and Publishing.
11. Dryden, Gordon and Jeannette Vos (1999). *The Learning Revolution, to Change the Way the World Learns* (updated international edition), The Learning Web.
12. Jensen, Eric (1995). *The Learning Brain,* The Brain Store.
13. Jensen, Eric (1998). *Teaching with the Brain in Mind,* Association for Supervision and Curriculum Development.
14. Jensen, Eric (2000). *Brain-Based Learning,* The Brain Store.
15. Greenfield, Susan (2000). *The Private Life of the Brain,* Penguin Books.
16. Greenfield, Susan (2000). *Brain Story,* BBC Worldwide.
17. Greenfield, Susan (1998). *The Human Brain, a Guided Tour,* Phoenix.
18. McCrone, John (1999). *Going Inside: A Tour Round a Single Moment of Consciousness,* Faber and Faber. p. 309.
19. ibid. p. 311.
20. Meighan, Roland (1981). *A Sociology of Educating,* Holt, Rinehart and Winston. Third edition with Iram Siraj-Blatchford, 1997. Cassell.
21. Holt, John (1969). *How Children Fail,* Penguin.
22. Postman, Neil and Charles Weingartner (1969). *Teaching as a Subversive Activity,* Delacorte.
23. King, Edith (1998). 'Ivan Illich', in Ginnis, Paul ed. (1998). *The Trailblazers,* Education Now Books.
24. Dryden, Gordon and Jeannette Vos (1999). pp. 37–83.
25. Handy, Charles (1996). *Beyond Certainty,* Harvard Business School Press.
26. Claxton, Guy (1999). *Wise Up: The Challenge of Lifelong Learning,* Bloomsbury Publishing.
27. Visit the British Computer Society website: www.bcs.org
28. Glines, Don (1989). In *National Association of Secondary School Principals Bulletin,* February.
29. Abbot, John and Terry Ryan (2000). *The Unfinished Revolution: Learning, Human Behaviour, Community, and Political Paradox,* Network Educational Press.
30. Government Green Paper (1998). *The Learning Age: A Renaissance For A New Britain,* Department for Education and Employment.

31.   Blair, Tony (2001). 'A Second Term to Put Secondary Schools First' in *The Times*, 5 September.

32.   Abbott and Ryan (2000). p. 35.

33.   Bruer, John T. (1993). *Schools for Thought*, MIT Press.

34.   Department for Education and Employment (1999). *All Our Futures: Creativity, Culture and Education*, the Report of the National Advisory Committee on Creative And Cultural Education.

35.   Robinson, Ken (1999). 'Our Future Must Be Creative', in *The Times*, 16 July.

36.   Robinson, Ken (2000). 'Creativity In Schools And Beyond', in Lucas, Bill and Toby Greany, eds., *Schools In The Learning Age*, Campaign for Learning.

37.   Estelle Morris interviewed in *Times Education Supplement*, 15 June 2001.

38.   Bentley, Tom (2000). 'Creativity, Community and a New Approach to Schooling', in Lucas, Bill and Toby Greany, eds., *Schools in the Learning Age*, Campaign for Learning.

39.   Bowring-Carr, Christopher and John West-Burnham (1997). p. 25.

40.   Harber, Clive (1998). 'Paulo Freire', in Ginnis, P., *The Trailblazers*, Education Now Books.

41.   Higham, Anita (1997). 'Something Significantly Different ...', in *Education Now News and Review*, Winter 1997/8.

42.   Lucas, Bill and Toby Greany, eds. (2000). *Schools in the Learning Age*, Campaign for Learning. p. vii.

43.   Bayliss, Valerie (1999). 'In my View', in *Insight*, Autumn 1999, pp. 18–19.

44.   Ball, Sir Christopher (1995). In *RSA Journal*, December.

45.   See Powell, Robert (2001). *The Danish Free School Tradition – a Lesson in Democracy*, Curlew Productions.

46.   Miller, Ron, ed. (2000). *Creating Learning Communities: Models, Resources, and New Ways of Thinking About Teaching and Learning*, The Foundation for Educational Renewal.

47.   Shotton, John (1993). *No Master High Or Low: Libertarian Education and Schooling 1890–1990*, Libertarian Education.

48.   Adcock, John (1994). *In Place of Schools*, New Education Press.

49.   Adcock, John (2000). *Teaching Tomorrow, Personal Tuition as an Alternative to School*, Education Now Books.

50.   Lucas, Bill and Toby Greany, eds. (2000).

51.   Meighan Roland (1997). *The Next Learning System: and why Home–schoolers are Trailblazers*, Educational Heretics Press.

52.   Sylwester, Robert (1993). 'What The Biology Of The Brain Tells Us About Learning', in *Educational Leadership*, December 1993–January 1994.

53.   Bodenhamer, Bob G. and L. Michael Hall (1999). *The User's Manual For The Brain*, Crown House Publishing.

54.   Brandes, Donna and Paul Ginnis (1986). *A Guide to Student-Centred Learning*, Stanley Thornes.

55.   Brandes, Donna and Paul Ginnis (1990). *The Student-Centred School*, Simon and Schuster.

56.   Abbott, John and Terry Ryan (1999). *Constructing Knowledge and Shaping Brains*, a paper that appeared on the 21st Century Learning Initiative website (www.21learn.org) and seems to have been reworked as Appendix 2 to *The Unfinished Revolution* (2000).

57.   Greenfield, Susan (1994). *Royal Institution Christmas Lectures*, available from the BBC.

58.   Churchland, Paul (1995). *The Engine of Reason, the Seat of the Soul*, A Bradford Book/The MIT Press.

59.   Hobson, J. A. (1994). *Chemistry of Conscious States*, Little and Brown.

60.   Jensen, Eric (1998). p. 15.

61.   Butterworth, Brian (1999). *The Mathematical Brain*, Macmillan.

62.   Gammage, Philip (1999). 'After Five, Your Brain is Cooked', in *Education Now News and Review*, Number 24, Summer.

63.   Boyer, Ernest quoted in Abbott, John (1993). *Learning Makes Sense*, Education 2000.

64.   Rosenthal, Robert and Leonore Jacobsen (1968). *Pygmalion in the Classroom*, Reinhart and Winston.

65.   Smith, Alistair (1998). p. 57.

66.   Howe, Michael J. A. (1997). *IQ in Question, the Truth About Intelligence*, Sage Publications. p. 161.

67.   Hart, Leslie (1983). *Human Brain and Human Learning*, Longman.

68.   Thompson, Richard F. (1985). *The Brain, a Neuroscience Primer*, W. H. Freeman and Company. p. 18.

69.   Healey, Jane (1994). *Your Child's Growing Mind: a Guide to Learning and Brain Development from Birth to Adolescence*, Main Street Books.

70.   Damasio, Antonio (1994). *Descartes' Error: Emotion, Reason and the Human Brain*, Grosset/Putnam.

71.   Abbott, John and Terry Ryan (1999). 'Constructing Knowledge, Reconstructing Schooling', in *Educational Leadership*, November.

72.   Glasser, William (1986). *Control Theory in the Classroom*, HarperCollins.

73.   Smith, Alistair (1998). p. 88.

74.   Jensen, Eric (1995). *Superteaching*, The Brain Store.

75.   Northamptonshire County Council (1998). *Ready for Revision*, Northampton, UK, Northamptonshire Inspection and Advisory Service.

76.   Jensen, Eric (1998). p. 46.

77.   Hobson, Allan. *The Chemistry of Conscious States*, Little and Brown (1994); *Consciousness*, Scientific American Library (1998); *Dreaming as Delirium*, The MIT Press (1999).

78.   Denney, Nancy W. 'A Review of Life Span Research with the Twenty Questions Task: a study of Problem-Solving Ability', *The International Journal of Aging and Human Development*, Volume: 21, Issue: 3.

79.   Sylwester, R. and J. Cho (1993). 'What Brain Research Says About Paying Attention', in *Educational Leadership*, January 1993: 71–5.

80.   Prigogine, I. and I. Stengers (1984). *Order Out of Chaos*, Bantam.

81.   Gleik, J. (1987). *Making a New Science*, Viking.

82.   Doll, W. E. J. (1989). 'Complexity in the Classroom', in *Educational Leadership* 47.1: 65–70

83.   Scottish Consultative Council on the Curriculum (1996). p. 9.

84.   For a briefing on CREB, go to http://www.sfn.org/briefings/creb.html

85.   Calvin, William (1996). *How Brains Think*, Basic Books.

86.   Gazzaniga, Michael (1996). *Conversations in Cognitive Neuroscience*, MIT Press; and (1998) *The Mind's Past*, University of California Press.

87.   Buzan, Tony quoted in Hughes, Mike (1999). p. 48.

88.   Ekwall, Eldon E. and Shanker, James L., (1988). *Diagnosis and Remediation of the Disabled Reader*, Third Edition, Allyn and Bacon.

89.   Neimark, Jill (1995). 'It's Magical. It's Malleable. ... It's Memory', in *Psychology Today*, January–February.

90.   McGaugh, J. L. (1989). 'Dissociating Learning and Performance: Drug Hormone Enhancement Of Memory Storage', in *Brain Research Bulletin*, 23.4–5: 339–345. See also (2000) 'Memory – a Century of Consolidation', in *Science* 287: 248–251.

91.   Fry, William F. (1997). 'Spanish Humour: a Hypotheory, a Report on Initiation of Research', in *Humour: International Journal of Humour Research*, Vol. 10(2), 165–172.

92.   Fry, William F. (1998). 'Thriveonline' interview at http://thriveonline.oxygen.com/serenity/humor/wfrychat.html

93.   Hannaford, Carla (1995). *Smart Moves, Why Learning is Not All in Your Head*, Great Ocean Publishers.

94.   Dennison, Paul E. and Gail E. Dennison (1988). *Brain Gym Teacher's Edition*, Edu-Kinesthetics Inc. Visit Brain Gym at www.braingym.com

95.   Hannaford, Carla (1995). p. 11.

96.   Anderson, Roy (1999). *First Steps To A Physical Basis Of Concentration*, Crown House Publishing.

97.   Patterson, Marilyn Nikimaa (1997). *Every Body Can Learn, Engaging the Bodily-Kinesthetic Intelligence in the Everyday Classroom*, Zephyr Press.

98.   Jensen, Eric (2000). *Learning with the Body in Mind,* The Brain Store.

99.   Goleman, Daniel (1996). *Emotional Intelligence, Why it Can Matter More Than IQ,* Bloomsbury. pp. 4–12.

100.   James, Oliver in *London Observer,* 8 June 1997, quoted in Smith, Alistair (1998). p. 45.

101.   Meighan, Roland (2001). 'How Many Peers Make Five?', in *Natural Parent,* March/April.

102.   Meighan, Roland (2001). 'In Place of Fear', in Natural Parent, May/June.

103.   Meighan, Roland (2001). *Natural Learning and the Natural Curriculum,* Educational Heretics Press in association with *Natural Parent.*

104.   O'Keefe, J. and L. Nadel (1978). *The Hippocampus as a Cognitive Map,* Claredon Press. Nadel, L. (1990). 'Varieties of Spatial Cognition: Psychobiological Considerations', in *Annals of the New York Academy of Sciences,* 608: 613–26. Nadel, L., J. Wilmer and E. M. Kurz (1984). 'Cognitive Maps and Environmental Context', in Balsam and Tomi, eds., *Context and Learning,* Lawrence Erlbaum.

105.   Find out about the work of the Institute at www.nimh.nih.gov

106.   Bergland, Richard (1993). In Restak, R., *Receptors,* Bantam Books.

107.   Mills, R. C. (1987). *Relationship Between School Motivational Climate, Teacher Attitudes, Student Mental Health, School Failure and Health Damaging Behaviour.* Paper at Annual Conference of the American Educational Research Association, Washington DC.

108.   White, Alan (1989). *Student-Centred Learning,* unpublished paper.

109.   Bowkett, Stephen (1999). *Self-Intelligence, a Handbook for Developing Confidence, Self-Esteem and Interpersonal Skills,* Network Educational Press. p. 7.

110.   Lewkowicz, Adina Bloom (1999). *Teaching Emotional Intelligence: Making Informed Choices,* SkyLight Training and Publishing.

111.   Brearley, Michael (2001). *Emotional Intelligence in the Classroom,* Crown House Publishing. p. v.

112.   Branden, Nathaniel (1994). *The Six Pillars of Self-Esteem,* Bantam Books.

113.   Opening comment on the Nathaniel Branden website: www.nathanielbranden.net.

114.   Jensen, Eric (1995). *Superteaching,* The Brain Store.

115.   Deci, E. and R. M. Ryan (1985). *Intrinsic Motivation and Self-Determination in Human Behaviour,* Plenum.

116.   Deci, E. et al. (1992). 'Autonomy and Competence as Motivational Factors in Students with Learning Disabilities and Emotional Handicaps', in *Journal of Learning Disabilities* 25: 457–471. Deci, E. et al. (1991). 'Motivation and Education: the Self-Determination Perspective', in *Educational Psychologist* 26: 325–346.

117.   Mager, R. F. and J. McCann (1963). *Learner-Controlled Instruction,* Varian Press.

118.   Dunn, R., J. Beaudry and A. Klavas (1989). 'Survey of Research on Learning Styles', in *Educational Leadership,* 46, 50–58.

119.   Sternberg, Robert (1994). p. 36.

120.   Keefe, J. W. (1979). 'Learning Style: an Overview', in Keefe, J. W., ed., *Student Learning Styles: Diagnosing and Prescribing Programs,* National Association of Secondary School Principals.

121.   Jensen, Eric (1993). *Learning Styles for the Nineties,* Turning Point. Three audio-cassette pack.

122.   Aviram, Aaron (1992). 'Non-Lococentric Education', in *Educational Review,* vol. 44, no. 1.

123.   Kirby, Patricia (1979). *Cognitive Style, Learning Style, and Transfer Skill Acquisition,* National Centre For Research In Vocational Education.

124.   Carbo, M. (1980). *An Analysis of the Relationship Between the Modality Preferences of Kindergartners and the Selected Reading Treatments as they Affect the Learning of a Basic Sight-Word Vocabulary,* Dissertation, St John's University, New York. Carbo, M., R. Dunn and K. Dunn (1986). *Teaching Students to Read Through their Individual Learning Styles,* Prentice-Hall.

125. De Bello, T. (1985). *A Critical Analysis of the Achievement and Attitude Effects of Administrative Assignments to Social Studies Writing Instruction Based on Identified, Eighth Grade Students' Learning Style Preferences for Learning Alone, With Peers, or With Teachers,* Dissertation, St. John's University, New York.

126. Della Valle, J. (1984). *An Experimental Investigation of the Relationship(s) Between Preference for Mobility and the Word Recognition Scores of Seventh Grade Students to Provide Supervisory and Administrative Guidelines for the Organization of Effective Instructional Environments,* Dissertation, St. John's University, New York. Della Valle, J. et al. (1986). 'The Effects of Matching and Mismatching Student's Mobility Preferences on Recognition and Memory Tasks', in *Journal of Educational Research,* 79.5: 267–272.

127. Hodges, H. (1985). *An Analysis of the Relationships Among Preferences for a Formal/Informal Design, One Element of Learning Style, Academic Achievement, and Attitudes of Seventh and Eighth Grade Students in Remedial Mathematics Classes in a New York City Alternative Junior High School,* Dissertation, St. John's University, New York.

128. Shea, T. C. (1983). *An Investigation of the Relationship Among Preferences for the Learning Style Element of Design, Selected Instructional Environments, and Reading Achievement of Ninth Grade Students to Improve Administrative Determinations Concerning Effective Educational Facilities,* Dissertation, St. John's University, New York.

129. Shipman, V. and F. Shipman (1983). 'Cognitive Styles: Some Conceptual, Methodological and Applied Issues', in Gordon, E. W., ed., *Human Diversity and Pedagogy,* Mediax.

130. Virostko, J. (1983). *An Analysis of the Relationships Among Academic Achievement in Mathematics and Reading, Assigned Instructional Schedules, and the Learning Style Time Preferences of Third, Fourth, Fifth and Sixth Grade Students,* Dissertation, St. John's University, New York.

131. White, R. T. (1980). *An Investigation of the Relationship Between Selected Instructional Methods and Selected Elements of Emotional Learning Style Upon Student Achievement in Seventh Grade Social Studies,* Dissertation, St. John's University, New York.

132. Gregorc, Anthony F. (1982, revised 2001). *An Adult's Guide to Style,* Gregorc Associates.

133. Tobias, Cynthia Ulrich (1994). *The Way They Learn,* Focus on the Family Publishing.

134. Vail, Priscilla L. (1992). *Learning Styles, Food for Thought and 130 Practical Tips for Teachers K-4,* Modern Learning Press.

135. McCarthy, Bernice (1980). *The 4Mat System, Teaching and Learning Styles with Right/Left Mode Technique,* EXCEL.

136. Gregorc, Anthony F. (2001). *Mind Styles FAQs Book,* Gregorc Associates. p. 23.

137. ibid. p. 25.

138. Vail, Priscilla L. (1992). p. 3.

139. Bellanca, James (1994). *Active Learning Handbook for the Multiple Intelligences Classroom,* IRI/SkyLight Training and Publishing.

140. McCarthy, Bernice (1980). p. 53.

141. Specific Diagnostic Studies Inc. of Rockville, Maryland has analysed 5,300 student responses from USA, Hong Kong and Japan to its Learning Channel Preference Checklist.

142. Hughes, Mike (1999). p. 41.

143. Comment on his website: www.gregorc.com

144. Gregorc, Anthony F. (2001). p. 13.

145. ibid. p. 1.

146. Gregorc, Anthony F. (1982). p. 5.

147. Gregorc, Anthony F. (2001). p. 15.

148. Gregorc, Diane F. (1997). *Relating With Style,* Gregorc Associates. p. 70 ff.

149. Perkins, David (1995). *Outsmarting IQ: the Emerging Science of Learnable Intelligence,* The Free Press.

150. Zohar, Danah and Ian Marshall (2000), *SQ: Spiritual Intelligence – The Ultimate Intelligence,* Bloomsbury.

151. Gardner, Howard (1993). *Frames of Mind,* Fontana Press.
152. Gardner, Howard (1999). *Intelligence Reframed,* Basic Books. p. 34.
153. Herrnstein, R. J. and C. Murray (1994). *The Bell Curve: Intelligence and Class Structure in American Life,* Free Press.
154. White, John (1998). *Do Howard Gardner's Multiple Intelligences Add Up?,* University of London Institute of Education.
155. ibid. pp. 2–3.
156. Craft, A. (1997). *Proceedings of Creativity in Education Colloquium on Multiple Intelligences and Creativity with Howard Gardner,* July 1997. Open University School of Education.
157. *Mensa Magazine,* March 2000, British Mensa Ltd, St John's House, St John's Square, Wolverhampton.
158. Northamptonshire County Council (1998).
159. Roberts, Mike (1994). *Skills for Self-Managed Learning: Autonomous Learning by Research Projects,* Education Now Books. pp. 55–56.
160. Visit Robert Fisher's website: www.brunel.ac.uk/faculty/ed/Robert_Fisher
161. Visit the Philosophy for Children website: www.p4c.net
162. McGuinness, Carol (1999). *From Thinking Skills to Thinking Classrooms: a Review and Evaluation of Approaches for Promoting Pupils' Thinking Skills (including ICT),* Department for Education and Employment Research Report 115.
163. Bowring-Carr, Christopher and John West-Burnham (1997). pp. 94–95.
164. Bowring-Carr, Christopher and John West-Burnham (2002) *A Curriculum for Learning,* Network Educational Press.
165. Bloom, Benjamin (1956). *Taxonomy of Educational Objectives,* David McKay.
166. Quellmalz, E. S. (1985). 'Developing Reasoning Skills', in Baron, J. R. and R. J. Sternberg, *Teaching Thinking Skillls: Theory and Practice,* Freeman.
167. Fogarty, Robin (1994). *The Mindful School: How To Teach For Metacognitive Reflection,* Skylight.
168. Costa, Arthur (1995). *Teaching For Intelligent Behaviour: Outstanding Strategies For Strengthening Your Students' Thinking Skills,* Bureau of Education and Research.
169. Fogarty, Robin (1994). p. xvii.
170. Perkins, David (1995).
171. Final report of the Advisory Group on Citizenship, chaired by Professor Bernard Crick (1998). *Education for Citizenship and the Teaching of Democracy in Schools,* Qualifications and Curriculum Authority.
172. Dewey, John (1916). *Democracy and Education,* Macmillan.
173. Final report of the Advisory Group on Citizenship (1998). p. 7.
174. Clarke, F. (2000). 'Democracy has to be Lived to be Learned', in *Times Educational Supplement,* 20 October.
175. Davies, L. and G. Kirkpatrick (2000). *The EURIDEM Project: Pupil Democracy in Europe,* Children's Rights Alliance.
176. Harber, Clive (2001). 'Not Quite the Revolution – Eight Problems with "Citizenship Education"', in *Education Now News and Review Feature Supplement,* Spring.
177. Alexander, Titus (2000). *Citizenship Schools, a Practical Guide to Education for Citizenship and Personal Development,* Campaign for Learning.
178. Final report of the Advisory Group on Citizenship (1998). p. 37.
179. Visit their website: www.clrc.com
180. Visit the Kagan website: www.kagancooplearn.com
181. Johnson, Johnson and Holubec (1984). *Circles of Learning,* Association For Supervision and Curriculum Development.
182. Baldaro, James (1995). 'The Benefits of Student Participation', in *Education Now News and Review Feature Supplement,* Summer.
183. ibid.
184. Harber, Clive, ed. (1995). *Developing Democratic Education,* Education Now Books.
185. Newman-Turner, Adam and Lee Jerome (2001). *Activate! – Teacher Starter File,* Nelson Thornes.

186. Maxted, Peter (2000). *Understanding Barriers to Learning,* Campaign for Learning.
187. Armstrong, Thomas (1987). *In Their Own Way, Discovering and Encouraging Your Child's Personal Learning Style,* G. P .Putnam's Sons. pp. ix–x.
188. Abbott, John and Terry Ryan (2000). p. 32.

Section 2: Tools for Teaching and Learning

1. Neelands, Jonothan (1984). *Making Sense of Drama, a Guide to Classroom Practice,* Heinemann. Neelands, Jonothan (1990). *Structuring Drama Work, a Handbook of Available Forms in Theatre and Drama,* Cambridge University Press. Neelands, Jonothan (1992). *Learning Through Imagined Experience,* Hodder and Stoughton.
2. Boal, Augusto (1979). *Theatre of the Oppressed,* Pluto Press.

Section 3: Tools for Managing Group Work, Behaviour and Personal Responsibility

1. Kohn, Alfie (1993). *Punished by Rewards,* Houghton Mifflin.
2. Brandes, Donna and Howard Phillips (1979). *Gamesters' Handbook, 140 Games for Teachers and Group Leaders,* Hutchinson. Brandes, Donna (1983). *Gamesters' Handbook 2,* Hutchinson. Brandes, Donna and John Norris (1998). *Gamesters' Handbook 3,* Nelson Thornes.
3. Bond, Tim (1986). *Games for Social and Life Skills,* Stanley Thornes.
4. Dynamix (2003). *Serious Fun, Games for 4–9 year olds,* part of the *Can Do* series edited by Annie Davy, Thomson Learning, *Serious Fun 2, Games for 10–14 year olds,* part of the *Can Do* series edited by Annie Davy, Thomson Learning.
5. Hohenstein, Mary (1980). *A Compact Encyclopedia of Games for People of all Ages,* Bethany Fellowship.
6. Brandes, Donna and Paul Ginnis (1986). *A Guide to Student-Centred Learning,* Stanley Thornes.
7. Brandes, Donna and Paul Ginnis (1990). *The Student-Centred School,* Simon and Schuster.
8. *Mensa Magazine,* March 2000.
9. Rosenthal, Robert and Leonore Jacobsen (1968). *Pygmalion in the Classroom,* Reinhart and Winston.

Section 4: Operating Tools

1. Abbott, John and Terry Ryan (200). p. 44.
2. Brandes, Donna and Paul Ginnis (1986).
3. Brandes, Donna and Paul Ginnis (1990).
4. Baldaro, James (1995).

Section 5: Audit Tools

1. Hughes, Mike with Andy Vass (2001), *Strategies for Closing the Learning Gap,* Education Network Press.
2. Humphreys, Tony (1998). *Self-Esteem: the Key to Your Child's Education,* Gill and Macmillan.
3. Stratton, Peter and Nicky Hayes (1993). *A Student's Dictionary of Psychology,* Second Edition, Edward Arnold. p. 175.
4. ibid. p. 176.
5. ibid. p. 175.
6. Youngs, Bettie B. (1992). *The Six Vital Elements of Self-Esteem and How to Develop Them in Your Students,* Jalmar Press.
7. Faber, Adele and Elaine Mazlish (1980). *How to Talk so Kids will Listen and Listen so Kids will Talk,* Avon Books.

8. Covey, Stephen R. (1989). *The Seven Habits of Highly Effective People,* Simon and Schuster.
9. Quinn, Robert E., Sue R. Faerman, Michael P. Thompson and Michael R. McGrath (1996). *Becoming a Master Manager: a Competency Framework,* John Wiley and Sons. p. v.

Select Bibliography

Abbot, John and Terry Ryan (2000). *The Unfinished Revolution*, Stafford, UK, Network Educational Press.

Adcock, John (2000). *Teaching Tomorrow: Personal Tuition as an Alternative to School*, Nottingham, UK, Education Now Books.

Anderson, Roy (1999). *First Steps to a Physical Basis of Concentration*, Bancyfelin, Wales, Crown House Publishing.

Armstrong, Thomas (1987). *In Their Own Way: Discovering and Encouraging Your Child's Personal Learning Style*, New York, G. P. Putnam's Sons.

Beaver, Diana (1994). *Lazy Learning, Making the Most of the Brains You Were Born With*, Shaftesbury, Dorset, UK, Element Books Limited.

Bellanca, James (1990). *Keep Them Thinking, a Handbook of Model Lessons*, Arlington Heights, Illinois, IRI/SkyLight Training and Publishing.

Bellanca, James (1994). *Active Learning Handbook for the Multiple Intelligences Classroom*, Arlington Heights, Illinois, IRI/SkyLight Training and Publishing.

Bellanca, James, Carolyn Chapman, Elizabeth Swartz (1994). *Multiple Assessments for Multiple Intelligences*, Arlington Heights, Illinois, IRI/SkyLight Training and Publishing.

Bellanca, James and Robin Fogarty (1991). *Blueprints for Thinking in the Cooperative Classroom*, Arlington Heights, Illinois, IRI/SkyLight Training and Publishing.

Bellanca, James and Robin Fogarty (second edition, 1993). *Catch Them Thinking, a Handbook of Classroom Strategies*, Arlington Heights, Illinois, IRI/SkyLight Training and Publishing.

Berman, Sally (1995). *A Multiple Intelligences Road to a Quality Classroom*, Palatine, Illinois, IRI/SkyLight Training and Publishing.

Boal, Augusto (1979). *Theatre of the Oppressed*, London, Pluto Press.

Bodenhamer, Bob G. and L. Michael Hall (1999). *The User's Manual For The Brain*, Bancyfelin, Wales, Crown House Publishing.

Bond, Tim (1986). *Games for Social and Life Skills*, reprinted 1990, Cheltenham, UK, Stanley Thornes.

Bowkett, Stephen (1999). *Self-Intelligence, A Handbook for Developing Confidence, Self-Esteem and Interpersonal Skills*, Stafford, UK, Network Educational Press.

Bowring-Carr, Christopher and John West-Burnham (1997). *Effective Learning in Schools, How to Integrate Learning and Leadership for a Successful School*, London, Pitman.

Bowring-Carr, Christopher and John West-Burnham (2002). *A Curriculum for Learning*, Stafford, UK, Network Educational Press.

Brandes, Donna and Howard Phillips (1979). *Gamesters' Handbook, 140 Games for Teachers and Group Leaders*, London, Hutchinson.

Brandes, Donna (1983). *Gamesters' Handbook 2*, London, Hutchinson.

Brandes, Donna and John Norris (1998). *Gamesters' Handbook 3*, Cheltenham, UK, Nelson Thornes.

Brandes, Donna and Paul Ginnis (1986). *A Guide to Student-Centred Learning,* Cheltenham, UK, Stanley Thornes.

Brandes, Donna and Paul Ginnis (1990). *The Student-Centred School*, Hemel Hempstead, UK, Simon and Schuster.

Brearley, Michael (2001). *Emotional Intelligence in the Classroom*, Bancyfelin, Wales, Crown House Publishing.

Burke, Kay (1992). *What to do with the Kid Who ... Developing Cooperation, Self Discipline, and Responsibility in the Classroom*, Arlington Heights, Illinois, IRI/SkyLight Training and Publishing.

Burnett, Garry (2002). *Learning to Learn: Making Learning Work for All Students*, Bancyfelin, Wales, Crown House Publishing.

Butterworth, Brian (1999). *The Mathematical Brain*, London, Macmillan.

Buzan, Tony (1986). *Use Your Memory*, London, BBC Worldwide Publishing.

Buzan, Tony (1993). *The Mindmap Book*, London, BBC Worldwide Publishing.

Caine, Renate Nummela and Geoffrey Caine (1997). *Unleashing the Power of Perceptual Change, the Potential of Brain-Based Teaching*, Alexandria, Virginia, Association for Supervision and Curriculum Development.

Chapman, Carolyn (1993). *If the Shoe Fits ... How to Develop Multiple Intelligences in the Classroom*, Arlington Heights, Illinois, IRI/SkyLight Training and Publishing.

Claxton, Guy (1999). *Wise Up, the Challenge of Lifelong Learning*, New York, USA, Bloomsbury.

Covey, Stephen R. (1989). *The Seven Habits of Highly Effective People*, London, Simon and Schuster.

DeAmicis, Bonita (1997). *A Daily Dose Integrating MI into Your Curriculum*, Tucson, Arizona, Zephyr Press.

Devlin, Keith (2000). *The Maths Gene, Why Everyone has it, but Most People Don't Use it*, London, Phoenix.

Dickinson, Chris (1996). *Effective Learning Activities*, Stafford, UK, Network Educational Press.

Dryden, Gordon and Jeannette Vos (1999, updated international edition). *The Learning Revolution, to Change the Way the World Learns*, Torrance, California, The Learning Web.

Dynamix (2002). *Participation, Not Just Ticking a Box*, Swansea, Wales, Dynamix and Save The Children Fund.

Dynamix (2003). *Serious Fun, Games for 4–9 year olds*, part of the *Can Do* series edited by Annie Davy, London, Thomson Learning.

Dynamix (2003). *Serious Fun 2, Games for 10–14 year olds*, part of the *Can Do* series edited by Annie Davy, London, Thomson Learning.

Fletcher, Mark (2000). *Teaching for Success: the Brain-Friendly Revolution in Action*, Folkstone, UK, English Experience.

Fogarty, Robin and James Bellanca (1986). *Teach Them Thinking*, Arlington Heights, Illinois, IRI/SkyLight Training and Publishing.

Fogarty, Robin (1994). *The Mindful School: How to Teach for Metacognitive Reflection*, Palatine, Illinois, IRI/Skylight Training and Publishing.

Fogarty, Robin (1997). *Brain Compatible Classrooms*, Arlington Heights, Illinois, SkyLight Professional Development.

Freire, Paulo (1970). *Pedagogy of the Oppressed*, New York, Seabury Press.

Fry, Ron (1996). *Improve your Memory*, Franklin Lakes, New Jersey, The Career Press.

Gammage, Philip and Rosalind Swann (1995). *Issues in Early Childhood Education*, Nottingham, Education Now Books.

Gardner, Howard (1993). *Frames of Mind*, London, Fontana Press.

Gardner, Howard (1993). *Multiple Intelligences, the Theory in Practice*, New York, Basic Books.

Gardner, Howard (1993). *The Unschooled Mind*, London, Fontana Press.

Gardner, Howard (1997). *Extraordinary Minds*, London, Weidenfield & Nicholson.

Gardner, Howard (1999). *Intelligence Reframed*, New York, Basic Books.

Ginnis, Paul, ed. (1998). *The Trailblazers*, Nottingham, UK, Education Now Books.

Goleman, Daniel (1996). *Emotional Intelligence, Why it can Matter more than IQ*, London, Bloomsbury.

Goleman, Daniel (1998). *Working With Emotional Intelligence*, London, Bloomsbury.

Greenfield, Susan (1998). *The Human Brain, a Guided Tour*, London, Phoenix.

Greenfield, Susan (2000). *Brain Story*, London, BBC Worldwide.

Greenfield, Susan (2000). *The Private Life of the Brain*, London, Penguin Books.

Gregorc, Anthony F. (1985). *Inside Styles: Beyond the Basics*, Columbia, Connecticut, Gregorc Associates.

Gregorc, Anthony F. (1982, revised 2001). *An Adult's Guide to Style*, Columbia, Connecticut, Gregorc Associates.

Gregorc, Anthony F. (1998). *The Mind Styles Model; Theory; Principles and Practice*, Columbia, Connecticut, Gregorc Associates.

Gregorc, Anthony F. (2001). *Mind Styles FAQs Book*, Columbia, Connecticut, Gregorc Associates.

Gregorc, Diane F. (1997). *Relating With Style*, Columbia, Connecticut, Gregorc Associates.

Handy, Charles (1996). *Beyond Certainty*, Harvard, Harvard Business School Press.

Hannaford, Carla (1995). *Smart Moves, Why Learning is Not All in Your Head*, Atlanta, Georgia, Great Ocean Publishers.

Harber, Clive (1992). *Democratic Learning and Learning Democracy*, Nottingham, UK, Education Now Books.

Harber, Clive, ed. (1995). *Developing Democratic Education*, Nottingham, UK, Education Now Books.

Hohenstein, Mary (1980). *A Compact Encyclopedia of Games for People of all Ages*, Minneapolis, Minnesota, Bethany Fellowship.

Holt, John (1969). *How Children Fail*, London, Penguin.

Howard, Pierce J. (2000). *The Owner's Manual for the Brain, Everyday Applications from Mind-Brain Research*, Austin, Texas, Bard Press.

Howe, Michael J. A. (1997). *IQ in Question, the Truth about Intelligence*, London, Sage Publications.

Hughes, Mike (1999). *Closing the Learning Gap*, Stafford, UK, Network Educational Press.

Hughes, Mike with Andy Vass (2001). *Strategies for Closing the Learning Gap*, Stafford, UK, Network Educational Press.

Humphreys, Tony (1998). *Self-Esteem: the Key to your Child's Education*, Dublin, Gill and Macmillan.

Illich, Ivan (1971). *Deschooling Society*, Harmondsworth, UK, Penguin.

Jensen, Eric (1995). *Superteaching*, San Diego, California, The Brain Store Inc.

Jensen, Eric (1995). *The Learning Brain*, San Diego, California, The Brain Store.

Jensen, Eric (1996). *Completing the Puzzle: the Brain Compatible Approach to Learning*, Del Mar, USA, The Brain Store.

Jensen, Eric (1998). *Teaching with the Brain in Mind*, Alexandria, Virginia, Association for Supervision and Curriculum Development.

Jensen, Eric (2000). *Brain-Based Learning* (revised edition), San Diego, California, The Brain Store.

Jensen, Eric (2000). *Different Brains Different Learners, How to Reach the Hard to Reach*, San Diego, California, The Brain Store.

Jensen, Eric (2000). *Learning with the Body in Mind*, San Diego California, The Brain Store.

Joyce, Bruce, Emily Calhoun, and David Hopkins (1997). *Models of Learning, Tools for Teaching*, Ballmoor, UK, Open University Press.

Kirschenbaum, Howard and Valerie Land Nenderson, eds. (1990). *The Carl Rogers Reader.* London, Constable.

Kohn, Alfie (1993). *Punished by Rewards*, New York, Houghton Mifflin.

Lashley, Conrad (1995). *Improving Study Skills, A Complete Approach*, London, Cassell.

Lazear, David (1991). *Seven Ways of Knowing: Teaching for Multiple Intelligences*, Arlington Heights, Illinois, IRI/Skylight Training and Publishing.

Lazear, David (1994). *Intelligence Builders for Every Student: 44 Exercises to Expand MI in Your Classroom*, Tucson, Arizona, Zephyr Press.

Lazear, David (1994). *Seven Pathways of Learning: Teaching Students and Parents about Multiple Intelligences,* Tucson, Arizona, Zephyr Press.

Lazear, David (1998). *Multiple Intelligence Approaches to Assessment, Solving the Assessment Conundrum,* Tucson, Arizona, Zephyr Press.

Lewkowicz, Adina Bloom (1999). *Teaching Emotional Intelligence: Making Informed Choices*, Arlington Heights, Illinois, SkyLight Training and Publishing.

Lucas, Bill and Toby Greany (2000). *Schools in the Learning Age*, London, Campaign for Learning.

Margulies, Nancy (1991). *Mapping Inner Space, Learning and Teaching Mind Mapping*, Tucson, Arizona, Zephyr Press.

Maxted, Peter (1999). *Understanding Barriers to Learning*, London, Campaign for Learning.

McCarthy, Bernice (1980). *The 4Mat System, Teaching and Learning Styles with Right/Left Mode Techniques*, Barrington, USA, EXCEL.

McCrone, John (1999). *Going Inside: a Tour Round a Single Moment of Consciousness*, London, Faber and Faber.

McKay, Matthew and Patrick Fanning (2000). *Self Esteem*, Oakland, California, New Harbinger Publications.

Meighan, Roland (1995). *John Holt: Personalised Education and the Reconstruction of Schooling*, Nottingham, UK, Education Now Books in association with Educational Heretics Press.

Meighan, Roland (1997). *The Next Learning System: and why Homeschoolers are Trailblazers,* Nottingham, UK, Educational Heretics Press.

Meighan, Roland and Iram Siraj-Blatchford (1997). *A Sociology of Educating,* London, Cassell.

Meighan, Roland (2001). *Natural Learning and the Natural Curriculum,* Nottingham, UK, Educational Heretics Press in association with Natural Parent.

Miller, Ron, ed. (2000). *Creating Learning Communities, Models, Resources and New Ways of Thinking About Teaching and Learning,* Brandon, Vermont, The Foundation for Educational Renewal.

Neelands, Jonothan (1984). *Making Sense of Drama, a Guide to Classroom Practice,* London, Heinemann.

Neelands, Jonothan (1990). *Structuring Drama Work, a Handbook of Available Forms in Theatre and Drama,* Cambridge, UK, Cambridge University Press.

Neelands, Jonothan (1992). *Learning Through Imagined Experience,* London, Hodder and Stoughton.

Northamptonshire County Council (1998). *Ready for Revision,* Northampton, UK, Northamptonshire Inspection and Advisory Service.

Orlick, Terry (1978). *The Cooperative Sports and Games Book, Challenge Without Competition,* London, Writers and Readers Publishing Cooperative.

Ornstein, Robert (1997). *The Right Mind, A Cutting Edge Picture of How the Two Sides of the Brain Work,* Orlando, Florida, Harcourt Brace and Company.

Parry, Terence and Gayle Gregory (1998). *Designing Brain Compatible Learning,* Arlington Heights, Illinois, SkyLight Professional Development.

Patterson, Marilyn Nikimaa (1997). *Every Body Can Learn: Engaging the Bodily-Kinesthetic Intelligence in the Everyday Classroom,* Tucson, Arizona, Zephyr Press.

Postman, Neil and Charles Weingartner (1969). *Teaching as a Subversive Activity,* New York, Delacorte.

Quinn, Robert E., Sue R. Faerman, Michael P. Thompson and Michael R. McGrath (1996). *Becoming a Master Manager: a Competency Framework,* New York, John Wiley and Sons.

Race, Phil (1995). *Who Learns Wins,* London, Penguin Group and BBC Enterprises.

Reif, Sandra F. and Julie A. Heimburge (1996). *How to Reach and Teach all Students in the Inclusive Classroom,* West Nyack, New York, The Center for Applied Research in Education.

Relf, Peter, Rod Hirst, Jan Richardson and Georgina Youdell (1998). *Best Behaviour, Starting Points for Effective Behaviour Management,* Stafford, UK, Network Educational Press.

Roberts, Mike (1994). *Skills for Self-Managed Learning, Autonomous Learning by Research Projects,* Nottingham, UK, Education Now Books.

Rogers, Carl R. (1951). *Client-Centred Therapy,* London, Constable.

Rogers, Carl R. (1961). *On Becoming a Person, a Therapist's View of Psychotherapy*, London, Constable.

Rogers, Carl R. (1983). *Freedom to Learn for the 80s*, Columbus, Ohio, Charles E. Merrill.

Rose, Colin and Louise Goll (1992). *Accelerate Your Learning*, Aylesbury, UK, Accelerated Learning Systems.

Rose, Colin and Malcolm J. Nicholl (1997). *Accelerated Learning for the 21st Century*, London, Piatkus.

Rowntree, Derek (1970). *Learn How to Study, a Guide for Students of all Ages*, London, Warner Books.

Scottish Consultative Council on the Curriculum (1996). *Teaching for Effective Learning, a Paper for Discussion and Development*, Dundee, Scotland, Scottish Consultative Council on the Curriculum. This group now call themselves Teaching and Learning Scotland and the second edition of the paper appears under their new name.

Shute, Chris (1994). *Alice Miller: The Unkind Society, Parenting and Schooling*, Nottingham, UK, Educational Heretics Press.

Smith, Alistair (1996). *Accelerated Learning in the Classroom*, Stafford, UK, Network Educational Press.

Smith, Alistair (1998). *Accelerated Learning in Practice, Brain-Based Methods for Accelerating Motivation and Achievement*, Stafford, UK, Network Educational Press.

Smith, Alistair (2002). *The Brain's Behind It*, Stafford, UK, Network Educational Press.

Smith, Robert M. (1983). *Learning How to Learn, Applied Theory for Adults*, Ballmoor, UK, Open University Press.

Stine, Jean Marie (1997). *Double Your Brain Power: Increase Your Memory by Using all of Your Brain all of the Time*, Paramus, New Jersey, Prentice Hall.

Teare, Barry (1997). *Effective Provision for Able and Talented Children*, Stafford, UK, Network Educational Press.

Teare, Barry (1997). *Effective Resources for Able and Talented Children*, Stafford, UK, Network Educational Press.

Teare, Barry (2001). *More Effective Resources for Able and Talented Children*, Stafford, UK, Network Educational Press.

Thompson, Richard F. (1985). *The Brain, a Neuroscience Primer*, New York, W. H. Freeman and Company.

Tobias, Cynthia Ulrich (1994). *The Way They Learn*, Colorado Springs, Focus on the Family Publishing.

Trafford, Bernard (1997). *Participation, Power-Sharing and School Improvement*, Nottingham, UK, Educational Heretics Press.

Vail, Priscilla L. (1992). *Learning Styles, Food for Thought and 130 Practical Tips for Teachers K-4*, Rosemont, New Jersey, Modern Learning Press.

Weber, Ellen (1997). *Roundtable Learning, Building Understanding Through Enhanced MI Strategies*, Tucson, Arizona, Zephyr Press.

White, John (1998). *Do Howard Gardner's Multiple Intelligences Add Up?* London, University of London Institute of Education.

Williams, Linda Verlee (1988). *Teaching for the Two-Sided Mind*, New York, Simon and Schuster.

Winebrenner, Susan (1992). *Teaching Gifted Kids in the Regular Classroom*, Minneapolis, Free Spirit Publishing.

Youngs, Bettie B. (1992). *The Six Vital Elements of Self-Esteem and How to Develop Them in Your Students*, USA, Jalmar Press.

Zohar, Danah and Ian Marshall (2000). *SQ: Spiritual Intelligence – The Ultimate Intelligence*, London, Bloomsbury.

Index

A

Abbott, John, 6–7, 12, 19, 60, 251, 338–339, 343

ability, 6–8, 15–17, 29–31, 34, 40, 47, 49, 53, 60, 86, 100, 114, 117, 127, 151, 177, 192, 208, 241, 251, 253, 262, 296, 307–308, 339
see also mixed-ability

able, 7, 10, 17, 25–26, 28–29, 37, 45, 51, 70, 85–86, 104, 114, 123, 137, 151, 153, 158, 161, 178, 181, 184, 208, 218, 222, 228–229, 231, 236–238, 241, 243–244, 246, 249, 257–259, 263–264, 274–275, 281, 286–287, 289, 298, 307, 309, 317, 319, 351

Abstract Random, 42–45, 117, 159, 228, 238, 247, 276, 280, 285

Abstract Sequential, 38, 41–45, 228, 238, 247, 276, 280, 285

accelerate, 334, 351

accelerated, ix, 4, 11, 27–28, 39, 251, 270, 280, 314, 317, 331, 334–335, 337, 351

accelerated learning, ix, 4, 11, 27–28, 39, 314, 317, 331, 334–335, 337, 351

achieve, 14, 22, 58, 85, 204, 218–219, 222, 234, 236, 267, 292, 296, 301, 307, 314, 317, 321

achievement, ix, vii, 1, 4, 17, 25, 35, 38–40, 48, 55–56, 189, 231, 234, 238, 242, 245–246, 253, 258, 261–262, 279, 290, 293, 295, 317, 337, 341, 351
see also underachievement

act, 2, 8, 13, 24, 26, 40, 53, 75–76, 173, 222, 241
see also role play, drama, dramatic

active, ix, 12, 18–19, 22, 24, 30–31, 37, 39, 54, 58, 64, 82, 114, 128, 137, 148, 151, 164, 177, 188–189, 276, 300, 310, 317, 341, 345

alternative, 6, 10, 51, 56, 106, 130, 148, 210, 221, 239, 266, 293, 331, 338, 341, 345

alternatives, 7, 11, 43, 204, 311, 315

amygdala, 24, 26

art, vii, 37, 44, 52, 65, 69, 71, 91, 101, 104, 110–111, 117, 124, 136, 139–140, 153, 164, 171, 238, 246–247, 250–251, 260, 283, 286, 296
see also creative, creativity

articulate, 20, 66, 91, 124, 157, 228, 300

articulation, 20, 58–59, 206, 265

assertive, 199–204, 291, 294, 313, 317

assertiveness, ii, 30, 105–106, 178, 181, 198–202, 204, 206, 262, 293–294, 296

assess, 52, 73, 99, 121, 131, 164, 220, 265–266, 293, 295, 317

assessment, 4, 8, 32, 36, 38, 47, 54, 57, 74, 85–86, 88, 92, 108, 126, 133–134, 153, 155, 167, 183, 188, 217, 220–222, 229, 236, 240, 246, 254–255, 257, 260, 265, 268, 274–275, 277, 289, 291–293, 295, 301–302, 309, 314, 334, 349

attainment, 4, 35, 55, 57–58, 184, 241
see also underattainment

attention, 7, 22–26, 30–32, 44, 51, 59, 68–71, 80, 90, 93, 102, 108, 115, 140, 164, 169, 172, 187–189, 192, 195, 203, 212–213, 223, 262, 283, 286, 297, 304, 308, 311–312, 322, 339

auditory, 11, 39–40, 63, 157, 228, 238, 250, 276, 280–281, 285

autonomous, 46, 50–51, 342, 350

axon, 13–14, 18, 27

B

behaviour, ii, 4, 6, 11, 16, 26–28, 35, 40, 46, 53, 56, 60, 80, 143, 175, 177, 181–183, 185–187, 189–191, 193, 195, 197–201, 203–205, 207, 209, 211, 213, 215, 217–219, 221, 223, 261–263, 270, 279, 287, 290, 293, 296, 301, 306–307, 309–311, 314, 318, 328, 337, 340, 342–343, 350
see also discipline

behaviourism, 198–199

behaviouristic, 22, 177, 204, 292

blood flow, 22, 25, 184

Bloom, Benjamin, 52, 342

brain-compatible, 12, 261, 280, 317

brain-friendly, 10–11, 334, 347

Brandes, Donna, v, x, 11, 28, 261, 338, 343, 346

C

Campaign for Learning, 9, 53, 331, 333, 338, 342–343, 349

cerebellum, 23–24

cerebral cortex, 18, 24, 31, 53

child-centred, 7

choice, 32–33, 44, 73, 88, 106, 201–203, 223, 228, 243, 246–247, 249, 251, 257, 267, 276, 279, 290, 296, 301, 304, 310, 325, 334

choices, 29, 33, 38, 40, 53, 57, 59, 86, 190, 199, 201, 205, 215, 221, 247, 249, 251–252, 255, 257, 267, 280–281, 290, 293, 295–296, 301–302, 304, 309, 311–313, 317, 322, 334, 340, 349

citizens, 50, 54, 63, 164

citizenship, 9, 28, 33, 50, 53–56, 63, 66, 82, 90, 92, 94, 124, 135, 138, 153, 164, 178, 188, 190, 198–199, 213, 215, 267, 270, 317, 326, 331, 342

cognition, 28, 340

cognitive, vii, 8, 15, 17, 23, 41, 46, 51–53, 55, 108, 317, 339–341 collaboration, 92, 146, 153, 181, 219

collaborative, 55, 126, 129, 131, 137, 151, 182, 185, 298

collective, 33, 58, 93–94, 133, 178, 190, 215, 244, 261–262, 270

concept, 6, 14, 18–21, 25, 43, 46, 55–56, 66, 71, 81, 89, 161, 173, 217, 259, 298
see also internalise, internalised, internalisation, pattern, patterning

conceptualisation, 18, 21
see also internalise, internalised, internalisation, pattern, patterning

Concrete Random, 38, 42–45, 228, 238, 247, 276, 280, 285

Concrete Sequential, 38, 41–46, 103–104, 153, 228, 238, 247, 276, 280, 285

constructivism, 19, 53, 251

cooperation, ix, x, 44, 53, 55, 58, 63, 69–70, 86, 89, 138, 153, 164, 193, 270, 285, 346

cooperative, 15, 55, 69, 90, 123, 129, 182–183, 270, 294, 322, 345, 350

corporate, ii, 20, 54, 78, 89, 134, 136, 181–183, 217, 276, 319, 329

Covey, Stephen, 3, 315, 325, 337, 344, 346

creative, 7–8, 22, 42, 45–46, 50–52, 93, 106, 139, 159, 168–169, 206–207, 247, 265, 285, 312, 319, 321–323, 329, 333, 338
see also art

creativity, x, xi, 8–9, 25, 44, 252, 266, 317, 338, 342
see also art

D

debrief, 52, 106, 137, 146, 153, 187–188, 192–194, 199, 209, 251, 281, 301–302, 318–319, 322

demeanour, 28, 292, 307

democracy, ix, x, 9–10, 33, 50, 53–55, 58, 161, 178, 262, 338, 342, 348

democratic, 6, 10, 21, 55–56, 63, 82, 149, 261, 270, 292, 317, 326, 342, 348

dendrite, 13, 18, 27

Dewey, John, ix, 12, 53, 297, 317, 342

differentiate, 92, 207, 296

differentiated, 33, 38, 86, 135, 146, 222, 229, 234, 236, 244, 251, 253, 257, 260, 275, 317, 325

differentiation, 19, 85, 102, 127, 134, 140, 151, 210, 227, 231, 234, 245, 290, 317–318, 327

disability, 56, 309

disabilities, 56, 340

discipline, xi, 45, 116, 153, 177, 303, 346
see also behaviour

discuss, 68, 70, 72, 80, 94, 126, 128–129, 137, 144, 150, 156, 164, 190, 202, 204, 208, 221, 247, 249, 262, 266, 281, 287, 295, 298, 303, 311–312, 319, 330

discussion, ii, 12, 19–20, 29–30, 32, 39, 44–45, 55, 71, 76, 83, 95–97, 106, 130, 138, 143, 150–151, 156, 169–170, 177, 180, 183, 186, 188, 190, 193, 195–199, 201–202, 207, 212–214, 218, 221, 255, 262–267, 270, 275–276, 282, 285, 287, 291, 298, 312, 315, 317–319, 321, 328–330, 351

drama, ix, x, 44, 52, 63–64, 97, 106, 121, 124, 137, 195, 283, 286, 293, 343, 350
see also act, role play

dramatic, 17, 22, 24, 43, 64, 105–106, 108, 117, 159–160, 307, 317, 327
see also act, role play

Dunn, Ken and Rita, 34, 40, 333–334, 340

E

Einstein, Albert, 13–14, 48, 117, 208

emotion, 19, 24, 26, 293, 326, 339

emotional, 11, 15, 17, 22, 24–26, 28–30, 33, 35, 46, 58–59, 76, 79, 160, 163–164, 177–178, 184, 186, 190, 206, 263–264, 270, 291, 294, 317, 334, 340–341, 346–347, 349

emotions, 24–30, 44, 58, 160, 178, 184, 206

engaged, 17, 22, 30
see also motivate, motivated, motivation

engagement, 128, 171, 261
see also motivate, motivated, motivation

environment, 15–17, 20, 22, 27, 34–36, 49, 58–59, 106, 169, 255, 274, 277, 289, 294, 296

excluded, 27, 38, 56

exclusion, 39, 193

expect, 7, 19, 40, 45, 86, 123, 191, 200, 222, 259, 263, 293–294, 297, 300, 311, 321, 323, 329–330

expectation, 36, 82, 151, 196, 327–328

experiential, 12, 44, 46, 53–55, 64, 79, 106, 178, 195, 297, 317

experientially, 33, 63, 181, 297, 322

extension, 73, 135, 142, 231–233

F

feedback, vi, 16, 21, 28, 36, 108, 154–155, 161, 182, 186, 230, 269, 274, 276–277, 279, 282, 289, 293, 295–296, 298, 307, 312–313, 316–317, 319, 322, 324, 328, 330

Fisher, Robert, 51, 317, 342

Friere, Paulo, 5

fun, vii, 9, 24, 27, 58–59, 63, 69, 73, 76, 94, 99, 112, 119, 131, 140, 157, 167, 169, 181, 185, 187, 192–193, 227, 231, 250, 261, 283, 286, 290, 293, 343, 347

G

game, 12, 17, 25, 43, 110, 127–128, 166–168, 170–171, 173, 192–194, 223, 238, 242, 244, 255, 290

games, ii, xi, 19, 21, 24, 44, 49, 124, 129, 157, 168, 178, 192–193, 195–196, 200, 250, 294, 298, 322, 343, 345–348, 350

Gardner, Howard, 8, 34, 37, 46–47, 63, 276, 285, 317, 332, 342, 347, 352

GCSE, 22, 27, 60, 95, 101, 106, 126, 139, 141, 146, 158, 170–171, 210, 222, 232, 241, 246, 259, 261, 297, 299

gestalt, 11, 18

gestalts, 18

gifted, 11, 352

GNVQ (General National Vocational Qualification), 67, 124–126, 210, 259, 297

Goleman, Daniel, 25, 29, 46, 178, 317, 332, 340, 347

Greenfield, Susan, 5, 13, 24, 337–338, 347

Gregorc, Anthony, 33–38, 41–43, 45, 63, 228, 247, 250, 276, 280, 284–285, 317, 332–334, 341, 347–348

ground rules, 28, 59, 80, 116, 159, 164, 179–180, 186, 188–190, 192, 194–195, 199, 218–219, 263, 266, 270, 277, 290–291, 294, 317, 322

group, ii, vi, 12, 14, 16, 27, 38–39, 43–44, 49–50, 54–55, 63–65, 78–80, 83, 86, 89, 91–96, 104–106, 109, 117, 119, 122–123, 126–127, 130, 137, 142, 145–146, 148, 150–153, 164, 171, 175, 177–187, 189, 191, 193, 195, 197, 199, 201, 203, 205, 207–219, 221, 223, 228, 240, 242, 250–251, 253, 255, 259, 263–270, 280, 285–287, 290, 296–298, 305, 317, 322–323, 329, 337, 342–343, 346, 350–351

grouping, 126

groups, ii, xi, 12, 18, 20, 55, 63, 65–66, 75–77, 79–80, 86, 89–94, 100, 106, 109, 117, 119, 122–127, 129–131, 136, 141–142, 145–148, 150–153, 158–159, 171, 177, 181–182, 185, 195, 197, 207–208, 211–212, 214, 216, 219–221, 223, 228, 233, 237–238, 250–251, 253, 259–260, 262–264, 266–267, 276, 280–281, 285, 296, 298–299, 305, 317, 319, 322–323, 329

H

habit, 3, 8, 36, 102, 114, 151, 163, 220–221, 247, 259, 266, 301–302, 305, 308, 312, 325

Handy, Charles, 6, 34, 46, 114, 270, 291, 337, 348

Hart, Leslie, 18–19, 26, 339

hemisphere, 334

hemispheres, 21, 34, 335

hippocampus, 23, 340

holistic, 11, 238

Holt, John, viii, 5, 27, 337, 348–349

homework, 8, 36, 51, 117, 127, 150, 160, 203–204, 206, 220, 229, 239–240, 259, 261, 266, 275, 297, 304, 306, 310–311, 330

Honey and Mumford, 36, 63, 250, 333–334

Howe, Michael, 17, 317, 339, 348

Hughes, Mike, 4, 39, 279, 335, 337, 339, 341, 343, 348

humanistic, ix, 11, 177, 204, 261, 292, 317

I

ICT, 6, 71, 104, 108, 119, 124, 141, 243, 275, 298–299, 319, 342
see also information and communications technology, technology

Illich, Ivan, 5–6, 337, 348

imagination, 24, 44, 52, 159, 255, 266, 283, 286

include, 9, 11, 20–21, 26, 35, 51–52, 67, 71, 79, 85, 87, 91, 108, 153, 180, 192–193, 201, 216, 239–240, 250, 266, 278, 298, 319

included, 93, 123, 152, 292

inclusion, 28, 35, 50, 56–57, 63, 80, 90, 178, 184, 193, 213, 228, 317, 326–327, 331

independence, 44, 49, 51, 58–60, 119, 127, 138, 227, 260, 297

independent, iii, 9, 30, 46, 50–51, 53, 58, 63, 66, 70, 86, 88, 92, 98, 101–102, 110, 112, 114, 119, 124, 136, 146, 160, 164, 233, 238, 245–246, 250, 257–259, 277, 297, 314, 317, 322–323

individual, vii, ix, x, 7, 9–10, 16, 19, 33–34, 41, 44–45, 48, 55, 58, 60, 63, 72, 76, 80, 85, 89, 92–93, 96, 98, 104, 117, 141, 143, 154, 172, 195, 199, 201, 208–210, 217–219, 223, 227–228, 244, 247, 250–253, 257, 260, 265, 267–270, 273–276, 280, 282, 287, 289, 296, 316, 319, 325, 330, 340

individualised, 9

information and communications technology, 6, 53, 76
see also ICT, technology

intelligence, x, 8, 10, 15–17, 19, 25, 29–30, 33–34, 36–37, 46–50, 53, 58–59, 63, 88, 124, 159–160, 164, 178, 184, 190, 206, 208, 270, 292, 308, 317, 334, 339–342, 346–350, 352

intelligences, 46–48, 50, 70, 76, 106, 138, 153, 238, 250, 308, 327, 335, 341–342, 345–347, 349, 352

intelligent, v, 28, 46–47, 53, 80, 141, 178, 317, 342

internalisation, 307
see also concept, conceptualisation, pattern, patterning

internalise, 3, 66, 264, 305
see also concept, conceptualisation, pattern, patterning

internalised, 16, 18–19, 32, 82, 208, 246, 262, 297, 307, 314–316
see also concept, conceptualisation, pattern, patterning

intrapersonal, 46–47, 49, 276, 285

intuition, x, 44, 266

intuitive, 12, 42, 46, 49, 52

investigation, 44, 50, 63, 240, 331, 341

investigative, 18, 22, 284

J

Jensen, Eric, 4, 14, 20–21, 25, 33, 35, 317, 332, 337–340, 348–349

K

kinaesthetic, 11, 38–40, 49, 63, 76, 106, 108, 119, 131, 144, 146, 157, 228, 238, 250, 276, 280–281, 285, 288
see also movement, physical

kinesiology, 25
see also movement, physical

L

leader, 76, 205, 211, 218, 237

leaders, vi, 185, 328, 343, 346

leadership, vii, 50, 91, 180–181, 337–340, 345

learning styles, iii, 33–40, 45, 50, 56–57, 59, 63, 76, 85–86, 88, 104, 106, 135, 153, 159, 228, 234, 238, 246–247, 250–251, 257, 276, 279, 283, 285, 287, 290, 295, 298, 302, 317–318, 322, 329–330, 332–333, 335, 340–341, 349, 352

learning-styles, 36, 38, 63, 228–229, 252, 279, 281, 283, 285–287, 292, 302, 318, 322, 330

Leat, David, 51, 317

life skills, 186, 192, 199, 343, 345

life-long learning, 33, 297

limbic, 25–26

linguistic, 46, 49, 80, 138, 238, 276, 285

listen, 21, 39, 49, 82, 91, 108, 172, 187–189, 196–197, 202–205, 223, 269, 281, 293–294, 298, 301, 303, 308, 311, 317, 330, 343

listening, ii, xi, 24, 28, 30, 39, 57–58, 69–71, 79–81, 85, 91, 94–96, 98, 101, 109, 115, 117, 138, 149, 151, 164, 178, 181–182, 187–189, 194–195, 200, 203, 205–206, 223, 255, 262, 277, 290, 299, 311, 317, 322

logic, 18, 38, 43, 67

logical, 21, 42, 44, 46–47, 49, 51–52, 67–68, 80, 93, 138, 152, 156–157, 208, 238

M

McCarthy, Bernice, 34, 37–38, 63, 284, 341, 349

McGuinness, Carol, 51, 317, 342

Meighan, Roland, v, x, 5, 10, 27, 317, 337–338, 340, 349–350

memories, ii, 16, 21, 23, 40, 129–130, 182, 187, 276, 303

memorisation, 98, 112, 128, 131, 167

memorise, 66, 97, 114, 131

memory, ii, 11, 16, 23–24, 31, 49, 55, 63, 74, 76, 98, 111, 117, 128–130, 142, 220, 275–276, 303, 339, 341, 346–347, 351

menu, iii, 22, 33, 38, 40, 43, 227, 238, 246–247, 249–252, 275–277, 281, 302, 318

metacognition, 52–53

metacognitive, 52–53, 55, 317, 342, 347

midbrain, 14, 24, 26

mind map, 87, 173, 233, 257, 277–278, 300

mind mapping, 349

mind maps, 20, 87, 98, 300, 302

Mind Style, 35–36, 43, 45

Mind Styles, 37, 43, 45, 63, 153, 228, 341, 348

mixed-ability, 74, 89, 92, 151, 251
see also ability

motivate, 49
see also engage, engaged, engagement

motivated, 17, 30–32, 68, 210, 227, 236
see also engage, engaged, engagement

motivation, xi, 3, 16, 24, 27, 33, 35, 57, 63, 80, 86, 104, 106, 112, 124, 142–143, 159, 180, 209, 238, 245, 257, 267–268, 270, 314, 324–325, 337, 340, 351
see also engage, engaged, engagement

movement, 10–12, 24–25, 38, 43–45, 64, 87, 121, 130, 134, 187, 194, 228, 266, 279
see also kinaesthetic, kinesiology, physical

multi-sensation, 58–59

multisensory, ii, 21–23, 40, 76, 130–131, 157, 276, 303

music, 15, 17, 44, 49, 52, 111, 151, 172, 187, 277, 283, 286, 290, 294, 301

musical, 46, 49, 111, 276, 285

N

negotiate, 40, 54, 276, 290, 295–296, 304, 317, 323

negotiation, 33, 38, 86, 188, 227–228, 261, 265

neocortex, 11, 18, 20–23, 25–26, 114, 124, 144, 251, 326
see also neurocortex and cerebral cortex

neural, 14–15, 18-19, 22–23, 25–26, 28, 31, 33, 46–47, 53, 55, 327

neurocortex, 25

Neuro-Linguistic Programming, 11, 39, 63, 307
see also NLP

neuron, 13–14

neurons, 5, 13–16, 18, 23–24, 31, 327

neuroscience, 5, 23, 59, 317, 339, 351

neuroscientific, ix, 7, 11–12, 326

neurotransmitter, 28

neurotransmitters, 13, 15, 22, 24

NLP, 11, 28, 39
see also Neuro-Linguistic Programming

note making, 92, 98, 114, 219, 302, 305

notes, 20, 65, 72, 78, 91, 96–98, 100, 113–114, 117, 121–123, 127, 131, 136, 151, 157, 166, 168, 188, 209, 218, 240, 265–266, 269, 298, 300, 302–303

O

objective, 41, 91, 150, 205, 228, 235–238, 246, 249, 313

objectives, 38, 44–45, 52, 85–86, 116, 120, 122, 150, 158–159, 196, 220, 222, 229, 234, 236, 244, 246, 249, 251, 253, 257, 260–261, 264, 274–276, 295, 317, 342

outcome, 33, 40, 150, 204, 206, 270, 319, 324

outcomes, 8, 10, 33, 43–45, 52, 54, 202, 227, 270, 281, 295, 297, 305, 307–308

P

participate, 163–164, 189

participation, 56, 80, 82, 84, 96, 151, 161, 164, 178, 184, 195–197, 342, 347, 351

pattern, 18–19, 76, 130, 239–240
see also concept, conceptualisation, internalise, internalised, internalisation

patterning, 19, 53
see also concept, conceptualisation, internalise, internalised, internalisation

peer, 20–21, 39, 44, 63, 86, 92, 124, 127, 134–136, 146–147, 177, 188, 204, 234, 237, 247, 255, 267, 281, 287, 291, 296, 300, 317, 322–323

peers, 17, 21, 27, 35, 115, 136, 177, 199, 216, 265, 295, 298, 300, 340–341

personal, ii, x, 4–5, 8, 10–11, 18–20, 23, 28–30, 32–38, 42–43, 47–49, 54, 56–58, 82, 88, 90, 94, 101, 106, 138, 148, 151, 160–161, 164, 172, 175, 177–179, 181, 183, 185–191, 193, 195–199, 201, 203–205, 207, 209–211, 213, 215, 217, 219, 221, 223, 233, 243, 245, 249, 253–254, 257–259, 261–262, 267–270, 276, 279, 281, 287, 289–290, 293, 296, 300, 302, 307–308, 310–313, 315, 317–319, 323, 326, 328–329, 333, 338, 342–343, 345

personal learning plan, 33, 233, 253–254, 257, 267–268

personalised, 44, 51, 295, 349

personally, 32, 50, 86, 172, 183, 186, 228, 265, 288

physical, 11, 16–18, 23–27, 32–35, 39, 41, 46, 49, 59–60, 79–80, 84, 131, 156, 166, 177, 186, 228, 250, 275, 284, 291, 296, 303, 339, 345
see also kinaesthetic, kinesiology, movement

Piaget, Jean, 53, 317

play, 8, 15, 18, 20, 25, 27, 49, 67, 76, 105–106, 108, 116, 130–131, 151, 159, 169, 171, 173, 177,

183–184, 186, 192, 223, 232, 264, 279, 294, 297, 315, 327

potential, vii, 6, 9, 13–16, 29, 47, 80, 117, 192, 194, 222, 224, 231, 236, 274, 287, 290, 292, 301, 304, 307, 311–313, 315, 317, 325–327, 346

praise, 293

problem solving, 44, 53, 55, 299–300

problems, 4, 6, 14, 22, 47, 50, 53–54, 56, 81, 139, 144, 151, 204, 208, 210, 219, 232, 239, 270, 283, 286, 293, 326, 342

progressive, 7, 10, 321

psychology, vii, ix, 5, 11–12, 17, 22, 25, 46, 59, 177, 204, 261, 289, 292, 296, 317, 331, 339, 343

punishment, 27, 195, 199

punishments, 177, 190, 198–199, 212, 262, 293, 301

Q

question, ii, 9, 20, 22, 48, 59, 72, 81, 89, 93–95, 99, 107, 110, 116, 118, 131, 133–134, 139–146, 154–155, 166–167, 170–171, 180, 185, 193, 197, 206, 214, 218, 220, 265, 275–276, 291, 299, 308, 310–311, 317, 329, 339, 348

questions, vii, 7, 9, 20, 22, 29, 44, 47, 49, 69, 71–72, 74, 81, 86, 91, 93–94, 99–100, 107–110, 116–120, 123–127, 133–134, 139–146, 151, 154–155, 159–160, 164, 166–167, 170–171, 179, 185, 188, 195, 203, 214, 220–221, 223, 233, 237–238, 241, 246, 253–254, 257, 259–260, 265, 273–274, 277–278, 281, 287, 299–300, 310, 318, 326–327, 334, 339

questioning, 55, 60, 70, 143, 255, 264, 299

R

RAS, 30–32
see also reticular activating system

reptilian, 26, 177, 201, 301

research, iii, 4–5, 7, 12, 18, 20, 21, 25, 27, 30–31, 34–35, 38–41, 43–45, 55–56, 58–59, 63, 66, 72, 77, 86, 98, 100, 104, 108, 117, 123, 125–127, 136, 142, 144–146, 150–151, 160, 165, 167, 210, 216, 227–228, 233, 240–241, 243, 247, 251, 253, 257–260, 276, 279–280, 284–285, 292, 297, 299–300, 307, 315, 317–319, 322–323, 326, 329, 331–332, 339–342, 348, 350

retain, 20, 24, 34, 166, 292, 326

retention, 23–24, 40, 55, 73, 303

reticular activating system, 30–33, 267, 314
see also RAS

revise, 73, 83, 95, 100, 131, 156–157, 321

revision, 8, 48, 72–73, 86, 88, 94, 98–99, 109, 112, 114, 124, 127, 129, 131, 136, 140, 146, 151, 156, 167–168, 170, 188, 198, 297, 299, 322, 339, 350

reward, 27, 317

rewards, 27, 56, 177, 199, 261–262, 293, 301, 343, 349

Robinson, Ken, 8, 338

Rogers, Carl, ix, 9, 11, 307, 317, 332, 349–351

role play, 49, 173
see also act, role play, drama, dramatic

Rose, Colin, 4, 334, 336, 351

Rosenthal and Jacobsen, 16, 208, 338, 343

rote, 114, 128

route, 26, 33, 38, 43, 76, 82, 86, 125, 133, 209, 238, 241, 244

S

scanning, 4–5, 145–146, 299, 302

self-assessment, 220–221, 236, 287

self-awareness, 29–30, 36–37, 199, 249, 251

self-belief, x, 16, 104, 199, 279

self-concept, 47, 289

self-esteem, iii, x, 11, 16, 29–30, 47, 56–57, 59, 164, 178, 181, 188, 196, 204, 208, 261–262, 273, 289–291, 296, 301, 307–309, 318, 326–327, 340, 343, 345, 348, 352

self-image, 16, 208, 289–290

self-managed, 50, 342, 350

sensate, 41, 284

senses, 23, 34, 39–40, 58, 130–131

sensory, 5, 18, 26, 31, 34–36, 39–40, 76, 108, 276

Smith, Alistair, 4, 17, 20, 27, 179–180, 317, 335, 337, 339–340, 351

social, vii, 5–9, 15–16, 20, 27, 29–30, 34–35, 47, 49–51, 53–54, 56, 60, 63, 81, 94, 106, 116, 127, 141, 159, 164, 178, 184, 192, 198–199, 201, 213, 270, 276, 298, 326–327, 329, 341, 343, 345

society, 6, 8–10, 52, 58, 60, 78–79, 178, 181, 199, 331, 337, 348, 351

socioeconomic, 5, 17, 43, 53, 58, 326

sociological, ix, 35, 317

sociology, 5, 55, 59, 66, 98, 143, 337, 350

spatial, 24, 46, 49, 55, 76, 153, 208, 276, 285, 340

student-centred, ix–x, 9, 11, 21, 28, 64, 106, 120, 196, 261–262, 270, 338, 340, 343, 346

study skills, 126, 146, 151, 270, 317, 322, 349

survival, 22, 26, 33, 177, 184

survive, 10, 26, 35

synapse, 13, 18, 27

synaptic, 13–14, 23

T

tactile, 15, 39–40, 68, 85, 281, 285

technology, 4–6, 9, 51–53, 65, 67–69, 71, 76, 88, 91, 93, 95, 97, 102, 104, 108–109, 117, 121, 124, 129, 136, 139, 141, 144, 156, 171, 218, 242, 244, 247, 249, 251
see also information and communications technology, ICT

thalamus, 14, 26

thinking, viii, ix, x, 6–7, 9–10, 12, 16–17, 20, 22, 25–26, 38, 40, 44–47, 50–53, 56, 58–59, 63–64, 68, 72, 80, 96, 109, 140, 148, 156–157, 159, 161, 164, 169, 181, 192, 206, 216, 236, 238, 242, 252, 255, 259, 265–266, 273–274, 277, 284, 295, 297, 300–301, 307–308, 312, 315, 317, 319, 321, 326–327, 338, 342, 345, 347, 350

threat, 26–27, 177, 186, 326

U

underachievement, 4, 39, 47
see also achievement

underattainment, 4
see also attainment

V

VAK, 37–38, 281, 285, 317, 333–335

varied, 35, 50, 146, 285, 302, 317, 327, 330

variety, ix, xi, 15, 22, 32–33, 35, 38, 51, 58–59, 63, 92, 118, 126, 139, 146, 167, 228, 231, 234, 236, 238, 250, 257, 276, 279, 281, 290, 317, 322

visual, 6, 11, 15, 37, 39–40, 63, 68–70, 79, 102, 106, 108, 110, 123–124, 131, 146, 153, 155, 157–159, 221, 228, 233, 238, 250, 270, 275–276, 280–281, 285, 288, 298, 319

W

West-Burnham, John, vii, 4, 9, 51–52, 337–338, 342, 345